The Mad King

The Mad King

The Life and Times of Ludwig II of Bavaria

GREG KING

A Birch Lane Press Book

Published by Carol Publishing Group

A Birch Lane Press Book
Published by Carol Publishing Group
Birch Lane Press is a registered trademark of Carol Communications, Inc.

Editorial, sales and distribution, rights and permissions inquiries should be addressed to Carol Publishing Group, 120 Enterprise Avenue, Secaucus, N.J. 07094

In Canada: Canadian Manda Group, One Atlantic Avenue, Suite 105, Toronto, Ontario M6K 3E7

Carol Publishing Group books may be purchased in bulk at special discounts for sales promotion, fund-raising, or educational purposes. Special editions can be created to specifications. For details, contact Special Sales Department, 120 Enterprise Avenue, Secaucus, N.J. 07094.

Manufactured in the United States of America

10 9 8 7 6 5 4 3 2 1

Library of Congress Cataloging-in-Publication Data

King, Greg.
    The mad king : the life and times of Ludwig II of Bavaria /
Greg King.
        p.   cm.
    ISBN 1-55972-362-9
    1. Ludwig II, King of Bavaria, 1845–86. 2. Bavaria (Germany)—Kings and rulers—Biography. 3. Bavaria (Germany)—History—1777–1918.   I. Title
DD801.B387K56 1996
943'.308'092—dc20
    [B]   96-24034
                                                                            CIP

To Gabe

Contents

Author's Note

Several different units of German currency are used throughout this book. Before the formation of the German Empire under Prussia in 1871, Bavaria used gulden as opposed to the Prussian mark. After Bismarck's unification, Bavaria converted her currency to the Prussian system, with one gulden being roughly equal to 1.75 marks.

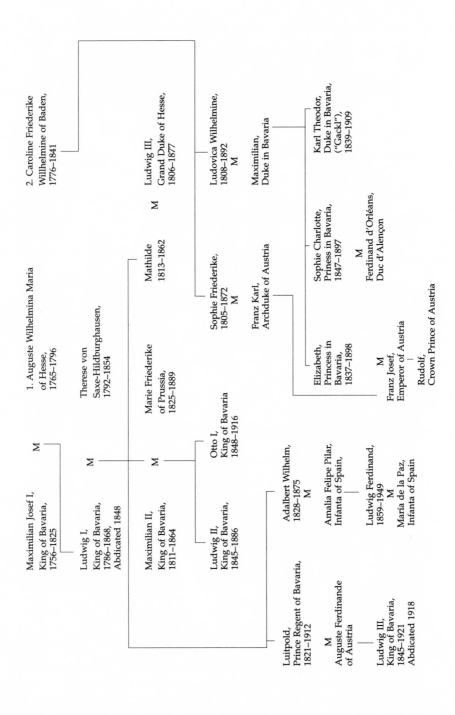

Maximilian Josef I,
King of Bavaria,
1756–1825

M

1. Auguste Wilhelmina Maria
of Hesse,
1765–1796

2. Caroline Friederike
Willhelmine of Baden,
1776–1841

Ludwig I,
King of Bavaria,
1786–1868,
Abdicated 1848

M

Therese von
Saxe-Hildburghausen,
1792–1854

Ludwig III,
Grand Duke of Hesse,
1806–1877

M

Ludovica Wilhelmine,
1808–1892

Maximilian II,
King of Bavaria,
1811–1864

M

Marie Friederike
of Prussia,
1825–1889

Mathilde
1813–1862

Maximilian,
Duke in Bavaria

Ludwig II,
King of Bavaria,
1845–1886

Otto I,
King of Bavaria,
1848–1916

Sophie Friederike,
1805–1872

M

Franz Karl,
Archduke of Austria

Sophie Charlotte,
Princess in Bavaria,
1847–1897

M

Ferdinand d'Orléans,
Duc d'Alençon

Karl Theodor,
Duke in Bavaria,
("Gackl"),
1839–1909

Adalbert Wilhelm,
1828–1875

M

Amalia Felipe Pilar,
Infanta of Spain,

Ludwig Ferdinand,
1859–1949

M

María de la Paz,
Infanta of Spain

Elizabeth,
Princess in
Bavaria,
1837–1898

M

Franz Josef,
Emperor of Austria

–

Rudolf,
Crown Prince of Austria

Luitpold,
Prince Regent of Bavaria,
1821–1912

M

Auguste Ferdinande
of Austria

Ludwig III,
King of Bavaria,
1845–1921
Abdicated 1918

The Mad King

1

The Wittelsbach Inheritance

Soft light from the late summer evening fell across Munich, casting lengthening shadows over the capital's ornately decorated buildings and large, cobbled squares. Above the city's cathedral and churches, a golden sea of cupolas and crosses sparkled in the last rays of sunset. The jagged profile of the distant Alps grew dark against the sky, their snow-capped peaks glistening in the pale pinks, scarlets, and blues that washed the twilight. One by one, lights appeared in windows, echoing the glow from flickering candles in the wrought-iron lamps standing along the streets. The warm air was scented sweet with the heavy fragrances coming from the honeysuckle and roses cascading over balconies. A contented current fell over the city, the noise of carriages and streetcars replaced by music and laughter from the sidewalk cafes, with whispered secrets exchanged between lovers as they strolled the banks of the Isar River and the sound of dinner conversations floating through windows left open to catch any passing breeze.

Some three miles from the center of the city, lost amid the twisting avenues and quiet suburbs, a mile-long canal sliced through a lush park shaded with linden, oak, and chestnut trees. At the end of the canal, reflected in its dark, shimmering surface like an enchanted vision, stood Nymphenburg Palace, summer residence of the kings of Bavaria. Against the dark summer night, the windows of the palace blazed like fires, their orange glow spilling across the graveled forecourt and the brightly uniformed sentries pacing back and forth on their rounds.

In the dim light, a lone figure stood silhouetted in one of the tall windows, nervously smoking cigarette after cigarette. Every few minutes, the polished double doors of the adjoining room swung open, breaking his solitary spell and allowing the briefest glimpse of the green, watered-silk wall coverings beyond. Now and then, Crown Prince Maximilian turned from the window, listening intently as doctors and midwives delivered their latest reports on his wife's struggle.

Hour after hour passed, the night growing longer as the crown prince awaited the birth of his first child.

Crown Princess Marie's confinement was a source of great concern. Just a year earlier, she had suffered a miscarriage. This second pregnancy, therefore, assumed a special significance, both to the expectant couple and to the Bavarian people. Anticipation centered exclusively on a boy: A son would ensure the Wittelsbach succession well into the twentieth century.

At half past midnight on Monday, 25 August 1845, the lusty cry of a baby dispelled the tension of that anxious night: Marie had given birth to a healthy, dark-haired dark-eyed son, an heir presumptive to the Bavarian throne. The baby's grandfather, King Ludwig I, immediately sent an equerry to convey the happy news, and within the hour, all of Munich was awoken by the pealing of church bells and the thunder of a hundred guns, announcing the birth of the boy born to one day be king.

The very next day, in the sweltering late summer heat, Archbishop Gubsattel of Munich performed the christening ceremony in the sumptuous Festsaal of Nymphenburg Palace. Beneath its high vaults, heavily embellished with frescoes, baroque arches, and gold leaf, the Bavarian royal family and their guests stood and watched as King Ludwig slowly approached an elaborate font placed in the middle of the great hall. In his outstretched arms he carried a velvet cushion holding his new grandson; from beneath the voluminous satin and antique lace folds of the Wittelsbach christening mantle, the baby kicked and cried. The crown prince and princess had selected an illustrious group of godfathers for their new son: Along with his grandfather Ludwig of Bavaria, they included his uncle King Otto of Greece and great-uncle King Friedrich Wilhelm IV of Prussia, who had come from Tegernsee with his consort, Elizabeth, for the occasion.

The archbishop gently lifted the infant, settled him in the crook of his left arm, and, with his ringed hand, sprinkled the downy head with holy water as he solemnly baptized him Otto Friedrich Wilhelm. Within a few days, however, King Ludwig asked his son and daughter-in-law to change the baby's first name. The feast day of St. Ludwig, patron saint of Bavaria, was celebrated on the day of his grandson's birth; it was also, by strange coincidence, the day of his own birth. In view of these omens, the king asked that his new grandson be renamed in his honor. And so Otto became the future Ludwig II, remembered to history as the Mad King of Bavaria.

Ludwig II was born into a world of wealth and privilege and raised in isolated splendor. At the age of eighteen, he acceded to the Bavarian throne as a beautiful, golden youth, captivating the hearts of his subjects and inspiring their hopes for a glorious reign. Twenty-two years later, the handsome Adonis had become a fat, bloated misanthrope, hidden away from the inquisitive eyes of his court and his countrymen in a succession of increasingly fantastic castles. Members of his family and the government, fearing for the financial security of the throne and the political stability of Bavaria, joined forces to remove him in a coup. Within a day of his forced deposition, his corpse was discovered floating among the reeds along the shore of Lake Starnberg, outside of Munich. His early promise and extraordinary beauty had made him a romantic hero among the people of Bavaria; his cloistered existence, lavish castles, nocturnal rides in gilded sleighs, and mysterious death turned Ludwig II into a modern myth.

Ludwig II stood apart from the world around him. Raised without warmth or affection, he grew into an aloof, emotionally starved young man, curiously detached from everyday life. In his loneliness, he found comfort in glowing accounts of life at the court of Louis XIV at Versailles, in the tales of ancient gods and dark Teutonic history, and in a world of dreams. He so hated his own century, his own surroundings, that he actively sought refuge in another, less hostile environment, one filled with granite and marble castles and palaces where he could relive the glories of past ages and peopled not with the unfriendly faces of the Munich court but with the ghosts of Parsifal and Lohengrin, Louis XIV and Marie Antoinette. Through the musical dramas of Richard Wagner, he managed to escape, however briefly, into a place and time where he felt himself truly accepted, an era of chivalry and fair maidens, of heroic knights and divinely inspired rule. All around him, the realities of his position—the political pressures and wars with Prussia, the intrigues of Bavarian politics, the impotence of the democratic monarch in Bavaria—drove him further and further into this world of illusion, and with the passing years, he severed all but the last links with the world beyond his own rarefied existence. His struggles, against Otto von Bismarck, against the court officials who blocked his friendship with Wagner, against his own desires for solitude, and against his homosexuality, crushed Ludwig's spirit. Misunderstood and alone, victimized by circumstance and by his own character, he sought comfort in his world of fantasy, in his midnight drives through the dark Bavarian forests, in his secret romances with a succession of grooms and soldiers. He was whispered about, called mad, plotted against, and betrayed—all because he refused to bow to convention, to live his life as expected. But there seemed little threat of this overwhelming tragedy when the future Ludwig II first appeared on that golden summer night, greeted with joy and expectation by his family and future subjects alike.

The year of Ludwig's birth, 1845, also witnessed his grandfather the king of Bavaria's silver jubilee celebrations, a rich panoply of brilliant parades and reviews, moving celebratory masses, and lavish balls marking the twenty-fifth anniversary of Ludwig's accession to the throne. From his birth, the new baby was heir to one of the most illustrious royal dynasties in all of Europe, the house of Wittelsbach. Ludwig I was the twenty-fourth in a line of Wittelsbach dukes and electors to rule in Bavaria, but only the second to hold the title of king. As a dynasty, they were often brilliant and artistic, with a stubborn determination to succeed, a trait perhaps inherited from their distant ancestor, the Holy Roman Emperor Charlemagne. During their years of rule, Bavaria prospered, and in 1918, when the end came for the Wittelsbachs, their country—alone among the German states ruled by Kaiser Wilhelm II—would retain an impressive measure of autonomy in the new Weimar Republic. But their beginnings were humble, buried in Teutonic history.

The Wittelsbachs traced their ancestry to the house of Scheyern, an aristocratic family which ruled a small, autonomous stretch of land from their castle at Pfaffenhofen. In 1180, while Europe was torn asunder by crusades and wars, Emperor Friedrich Barbarossa selected the head of the Scheyern family, Count Otto, as the new duke of Bavaria. On learning of his good fortune, for the Wittelsbachs never gained their power through war or revolution, Otto von Scheyern packed up his entire court and moved them from Pfaffenhofen to Wittelsbach Castle. He assumed the name of the castle as his own, and a royal dynasty was born.

Wittelsbach rule reached its zenith in 1314, when one of their own was proclaimed Ludwig III of the Germanic states. Though known to history simply as Ludwig the Bavarian, at the height of his power, in 1328, he assumed the title of Holy Roman Emperor. His reign was marked with troubles: An attempt to control the destinies of Italy brought him into conflict with Pope John XXII, who, in desperation, excommunicated Ludwig and tried to revoke his imperial dignity and titles. Ludwig, however, proved too crafty to fall victim to the intrigues of the Vatican: He simply gathered an enormous army, marched at its head over the Alps, and deposed the troublesome pope. Thereafter, their centuries of rule found the Catholic Wittelsbachs in frequent conflict with the Holy See over questions of religious influence and government policy.

The family only gained their kingdom in 1806, after holding the positions of duke and elector for hundreds of years. Having formed a propitious alliance with Napoléon, Elector Maximilian Josef I further cemented relations with the powerful Bonaparte and married his daughter Amelia to the emperor's stepson Eugene de Beauharnais. Maximilian Josef's soldiers marched with Napoléon's Grande Armée as it swept triumphantly across Europe, and his loyalty was rewarded with a grant of sovereignty over Bavaria.

The new king's successes, however, did not end with the single marital union with the French emperor's family, for he married his other daughters into equally distinguished positions. Elizabeth, as the wife of the head of the Hohenzollern family, became queen of Prussia; Marie wed the king of Saxony; Caroline married Emperor Franz I of Austria; and Sophia, in a rather complex turn of events, married her own nephew, the heir to the Austrian throne. She thus became daughter-in-law to her own sister Caroline. For the Wittelsbachs, this highly incestuous degree of intermarriage had long been a way of life, in spite of the marked eccentricity which it often produced. During Maximilian Josef's reign as king of Bavaria, his relatives filled the royal courts of Hesse, Baden, Prussia, Saxony, and Austria; as the nineteenth century progressed, there were further links through marriage to the royal houses of Spain, Romania, Greece, Russia, Sweden, Denmark, and Great Britain.

The Bavarian kingdom in the nineteenth century was one of thirty-nine independent states which together formed the German Bund, or Confederation, created in 1815 at the Congress of Vienna from the remnants of the old Holy Roman Empire. Bavaria was the largest country, with boundaries encompassing the great sweep of the rugged Alps along the Tyrolian frontier; Franconia and parts of Swabia; and the twisting paths of the Danube, Inn, and Isar Rivers. Most of the land was agricultural. Farmlands spilled across the rolling hills and endless plains in the north, bordered by the black forests of Bohemia and Prussia. In the south, lakes and marshes stretched over the lowlands, ending abruptly in the forbidding Alps. Every few miles, hamlets and peasant villages clustered round whitewashed rococo churches with onion domes. Throughout the land, frescoed medieval buildings and cobblestone squares echoed the Dark Ages of European history, their somber character enlivened with carved gables and an abundance of bright flowers spilling from window boxes all through the summer.

Some four and a half million people lived in Bavaria under Wittelsbach rule. Many were peasants, hardworking, simple people tied to the land and dedicated to the two forces which ruled their lives: the temporal influence of the Wittelsbach dynasty and the spiritual power of the Catholic Church. By the middle of the nineteenth century, the rise of Protestantism had cut into Rome's traditional hold on the Germanic peoples, and nearly a third of them converted to the Lutheran Church. Even so, the Catholic tradition remained deeply ingrained, especially in Bavaria: Feast and fast days were celebrated by both sides of the population, every village boasted a roadside shrine to its patron saint, and the liturgical calendar dominated the days and months of the people's lives. The Catholic Church, along with the throne, provided an element of stability in a rapidly changing world, and most Bavarians remained true to the ideals handed down through the centuries of a generally peaceful existence: church, throne, family, and country. Although the kingdom was surrounded on all sides by other members of the German Federation, Bavarians, on the whole, tended to regard these fellow Bund states with a degree of mistrust, reflecting the xenophobic attitudes prevalent in the countryside as well as in the cities.

At the center of Bavarian life was Munich, capital of the kingdom. In the nineteenth century, Munich was a curious mixture of ancient and modern. Sprawling alongside the flat, marshy lands bordering the Alps, the capital boasted medieval half-timbered houses and cobblestone squares; yet, at the time of the future Ludwig II's birth, it also encompassed a rapidly growing industry. Visitors were often struck by Munich's dichotomy, for in spite of its fine buildings and high academic and cultural reputation, the city still possessed more than a hint of the provincial. This could be seen in its street fairs, where peasants from the surrounding countryside came to sell their goods at makeshift stalls; in the horse-drawn carts that filled the broad avenues and prospects; and in the slightly bourgeois amusements of the beer halls, with their thumping brass bands and Tyrolian dancers. Nevertheless, these diverse elements lent to the city a peculiar charm, quite unlike the somewhat somber and oppressive atmospheres prevalent in neighboring Vienna to the south and in Berlin, far to the north.

Munich was founded in the eleventh century as a place of asylum for the Catholic Church. Because of its geographical position in the center of Europe, Munich often found itself in the path of invading armies from both the north and south. As a consequence, it was frequently occupied by foreign powers. Munich was burned and looted by Austrians, Italians, and Swedes as well as the Dutch and French. Seven fortified towers with stout gates stood tall in the walls that still ringed the center of the city, their battlements and merlons mute testimony to its uncertain past.

Bordering the outer city, the fast-flowing waters of the Isar River wound past parks and palace gardens; it was crossed by ornate stone bridges, banked by granite quays, and lined with broad avenues shaded by stately rows of pleached linden trees. Munich, on clear days, enjoyed marvelous views of the nearby Alps to the south. Winds from the mountains swept through the city, bringing relief from the humid heat in summer and from the icy rain and snow which froze the inhabitants in winter.

Matching the jagged silhouette in the distance, the capital's skyline, dominated by spires and cupolas, reflected the deeply held Catholic and Protestant faiths of the Bavarians. The styles of these elaborate houses of God, ranging from the Italian Renaissance lines of St. Michael's Church, with its enormous stucco barrel vaults, to the heavy baroque details of the Theatinerkirche, built by Electress Henrietta Adelaide to commemorate the birth of her son Maximilian, reflected the diverse nature of the city. The grandest of the capital's churches, the Frauenkirche or Cathedral of Our Lady, had been erected in the fifteenth century in the High Gothic style. Twin towers, topped with low domes, rose more than three hundred feet above the tiled roofs of the sprawling city below, giving breathtaking views across the capital and over the verdant and fertile countryside. In the church's dark burial vault stood the elaborate tomb of Ludwig the Bavarian, the greatest of all the Wittelsbach sovereigns.

The people of Munich loved pleasures; principal among these was the celebration of the city's favorite beverage, beer. On the Platzl stood the Hofbräuhaus, the first state brewery, founded in 1585 by Duke Wilhelm V. At all hours of the day and night, in winter and summer, people gathered in the halls, open-air cafes, darkly paneled private clubs, and fashionable bars to raise a stein of freshly brewed beer. It was the great common link among all classes, from the aristocracy to the peasantry. Gossip, the latest news, and family discussions could be heard in these gathering places. Lovers came to meet and celebrate, businessmen to seal deals and set agendas, and politicians to coerce and argue with their constituents. At the end of the day, they were all Bavarians, linked by loyalty to country, crown, and church.

In the middle of the nineteenth century, Munich took on an appearance and a character entirely dictated by its reigning sovereign, King Ludwig I. A man of great artistic and intellectual sensibilities, the king had for many years nursed a love of the art and architecture of ancient Greece. Wittelsbachs had always taken a passionate interest in art, acting as patrons to the great artists and architects of their day, and Ludwig was no different. Shortly after mounting the throne in 1825, he declared his intention of turning Munich into a German showplace. By trimming court costs and living frugally, he managed to save some 20 million gulden from the royal civil list, an annual stipend for the royal family's household expenses. With these funds, along with money culled from the state treasury and the genius of architect Leo von Klenze, Ludwig virtually transformed his Alpine capital into a second Athens.

Set on an elaborate stone base, a bronze equestrian statue of the king appeared to gaze with pleasure down the long and majestic Ludwigstrasse. At the end of the avenue lay his massive Siegestor, a triumphal arch copied from that of Constantine in Rome. Beyond this lay Schwabing, the university district, where students crowded the sidewalk cafes and beer halls and haunted the Bavarian State Library, the largest of all such German institutions. Musicians played on street corners and artists sat on the rims of fountains and in the brick-paved squares, sketching and painting the medieval scene spread before them.

The Königsplatz, a broad, paved square, was dominated by two imposing architectural monuments erected at the king's orders. At one side stood the Propylaen, an immense marble gate copied from the Propylaea at the Acropolis in Athens. Opposite this, von Klenze built the templelike Glyptothek, a museum devoted to the king's prized collection of ancient Greek and Roman antiquities. To this, the king added two further museums, the Alte and Neue Pinakotheks. The Neue Pinakothek was reserved primarily for the works of current court painters, while the Alte Pinakothek housed the great Wittelsbach collection, begun in the sixteenth century by Duke Wilhelm IV. In the Alte Pinakothek were works by Albrecht Dürer, Leonardo da Vinci, Raphael, Fra Angelico, Fra Filippo Lippi, El Greco, and more than a hundred canvases by Peter Paul Rubens.

Ludwig's Munich became a city of great spaces and neatly manicured gardens. The greatest of all the capital's parks was the famous Englisher Garten, a peaceful haven which owed its existence to an American, Benjamin Thompson, a native of Woburn, Massachusetts. During the American Revolution, he had sided with the British; when hostilities ceased, he fled to London. After being ennobled by a grateful King George III, he worked in the Foreign Office and was eventually posted to Munich. The Bavarian elector named Thompson Count Rumford, and it was in this position that he influenced the court gardeners to lay out a park in the naturalistic style made popular in England in the mid-eighteenth century by the famous Lancelot "Capability" Brown. The park had immense stretches of lawns, specimen trees, and several man-made lakes, the largest of which, the Kleinhesseloher See, was used for swimming and boating in summer and ice skating in winter.

Above all else, Munich was a royal capital, and in the center of the city was the Residenz, the Wittelsbach palace. A rambling complex of buildings, enlarged over the centuries by a succession of dukes and electors, the Residenz represented a curious mixture of architectural styles, including Romanesque, Gothic, Italian Renaissance, high baroque, and Bavarian rococo as well as Ludwig's favorite neoclassical and Empire designs. It first became a royal palace in the fifteenth century, when Duke Wilhelm V added new wings to an existing structure and took up residence there with his court. Over the next two hundred years, the Wittelsbachs built two court chapels, two theaters, state suites, ballrooms, and galleries until by the middle of the nineteenth century the Residenz encompassed nearly five hundred rooms, spread across several acres, and wrapped round nine interior courtyards.

The Residenz was a treasury of diverse architecture, elaborate interior decoration, and fabulous works of art. Beyond the arcaded courtyards, with their splashing fountains and complicated parterres of golden box, lay a world of great luxury. In one corner of the palace was the famous Altes Residenztheater, built by the famed eighteenth-century court architect François Cuvilliés. This was a rococo fantasy in white, crimson, and gold decorated with caryatids, cherubs, swags, and velvet brocades, an intimate setting for ballets and concerts. Mozart's *Idomeneo* had first been performed in the Altes Residenztheater in 1781, and the Wittelsbachs continued the tradition of hosting royal command performances within its magnificent walls.

From the top of the Imperial Staircase, long suites of state apartments opened in brilliant succession. The Hall of the Four White Horses took its name from the ceiling panels painted in the seventeenth century by Peter Candid, while the walls of the state dining room were decorated with murals depicting Aeschylus, Aristophanes, and Anacreon. Ballrooms, reception rooms, and cabinets were filled with splendid eighteenth-century French furniture embellished with tortoiseshell, mother-of-pearl, and ormolu. Floors were inlaid in intricate patterns with palmetto, mahogany, rosewood, and ebony in geometrical designs; above these gleaming surfaces, chandeliers in silver, bronze, gilt, and porcelain dripped with delicate crystal prisms which sparkled brightly in the light of thousands of candles. These rooms were filled with history: Here, Pope Pius VI had stayed as a guest of the Wittelsbach family in the sixteenth century; Marie Antoinette and her suite of 250 retainers had spent the night during her ill-fated journey to France for her wedding; and later, Napoléon had planned his southern campaigns amid its gilded splendor.

The Rich Apartments, twelve of the most beautiful rooms, had been decorated in the Bavarian rococo style by François Cuvilliés, Josef Effner, and Johann Baptist Zimmermann; their fine stucco work, inlaid floors, gilded decorations, and carved furnishings were of incomparable splendor. The Ancestors' Gallery, a lavish corridor on the first floor, contained more than a hundred portraits of the rulers of the house of Wittelsbach; it led to the Grotto Court, a favorite place for strolls during court balls and for relaxing among tinkling fountains, marble loggias, and the whimsical rococo shell designs covering the walls.

At the end of the suite lay the sanctum sanctorum of the Residenz, the Throne Room, decorated with blue watered silk and white stucco to reflect the national colors of the kingdom. Twelve tall, gilded iron standards depicted the coats of arms of the Wittelsbach dynasty; they had been made from cannons seized from the Turks during the Battle of Navarino.[1] On nights when there were balls, seemingly endless lines of elegant courtiers and beautiful women paraded through the room, pausing to bow or drop a curtsy before King Ludwig, seated on a red velvet dais. Here, from his silver-gilt throne, the king could survey his court, rejoicing in his achievements and content in the knowledge that he would leave an enduring legacy in his capital.

For all of their regal trappings, the Wittelsbachs ruled Bavaria as enlightened and progressive-minded monarchs. Maximilian Josef I granted his country a written constitution in 1818, establishing the democratic principles which were to govern Bavaria during the years of Wittelsbach power. When he died in 1825, the crown passed to his eldest son, who assumed the throne as Ludwig I. A godson of the doomed king Louis XVI of France, Ludwig was an artistic, thoughtful man, dedicated to his role as sovereign. His energy for even the unglamorous duties of a monarch was tireless. "My lamp is the first alight," he once proudly declared. "When I look from my window in the early dawn, the Max Josef Platz is in darkness, and by the time the clerks have come to the Treasury Office, I have got through half the work."[2]

Ludwig was married to the beautiful princess Thérèse von Saxe-Hildburghausen, a woman glowingly described by one who knew her well as "a model for all wives and mothers."[3] Her life at court, however, was not happy. Her husband, for all of his devotion, had a roving eye and a notorious obsession with beautiful women. He commissioned artists to paint portraits of the loveliest women at the Bavarian court, which soon became famous throughout Munich. It was this preoccupation with the physical charms of the women at his court which eventually led to the king's downfall. When he was sixty years old, his romantic gaze fell upon the bewitching twenty-eight-year-old Irish-woman known to history as Lola Montez; the Wittelsbachs nearly lost their throne as a result of his romantic folly.

Lola Montez, that legendary, hypnotic, and exotic beauty who so captivated and scandalized Europe in the middle of the nineteenth century, was born Eliza Gilbert, a native of Limerick. Fancying herself a descendant of Spanish nobility, she adopted her stage name in an effort to disguise her more humble origins. A Spanish dancing master taught her the flamenco of his country, and once proficient, she quickly learned to use her charms to cast a spell on the men in audiences across the continent.

Her first public appearance, at Her Majesty's Theatre in the Haymarket in London, caused a riot. In the audience was a certain Lord Ranleigh, who watched carefully as Lola danced seductively across the stage. He recognized her not as the mysteriously billed exotic dancer from Spain but as the former wife of a comrade in an Indian regiment. Rising from his seat, Ranleigh hurled insults at the startled dancer, accusing her of deception and immorality. His cries were soon taken up by others in the audience, and Lola was hissed from the stage in tears.

Her career seemingly in ruins, Lola fled to the continent. After many months, she finally found an agent willing to book an appearance in Warsaw. She enjoyed great success in the Polish capital until she made the mistake of spurning the amorous advances of the Russian viceroy, General Field Marshal Prince Ivan Paskeievich. He retaliated by ordering the dancer expelled from the country; the public learned of the incident and was so outraged by her behavior that crowds rioted in the streets of Warsaw, forcing Lola once again to flee in shame.

She eventually settled in Paris, naively believing that she could begin her life anew, but her notoriety had preceded her. Lola was unable to resist the temptations offered in the French capital. She engaged in a number of flaunted love affairs with the leading men of the day, including composer Franz Liszt and writer Alexandre Dumas. Men were enthralled with the beautiful Lola Montez, even fighting duels over her, and newspaper headlines screamed her name across their front pages. In shame, Lola found herself forced to give evidence at the criminal trial of the man who had killed her lover in a jealous rage. Once again, Lola fled from the havoc she invariably created around her.

Lola arrived in Munich at a politically tenuous time. In 1837, the Jesuit Party had come to power, with Karl von Abel as their prime minister. Although Bavarians were on the whole deeply religious, this incursion into the political realm worried the liberal king Ludwig. His opposition, and that of his supporters, soon earned the hatred of the Jesuits, who attacked the king and his policies as anti-Catholic, a damning condemnation in a country largely still loyal to Rome. Von Abel's Jesuit government soon set about disrupting the political climate even further: According to the Bavarian constitution of 1818, all religious groups were accorded equality, but the Jesuits instigated a widespread plan of Protestant persecution, waiting for an opportunity to discredit the king and his liberal ministers serving in the opposition. Unwittingly, Lola handed them their chance when she came to Munich.

Following the announcement that she was to appear in a command performance at the court theater, the Jesuits denounced Lola Montez as an immoral adventuress. However, despite the political and religious scandal his presence would create, the king was determined to see for himself this enigmatic woman who had caused such disruption in London, Paris, and Warsaw. Like others before him, Ludwig was intoxicated by the dancer's sensual movements and great physical charms. Following royal tradition, he received Lola, as a foreign artist, in a private audience; rumors flew across Munich that she had taken full advantage of the situation, ripping open her bodice once the doors of the rooms were closed. In truth, Ludwig needed little encouragement and foolishly declared to one of his ministers that he was "bewitched" by Lola Montez. By the time of her second—and final—performance in Munich, he had to order the police to fill the orchestra pit to protect the dancer from the howling mobs of scandalized Catholics.

Ludwig granted Lola endless audiences, which infuriated both the Jesuits in the government and his Catholic subjects. He asked Friedrich August von Kaulbach to paint her portrait; when it was completed, he ordered it hung in a prominent position in his famous Gallery of Beauties, a public declaration of his infatuation. He incurred further criticism by buying Lola a large mansion on the fashionable Barerstrasse and granting her an annual allowance of 2,000 gulden from the royal treasury, money culled from public taxes and revenues.

The king did not stop at an allowance and a mansion. He compounded his disregard of public opinion by expressing a wish to ennoble the dancer. Knowing that only Bavarian citizens could hold ranks in the country's peerage, the king demanded that she be naturalized. For the Jesuits, this humiliation proved the last straw. At an audience with the king, von Abel demanded, as leader of the government, that the king expel Lola Montez from Bavaria. But the prime minister had not counted on the degree of the king's infatuation, for instead Ludwig abruptly dismissed von Abel from office. When the Cabinet of Ministers learned of this, they signed a joint resolution, saying that the king must renounce the dancer or the government would resign. Faced with this threat, Ludwig did the unthinkable: He dismissed the entire Cabinet of Ministers and prorogued the Bavarian parliament.

The king replaced von Abel with Ludwig von Maurer and ordered him to form a new government. The new prime minister's first act was to sign the naturalization papers granting Lola Montez Bavarian citizenship. Ludwig immediately named the former Eliza Gilbert of Limerick the countess of Landsfeld and Baroness Rosenthal; he also raised her to the rank of a canoness in the Order of St. Thérèse, an honor reserved solely for Bavarian princesses. On reading this startling piece of news in the court calendar, the aristocracy joined the Jesuits in protest and, rebelling at this intrusion, deliberately snubbed the court. The archbishop of Munich declared that any priest offering to hear confession or say mass for Lola Montez faced immediate excommunication.

In the midst of this furor, Lola herself behaved with something short of the dignity befitting her new rank. One evening, as she strolled along the streets of the capital, she encountered a group of Catholics who recognized her as the king's favorite and began to shout names and hurl stones. Fearing for her safety, the dancer quickly turned and ran, chased by the mob along the Ludwigstrasse to the door of the Theatinerkirche across from the Residenz; only when she was safely inside the sanctuary did the crowd disperse. On another occasion, a group of drunken university students stormed through the streets of the capital, intent on reaching the house of the infamous dancer. They gathered before her mansion on the Barerstrasse, shouting her name over and over again; when Lola finally appeared, she behaved as if the entire drama were simply a command performance. From her balcony, she waved to the screaming students, who greeted her with hisses and threats. Unperturbed, she foolishly brought out a bottle of champagne and, while toasting the angry crowds below, showered them with expensive chocolates.

Infuriated by such scenes, Ludwig retaliated not against his beloved Lola but against the university students themselves. His eyes blinded to the political realities of the crisis, the king ordered the University of Munich closed, expelled the students, and dismissed all Jesuit instructors. Although he had taken office at the king's request, von Maurer could no longer tolerate the disintegration of the government; he called a special session of the Landtag, or Bavarian parliament, and declared his intention to introduce a resolution calling for Lola Montez's expulsion from the country. The king heard of this plan and ordered his army into the streets. When his ministers reported to Parliament, they found the doors locked and the legislature dissolved. The entire Bavarian government had been brought to its knees by the king's romantic obsession: The capital was in an uproar, people rioted in the streets, and soldiers in the army threatened mutiny or a coup d'état. It was only at this last moment, when it truly appeared that his country was on the verge of civil war, that Ludwig finally relented. Fearing that he was about to lose his throne, he ordered the immediate expulsion of his calamitous mistress from his country. Shocked at this sudden and unexpected loss of royal favor, Lola fled in disgrace. She died thirteen years later, in obscure poverty, and was buried in New York.

It seemed as if the Montez scandal had passed, but the sense of restored serenity did not last. Ludwig's ineptitude and imperious behavior had alienated most of his Protestant subjects, while the Catholics were incensed by his flaunted offenses. Through the adventure of the Irish dancer, the king had created an impossible situation in the Bavarian government. Too many reputations had been ruined and egos trodden on for the country's politicians to carry on with the king at the helm. Unfortunately for Ludwig, 1848 was the year of European revolutions: King Louis Philippe of France was forced to abdicate, as was the emperor of Austria; the crown prince of Prussia fled to London; and even the pope was driven into exile by angry crowds. On 21 March 1848, under intense pressure from his entire family and government, Ludwig I abdicated the Bavarian throne.

2

Childhood

Ludwig was just two and a half years old when his grandfather abdicated. He could not understand the political turmoil surrounding the Lola Montez affair, but there was no escape from the sounds of the noisy street demonstrations which filtered through his nursery windows, the anxious looks of his parents, and the tears of his mother as Bavaria stood poised at the edge of revolution. Although no one realized it at the time, King Ludwig I's romantic foible was to have dire implications for his young grandson, depriving him of any chance to enjoy a normal childhood.

His father, Bavaria's new king, Maximilian II, was a shy, unassuming man whose slight stoop, receding hairline, and delicate health belied his thirty-eight years. An intellectual with serious tastes and conservative, traditional views, Maximilian had little in common with the dilettantish aesthetes and sophisticated politicians of his father's court. The king once declared that under different circumstances he would have been a university professor, and he enjoyed nothing more than joining a group of academics in one of Munich's beer halls, arguing science and philosophy until the early hours. Not the romantic figure that his father had been, the new king suffered from fits of nerves and crippling self-doubt. Nevertheless, he managed to win the support of his people and restore the Bavarian throne to its former prestige following the Lola Montez scandal.

In 1842, Maximilian, as crown prince, married the niece of King Friedrich Wilhelm III of Prussia. King Ludwig I wrote happily of his son's wife: "She is the very essence of good-nature, very pretty, and has beautiful eyes. . . . I now have in Marie a second, charming little daughter-in-law."[1] The king's words were true enough, for Marie of Prussia was indeed a beauty, with jet-black hair and piercing blue eyes, but she was not an altogether popular choice as future queen. Her Prussian background caused some resentment among the xenophobic Bavarians, who would have preferred a suitable princess from their own land. Not only did they resent Prussia as a German state, with its northern arrogance and cold demeanor, but their future queen was also a devout Protestant who refused to convert to Catholicism. Over the years, however, Marie managed to ingratiate herself with her adopted people, and she won Bavaria's affections by providing the kingdom with an heir to the throne, Ludwig, and with a second son, Otto Wilhelm Luitpold Adalbert Waldemar, who arrived on 27 April 1848, scarcely a month after Maximilian II acceded to the throne.

Although he was to be, as time passed, a less than ideal father, Maximilian was filled with pride at the birth of his first son. Four days after Ludwig's birth, the crown prince wrote to his brother-in-law, Prince Adalbert of Prussia:

> These lines will bring you the happy news that the Lord has blessed our dear Marie with a strong little boy on the birthday of my father, who is very happy indeed about it. . . . About four o'clock in the morning the pains began, at six o'clock Marie told me, and only at half-past twelve in the night were they over, when the little one first saw the light of this world. The moment when the child gave its first cry was wonderful. The good Marie suddenly forgot all her pains. . . . [2]

The first few years of young Ludwig's life were peaceful. His early view of the world was largely confined to the royal nursery, a humble suite of rooms at the top of the palace. He was raised according to the spartan principles of the upper classes of the Victorian era, whereby children were often denied even the most common of creature comforts in an effort to build character and avoid indulgence. He moved from the crib to an army camp bed with woolen blankets and horse hair pillows. There were, it is true, fine toys: model castles and tin soldiers and wooden slides, but, from his earliest days, the young boy was subjected to cold baths, an exhausting educational agenda, royal duties which took up much of his already limited leisure time, and even hunger. Food at the royal table was kept to a minimum, and Ludwig's elderly nurse, Lisel, frequently resorted to sneaking provisions from the kitchen to her hungry young charge.[3]

At the time of Ludwig's birth, children were raised apart from their parents, tucked away with nurses and nannies, and cared for by a succession of foreign governesses; royal parents also supplied their young sons with military instructors. In Ludwig's case, the effects of this isolation were multiplied by the fact that his parents were sovereigns. When the children were young, Queen Marie always tried to set aside an hour each day to spend with Ludwig and Otto, but as they grew older and she undertook more royal duties, even this minimal time was often sacrificed. The only time Ludwig and his parents shared usually came at lunch, teatime, or dinner, but even these occasions were ritual concessions to family duty. The children were brought down from their rooms, brushed and scrubbed and carefully dressed in their best clothes, only to be kept quietly in a corner, their presence clearly more ornamental than familial.

His father and mother were often absent during Ludwig's childhood, compelled by duty to serve the public and the state to the detriment of their own private lives. This isolation perpetuated itself. Having themselves been raised in the same fashion as they now raised their children, neither Maximilian nor Marie saw any need for change. To stray from royal tradition would have meant acknowledging their own failures. They felt hopelessly awkward in their children's presence: Maximilian and Marie knew nothing of their interests and could never make more than the most shallow conversation with them. In turn, Ludwig and Otto responded with acute discomfort, and neither side knew how to overcome the embarrassing silence which usually followed any attempts to communicate. The fact that the children looked with great affection and warmth upon their nanny and the servants who filled the nurseries and yet were very nervous with their own parents was so painful for the king and queen that they simply avoided the young boys. Unable to understand his parents' lack of warmth, and feeling himself unloved and ignored, Ludwig increasingly withdrew from those around him to a world of fantasy.

Maximilian II was not a very doting parent. Even had he not been king, with the duties and restrictions on his time which the position imposed, it is doubtful that his taste for intellectual pursuits and unbending seriousness would have endeared him to his young sons. Like his wife, he clearly favored Otto; with his unerring sense of duty, Maximilian felt compelled to treat his elder son and heir differently, and their relationship was always marked with a stiff, if friendly, formality and noticeable lack of affection. He was never able to understand Ludwig's brooding melancholy or his romantic dreams.

His father raised Ludwig as most nineteenth-century European heirs were raised. All of the sovereigns of Europe seemed to have agreed that their sons should be beaten into the realization of their future responsibilities. There was nothing unusual in his puritanical views or exaggerated expectations. A comparison of King Maximilian with two other royal fathers of the same period, Emperor Franz Josef of Austria and Albert, England's prince consort, illustrates that he was guilty of no more or less than any other man in his position. All three prominent Victorian fathers set unreasonably high expectations for their children, and especially for their heirs. Crown Prince Ludwig, along with his contemporaries Crown Prince Rudolf of Austria and Albert Edward, the Prince of Wales, had to be better than everyone else, with higher ideals, greater intelligence, and more dignity than other children, in order to serve as moral examples to their future subjects. Inevitably, such hopes were dashed. When the sons failed to live up to their fathers' stringent standards, their failure was taken as obstinacy and rebellion. Crown Prince Rudolf virtually severed relations with his father, Emperor Franz Josef, and even conspired with his political enemies; the Prince of Wales responded to his father's harshness by becoming the antithesis of what was expected. Rudolf rebelled through his political involvements, the Prince of Wales through his numerous affairs and questionable private life.

In Ludwig's case, his own failures were met with frequent beatings and, as he grew older, harsh verbal reprimands from his humorless, martinet father. Maximilian made no effort to include his children in his life and was so uncomfortable in his elder son's presence that he deliberately avoided Ludwig. Their relationship was stilted and strained, devoid of any natural affection. One of the king's government ministers later wrote:

> He rarely visited the rooms where they were growing up; when he did he usually just held out his hand in greeting and took his leave as quickly as possible. It needed long and hard efforts to persuade the King to take his eldest son with him on his morning walk in the English Garden between nine and ten o'clock. But even so, it only happened a few times.[4]

Unfortunately for Ludwig, his relationship with his mother was scarcely better. Queen Marie had no intellectual curiosity and was completely isolated from the sympathies of her eldest son. King Maximilian's cabinet secretary, Franz von Pfistermeister, later remarked that "the Queen had little knowledge as to how to draw her little sons to her. She visited them only fleetingly in their rooms, and scarcely even knew how to treat them as children ought to be treated. Nor did the little sons know how to treat their mother."[5] Unlike her elder son, Marie found pleasure in simple entertainments: needlework, hiking, gossip, and gardening. Whereas Ludwig became a voracious reader from the moment he learned to read, the queen once proudly declared, "I never read a book, and I don't understand how anyone can incessantly read."[6] Their relationship eventually grew so cold during his growing-up years that, after he succeeded to the throne, Ludwig once caustically referred to his mother as "the widow of my predecessor."[7]

Deprived of the natural parental warmth and affection which he so craved, Ludwig turned increasingly to his governess, Fräulein Sibylle von Meilhaus, for comfort and reassurance. A warmhearted, sympathetic woman, she understood the shy, melancholy boy and he, in turn, trusted her completely. One of his earliest poems, written at the direction of his religious tutor, was dedicated not to his parents but to his governess:

> Dear Meilhaus!
> Could I more than wish, could I give
> dearest Meilhaus, how quickly and pure
> would all your days pass by,
> how happy this high feast would be!
> But as I have nothing better now
> take my thankfulness as a gift.
> My heart is full of love for you
> and hopes that you will love it, too.[8]

But Fräulein von Meilhaus, in addition to providing her young charge with the affection he so craved, also foolishly added to his weighty inheritance by inadvertently introducing two of the mottoes which would occur with great regularity in his later letters and diaries: Louis XIV's proud boast *"L'état, c'est moi!"* and *"Car tel est Notre bon plaisir!"* Fräulein von Meilhaus invoked the specter of Louis XIV as an example of kingship, responsibility, and sovereign power. It was an unfortunate choice, however; soon Ludwig took these words to heart, finding in them a means to express his conception of his future position.

In 1854, Fräulein von Meilhaus became engaged to Baron M. Leonrod and left her position at the Wittelsbach court; her departure created an immense void in the nine-year-old boy's life. She had been the only person who had understood him and given Ludwig the affection and sympathy he craved. On her departure, he became more withdrawn, finding comfort only in his own future inheritance and in his lonely dreams. Until her death in 1881, Ludwig would regularly correspond with his "dear Meilhaus," confiding his hopes and fears to her in a way he refused to do with members of his own family.

Ludwig was a lonely child. Solitary pursuits suited his character. Although only three years separated him from Otto, the gulf between the two brothers was great. They were never very close as children, and this distance was deliberately enforced: Queen Marie habitually dressed Ludwig in royal blue, while Otto was relegated to wearing the more egalitarian red, and she allowed few exceptions to this rule of fashion.[9] The two boys were utterly different in character: With his pensive and melancholy temperament, Ludwig contrasted strongly with the warm and unassuming Otto. As crown prince, Ludwig was raised according to stringent standards, while Otto was indulged by his parents and never suffered the reprimands and pressures his elder brother had to endure. Even as a young boy, Ludwig was painfully aware that his parents favored his brother Otto: "Otto is a good boy, and I will be good also," he once pitifully wrote to his mother.[10] But no matter how hard he tried, no matter how well he behaved or how emotional his pleading letters, Ludwig failed to win the parental acceptance and affection he so desperately craved.

The enforced differences in their positions strained relations between the two brothers. Ludwig never let Otto forget that it was he who would one day be king, and he took advantage of every opportunity to assert his own position over that of his younger brother. Once, Ludwig tied Otto up and threatened to behead him before a servant came to the rescue. On another occasion, Otto showed Ludwig a snowball which he had made, and his elder brother promptly took it away from him. In tears, Otto rushed to an attendant, who asked Ludwig for the snowball. But Ludwig refused. "What? Why can't I take the snowball? What am I Crown Prince for?"[11] When the royal family was in residence at the summer palace in Berchtesgarten, a member of the household appeared just in time to see Ludwig standing over his brother, whom he had bound and gagged. Ludwig was twisting a rope round his brother's neck, and Otto was coughing and turning purple from strangulation. When the official intervened, Ludwig cried out in indignation, "This is no business of yours! This is my vassal and he has dared to resist my will! He must be executed!" The servant duly rescued Otto, and Ludwig was soundly beaten by his father. This punishment forever colored Ludwig's memories of Berchtesgarten: The Alpine town would always remind him of this humiliating experience.[12]

Despite such arrogant displays, Ludwig was a shy, sensitive child. He preferred to play alone, and his favorite toys were building blocks. Architecture fascinated him. At Christmas in 1852, when he was seven, the former king Ludwig I gave his namesake a model of the famous Siegestor, Munich's Arch of Triumph. "He loves building," his grandfather proudly reported. "I was quite surprised to see excellent buildings in good taste made by him."[13]

In addition to architecture, Queen Marie noted her eldest son's fascination with the Catholic Church and its elaborate rituals. Ludwig eagerly awaited Fasching, the traditional celebrations preceding Lent, when the entire royal family attended glorious masses in Munich's

Frauenkirche and Theatinerkirche. Dressed as a nun, he would sneak into the private chapels of the palaces, staring for hours at the rococo altars with their gold-leafed scrolls, gilt, and cherubs beneath the frescoed ceilings.[14] It was the theatrical atmosphere of the church which he loved, the ornate solitude in the great cathedral, the pomp and pageantry, the rich robes of the priests, the hidden choirs, and the magic of fragrant incense and flickering votive candles.

More and more often, Ludwig took refuge in this world of illusion and fantasy, losing himself for hours in the pages of books where he learned of the splendors of Versailles and the court of Louis XIV, of the ancient heroic Teutonic sagas, and of the long-forgotten days of chivalry and knighthood. The more he read, the greater Ludwig's distaste for his own surroundings became: He hated the nineteenth century, with its prosiac styles of life and bourgeois entertainments. To escape, he wandered through his father's palaces, allowing his imagination to take inspiration in those rooms and immersing himself in an earlier world of autocratic power. The exuberant decoration of Cuvilliès and Zimmermann in the Residenz captivated him with its gilt, silks, brocades, inlaid floors, and crystal chandeliers; here he could relive the glories of Louis XIV and the vanished court at Versailles. Most of all, however, he was influenced by a suite known as the Nibelungen Apartments. Contained along the first floor of the Residenz's Königsbau, these marble rooms were decorated with immense murals by Julius Schnorr von Carolsfeld depicting the saga of the Teutonic gods. It was Ludwig's introduction to the epic characters of Wotan and Siegfried, Brünnhilde and Sieglinde, and to the mythical world of the Nibelungen, a world which Richard Wagner would later bring to life in his musical dramas.

Above all other places, Ludwig loved Hohenschwangau Castle, in the foothills of the Bavarian Alps just a few miles north of the Austrian border near the town of Füssen. The castle held a special place in Teutonic lore. The fiercely proud Knights of Schwangau first raised its battlements in the eleventh century; it was later occupied by Hiltebold, a crusader and a member of the legendary body of minnesingers, and Emperor Friedrich Barbarossa halted there with his entourage on his first journey to Rome. But it was the mythical figure of Lohengrin, the Swan Knight, who was most closely associated with Hohenschwangau. From these battlements, according to legend, the young knight had set out for the Rhine on his great quest to save Elsa of Brabant. Even the castle's name, Hohenschwangau, spoke of the legend, translating loosely as "the High Country of the Swan."

The Knights of Schwangau died out in the sixteenth century, and their castle fell into disuse and decay. During the Napoleonic Wars, the castle suffered further damage: In 1800 and 1809, Napoléon himself laid seige to the castle during his campaign against Austria. By the time Crown Prince Maximilian discovered the castle in 1832, it was little more than a romantic ruin, overgrown with ivy and wild roses. Impressed by its situation, he immediately set about restoring the fallen walls and battlements. The result was a Gothic Revival jewel, a fairy-tale castle bristling with stained-glass windows, soaring towers, merlons, and balconies.

Hohenschwangau crowned a mountain crag high above the Füssen plain, its ochre-colored walls and red-tile roofs glowing against the face of the dark fir and pine-clad slopes of the nearby peaks. Terraces complete with splashing fountains and old rose gardens surrounded the castle walls; below its battlements stood the twin lakes of Alpsee and Schwansee, their clear blue waters reflecting the sweep of the Alpine sky. From the shores of the Alpsee, where a small village had grown up to house those connected with the Bavarian court, a steep driveway wound up the slope of the mountain, twisting beneath a massive, arched gateway emblazoned with the Wittelsbach coat of arms, to open at the top to a paved square before the Castle.

Hohenschwangau was not a large castle. Its main apartments, grouped on the second and third floors, were relatively modest rooms because this was far less a royal residence than it was a large country house. The somber effect of its low-ceilinged rooms was relieved by tall windows and glass doors which flooded the interior with light. Stairways twisted through towers, and sunlight streamed through panels of stained glass, casting the stone landings in rainbow hues. Maximilian commissioned the artists Dominick Quaglio and Moritz von Schwind to decorate the walls of his newly rebuilt castle with murals recalling the building's legendary past and the heroic figures of Parsifal and Lohengrin. The walls of the Schwanrittersaal, the Hall of the Knights of the Swan, which served as the castle's dining room, were covered with murals depicting the tale of Lohengrin. But there were other mythical references at Hohenschwangau. Ludwig was fascinated by his father's bedroom, a highly romantic chamber which greatly influenced his taste for the exotic. It featured murals showing the enchanted garden of the fictional Armida and her seduction at the hands of Rinaldo, from the sixteenth-century Italian poet Torquato Tasso's romantic epic *Rinaldo*.[15]

Ludwig loved the outdoors and took full advantage of his summer holidays at Hohenschwangau to explore the surrounding mountains and forests. He and Otto often swam in the Alpsee below the castle's battlements and rode across the open fields to the Forggensee or up into the Alpine trails, taking picnics into the countryside with their governess or military instructor. The entire royal family loved to hike. Queen Marie took a keen interest in these rough climbs through the mountains and personally helped lay out many of the trails and paths which wound through the hills above her husband's castle. She wore a curious costume of her own design: a large, knee-length crinoline with matching hat, worn over men's trousers to make the climb easier. Maximilian himself was no less a sight, dressed in a green Tyrolian suit with green stockings and cap, while the two boys were dressed in Bavarian peasant costume.[16] Queen Marie, though accompanied by a lady-in-waiting and a few servants, took charge of all details, unpacking picnic baskets, cooking over an open fire, carrying plates of venison, roasted potatoes, and bread, and, afterward, standing over a mountain stream, happily washing the dirty dishes.

There were less pleasant experiences, however. Ludwig's military instructor, Major Emil von Wulffen, often took his young charge up the paths above the Alpsee to Pollat Gorge, a narrow channel below Sauling Mountain where a waterfall crashed 150 feet into the ravine below. From this point, the majestic spread of the Alps and the Füssen plain opened up, stretching to the north across the rolling hills. Ludwig genuinely liked von Wulffen, a kind, unassuming man who stood out among the self-important courtiers who formed the royal household. Unfortunately, von Wulffen suffered from epilepsy. One day, during an Alpine excursion, the major, while picking flowers, went into a seizure, fell from a mountain crag, and broke his neck before the boy's horrified eyes.[17] The memory of this tragedy haunted Ludwig for many years.

The Allgau (the region bordering the Alps in Bavaria) where Hohenschwangau stood became Ludwig's favorite refuge. He adored the countryside, the long walks, the bracing air scented by the sweet honeysuckle falling over the castle battlements, and the open, simple character of the local peasants. More than anything else, he loved the tranquillity induced by wandering in the mountains. Walking alone along the shore of the serene lakes or sitting in an arched window looking out over the mountains toward Austria, Ludwig allowed his imagination free rein. At the Residenz he had already been introduced to the world of the Nibelungen, the saga of the gods which Richard Wagner's music would later make vivid; at Hohenschwangau, he encountered the heroes of Teutonic legend, figures whom Wagner would also cloak in flesh and blood on stage: Parsifal and Lohengrin, and the quest for the Holy Grail. Dominating all was the pervasive image of the swan. From the coat of arms of the Knights of Schwangau, carved in stone above the arch of the castle's porte cochere, to the swans floating on the waters of the Alpsee and Schwansee below its ramparts, Ludwig was surrounded by these proud and graceful birds with which he was to identify. His childhood letters, filled with exaggerated flourishes, intertwined *L*s, and fleurs-de-lis, often ended with a swan, drawn by Ludwig as his personal emblem.[18]

Ludwig disliked the company of other children. His parents tried to introduce some normality into his life by bringing the young sons of the Bavarian aristocracy to court to play with him, but the experiment failed. Ludwig refused to participate in their games and could not forget that he was crown prince. He found it difficult to behave normally in their company, so acutely aware was he of his own unique position. When a servant discovered the son of Count Arco beating Ludwig over the head during a game, these visits ceased. Ludwig was most often to be found alone, sitting in silence. Once, the famous Bavarian theologian Ignaz von Döllinger discovered the boy in the corner of a darkened drawing room, staring vacantly into space.

"Your Highness should have something read to you, which would help pass these boring hours," Döllinger suggested.

"But I am not bored at all!" Ludwig exclaimed. "I imagine various things and keep myself quite amused."[19]

The peculiar behavior of both brothers did not escape the notice of certain courtiers, among them Dr. Geheimrat Gietl, the royal physician. According to a report by Gietl, even as a small child Otto showed clear signs of serious hallucinations, and he began to watch Ludwig for the same symptoms. He noted, for example, that once, while playing billiards, Ludwig had imagined that he heard voices taunting him. From that moment on, rumors slowly began to spread through the court that the future king might have inherited the well-known Wittelsbach eccentricity.

3

The Education of the Heir

Until he was eight years old, Ludwig remained isolated in the royal nursery with his governess, Fräulein von Meilhaus. The sympathetic woman had provided the sensitive young boy with the only attention and affection in his otherwise emotionless and sterile world, sitting with him, reading to him, teaching him to write, and telling him Bible stories. In 1853, she was joined by Dean Reindl, whom King Maximilian had summoned to court to give his eldest son religious instruction. A year later, when Fräulein von Meilhaus left, the king seized upon the opportunity to appoint an entirely new staff to oversee the education of his heir. Suddenly, the young, romantic boy who had dreamed of knights and heroes and sought love in the arms of his understanding governess was torn from her comforting presence and abruptly thrust into the hands of an intimidating group of men commissioned by his father to shape Ludwig into a good prince and king.

Ludwig's education was laid out by his father. Like other European heirs, he had lessons in riding, fencing, drawing, swimming, and dancing, but the majority of Ludwig's courses were devoted to languages, history, and the sciences, later supplemented with political and military instruction. Maximilian approached this plan with a certain relief, for it relegated Ludwig to the company and supervision of tutors and military instructors; this imposed academic isolation spared the king what was often a forced and uncomfortable relationship with his son. His stringent code of behavior, unreasonably high academic expectations, and reactionary discipline demanded Ludwig's complete obedience and attention. Weary of his melancholy son's penchant for fantasy, Maximilian was determined to fill his hours with lessons and supervised activities in an effort to transform Ludwig into a paragon of moral virtue and superior intellect.

Maximilian meant to shape his eldest son into a model monarch. This plan allowed for no individuality: To make Ludwig a good king, his father believed it was necessary not only to subdue his son's character but to crush it as well. Such a plan might have succeeded had Ludwig cooperated, but Maximilian had not reckoned with his son's character. Ludwig was too stubborn and arrogant to give in to his father; he was also ingenious when it came to the manner of his rebellion and did not retaliate with unacceptable behavior, which was certain to draw his father's displeasure. Instead, Ludwig simply complied with his father's every wish: No desire on the king's part was met with resistance. Ludwig did all that was required of him, but no more. He never expressed any enthusiasm or interest in any of his subjects, save for history and literature, and did only that which was necessary to pass his examinations. He sat through his lectures without comment, appearing dutiful on the exterior, but was actually lost in a world of dreams. He developed at an early age the ability to close out the more disagreeable realities of his daily existence; he would smile, nod, make polite conversation, and study his lessons, but, in reality, Ludwig found comfort only in the world of his imagination. The more the king demanded from his son, the less Ludwig was willing to give.

To supervise Ludwig's education, Maximilian commissioned Count Theodor Basselet de la Rosée, a fifty-three-year-old former cavalry officer with an unerring sense of loyalty to the throne and love of military discipline. Although the king was pleased with his choice, the count's commanding presence and booming voice intimidated Ludwig, who disliked him immediately. Nor were de la Rosée's impressions of Ludwig more favorable: He faced a pupil who appeared to care for no one but himself, a self-absorbed romantic who rebelled at the very idea of being corrected as an infringement on his royal dignity.

The count soon discovered that Ludwig could behave in an imperious and autocratic manner. Just before her departure from court, Fräulein von Meilhaus had accompanied her young charge on a shopping expedition to Füssen during which she saw him steal a small purse from one of the stores. Once outside of the shop, she confronted Ludwig and insisted that he return the purse and apologize to the store owner at once. But instead of appearing ashamed or chastized, Ludwig was incredulous. "What have I done wrong?" he asked with all sincerity. "Why should it be a sin? One day I will be King of this country, and all that belongs to my subjects belongs to me."[1]

Count de la Rosée encouraged Ludwig's belief in his own superiority and indulged this snobbery. He insisted that both Ludwig and Otto should associate only with their Wittelsbach cousins and with the children of the Bavarian aristocracy. According to a long-standing tradition at the Munich court, no member of the Bavarian royal family was to be addressed as Royal Highness until reaching his or her eighteenth birthday; even after the eighteenth birthday, the simpler title of

Highness was preferred. But de la Rosée would have none of this: He was adamant that Ludwig, as crown prince, be styled as Royal Highness and addressed as such within the royal household. Maximilian agreed, and Ludwig was soon surrounded by bowing and scraping courtiers.[2]

De la Rosée supervised a staff drawn from the University of Munich, the University of Göettingen, and the Bavarian Military Institute. These men were all leading authorities in their respective fields and included Father Ignaz von Döllinger, a famous Catholic theologian who instructed Ludwig in religion; Professor Julius von Liebig, a renowned chemist who taught at the University of Munich; his colleague, Professor Philipp von Jolly, who instructed Ludwig in physics; Johannes Huber, who lectured on philosophy and contemporary problems; Franz Trautmann, who oversaw the crown prince's languages; and Michael Klass, an influential Bavarian educator and reformer.

Each morning, a servant woke Ludwig at half past five; after bathing and dressing, he was required to immediately sit down and complete an hour of homework before his breakfast. For the next twelve hours, he was drilled in his regular subjects, with several hours set aside for homework, reading, and exercise. The young boy's day was strictly planned out, and there were few deviations from this intensive schedule: Leisure activities were required to be constructive, and indolence was not tolerated. This schedule, which was in effect six days a week, was broken for tea at ten o'clock, lunch at one, and tea in the afternoon at four with his parents; in the summer, special allowance was made for half days and for the royal family's frequent holidays at Hohenschwangau and Berchtesgarten.[3] Even so, the lessons were never discontinued for more than a few days at a time, and Ludwig was forced to work harder and longer than any other student in his father's kingdom.

Ludwig's preliminary instruction included lessons in mathematics, German language and grammar, and German history. This carried on for three years and followed the normal grammar school course which every Bavarian youth had to complete. In addition, he received religious instruction several times a week from Father Ignaz von Döllinger, who succeeded Reindl. When Ludwig was eleven, his father directed that his son's education be intensified. Working with a group of court officials and military representatives, Maximilian laid out a new and even more demanding schedule for Ludwig, based in part on the system completed by Emperor Franz Josef of Austria. At first, it was suggested that Ludwig complete the normal eight-year course of secondary education within a five-year period; eventually, this was deemed too excessive, and he was allowed seven years to complete the scheme.

The secondary phase of Ludwig's education expanded to encompass more mature subjects, which included French, English, Latin, and Greek. These lectures were supplemented with required reading: the Greek classics, William Shakespeare's *Romeo and Juliet*, and the plays of Jean-Baptiste Poquelin (Molière), all in their original languages. He soon learned French but could only stumble through a conversation in English. Ludwig's great love of reading served him well in his lessons, as did his exceptional memory: He could recite, without prompting, entire passages and scenes from the works of his favorite authors, including Friedrich von Schiller and Lord Byron. There were also classes in general world and European history, which Ludwig greatly enjoyed. For him, history was the story of his ancestors and their achievements. Through his examination of the lives and careers of Charlemagne, Ludwig the Bavarian, and Friedrich the Great, he discovered heroic figures upon whom he could model his own future reign. Further lessons in arithmetic, geography, science, astronomy, chemistry, and physics appealed to him far less; Ludwig had little interest in things scientific or practical, for his was a world of imagination and history.

Michael Klass, brought to the palace to teach the crown prince German and grammar, has been described by one of Ludwig's biographers as a "good-natured mediocrity."[4] Klass came to his position with a fine reputation as an educator, respected by his university colleagues; prior to his appointment, he had authored a book proposing reforms in the Bavarian educational system and was largely held to be an advanced, enlightened teacher. Of all Ludwig's instructors, it was Klass who was to have the most influence. Unfortunately, this influence was disastrous. For all of his enlightened, egalitarian thinking and proposals concerning the state of Bavarian education, Klass proposed an entirely different set of principles where members of the royal family were concerned. He was in awe of the king and his family and held fast to an almost medieval belief in the purity of sovereignty. According to Klass, the monarch was called by God to rule over his people, infused with divine authority, and thus above earthly justice and reproach. The sovereign, Klass taught Ludwig, was the link between God and people, between church and state.

Ludwig had long been exposed to such ideas. Fräulein von Meilhaus had introduced the boy to the phrases and philosophies of Louis XIV, while de la Rosée reinforced the sycophantic attitudes surrounding him through his orders for the court pertaining to royal etiquette. From the time he became crown prince, Ludwig had been subjected to a constant stream of exhortations concerning his supremacy over his future subjects; the autocratic behavior noted by many was a natural outcome of this childhood indulgence. Klass's lectures only confirmed what Ludwig himself believed to be true. He obviously took these lessons to heart: Many years later, Ludwig reported some of Klass's advice to his cousin Crown Prince Rudolf of Austria: "The monarch is the Lord's anointed, but at the same time he is the father of his subjects. It is religion that keeps the masses of people in order, and it is religion that brings out all the love and attachment of the people for their sovereign just as it is religion that inspires the love of the sovereign for his people; religion is the eternal bond between them."[5]

Ludwig was overwhelmed by the intensity of his education. Like any other young boy, he longed to escape the confines of the schoolroom and the watchful eyes of his tutors and play or read. But Maximilian insisted that his son not be indulged, and the continual lessons, increasingly difficult assignments, and constant supervision soon took their toll on the young boy. His tutors noticed Ludwig's nervousness and growing fatigue; he often sat slumped over his desk, unable to concentrate. Neither Maximilian nor Count de la Rosée recognized that Ludwig was suffering from nervous exhaustion; fearing that he simply had too much leisure time, they responded by increasing his studies, further aggravating the boy's fragile emotional state.

His carefully maintained reserve kept even de la Rosée at a distance, and it took many months before he could truthfully report any progress to the queen. In 1857, he wrote to Ludwig's mother:

> I submitted the Crown Prince to a little examination and am satisfied with the result. It gave me fresh hope that a good deal can still be done-which I had begun to doubt. Only those who know the Crown Prince well are in a position to see the noticeable changes in him. The last Confession had an extraordinarily good effect; never before have I seen the Crown Prince in such a happy and open mood as at that time.[6]

De la Rosée believed that he had a clear duty to instill in his charge a moral sense of right and wrong, and his puritanical influence spilled onto the pages of Ludwig's schoolboy essays. At the age of thirteen, he wrote:

> Vanity can also be the consequence of flattery. If one is, from one's youth, surrounded by people who do nothing but flatter, one very easily becomes vain and when one grows older it is very hard to give it up. Very often vanity is the cause of egotism which is very bad for men because one thinks only of oneself and forgets one's neighbours. The vain man might be said to have a poisonous snake gnawing at his heart.[7]

No one seems to have commented on the irony of the haughty Ludwig composing such a piece, but many noted his insolence. One day, Franz von Kobell, a professor at the University of Munich, happened to be at Hohenschwangau waiting to see King Maximilian when he spotted Ludwig playing somewhat dangerously on a stairway railing. When it appeared that the boy was about to fall, the professor reached out and pulled him to safety, but the prince only shot him an angry glare and walked away without comment. Many years later, Kobell met the then king Ludwig II. When he greeted the king, Ludwig icily said to him, "You have touched me!" and turned his back on the startled man.[8]

De la Rosée noted the boy's frequent changes in mood and overwhelming melancholy. To the queen, he wrote:

> Most of all is to try to develop the Prince's self-confidence without letting it grow into self-conceit. The Prince ought to develop a strong courage to live: he is to be kept from brooding; he must not linger over disagreeable impressions but try to be less sensitive towards them. . . . Special care is to be taken to train the Prince's will because the strength of the will can be trained; it is all the more necessary to emphasize this because ours is an age in which the imagination and the mind are fostered, but the will to act and live are neglectful.[9]

There is also a puritanical note in a letter which the count sent to his young pupil, warning against the evils of giving in to temptation:

> Therefore, try to unceasingly train your mind and body. If the evil tendencies come up again, suppress them, with a strong will you can achieve anything. Weakness is not dignified in a man-and that is what you want to become: a man who shall be an example to his people. Be kind and you will win all hearts, but be obedient. Because it was disobedience that brought man to misfortune. Honour your father and mother because, next to God, you have to thank them for all you have and all you are; then God's blessing will always be with you.[10]

No one knows the nature of the "evil tendencies" mentioned by de la Rosée, but such warnings had a dire effect on Ludwig. He apparently took them to heart; and they later contributed to the overwhelming sense of guilt which he expressed over his homosexual desires.

Ludwig received an allowance of twelve gulden a month, with the stipulation that he keep a careful record of how he spent it. By making him maintain a ledger, de la Rosée thought that the boy would learn the value of money. But Ludwig, having been raised in complete isolation, had no concept of prices or values. He often spent his entire allowance in a single day without realizing that he had done so. By the time of his sixteenth birthday, Ludwig's allowance had increased to twenty-five gulden a month, a figure roughly equivalent to a fortnight's wages for an average Bavarian worker. This allowed him to buy jeweled pins, swan cuff links, and books by his favorite authors: Schiller, Shakespeare, and Byron. Even so, he was often short of money. Otto, as a second son, received even less than Ludwig. Once, the younger prince, hearing that a healthy set of teeth were worth good money, offered the court dentist the choice of several of his own molars for a certain sum. This offer was promptly reported to the king, and Otto was beaten for his indiscretion.[11] Ludwig's frequent financial shortcomings as crown prince almost certainly contributed to his later carelessness as king where money was concerned.

By the age of seventeen, Ludwig had completed his secondary education. According to the general plan for his education, he was to have begun courses at the University of Göettingen in the fall of 1864, but his premature assumption of the Bavarian throne put a halt to this scheme. Instead, his only experience with higher education came from a series of lectures he attended at the University of Munich. The results of this attempt were mixed: While Ludwig took an intense interest in the lectures themselves, he was the only pupil who demanded a separate seat, away from the other students.[12]

Ludwig's education helped form him into an intelligent, thoughtful young man. He spoke German, French, and, somewhat less fluently, English. He was a graceful dancer and possessed impeccable manners. Ludwig cut a superb figure on a horse: His height and natural poise enhanced the effect when he rode, and he enjoyed nothing more than spending endless hours in the saddle, touring the Bavarian Alps near Hohenschwangau. He loved speed and frequently raced his mount through dangerous, wooded paths without concern. A great devotee of physical exercise, he often swam the mile width of the Alpsee below Hohenschwangau, impressing everyone with his strength and endurance.

Ludwig certainly had his admirers at court, but there were also many who witnessed his less enviable traits. His penchant for brooding had only grown with age. His strenuous education made him highstrung and over-sensitive, frequently causing him to take offense at an innocent gesture or look, condemning the often unaware culprit for years. Worst of all, he was absolutely convinced of his own superiority over the lesser mortals whom he would one day rule.

Aside from periodic lectures and meetings with government officials, Ludwig had no exposure to state duties prior to his accession to
the throne. His father saw no immediate need to introduce him to his
eventual responsibilities: Maximilian, after all, was still only fifty-one,
and, in spite of his sometimes delicate health, there was every expectation that he would continue to reign for many years to come.
Ludwig's only ideas regarding his future role as king had come from
two sources: the teachings of de la Rosée and Michael Klass. From both,
he came to believe that the very basis of kingship rested not in understanding the political system or in the day-to-day mechanisms of the
government. Rather, for Ludwig, it lay in a spiritual bond which he
believed existed between sovereign and subject. Ludwig's education
had been concerned with instilling in him a sense of his destiny as
future king; this had certainly been achieved, but at the price of sacri-
ficing any vestige of democratic tendencies. From his birth, Ludwig
believed he had been anointed by God to rule over the people of
Bavaria; his was a divinely inspired role. As such, his thoughts for the
future were tinged not with anticipation of working with government
ministers but of manifesting to his people and to history his destiny as
a Wittelsbach ruler. Thus, Ludwig came to identify with Louis XIV's
statement, *"Létat, c'est moi!"* He felt himself to be, if not a temporal
descendant, then at least a spiritual descendant of the Bourbon monarchs, an heir to the ancien régime of the Sun King.

While Ludwig disliked court officials and members of the Bavarian government, he had a fondness for the peasants whom he often
encountered in the countryside. Ludwig could maintain an icy silence
with a member of the royal household, insisting on bows and correct
titles and etiquette. But the men and women of the Alps treated him
naturally, with an unpretentious deference which came from their
hearts. To Ludwig, they were the "real Bavarians," loyal to the church
and to the throne, simple in their tastes, and without the malicious
streak which he detected in many of the courtiers in Munich. Michael
Klass had taught him that as future sovereign he enjoyed a real, spiritual link with the common people; it was they whom he should serve
once he came to the throne, and they, in turn, would respond with loyalty and affection.

De la Rosée considered the part he had played in educating the
future king a success. To the queen, he reported: "I had to fight many
a battle with the Crown Prince until we established the existing relationship."[13] Ludwig, however, had no such illusions. He had been obedient and had succeeded in his lessons, but without any real effort and
with little feeling. His heart lay elsewhere. In a letter to his cousin
Crown Prince Rudolf of Austria, Ludwig reflected on his education: "It

was your good fortune that you enjoyed so thoroughly excellent an understanding and upbringing and, what is more, that the Emperor took such a keen personal interest in your education. In the case of my father it was unfortunately quite different. He always treated me *de haut en bas*, and, at best, bestowed on me *en passant* a few cold words of favour."[14] Although Ludwig was mistaken about the bond between Rudolf and Emperor Franz Josef, his own comments leave little doubt as to the lack of feeling between him and his father.

At this sensitive moment in his life, Ludwig first discovered the works of Richard Wagner. The king would not allow his son to attend any of the composer's operas, but the crown prince managed to obtain the librettos of both *Tannhäuser* and *Lohengrin;* soon he knew both works by heart. The operas of the liberal, Prussian-born Richard Wagner were regarded at the time with some suspicion by the conservative, xenophobic Bavarians, and Ludwig had to struggle not only against his parents' refusals but also against the prevailing attitudes toward the composer. While Ludwig was young, the king could forestall his son's desire to see Wagner's operas. But in February of 1861, at the age of fifteen, Ludwig was finally given permission to attend a Munich performance of *Lohengrin*. That one event would change the course of his life.

4

"His Reactions Were Almost Morbid"

Although the music of Richard Wagner was to play an enormous part in the life of King Ludwig II of Bavaria, the details of his first acquaintance with it remain veiled in mystery. From his earliest days, Ludwig had been surrounded by the legends of Tannhäuser, Parsifal, and, especially, Lohengrin, the Swan Knight. That Wagner brought these tales to life onstage certainly interested the young prince. But there was more to Ludwig's fascination than mere hero-worship. These were his childhood fantasies brought to fruition with stirring music, dazzling costumes, and an atmosphere filled with the influential themes of German leadership and divine authority. They were, in the words of one biographer, "the concrete expression of what he had only been able to imagine."[1] Ernest Newman, the great biographer of the composer, wrote, "even as a boy Ludwig had a romantic vision of himself as king, leading the German people along ideal paths, and Wagner's writings simply happened to strike into that vision at the crucial time and with tremendous impact."[2]

It seems that Ludwig first learned of Richard Wagner from Baroness Leonrod. In February of 1858, she attended a performance of *Lohengrin* at the court theater in Munich and later described the opera in a glowing letter to her former charge. Knowing that Ludwig would be enraptured, she urged the young boy to see *Lohengrin* for himself. Ludwig begged his parents to be allowed to attend the performance; Maximilian, however, considered the composer's operas too controversial, too sensual for his high-strung thirteen-year-old son. This denial made Ludwig all the more determined to learn everything he could about the mysterious composer who aroused such violent reactions.

On his fourteenth birthday, Ludwig received a rather curious assortment of gifts, many of which addressed his intense interest in the story of Lohengrin. These included a painting of the Lohengrin mural in the dining room at Hohenschwangau, etchings of the castle itself, and another pair of swan cuff links. One of the prince's tutors, Professor Steininger, gave his pupil a book about the Holy Grail, which foreshadowed Ludwig's interest in the story of Parsifal and Wagner's later opera. Steininger also presented the boy with a copy of Richard Wagner's *Opera and Drama*; although Ludwig had never expressed much interest in music theater before, he quickly devoured this rambling treatise on the state of opera in Germany. He learned that Wagner had written many other prose works describing the problems faced by contemporary composers, and began a determined effort to read them all in order to absorb their thoughts.

By coincidence, Ludwig discovered more of the composer's works during a visit to the Munich palace of his great-uncle Duke Max in Bavaria. Max, who had married Ludovica, daughter of King Maximilian Josef I, was known in the capital as a bohemian and an artistic man. One afternoon, Ludwig apparently found his uncle's copies of Wagner's *Art Work of the Future* and *Music and the Future*. These two prose works were longer pieces dedicated to the composer's analysis of the state of music and art in nineteenth-century Germany. Soon Ludwig added these volumes to his growing Wagner collection.

Ludwig had yet to attend a performance of one of Wagner's operas. He knew the music from practicing it on the piano, but the pageantry of music, costume, drama, and art had yet to weave its magical spell upon him. Nonetheless, even without seeing for himself the spectacles of *Lohengrin* or *Tannhäuser*, Ludwig was truly enraptured with the composer's work. The idea of seeing the fantastic murals at Hohenschwangau and the Teutonic legends come to life greatly appealed to him. But in reading Wagner's prose, Ludwig also felt a stronger attraction, a sense of destiny. In 1863, Ludwig asked a Munich bookseller, Christian Kaiser, to draw up a list of Wagner's prose works; soon he filled the gaps in his collection as each became available. When the books arrived at the Residenz, Ludwig lost no time in reading through them. Ernest Newman commented that the prince "had studied Wagner's prose writings perhaps more ardently than anyone else in Germany or Austria outside the small circle of the elect."[3] Ludwig eagerly read of the destinies of the German people, of the need for a national leader to show by example the beauty and truth in art, of the spiritual bond between art and religion and those empowered to achieve its unification. He immediately recognized Wagner's call. The composer had created a world of dreams which not only reflected Ludwig's boyhood fantasies but mingled them in the most powerful way with the more adult themes of temptation, betrayal, and the love of the German people in their common bond, a kind of spiritual force uniting them with their leaders. As future king, Ludwig saw himself precisely in these terms: as a leader destined to inspire, to utilize his divine authority to transcend the commonplace and restore the glories of previous centuries.

At the time of Ludwig's awakening interest, Wagner's music still suffered from the conservative, anti-Prussian mood which predominated in Munich. King Maximilian II patronized painters and poets, but he left it to his music directors to sort out the details of who would or would not receive the favor of performance in the capital's theaters, and Munich remained Europe's lone holdout by rejecting the almost universal popularity of Wagner's works. In 1841, when Wagner had sent the director of the Munich Opera the score of his work *Der fliegende Holländer*, it was returned to the composer with the comment that it had been found "unsuitable for the German theatre and the tastes of the German people."[4] However, with the universal acclaim granted to the productions of both *Tannhäuser* and *Lohengrin*, Munich finally opened itself up to the world of Wagner's creations: On 12 August 1855, Munich witnessed its first production of *Tannhäuser*.

Ludwig's parents had little interest in opera in general, and Wagner's operas in particular. But they could only deny their headstrong son for so long. He had to wait for three years after reading Baroness Leonrod's enthusiastic letter, but on 2 February 1861, Ludwig finally received permission to attend a Munich performance of *Lohengrin*.

On that cold February evening, as scurries of snow swept across the red tile roofs of Munich's shops and halls, the sixteen-year-old prince walked through the long marble corridors of the Residenz, surrounded by portraits of his stern-faced Wittelsbach ancestors and medieval heroes, and made his way to the court theater. He entered the royal box and sank into a gilded armchair; within a few minutes, the intoxicating magic of Wagner's music began to surge through the theater and his soul. The richly fringed curtains swept aside, revealing a world which Ludwig had only been able to imagine in his dreams.

The setting was a square in medieval Brabant. Ludwig watched as a chorus of knights and their ladies filled the stage, their brilliant cloaks, shining armor, and swirling gowns combining to create a wildly kaleidoscopic scene. The festivities soon gave way to tragedy, as Elsa, a young princess, was falsely accused by her evil guardian Telramund of murdering her brother Gottfried. In desperation, she pleaded her case before King Heinrich, praying that God would send a champion to defend her and pledging her hero the kingdom and herself as a wife. Suddenly, as Ludwig watched the stage, he saw the vivid murals in Hohenschwangau brought to life: Lohengrin arrived in a boat drawn by a swan. For years, Ludwig had fantasized about the Swan Knight; he read of Lohengrin in books, gazed upon him in paintings, drew him in pictures, and imagined his great deeds. Now this mythical hero appeared before him in shining armor, an embodiment of the young man's dreams of chivalry and honor. He watched as Lohengrin declared that he had been sent to restore Elsa's lost honor, and challenged Telramund to battle; after having defeated the princess's wicked guardian, the heroic knight allowed him to live.

The people of Brabant heralded the mysterious knight, who declared that he would remain to marry Elsa and rule over them as long as she refrained from asking his name, where he had come from, and his lineage. Lohengrin and Elsa eventually married, but on their wedding night, their blissful, unearthly happiness was destroyed when, unable to resist temptation any longer, Elsa broke her pledge and begged her lover's identity. As the music rose over the great theater, suffused light flashing against the prisms of the crystal chandeliers, Ludwig perched at the edge of his seat, watching as the magical spell was broken: The mysterious swan boat reappeared and the knight was forced to leave Brabant. Before he departed, he told Elsa that he was Lohengrin, son of Parsifal, the king of the Temple of the Holy Grail. Ludwig took his parting words to heart: As a god, he could never hope to share in the earthly love of a mere mortal, and the relationship was doomed from the beginning. At the end of the evening, Ludwig returned to his rooms in the Residenz, overwhelmed by what he had just seen. Not only had his childhood fantasies been brought to life in action, costume, and song, but his own personal hero, Lohengrin, now appeared as a flesh-and-blood character, an honorable knight whose very status elevated him above all men and condemned him to a life of loneliness. Ludwig identified more closely with Lohengrin than with any other character, finding in his unique position, emotional turmoils, and ultimate self-sacrifice an echo of his own innermost thoughts. After Ludwig's death, a costume of the Swan Knight was discovered among his personal effects, a sad testament to his own struggles to come to peace with himself.

On 22 December of the following year, Ludwig attended his first performance of *Tannhäuser*. Wagner had based his opera on E. T. A. Hoffmann's epic, which in turn came from the medieval German legend. It was a story of love and temptation and man's inability to choose between spiritual fulfillment and the pleasures of the flesh. According to Franz von Leinfelder, the court secretary who accompanied him to the performance, Ludwig sat in silence throughout the opera; at times, he leaned forward to the edge of the royal box, straining to see and hear every action and word being played out before him. Tannhäuser, a medieval knight, fell in love with the beautiful and pure Elizabeth, a princess who lived high above her subjects in Wartburg Castle. During his courtship with the virginal princess, the knight was tempted and seduced by Venus, the queen of love, who inhabited the Venusberg, a grotto dedicated to sensual pleasures far below Wartburg's battlements. Throughout the opera, he struggled with his desires for both women, with his choice between purity and carnal delights. At times during the performance, von Leinfelder noted, the effect of the music on Ludwig was "almost demonical. . . . It made an overwhelming impression on his nervous system, and at times during the performance his reactions were almost morbid."[5] By the time the opera reached its climax and Tannhäuser abandoned Elizabeth to return to the Venusberg grotto, Ludwig, according to the secretary, "was thrown into such convulsions that I was afraid he might have an epileptic seizure."[6]

Much has been made of Ludwig's supposed lack of musical sense. In 1861, for example, de la Rosée, on the advice of Ludwig's music instructor reported to the king: "The lessons in playing the piano may be stopped as His Royal Highness the crown prince has neither talent for music nor does he like it."[7] Ignaz von Döllinger reported that Ludwig lacked "a musical ear."[8] Wagner himself later made several comments to the effect that Ludwig was completely unmusical. But the evidence suggests otherwise. Although, particularly with Wagner's operas, Ludwig enjoyed the spectacle and quasi-religious experience he derived from seeing tales of medieval Germany enacted, he also frequently attended symphony performances of works by artists such as Ludwig van Beethoven, Johann Sebastian Bach, Christoph Willibald Gluck, Wolfgang Amadeus Mozart, and Carl Maria von Weber. There was little drama involved in a night at the symphony, particularly as Ludwig never enjoyed parading himself before the inquisitive eyes of the public. Some of Wagner's criticism undoubtedly stemmed from Ludwig's lack of musical knowledge; he understood nothing of the components of the operas, caring instead only for the effect of the music and the mood it produced. The comment of the piano teacher almost certainly reflects this as well: Ludwig was no musician, and he had little talent where his own attempts were concerned. But the suggestion that he did not enjoy Wagner's operas for their musical content—or, indeed, the works of any other composer—is without merit. Ludwig himself wrote that "only the heavenly, God-born art of music was able to make clear to me the blissful emotions that fill my soul; the eternal cannot be laid hold of in words; to try to do that would be a profanation."[9]

The only Wittelsbach rulers Ludwig cared for were those who had recognized early on the genius of artists who later acquired critical and general approbation throughout Europe: Johann of Wittelsbach, who sponsored Jan van Eyck; Albert V, who counted among the members of his court Vischer, Krafft, and Albrecht Dürer; Maximilian Josef I, whose court architects Cuvilliés and Zimmermann created the exuberant Bavarian rococo style found in the Residenz and Nymphenburg Palace; and his own grandfather, King Ludwig I, who had changed the face of the Bavarian capital forever. Even his own father, the somewhat staid and unimaginative Maximilian II, had imported groups of artists and musicians from Prussia to add a touch of refinement to his capital. In art and architecture, Ludwig found what he believed to be not only his Wittelsbach heritage but also the purpose which would one day rule his life when he became king. Other monarchs had sponsored artists and builders; Ludwig would turn to Richard Wagner, and by doing so, he would help create a world which he found infinitely more enriching than the grim and stilted atmosphere of his parents' court. Through his efforts, Ludwig would also assist in the larger struggle which Wagner had described, the unification of the German people through a common bond of nationalistic art.

Ludwig had been nursing a growing distaste for the nineteenth century, not only for the world of his parents but also for the cold, unfriendly, and harsh realities of modern life throughout Europe. He hated it all: the beer hall entertainments which kept his father so amused; the industrialization of the cities, with their factories and smokestacks puffing black clouds of waste into the blue sky; the lack of the manners and chivalry which had marked earlier ages; the egalitarian attitudes which celebrated such horrible events as the French Revolution and the idea of regicide; and the usurping of European crowns, offices Ludwig held to be divinely ordained, by such parvenus as the monarchs of the Bonaparte dynasty. In Wagner's art, Ludwig could escape these modern realities and immerse himself in a world of ancient, pure, and holy fantasy.

The operas proved to Ludwig that art was, in and of itself, a separate reality, which could be shaped according to the wishes of the artist and patron. By submerging himself in a world of art, Ludwig could create his own environment, not only giving substance to his dreams but triumphing over the frailties of love and temptation. It was a message which he clearly took to heart, for it later shaped his own desire to build castles and palaces as places of refuge from the world in which he lived, artificial settings made concrete through the reality of art itself.

Wagner himself saw in his operas the same spiritual overtones for the German people which so captivated Ludwig. These were not mere works of art, as ordinary people understood such things. Wagner was providing the German people with a kind of alternate religion, a secular forum in which to display the lofty ideals of romantic love, spiritual temptation, and triumph, and the purity of national art. True art—the best art, according to Wagner—should educate and enlighten, uplift and purify as well as entertain, and through his operas he intended to guide the German people back to their forgotten past.

That Ludwig held Wagner the artist as a model for his own life, a man to guide and influence his actions, is beyond doubt. In one schoolboy essay, he wrote that this is precisely what he intended for the future once he came to the throne.

> . . . to take as a model a real man who is good and energetic in every respect and make him the guide. One should make it one's task and duty to follow this man and, in order to be able to do that, one must know and understand him thoroughly and study his whole life. By this means one is inspired to follow his footsteps as closely as possible until, at last, one is completely animated by him, and inspired by his whole way of life.

His tutor dismissed this paper with a single word written across its top: "Rubbish."[10] Yet here he laid out the plan which he meant to follow, including his specific intentions involving Richard Wagner. His other essays began to take on a hint of obsession, with such titles as "The War of the Wartburg" and "The Nibelungen Saga," but at the time of their composition, no one seemed to have been seriously concerned as to the direction in which they pointed.

Ludwig's dedication to Wagner and his works soon spread to every aspect of his life. It provided his favorite entertainment at the theater, furnished him with reading materials which filled his head with thoughts of his future position, spilled onto the pages of the essays and letters which he wrote, and began to dominate the decoration and furnishings of the rooms in which he lived.

Barely a year after the performance of *Tannhäuser*, a copy of the poem *Der Ring des Nibelungen*, with a preface by Richard Wagner, was given to Ludwig by one of his mother's ladies-in-waiting, Countess Fugger. In this preface, the composer denounced the current state of German opera; for his own works, Wagner hoped for better productions with higher standards and trained musicians, singers, and actors working together in a creative community. But Wagner despaired of ever reaching his goal, pointing out what he saw as the sad state of financial support for the arts in Germany. He did, however, hint that a German prince could lend his support as a patron to such a cause, thus ensuring the purity and survival of German art for generations to come. He ended the preface with this question: "Will this Prince be found?"[11] Reading these words, Ludwig was overcome with emotion. Here lay his destiny, his purpose as a monarch, his role in adult life. Given the opportunity, Ludwig vowed to himself, he would be this patron prince, come to the rescue of German national art.

5

"The Most Beautiful Youth I Have Ever Seen"

At the age of eighteen, Ludwig towered over his father. He stood six foot four, a slender young man whose exceptional looks captivated all who saw him. He had his mother's dark blue eyes and pale, ivory complexion; his finely chisled features reflected his Wittelsbach heritage. His dark hair, naturally straight, was tonged into dramatic waves each morning by the court barber; once, Ludwig vainly went so far as to declare, "If I didn't have my hair curled every day I couldn't enjoy my food."[1]

He made a lasting impression on all who saw him. The Austrian writer Klara Tschudi recorded:

> He was the most beautiful youth I have ever seen. His tall, slim figure was perfectly symmetric. His rich, slightly curling hair and the few traces of a mustache gave his head a similiarity to those great antique works of art through which we have our first ideas of Hellenic manly strength. Even if he had been a beggar, I would have noticed him. Nobody, old or young, rich or poor, could have been left untouched by the charm which radiated from his personality. His voice was agreeable. The questions which he asked were clear and definite. The subjects of his conversation were well chosen and spiritual; he expressed himself with ease and naturally. The enthusiasm with which he inspired me never diminished but, on the contrary, increased with the years.[2]

Years of rugged physical exercise, along with his compulsory military training, left Ludwig a strong, powerfully built young man. His favorite exercise was riding: He was known in his family as a tireless, if somewhat reckless, rider. An English witness recalled that Ludwig "sits with perfect ease on his horse, and, for a youth of his age, he carries himself with an extreme dignity, his beautiful eyes look straight ahead. Alas, nobody, except perhaps an enthusiastic young girl, would say that that beautiful young horseman looks very militaristic—because he might have got his hair cut."[3] His courage was undoubted: Once, Ludwig and his mother were taking a drive in a four-in-hand near Nymphenburg Palace, the prince riding in the postilion position. Halfway through the ride, Marie expressed concern at their swift speed, but Ludwig reassured her that everything was fine. When they reached the courtyard of the palace, however, Marie saw her son reach forward and grab the flowing manes of the horses to stop them: The reins had come loose from the bits during the ride, and Ludwig, using a whip, had managed to control the breakaway animals through sheer skill alone.[4]

Ludwig's physical appearance was unusual. His complexion was just a little too pale; his forehead, like that of his father, a little too high; his ears a little too prominent; his height an incongruous match to his slender build, so that his clothes often seemed too large. Yet, in spite of these peculiarities, Ludwig possessed a presence and bearing entirely in keeping with his regal station. A graceful dancer, though he cared little for dancing, he made a lasting impression on his future subjects whenever he attended his parents' court balls. Shy and uncomfortable in social situations, he often bowed his head, casting sidelong glances at unfamiliar faces in an effort to avoid their inquisitive stares.

His personality was a curious mixture of warmth and reserve. With those few people he embraced as intimates, he could be smothering in his affections and obsessive in his need for acceptance. At the same time, he treated most people with a cool disdain: He had no time for the officials who inhabited the world of his parents' courts. De la Rosée had drilled into Ludwig the need to hide his emotions; royalty was expected to appear distant and dispassionate. Ludwig, however, was never able to master his feelings, and many of those who surrounded him were later to comment on his seemingly violent changes of temper. His mercurial moods reflected his emotional immaturity; raised in splendid isolation, he had enjoyed no opportunity to experience regular friendships and their stabilizing influences.

As a youth, he was confined to a world of tutors, military instructors, and court officials, all of whom treated Ludwig with exaggerated deference; this rarefied life deprived him of any opportunity to measure his own position against the world outside his father's palace. Ludwig longed for companionship, for a confidant with whom he could share his dreams, but Count de la Rosée had told him to trust no one: No one was equal to his position, and no one could understand his difficulties. The count had allowed no friendships to develop; instead, Ludwig was taught that friends were a luxury which royals had to do without. Members of the royal family could be trusted as intimates, but no one else.

Ludwig always believed himself called to higher ideals. "He placed great value on feeling that his heart was pure and that his soul was chaste and unsullied" wrote one member of the government. "He gloried passionately in everything beautiful, great and noble, in the most exalted ideals."[5] Although he was naturally kind, it was a kindness tempered with an absolute conviction of his own superiority. More important, his seclusion had left him amazingly naive. He had to have the term "rape" explained to him soon after he became king, such was the prudish isolation in which he had been raised.[6] Summing up his years of training, Count de la Rosée reported: "He is lively and very gifted. He has learned a good deal, and already has a range of knowledge far beyond the ordinary. He has a wealth of imagination that I have seldom met with in so young a man. But he is hasty and passionate; an exceptionally developed willfulness points to an obstinacy which he has probably inherited from his grandfather and which it will be difficult to master."[7]

On 25 August 1863, Ludwig celebrated his eighteenth birthday at Hohenschwangau with his parents and Otto. He rose early that morning and took to his beloved countryside, strolling the trails and fishing on the Alpsee. When he returned to Hohenschwangau, Ludwig eagerly opened the stacks of carefully wrapped packages which stood waiting. Among his presents were several paintings of the Nibelungen saga and a swan-shaped pin studded with diamonds. In a rather extraordinary gesture, Maximilian arranged for the Füssen Choir to serenade his son in the courtyard of the castle. Ludwig and his family sat in the warm breeze on the terrace, listening with enjoyment to the gathered choir; their voices floated over the tiled battlements and on into the lengthening night as the sun set over the Bavarian Alps, turning their sharp peaks into a brilliant range of crimson fires silhouetted against the darkening sky. Somewhat wistfully, Ludwig wrote to his former governess: "How quickly these eighteen years have passed away. My childhood reminiscences are so vivid before my eyes—all those beautiful days which we spent together."[8]

A number of small but significant changes marked Ludwig's birthday. His annual civil list, paid out by the royal treasury, was increased to a more suitable amount, and the king appointed a small suite to look after his son, including a private secretary and two aides-de-camp, Lieutenant Baron Karl Theodor von Sauer and Lieutenant Prince Paul von Thurn und Taxis. The crown prince's personal staff also grew to include a valet, butler, and his own barber. More important for Ludwig, he was given his own suite of apartments in the

Munich Residenz. Reached by a private entrance from the Hofgarten, his rooms were on the top floor of the northeastern corner of the palace, just above those of his parents.

He could now schedule his own days and, for the first time, choose his own friends. He maintained a constant correspondence with his cousin Princess Anna of Hesse and By Rhine, confiding his interests and fears to her in the knowledge that she would never reveal his secrets. Ludwig's first attentions fell upon his cousin, Prince Karl Theodor in Bavaria. Known in the Wittelsbach family as Gackl, he was a handsome, good-natured young man, the son of Ludwig's bohemian uncle Duke Max. Ludwig confided to Baroness Leonrod:

> Knowing your good heart, which takes such a lively interest in everything I do, I feel I ought to tell you that I have found a true and faithful friend, whose only friend I am; it is my cousin Karl, the son of Duke Max. He is hated and misunderstood by almost everybody; but I know him better, and know that he has a good heart and soul. Oh, it is so beautiful to have a true and beloved friend to whom one can cling in the storms of life and with whom one can share everything.[9]

Ludwig wrote these lines at the beginning of spring 1863. Although he expressed great ardor over the friendship, his feelings for his cousin amounted to little more than an innocent and romantic schoolboy crush. Far more serious, and lasting, were Ludwig's affections for his aide-de-camp, Prince Paul von Thurn und Taxis.

Prince Paul was twenty years old, a tall, slender, handsome young man, polite and congenial. He boasted an illustrious heritage. The Thurn und Taxis family had served as postmasters general to the Holy Roman Empire for centuries, a position which brought with it great wealth and prestige. Their palace in Regensburg was a showplace of art treasures, and they were a renowned, cultured, and artistically inclined family. In addition, Paul was actually married to Ludwig's second cousin: His brother by his father's second marriage, Prince Maximilian, had married Hélène, daughter of Duke Max and sister of both Ludwig's beloved cousin Gackl and Empress Elizabeth of Austria. This fact recommended him to the king as a suitable companion to the crown prince. More important, he was loyal, devoted, and, above all, discreet—qualities which Ludwig would soon test to their very limits.

In the late summer of 1863, Ludwig and Paul spent a considerable amount of time alone in the Alps during the royal family's usual holiday. They soon abandoned the king and his family at Hohenschwangau for the remote pleasures of an old castle at Berchtesgarten. Here, amid the open meadows and thick forests, their friendship took a more intimate turn. They spent most of their time wandering through the mountains, riding, hiking, and reading poetry to each other. By the time he returned to the capital, Ludwig was enraptured; to his cousin Princess Anna he confessed: "After dinner . . . I went to see Prince Taxis. I only got to know him properly in Berchtesgarten, but have grown very fond of him."[10] Paul was unable to resist the overwhelming attentions of the beautiful young crown prince; soon enough, he fell under Ludwig's magical, romantic spell.

Ludwig's fondness for the young aide-de-camp quickly took on a more obsessive tone. Once the friendship was established, Ludwig showered Paul with emotional notes and letters, pledging his undying devotion. When they were separated, the frequency and intimacy of their letters reached a fever pitch. To have him nearer, Ludwig schemed to install Paul in a suite of rooms in the Residenz and appoint him chief aide-de-camp.

Paul feared that the intimate nature of the friendship would become known to members of the Munich court, and that he would be accused of taking advantage of the crown prince's affections to secure his position. Eventually, however, Paul could not resist Ludwig's intense pressure.

It did not take long for the gossip about Paul's style of life to reach Ludwig's ears. It was perhaps inevitable that the new favorite would suffer from the petty jealousy of royal servants and members of the Household whose families had served the Wittelsbachs for centuries. Rumors soon reached Ludwig that his friend was sharing his affections with any number of unnamed women. This upset Ludwig's fragile emotional balance, and he accused Paul of treachery. Paul wrote a plaintive letter to his friend, begging him not to listen to gossip. Paul's sensible words calmed Ludwig's distrustful nature and healed the threatening rift. Back in favor, he wrote:

> My Dear Ludwig!
> I dare to address you thus as you have asked me to do so. A thousand thanks for your dear and impatiently expected letter which I received yesterday. . . . I must confess that while saying goodbye to you at the station my eyes were moist, and that my thoughts have always been with you ever since. I often think of what you are doing and wonder whether you think of me. . . . I always wear your chain and consider it a symbol of the faith with which our friendship is bound together.[11]

*   *   *

De la Rosée's warnings to trust no one had deeply affected Ludwig, and he never knew if his friends were at his side by choice or were influenced by his position. This constant questioning of motives undermined all of Ludwig's relationships. He never had a circle of intimates to whom he could turn for support or advice. When he did form friendships, inevitably his affections fell on handsome young soldiers or members of the court, and his devotion always bordered on the obsessive. He entered into each of his friendships with a romantic optimism which temporarily blinded him to the realities of the situation. He gave himself wholly and expected the same kind of devotion in return. Because he lived in a world of dreams, Ludwig's ideas and expectations were always unrealistic, and never more so than when it came to his relationships. When reality intruded, Ludwig, filled with disappointment, would overreact and ruthlessly dismiss his new friend as insensitive and unworthy of his royal favor.

Ludwig longed for what he termed a "true friend" and, in Paul, believed that he had at last discovered his spiritual confidant. It began as a typical romantic friendship. Although there is substantial evidence of Ludwig's later homosexual desires, at the time of his relationship with Paul, he appears to have been entirely ignorant of all sexual matters. The intensity and obsessive quality of the friendship, with its declarations of undying love, certainly emphasize Ludwig's romantic nature, and it is likely that he had fallen in love with Paul without ever recognizing his own passions. But the relationship between Ludwig and Paul, whatever their romantic feelings, was almost certainly, at least in the first few years of its existence, not a sexual one.

To certain members of the royal court, however, the entire friendship was far too suspicious to pass without comment, and inevitably this affected the relationship. Rumors flew in Munich of the midnight meetings between the crown prince and his aide-de-camp at the latter's private house on the Turkenstrasse, a few blocks from the Residenz; of the lights burning in windows through the long nights; of the endless exchange of letters between the two young men; and of their unquenchable desire to be together. Ludwig's excessive devotion and need for his new friend colored their relations. Paul's failure to live up to Ludwig's stringent standards and reciprocate the devotion he received meant that he again found himself suspected of betrayal. Ludwig could not tolerate any rival. Soon, he was again besieged with tales of his friend's "frivolous life."[12] Although, this time around Ludwig dismissed the rumours, this malicious gossip against his beloved friend, and the petty jealousy at its root, solidified Ludwig's hatred of the Munich court and the incessant intrigues surrounding his future throne.

6

"God Has Taken a Good King from Us"

Ludwig made his first formal appearance before the public on his seventeenth birthday. On that clear, cloudless August day in 1862, he joined his parents and the entire royal family as they dedicated a statue to his grandfather King Ludwig I. Flags hung miserably in the windless, humid heat. A brass band played the national anthem as Ludwig watched his father unveil the new statue. He walked at Maximilian's side, head slightly bowed from self-consciousness. Ludwig had little enthusiasm for the public side of royal life, with its reviews, parades, dinners, and balls. In a letter to his cousin Anna of Hesse at the end of 1862, he noted with apparent satisfaction: "I do not think that I will be allowed to dance very much until next year because today my throat is again rather swollen. But I may go to the Theatre, and I like that much more than all the balls."[1]

In spite of his powerful build, Ludwig had always suffered from somewhat delicate health. Minor illnesses often plagued the crown prince, but he never appeared to mind. He sat for hours by the fire, reading his favorite authors. Nevertheless, he was still expected to participate in functions at his father's court. It was at one of these, in the fall of 1863, that Ludwig first met the man who was about to change the face of German politics and dominate the destiny of Bavaria for the next twenty-five years, Count Otto von Bismarck, chancellor of Prussia.

A banquet was given for Bismarck at Nymphenburg Palace. Ludwig, as crown prince, sat next to the chancellor, who later wrote a telling account of the evening.

> It seemed to me that his thoughts were far away from the table and only now and again did he remember his intention to talk to me; our conversation did not go beyond the ordinary court subjects. But even so I thought I recognized in his remarks a talent, a vivacity, and a good sense realized in his future career.

In the pauses of the conversation he looked past his mother to the ceiling, now and again hastily emptying his champagne glass, the filling of which was, as it seemed to me by his mother's directions, somewhat slowly performed; thus it happened that the Prince very often held his glass over his shoulder, behind him, where it was hesitatingly refilled. Neither then nor later did he overstep the bounds of moderation in drinking but I had the feeling that the surroundings bored him and that the champagne aided the play of his independent fancy. He made a sympathetic impression on me, although I must confess with some vexation that my efforts towards a pleasant conversation with him at the table were unsuccessful.[2]

Bismarck left Munich just as a major crisis threatened to erupt. Along the Elbe to the north lay two duchies, Schleswig and Holstein. Both Denmark and the German Confederation claimed sovereignty over the contentious lands, and a conflict over their eventual control seemed inevitable. Though efforts were made through negotiations to forestall such an outbreak, hostilities eventually erupted in February of 1864.

The crisis over the Schleswig-Holstein question took its toll on King Maximilian's already frail health. For most of his adult life, he had suffered from nervous exhaustion and debilitating headaches. It was whispered that he had contracted syphilis as a youth on a visit to Hungary, and was plagued with the symptoms of the disease, including mental instability, prior to his last illness.[3] In the last months of 1863, Maximilian increasingly complained of feeling unwell; a handful of royal physicians diagnosed severe rheumatism and advised the king to move to the warmer climate of Italy to rest through the harsh Bavarian winter. For a time, his ministers made the lengthy journey to Italy to consult with the king and receive his decisions, but as the Schleswig-Holstein crisis heightened, the Bavarian populace grew anxious. It was contrary to the etiquette of the Bavarian court to mention the health of any member of the royal family except in the most grave of circumstances, and none of Maximilian's subjects knew that he had gone to Italy on his doctors' orders. They felt that he was evading his duty at a time of crisis, and there were demonstrations in the streets outside of the Residenz calling for his return. Ever dutiful, and against the strong warnings of the royal physicians, Maximilian returned to the chill climate of his capital for the winter.

On 10 February 1864, King Maximilian and Queen Marie presided over a ball in the Altes Residenztheatre. Through the heavy falling snow, the windows of the Residenz blazed with candlelight as long lines of carriages and gilded sleighs drew up at the palace entrance, depositing their passengers, who gratefully handed over their fur wraps and heavy greatcoats and ascended the marble staircase to the warmth of the state apartments. All of the guests came in elaborate eighteenth-century-style costumes; they swept deep curtsies and bows to the king and to the queen, who wore a mauve velvet gown trimmed with ermine and embroidered with gold thread and diamonds. But Maximilian was so weak that he could barely last out the evening; no one guessed that this was to be his last public appearance.

The doctors believed Maximilian to be suffering merely from exhaustion, and ordered several days of bed rest. Under their supervision, he at first seemed to be recovering from his illness. But the ball he had hosted with the queen had worn him out. A few days after the affair, he took his usual walk in the Hofgarten, hoping that the fresh air would improve his condition; instead, he caught a cold. As the king was already fatigued and physically weak, the seemingly innocuous cold quickly turned into pneumonia.

Word of his illness soon reached the ears of the public. When the physicians began to issue regular medical bulletins on the king's condition, the entire capital suddenly realized the gravity of the situation.

> Although His Majesty the King did not go out during the last few days he had a fever yesterday which became worse toward the evening. This morning the fever is a little better, but it is not yet gone. The local disturbances are a catarrh of the nose, throat and trachea.[4]

The next bulletin, issued a few days later, seemed hopeful:

> His Majesty the King is better in every way.[5]

And, finally, on 27 February, the court physicians felt confident enough to declare:

> The fever of His Majesty the King has completely gone and the catarrh is getting better.[6]

Believing his father out of danger, Ludwig went to the court theater. He wanted to hear Albert Niemann sing the title role in *Lohengrin*, and was so overwhelmed by the magnificence of his voice that he immediately summoned the artist to a private audience in his apartments in the Residenz. To his cousin Anna he reported:

Lately I have been reading a great deal of Goethe, and was occupied with Niemann the singer that I really could not find time to write letters. . . . The other night I got somebody to throw lots of flowers to him, and I sent him a pair of cufflinks with swans and brilliants. Also a cross which gave him great pleasure. *Gardez silence! Je vous supplie!*
He wrote in my book:

No colours, no flowers,
No soul, no song![7]

Eventually, word of this questionable indulgence on Ludwig's part leaked out. Although the royal physicians had seemingly declared Maximilian to be out of danger, it appeared both in doubtful taste and disrespectful to his father that the crown prince should lavish such attention on an opera singer at a time of crisis. Ludwig had gone to the theater with the full assurance that his father's health was in no way imperiled, but this occasion, the first of many when he would ignore public opinion in favor of both Wagner's music and personal desire, caused some unfavorable whispers at his father's court.

Just a week after the royal physicians had pronounced Maximilian out of danger, the king suffered a relapse. On the afternoon of 7 March, he left the Residenz to take his regular stroll round the Hofgarten; by the time he returned to the palace, Maximilian could barely stand. He entered the Residenz, breathing heavily, and collapsed into the arms of his wife. Within two days, the royal physicians had confined Maximilian to his bed. His fever rose dramatically, and his gasps for breath filled the bedroom, frightening members of his family.

Like everyone else, Ludwig had believed that his father's illness had passed. Now his mother tearfully informed him that Maximilian's life was in danger. Although Ludwig appeared to have feared more than loved his father, he dutifully joined the queen and Otto at their vigils throughout the night. As the hours slipped away, Maximilian's fever rose and fell, making him delirious; his breathing became more difficult, and his only respite from the pain came when he lost consciousness. Throughout the ordeal, Marie and Otto remained at the king's bedside, but Ludwig wandered in and out of the room, lost in his own thoughts. The possibility that he would succeed his father was now imminent, a circumstance which overwhelmed the eighteen-year-old.

At four the next morning, Thursday, 10 March 1864, Archbishop Gregorios Scherr was summoned to administer the last rites. In a voice scarcely above a whisper, Maximilian asked to speak with Ludwig in private; Marie, Otto, and the rest of the family reluctantly left the gasping king alone with his uncertain heir. Members of the royal family who hovered beyond the doors were close enough to hear the king's last words: "My son, when your time comes, may you die as peacefully as your father."[8] With this, Maximilian closed his eyes in exhaustion. Ludwig and his mother and brother knelt at the side of the bed, awaiting the end; just after eleven-thirty that morning, with Marie holding his hand, Maximilian died.

Members of the court and royal household waited beyond the bedroom, filling the corridors and drawing rooms with their whispers and faintly muttered prayers. Finally, Archbishop Scherr, with head bowed and hands clasped, emerged from the royal chamber and was immediately asked, "Is the King still alive?"

"Yes," the archbishop replied, his voice choked with emotion. "He lives in Heaven. God has taken a good King from us, let us pray to Him that He sends us such another again."[9] A hush fell over the courtiers. In the Hofgarten, soldiers manned their guns to fire a last salute to the dead monarch, shattering the sleepy, late morning silence; soon the bells of the capital's churches and cathedral began their monotonous tolling. Just after noon, the doors of the late king's bedroom swung open. The gathered crowd bowed or sank into deep curtsies as the tall, shadowy figure of King Ludwig II appeared. He paused, silhouetted against the brilliant spring light pouring into the room behind him, his head bent and his eyes filled with tears at the thought of the new and overwhelming responsibilities facing him. It was a sad and heavy moment for everyone.

The eighteen-year-old youth who walked through that doorway and humbly held out his hand to the kneeling courtiers was a complete enigma: beautiful and proud, also reserved and shy. No one knew anything about his character, his thoughts, or his dreams. But Ludwig, the melancholy, sullen crown prince, was now the great and respected king, following in the footsteps of Charlemagne, Barbarossa, and Ludwig the Bavarian.

Bavarian monarchs had no coronation ceremony; instead, Ludwig made his first official appearance as king at his accession council, where he was invested with the royal regalia and took a simple oath of allegiance to the constitution. On 12 March, as the body of the late king lay in state in the Hofkapelle of the Residenz, his son's accession council was held.

Early that morning, hundreds of specially invited guests began arriving at the Residenz to witness the procession and the oath of allegiance. Government ministers, army field marshals, civil servants, clerical representatives, and courtiers crowded the long marble corridors and rococo drawing rooms of the palace, awaiting the king's appearance. The heavy black crepe draping the chandeliers and gilded pelmets fluttered softly as occasional breezes passed through the cavernous palace. Members of the diplomatic corps stood silently in the halls, their severe mourning clothes a somber contrast to the shining medals and orders decorating their chests and hanging from their necks. The whispers, the veils of the women, and the black drapes everywhere lent to the occasion a solemn, haunting quality.

Shortly before eleven, the doors of the private apartments opened and the grand marshal of the court appeared, signaling the approach of the new king. Ludwig walked with members of his household and suite. He wore the uniform of a general in the Bavarian army, with white breeches and a long blue tunic with crested silver buttons and silver epaulets. Across his chest stretched the red ribbon of the Order of St. George; the chain of the Order of St. Hubertus hung from his collar. Over his youthful shoulders hung the heavy, ermine-lined royal mantle of crimson-and-gold cloth. Slowly, he ascended the Imperial Staircase between ranks of Chevalier Gardes in silver breastplates, Uhlans in blue uniforms and plumed helmets, and Lancer Guards, all of them with swords drawn and raised in salute.

Ludwig entered the Throne Room preceded by pages carrying the regalia on velvet cushions: the state crown, scepter, orb, and chain of office. Another page carried the sword of state, its hilt studded with diamonds that flashed fire with every step. As Ludwig moved through the enormous room, the crowd standing against the walls bowed or dropped deep curtsies, the soft rustling of silk gowns breaking the silence of the moment. He climbed the steps of the dais to the gilded throne and turned to face the privy councillors, ministers, and court officials, raised his hand, and read the oath of allegiance from a gilded book held by an equerry. Ludwig then took his accession speech from a page and, with moist eyes, began to read in a slow and unsteady voice.

> It has pleased Almighty God to call away My Beloved Father from the Earth. It is impossible for Me to tell you what feelings are passing through My Heart. The task which lies before Me is a difficult and heavy one, but I build My Hopes on God that He will send Me the understanding and strength with which to fulfill it. I will reign true to the oath I have just taken and to the spirit of Our Constitution. All My efforts will be devoted to furthering the welfare of My People, and the greatness of Germany. I ask You to accord Me Your assistance in the carrying out of these, My difficult duties.[10]

Two days later, the state funeral for the late king took place. Building fronts and lamp standards were draped in heavy black crepe which hung limply in the misty air. The mournful tolling of church bells, the muffled beats of drums, and the steady rhythm of the funeral march accompanied the long cortege as it wound its way slowly through the streets to the Theatinerkirche, where the king's remains would be laid to rest in the Wittelsbach crypt. Ludwig, dressed in the dark blue uniform of a colonel in the Bavarian infantry but bareheaded, walked with his brother immediately behind the wreath-covered hearse, drawn by horses draped in black. He seemed unaware of the people who, with respectfully bowed heads, waited anxiously to catch a glimpse of their new monarch. One witness recalled:

> The pale young King walked in the middle of the procession beside his chubby younger brother. Ludwig's sad expression naturally aroused the sympathy of everyone and immediately won the hearts of the citizens, who shared his grief. If only you could have seen him, this pale young man, as he walked with bowed head and faltering steps behind the coffin of his beloved father. He had extraordinarily expressive eyes. . . . The whole impression of his appearance was both moving and regal.[11]

Such were the general thoughts of the citizens of Munich who celebrated the beauty and youth of their new king. But those who knew him better had a different view. Two days after Maximilian's funeral, the court secretary, Franz von Leinfelder, met Ludwig's former tutor de la Rosée on the Imperial Staircase of the Residenz. Leinfelder seemed optimistic about the new reign, declaring that "we now have an angel on our Throne." But the count's only comment was that Maximilian II's death was the worst possible tragedy which could have befallen Bavaria.[12]

7

The New Reign

The day after his father's funeral, Ludwig settled down to his task in earnest. "In difficult times you succeed to the Throne too early," his grandfather wrote to Ludwig soon after his accession. "May God lead you in the right paths and may religion always be with you."[1] He was only the latest in a long line of Wittelsbachs to rule in Bavaria and, as king, was at first determined to follow in the somewhat cautious footsteps of his father. His intentions were clearly honorable. To his former governess Baroness Leonrod he wrote: "I carry my heart to the Throne—a heart which beats for my people and which glows for their welfare—all Bavarians may be assured of that. I will do everything in my power to make my people happy; their welfare, their peace are the conditions of my happiness."[2]

Ludwig's character was a mystery to his new ministers. Because of his youth and lack of experience, many politicians in the Bavarian government expected the new king to be pliable and easily impressed. Instead, he soon proved obstinate and determined to have his own way in all matters. Ludwig brought to the throne an extraordinary degree of dignity and pride in his royal office, an unshakable belief in the providential nature of his position. Throughout the twenty-two years of his reign, no one—not his ministers, not Bismarck, not even Richard Wagner—ever managed to manipulate Ludwig. Inevitably, during the first years of his reign, Ludwig faced ministerial revolt and attempts to make political capital of his näiveté, but he met such threats with unexpected demonstrations of his imperious will. The king's ability to stand his ground was all the more surprising given the disorganized nature of the Bavarian government.

At the time of his accession, the king ruled with the benefit of the Landtag, which consisted of two chambers, the House of Peers and the House of Deputies. The Council of Ministers was led by the prime minister, with the heads of the various ministerial departments and their staffs working under him. But Ludwig's contact with the leading political figures of the day was limited by the structure of the government: Instead of communicating directly with the head of the government, Ludwig had to seek the intervention of a third party, the cabinet secretary, the most important person in the king's private cabinet.

This curious system was a legacy of Ludwig I, who, preoccupied with his own building projects in Munich, created a second set of officials to act as intermediaries between crown and government. The Cabinet Secretariat was thus composed of men who were members of the king's personal household and, at the same time, government officials. This group was headed by the cabinet secretary, a man who held perhaps more authority than the prime minister himself. All official matters were directed through the cabinet secretary, a position filled by Franz von Pfistermeister. Pfistermeister was sixteen years older than Ludwig, an old-school, hard-line conservative who supported Catholic tradition and the principle of service to the state.

The role of cabinet secretary was all-important: It was he who determined what issues were to be raised with the king, he who scheduled ministerial meetings, he who advised Ludwig on proposed legislation and official matters. As sovereign, Ludwig held no real power. According to the Bavarian constitution, he possessed rights similiar to those claimed by the British Crown: the right to be consulted, the right to encourage, and the right to warn, in the words of the English constitutional historian Walter Bagehot. To some extent, the degree of authority exercised by Bavarian sovereigns depended upon the personality of the king and the composition of his government. In the nineteenth century, with the formal declaration of the kingdom and the granting of a constitution, sovereign power slowly began to shift from the Residenz to the Landtag. Official questions required royal assent as a matter of course, but this was a mere formality. If the king protested against a government policy or involved himself directly in the affairs of state, his interest evoked the specter of a constitutional crisis. Thus, Bavarian monarchs met with officials, read through state papers, listened to the counsel of the cabinet secretary, and discreetly advised ministers but undertook few political decisions. While the king, therefore, could not function constitutionally without the intervention of the Cabinet Secretariat, the government, in conjunction with the secretariat, could function without the presence of the king. It was this aspect of the government's structure which later allowed King Ludwig II to ignore the affairs of state and concentrate his attention on building schemes.

The other important group of officials surrounding the king was his Court Secretariat, which operated separately from the rest of the Bavarian government. While the Cabinet Secretariat functioned as an arm of the government, the Court Secretariat consisted of members of the king's personal household. This included the department of the royal treasury and control of the civil list, from which the king derived his annual income from the state. In general charge of this group was the court secretary, who acted as head of the king's household and keeper of the privy purse, a position occupied by Julius von Hofmann. A number of other politicians who were to play important roles in the king's reign held minor posts at the time of his accession to the throne. Chief among these were Pfistermeister's undersecretary, Johann von Lutz; Count Maximilian von Holnstein, who held the post of *Oberstallmeister* or chief master of the royal horse; and Baron Ludwig von Pfordten, the foreign minister and head of the Cabinet of Ministers.

Ludwig II regularly began his days quite early, and by nine each morning he was at his immense desk, ready for his first audience. Each morning, he met with Pfistermeister, who advised the king of any scheduled engagements. There were the usual round of ceremonies to attend, including the less-than-glamorous activities of school openings, bridge dedications, and factory inspections. Still, the impressions left by the king as a political leader and monarch were, at least in the early days, glowing. The poet Paul Heyse later recalled: "The look in his beautiful, shining eyes was free and unselfconscious. He possessed an exceptionally sure knowledge of human nature which is remarkable considering that he had been brought up so alone and far from the world."[3] Even Bismarck, who prided himself on being a shrewd judge of character, wrote: "At all times he impressed me as being an active and clear-headed ruler of German-nationalist sympathies, even if his efforts were mainly directed towards the maintenance of the State federalist principle and of his country's constitutional rights."[4]

One or another of the government ministers generally met with the king to update him on the important issues of the day. The minister of justice, Eduard von Bomhard, later wrote:

> These sessions took place every week on the day allocated. One took one's seat on the sofa beside the King, and it was a pleasure to see the wide, open expression in his eyes when some part of the conversation specially interested him. The King's demeanour had a certain degree of natural youthful shyness, which became him, but it was at the same time impressively regal. He listened to one's discourse with great attentiveness, often looking searchingly into one's eyes. Afterwards he would talk about general things, but always the loftier questions of the day, never about mundane gossip of court or town. . . . He was

mentally gifted in the highest degree but the contents of his
mind were stored in a totally disorganized fashion.[6]

Bomhard also noted the peculiar nature of the young king during the
audiences.

> I was struck by the way in which every now and then, just
> when his expression and whole demeanour seemed to show
> contentment, he would suddenly straighten up and—looking
> around him with a serious, even stern expression—would
> reveal something dark in himself that was in complete contrast
> to the youthful charm of a moment before. I thought to myself:
> "If two different natures are germinating in this young man, as
> it has seemed to me from the very first conversation with him,
> may God grant that the good one may be victorious."[6]

Although von Bomhard was generally favorable to Ludwig, he
also noted his lack of organization. There was often a sense among his
ministers that Ludwig was only going through the motions of being
king and that his mind was elsewhere. It was Ludwig's misfortune that
he did not possess the self-restraint necessary to hide his feelings. As
von Bomhard indicated, the king often let his mind wander during his
audiences, and when he spoke, he did so in such a pompous manner
that he frequently left his listener confused as to his real meaning.

Ludwig's throne speech at his accession council in the Residenz,
brief though it was, laid out a careful set of political priorities, although
in abbreviated fashion. The most important line had been written with
the growing tensions between Austria, Prussia, and the two Elbe
duchies in mind: "All My efforts will be devoted to furthering the welfare of My People and the Greatness of Germany." Subtly, Ludwig reinforced the idea that the sovereignty of Bavaria was his first concern.
There lay in the same speech the seeds of an alternative policy, when
the new king discussed the greatness of Germany and his desire to
unify the people over whom he ruled. Advisers wondered if perhaps
the new king cherished the same dream as his grandfather, Ludwig I,
who had expressed the wish to form a united German empire. No one
knew enough about Ludwig II to decide which policy he sought to
pursue, and only in time, when circumstances forced the king's hand,
would he reveal which of these two conflicting concerns he believed
most worthy of his government.

Nominally, the king appeared to follow in his father's footsteps,
which proved a relief to many in the country's government. All of
Bavaria had mourned the death of Good King Max, and everyone

believed that this inexperienced youth would leave the affairs of state to his ministers. Indeed, it is recorded that early on in his reign several ministers who posed policy questions to the king were met with a polite and tenuous, "How would my father have acted in this case?"[7] But Ludwig began to quietly break away from the cautious, conservative policies of the late king. He could behave imperiously. A few weeks after Maximilian had died, the court marshal suggested to Ludwig that he, as the new king, might wish to take up residence in his father's former suite of rooms, which were more suitable in size than the apartments which he had occupied as crown prince. But to this suggestion, Ludwig angrily replied, "If it pleases me I shall tell you!"[8]

As king, Ludwig relied chiefly upon his own instincts when it came to policy decisions. Because he lacked a circle of intimates, he was rarely subject to outside influences. He was close to no one in his immediate family. He feared and avoided his late father's two brothers, Luitpold and Adalbert, although he often deputized the latter in his place for social functions. His elderly great-uncle Prince Karl held the post of field marshal and commander in chief of the Bavarian army and had little in common with his romantic great-nephew. The king maintained good relations only with his grandfather Ludwig I. The former king, now living in exile in Nice, never tired of giving his young grandson advice on how to govern, relishing the chance to relive, if only as a surrogate, some of the power he had once enjoyed. His grandfather's advice was somewhat conservative and reactionary. "Don't give up any Rights of the Crown," he warned Ludwig on one occasion. "For a short time you will be praised for it—but the loss remains. How changeable the *aura popularis* is! Your grandfather has had his lesson!"[9]

Such advice clearly found favor with Ludwig. One day, he had a curious conversation with his uncle Grand Duke Ludwig III of Hesse and By Rhine. He told the grand duke that his position as king must naturally move toward an autocratic one, and that the only sovereign in all of Europe he considered worthy of the title of monarch was the grand duke's own brother-in-law, Emperor Alexander II of Russia. Hearing this rather alarming news, the grand duke cautioned his nephew, "If you believe that, Your Royal Majesty, my dearest nephew, you'll get awfully bruised!"[10]

In accordance with these privately expressed views and his strength of will, Ludwig laid out his full political policy to the government. On 17 May 1864, he presented the prime minister with the document outlining his intended course of action. Among other points, the king declared that he intended to "keep Parliamentarianism in check, maintain the balance of power in the monarch's hands; to preserve the principles of Maximilian II, to pursue a truly German policy without acting in any way detrimentally to the integrity and independence of Bavaria which must remain at the head of the Central States and maintain its existing importance in foreign policy."[11] Ludwig intended to rule Bavaria without the benefit of increasing the power of the Landtag. He had fallen short of declaring that he intended to circumvent the legal machinery of the government, but after reading this document, no one in the kingdom could doubt that king's strength of character and youthful determination.

Ludwig had made clear his policy of Bavarian independence while at the same time aiming for a closer unification of the various German states. He believed that it would be possible to steer his government on both courses of action. While complete and guaranteed freedom for Bavaria was his top priority, he was at the same time willing to seek out a strengthening of the old alliances which had existed in Germany for many decades. This was the Triad, the hope of uniting together the three largest states—Bavaria, Prussia, and Austria—as a guarantee against any unchecked aggression by any one of the partners. Just how far this policy could progress depended to a large extent upon the intentions of Chancellor Bismarck of Prussia with regard to the two duchies of Schleswig and Holstein. Bavarian foreign policy therefore became a tense waiting game during the first few months of Ludwig's reign.

The roots of the Schleswig-Holstein crisis stretched back decades. In 1815, following the defeat of Napoléon at Waterloo, the Congress of Vienna convened to redress the balance of power in Europe. Under the leadership of Prince Klemens von Metternich, the remnants of the old Holy Roman Empire—some three hundred kingdoms, principalities, grand duchies, dukedoms, and electorates—were reconstructed to form a new Reich. This affiliation resulted in the federal Deutscher Bund, a collection of thirty-nine German states, loosely controlled by a representative Diet headquartered at Frankfurt.

Through the careful machinations of Metternich, Austria reigned supreme in the federal Bund for the first fifty years of its existence. At the time of the Congress of Vienna, Austria was the only confederation member prestigious enough to take a leading role. But over the following years, Prussia worked diligently to improve its condition within the Bund. Her population grew; her army gained respect for its spartan, effective principles; and industrial growth presaged her expansion as a European power. Fifty years on, it was Prussia which held in its hands the power to change the course of German history. The only thing missing was a man of vision to show them the way. Then, in September of 1862, a former civil servant from Pomerania, Count Otto von Bismarck, was appointed chancellor of the Prussian kingdom.

Bismarck was forty-eight when the Schleswig-Holstein crisis erupted. For most of his life, he had lived in relative obscurity, his forceful character and unchecked ambitions lying hidden. But Bismarck was manipulative, shrewd, and arrogant, characteristics which served him well when the Prussian king, Wilhelm I, threatened to abdicate owing to the turmoil in his government. Bismarck stepped in and offered to take the chancellorship and form a new government which would respect the royal dignity; Wilhelm accepted, and Bismarck was firmly in place as the most powerful man in all of Prussia. A few days later, he made his famous and ominous remarks which sounded through the chancelleries of Europe: "The great questions of the time will not be solved by speeches and majority votes but by blood and iron."[12]

The duchies of Schleswig and Holstein occupied a strategically important position to the north of the German Confederation, extending along the Elbe River at the base of the Jutland Peninsula. The population of Schleswig was a mixture of Germans and Danes, while that of Holstein was predominately German. They had been loosely affiliated with the Danish crown for hundreds of years, but there was no formal treaty of incorporation, and questions of their sovereignty had troubled Europe for centuries. The situation was made even more complicated by the fact that, while Schleswig remained tied to Denmark, Holstein was a member of the German Confederation. In 1848, the largely German Holsteiners revolted against Danish rule, and Prussia, with the full approval of the federal Diet in Frankfurt, dispatched troops to aid in their struggle. When Imperial Russia protested, Prussia reluctantly withdrew her soldiers.

This incursion led to the Treaty of London in 1852, which placed the duchies under nominal Danish control. The treaty forbade the king of Denmark, however, from attempting to incorporate the duchies into his own kingdom. Because King Friedrich VII of Denmark was without heirs, the Treaty of London also appointed a distant relative descended through the female line of the Danish royal family, Prince Christian of Schleswig-Holstein-Sonderburg-Glucksburg, as his eventual successor. Both Schleswig and Holstein refused to accept Christian, citing the Salic Law as an inviolable part of their history and championing their own candidate, Prince Friedrich, duke of Augustenburg, a man with a strong hereditary claim to the disputed territories. The Treaty of London had awarded considerable financial compensation to the duke for his renunciation of any claims to the two duchies, and the matter seemed settled. But the German-speaking majority population, especially that of Holstein, resisted the enforced subjugation. On their behalf, Prussia protested against Danish influence, but neither country was prepared to resort to violence to firmly establish sovereignty.

There the matter might have rested had it not been for the ambitious king Friedrich VII. In 1855, he had tried to circumvent German authority and form a new parliament to rule over the duchies from Copenhagen, but the federal Bund in Frankfurt declared that this was a violation of the German constitution. Denmark chose not to push her position; however, in the passing years, the king continually waved the specter of a separate parliament in Frankfurt's face, further aggrevating tensions. Denmark seemed to revel in making these threats, and over the following years the Diet continually issued warnings that a breech of the Treaty of London would lead to hostilities. Disregarding these ominous predictions, Denmark flaunted its contempt for the Bund: on 30 March 1863, she created a separate parliament for Holstein and placed it under her authority, thus establishing a de facto Danish government.

This created serious diplomatic problems for the states joined together in the Deutscher Bund. Denmark's repeated disregard of the federal declarations amounted to a severing of political, economic, and diplomatic ties with the other German countries. Three months later, on 9 July, the federal Bund in Frankfurt, on behalf of all member states, formally issued a resolution demanding the dissolution of the illegal Holstein parliament. King Friedrich VII rejected this and instead threatened to forcibly incorporate the two duchies. As with the establishment of the Holstein parliament, such a move was illegal, according to both the Treaty of London and to the German federal constitution, by whose terms Denmark had previously agreed to abide.

The tense situation continued throughout the summer of 1863. Then, within the space of forty-eight hours that autumn, the crisis erupted. On 13 November, King Friedrich VII forcibly annexed the two duchies. Two days later, an unforeseen royal event occured which had dire consequences for the peace of Europe: On 15 November, King Friedrich died, and his distant relative acceded to the throne as King Christian IX. Not wishing to make the first act of his reign a concession, the new king promptly made good on the Danish threat and commanded that the forcible incorporation of the two duchies into his kingdom continue, ignoring both the protests and concerns of German confederation members and the terms of the Treaty of London. Christian's declaration brought the smoldering question to a crisis point: Should the two duchies fall under Danish or German control?

Bismarck showed little concern for the fate of the two duchies throughout the early months of the crisis. As a calculating, blunt politician, he was not interested in sentimental claims to the territories nor in the pattern of alliances which laid out the opposition. The chancellor operated according to the principles of realpolitik, a ruthlessly intel-

lectual view of government. Power, and the right to that power, were
Bismarck's only concerns. "In this manner," wrote one analyst, "Bis-
marck returned to the tradition of such eighteenth-century rulers as
Louis XIV and Friedrich the Great."[13]

King Friedrich's illegal incorporation of the duchies, and Christian IX's continuation of this policy, brought Bismarck to the forefront
of the argument. He knew that Prussia as a state had no claim to the
duchies; they properly fell under the joint authority of the Deutscher
Bund. But an opportunity had presented itself, and Bismarck was quick
to seize the chance which lay before him to assert Prussian influence
and power in northern Germany. At first, he was content to turn the
matter over to the German Bund for consideration, certain that they
would find against Denmark. Indeed, the confederation protested
Christian's move. But, at the same time, Bismarck was crafty enough
to plan for contingencies and waited to see how the situation would
play out before committing himself and his country's resources.

The population of Holstein immediately protested Christian IX's
accession and refused to swear allegiance to the Danish crown. They
appealed to Frankfurt for assistance, campaigning for the return of the
duke of Augustenburg. The Deutscher Bund was in an uproar, and all
of Germany was swept up in war fever. The Bund eventually passed a
resolution lending its support to the duke's claims and to the formation of an independent kingdom under his rule.

Bismarck was eager for Prussia to assert herself and desired a test
of her armies. If Prussia could gain control of the contentious lands,
she would have free access to the port of Kiel, a center of great strategic importance for her expanding naval forces. The chancellor was able
to convince Austria that the question over the duchies needed to be
dealt with in a forceful and direct manner. The two countries agreed to
act in unison against Denmark, ostensibly to support the 1852 Treaty
of London. The Austrians found the claims of the duke of Augustenburg intolerable "since his cause depended on a claim of national self-
determination," noted one historian, "a principle totally alien to the
Habsburgs."[14]

On Christmas Eve, 1863, Prussian and Austrian troops entered
the Duchy of Holstein. A week later, the German Confederation dispatched troops from Hanover and Saxony to join them in ousting Denmark. The German Confederation was still divided, with Prussia and
Austria favoring incorporation into the Bund, while Frankfurt was willing only to promote the claims of the duke of Augustenburg. But Bismarck refused to wait for unanimity. On 29 January 1864, he issued an
ultimatum to King Christian IX, demanding that Denmark withdraw
all of her soldiers and officials from Schleswig and Holstein. The chan-

cellor gave the king forty-eight hours to reply. Denmark refused to concede, and on 1 February 1864, Prussia, supported by Austria, declared war on Denmark.

Such was the history of the tangled conflict into which Ludwig was plunged from his very first days on the Bavarian throne. Bavaria, geographically sandwiched between Prussia to the north and Austria to the south, made no secret of her support for an independent Schleswig-Holstein, under the rule of the duke of Augustenburg. Politically, this was the most favorable solution to the problem for Bavaria. She did not wish to encourage either Prussian or Austrian aggression, fearing the results of such moves on her own future sovereignty. Nor did Denmark's imperious conduct find favor in Munich. Bavaria's encouragement of the duke of Augustenburg, however, did not extend beyond expressions of moral support. No one in Munich had any wish to see Bavarian soldiers embroiled in a military conflict in the north. Still, nearly everyone recognized the potential consequences: Prussia was anxious for a test of her military strength and intended to discover exactly how far she could push the members of the German Confederation.

The Bavarian policy of moderation was that of Maximilian II. He had participated in a conference the previous year on the Schleswig-Holstein problem hosted by Emperor Franz Josef of Austria, and made diplomatic pleas to all sides to contain the conflict. This was the legacy he left to his son Ludwig. But while Maximilian worried over the situation, Ludwig was absolutely bored. He cared little for politics and could not understand how anyone could be so caught up in the question of the two duchies. A few weeks before he came to the throne, he confessed to his cousin Anna: "I am *sick to death* of this eternal Schleswig-Holstein business. . . . *Please don't show this letter to anybody!*"[15]

Danish troops proved no match for the combined forces of Prussia and Austria, and King Christian IX quickly surrendered. In April, peace negotiations took place in London. The London Conference afforded Ludwig his first opportunity to influence the political composition of a greater Germany. He directed Bavarian officials to demand the inclusion of representatives for the duke of Augustenburg, naively hoping that this relatively neutral third option would prevent the domination of either Prussia or Austria in the German Confederation. But this suggestion came to nothing, leaving the king infuriated. At the end of the London Conference, Prussia and Austria emerged victorious, Denmark being held responsible for having instigated the entire conflict through her illegal maneuvers. Bismarck's triumph meant an end to the hostilities. But with this Prussian victory, Ludwig began to fear for the future sovereignty of his country. Within two years, he would see this fear realized.

8

The Eagle and the Dove

$\mathbf{A}$lthough Ludwig came to the throne filled with good intentions and surrounded by the highest hopes of his subjects, the realities of his new position soon began to bore him. He had never been very fond of Munich, and in the early weeks of his reign, he began a pattern of spending more and more time away from his capital. In spite of the mutual loss which they both had suffered with the death of King Maximilian, Ludwig did his best to avoid his mother. They had never been very close, and Ludwig had little tolerance for the queen's constant mourning. As she still lived at Hohenschwangau in the summers, he sought out another residence.

Eventually, he settled on Castle Berg, fifteen miles southwest of Munich. Like Hohenschwangau, Berg had been romanticized in the Gothic fashion, with crenelated walls, wrought-iron balconies, and tall towers. It was much smaller than Hohenschwangau, with only a half-dozen low-ceilinged rooms scattered across each of its three floors. But the location of the castle was excellent: It lay on the shores of Lake Starnberg, quiet and secluded, and its isolation suited the king. He loved to stroll the graveled paths edging the reed-choked shoreline, listening as the stillness of the early morning broken with the singing of birds or to the sound of waves against the rocky beach. Above the morning mist of the lake, he could see the distant Alps, still covered in newly fallen snow in summer.

Berg offered other advantages. Some three miles across Lake Starnberg, almost directly opposite Castle Berg, stood Possenhofen, the summer home of Ludwig's great-uncle Duke Max in Bavaria. Possenhofen, like Berg, was a country house rather than a palace, its walls overgrown with honeysuckle and wisteria. The castle was comfortable, though slightly shabby, with threadbare carpets; cows wandered freely in the rose garden.[1] As a child, Ludwig had often visited his cousins at Possenhofen; compared with his rigid life at court, Possenhofen must have seemed like paradise to the crown prince. It was first and foremost a family house, filled not with bowing courtiers but with laughter and wild games.

Duke Max came from the junior Wittelsbach-Birkenfeld-Geinhausen line of the royal family and, as such, was regarded as something of a poor country cousin. He was well-read, liberal in thought, and artistic by nature; both Possenhofen and his palace on the Ludwigstrasse in Munich were frequently filled with groups of painters, actors, and musicians. His egalitarian leanings and well-known eccentricities made him one of the most popular of all the Wittelsbachs.

Duke Max had married well, winning the hand of Princess Ludovica, daughter of King Maximilian Josef I and sister of Ludwig I. Ludovica was refined, cultured and reserved, and she and her husband had little in common except their eight children, who grew up largely under the influence of their regal mother. Ludovica ensured that they received proper educations, though her efforts to instill in them her own royal bearing were often thwarted by her husband. As a consequence, the children were a curious mixture of aristocratic manners and bohemian thoughts. None cared greatly for etiquette, which endeared them to their father but caused their punctilious mother endless worry.

To compensate for this somewhat chaotic existence, Ludovica carefully groomed her daughters for marriage. Hélène, the eldest, was a beautiful, intelligent, thoughtful young girl, unaffected by her regal position, and her mother was determined to find for her a reigning European monarch. Fortunately for Ludovica, she had to look no further than her own family. The duchess's elder sister Sophia had married the heir to the Austrian throne, Crown Prince Franz Karl, and their son, Archduke Franz Josef, was widely regarded as one of the most handsome and eligible of European heirs. In 1848, when revolution gripped Europe, Emperor Ferdinand I of Austria abdicated. Sophia's husband, Franz Karl, also renounced his rights, leaving their eighteen-year-old son Franz Josef to ascend the Habsburg throne.

Archduchess Sophia, like her sister Ludovica, was a forceful mother, and the two sisters arranged a meeting between Emperor Franz Josef and Princess Hélène at the Alpine resort Bad Ischel. On this occasion, Hélène's fifteen-year-old sister Elizabeth, known in the family as Sissi, accompanied her mother and inadvertently managed to bewitch the visiting emperor. Franz Josef was captivated by the beautiful, unpretentious, and vivacious young girl; he ignored his mother's plans for the older, more refined Hélène and proposed instead to her younger sister. Both Sophia and Ludovica were startled, and the archduchess in particular worried that the unconventional Elizabeth would find the change in status a difficult adjustment. But Franz Josef was adamant.

Shortly after her sixteenth birthday, Elizabeth and her family boarded a steamer and sailed down the Danube to join her fiancé in Vienna. They needed special papal dispensation for their wedding: The union between Franz Josef and Elizabeth in Bavaria was the twenty-first alliance between the Wittelsbachs and the Habsburgs.[2]

Elizabeth was eight years older than her cousin Ludwig of Bavaria. Often called the most beautiful woman in Europe, she captured the hearts of countless men. She had classical features, a rose-petal complexion, and the deepest blue eyes before whose gaze men melted. But her crowning glory was her hair: Very long and lustrous, it was of a deep chestnut color and it took an entire day to wash and dry. She wore it plaited into a thick braid which she coiled round her head like a halo; on festive occasions, ribbons and sometimes flowers were woven into the braid. Franz Xavier Winterhalter's famous portrait of the radiant empress showed her in a voluminous-skirted tulle ball gown, with diamond stars scattered through her hair. It was a breathtaking painting of this enigmatic woman, an attempt to depict the beauty and charm of the empress, who possessed not a small touch of the Wittelsbach's eccentricity.

Although slim and with an unusually small waist, Elizabeth starved herself to maintain her youthful figure and had to be forced to eat in later years after she had developed anorexia. Before that, however, she kept herself trim by exercising regularly on gymnastic equipment she had installed in her rooms. As well, she rode with a passion, spending long hours on her fine thoroughbreds or galloping to hounds in the Godollo Forest in Hungary; she also went to Ireland regularly to hunt. To show off her perfect figure, she was sewn into her skintight riding habits so that no wrinkle would appear in her clothes. Like Ludwig, she was seemingly indefatigable in the saddle and was believed to be the best horsewoman on the European continent.

Franz Josef loved and worshiped his exquisite wife, whom he indulged and spoiled, and she fulfilled her main duty as empress by giving the Austrian nation an heir, Crown Prince Rudolf, but Elizabeth was not happy. Her mother-in-law, Archduchess Sophia, virtually kidnapped her children in order to raise them according to her own old-fashioned standards. The free-spirited Elizabeth, having grown up in the bohemian atmosphere of her artistic father's unconventional establishment, felt imprisoned by the rigid Spanish-style etiquette of the Habsburg court. She disliked, and always fought against, those who expected her to perform to perfection every time she appeared at court functions, and her public boredom masked a private agony. For all of his adoration of his wife, Franz Josef could not resist the charms of other women, and his numerous affairs provided the Viennese gossips with hours of endless speculation. Elizabeth suffered this public humiliation in silence; then, to her horror, she discovered that her wayward husband had infected her with venereal disease, and fled in shame to Madeira. Franz Josef followed his wife to her place of self-imposed exile and, after much pleading, managed to persuade her to return to Vienna to avoid a scandal. But she never forgave her unfaithful and indiscreet husband.

Elizabeth roamed Europe, seeking purpose in an otherwise sad and empty life. She suffered from uncontrollable depression followed by fits of nervous energy which left her exhausted and high-strung. This erratic and unpredictable behavior soon had the long-tongued members of the Habsburg court whispering that their beautiful empress might be mad. Elizabeth heard the rumors and took a perverse pride in remaining an enigma to those around her. "I know that sometimes I am considered mad," she declared to members of her suite, a smile on her lips but with a dead-serious face. It became a game, an amusing way of passing endless hours at the Hofburg. She delighted in making outrageous statements and then examining her listener's face to see if they could discern truth from fantasy.[3] It was a trait she shared with her cousin Ludwig of Bavaria.

In the summer of 1864, Ludwig paid a long visit to Bad Kissingen, a spa resort popular among the fashionable aristocracy. The resort was filled with important members of several European royal families: In addition to Ludwig, the emperor and empress of Austria had come to Kissingen, as well as Emperor Alexander II and his consort Marie Alexandrovna. When Ludwig arrived, the streets of Kissingen were filled with speeding carriages and marching soldiers, brass bands playing national anthems, and crowds hoping to catch a glimpse of Bavaria's handsome young monarch. Soon after his arrival, Ludwig paid a call on Emperor Franz Josef and his wife; it was the first occasion on which Elizabeth had met her cousin since his accession to the Bavarian throne.

Although they had not been particularly close as children, Ludwig and Elizabeth shared a number of characteristics which quickly drew them together at Kissingen. Both were brooding, melancholy figures, isolated from the world around them, dissatisfied with their lives, and disliking their duties at court. Despite their eight-year age difference, Ludwig and Elizabeth truly understood each other, recognizing their mutual longing for beauty and their sense of loneliness, sadly enigmatic qualities which made them ideal confidants. The pair spent long hours together, strolling slowly up and down the picturesque promenade of the town; they were scarcely an anonymous couple, but they seemed so far removed from the cares of the world that no one dared approach. It was obvious to anyone who saw them together that Ludwig was enraptured with his beautiful second cousin.

Ludwig displayed more affection for empress Elizabeth than for any other woman in his life. After one of his visits at Possenhofen, the Empress wrote to her daughter:

> Yesterday the King paid me a long visit and if Grandmama had not come in at last he would still be here. He is quite reconciled to me. I was very nice and he kissed my hand so often that Aunt Sophie, who was peering through the door, asked me afterwards whether I had any hand left. He was wearing an Austrian uniform again and was scented with perfume.[4]

The matter of the Austrian uniforms caused a great deal of embarrassment. When Elizabeth paid a private visit to her parents at Possenhofen, Ludwig destroyed the secrecy by meeting her at the railway station in Munich wearing full Austrian dress uniform and had the entire siding decorated with white lilies.[5] While Ludwig loved dressing up and considered wearing a uniform a sign of respect to the empress, he was careless with the details. On one occasion he wore an Austrian uniform with the grand cross of the Order of St. Stephen upside down, the sash worn inside out and running in the wrong direction across his torso.[6]

Ludwig eagerly awaited Elizabeth's frequent return visits to her family at Possenhofen. When she arrived, he rode one of his horses round the perimeter of Lake Starnberg to leave a bunch of roses at the door before she awoke. They often sailed the length of the lake in his small steamer, *Maximilian*, or escaped to the Roseninsel, an island owned by Ludwig which lay in the center of the lake. Maximilian had planted the island with nearly thirty thousand rosebushes and, through the summer, they exploded in riots of color and sweet fragrance. In the midst of this garden stood a small, Swiss-style chalet with a tall watchtower; here Ludwig and Elizabeth spent endless hours alone, talking, reading poetry to each other, and, when one of them was absent, leaving letters for the other in the secret hidden compartment of a desk in a sitting room overlooking the lake. They wandered alone through the woods, riding and walking, taking picnics and reading aloud to each other beneath the shade of the pine and chestnut trees.

Ludwig cherished these private afternoons with his beloved cousin. After one of their meetings on a train, he wrote breathlessly to Elizabeth:

You can have no idea, dear Cousin, how happy you made me. The hours recently passed with you in the railway carriage were among the most wonderful of my life. Never will their memory fade. You gave me permission to visit you at Ischel—when that time comes I shall be of all men upon earth the most blessed, for the feelings of sincere love and reverence and faithful attachment to you which I have cherished in my heart since my early youth make me imagine heaven on earth when in your company, a feeling which will be extinguished by death alone. . . . I beg you to forgive the contents of this letter, but I could not help myself.[7]

These long afternoons together, numerous private letters, barely disguised admiration, and obvious attraction caused much comment, not only among members of the cousins' respective families but at the Munich and Viennese courts as well. Inevitably, there were rumors that Ludwig and Elizabeth were lovers. Their soulful friendship certainly extended beyond the normal bounds of familial love. Both Ludwig and Elizabeth, desperately seeking beauty and happiness and an escape from the dreary world of the mid–nineteenth century, found in each other a romantic soulmate, a deep understanding born of a shared heritage and self-enforced isolation. They dwelt in a world of dreams, each giving access to the other but denying the rest of humanity.

In this world, there was no place for worldy love, no sensual temptation. Ludwig abhorred such thoughts, such pressures, which threatened his fragile sexual identity. He had not yet come to realize or accept his homosexuality, but he once tellingly explained that he had no physical desire for women—"thank God"—and that this made his "adoration for the purity of women all the more deeply felt."[8] His love for his cousin Sissi was pure and chivalrous, a return to the ancient days which Ludwig so admired. In their letters he signed himself "The Eagle," she, "The Dove," names reflecting the celestial nature of their bond. Ludwig loved Elizabeth because she understood him, never sought to intrude into his own world, and never tried to force him into a role which he could not fulfill. He could dismiss the cares of the world in her presence, losing himself in her beauty, all the while knowing that there was never any danger that he would have to respond to her in any way which threatened his own uncertain sexual feelings. As a married woman, Elizabeth was a safe confidant for the king. Nevertheless, members of both the Wittelsbach and Habsburg families continued to whisper about the unnaturally close relationship which the two cousins seemed to share, further fueling gossip and scandal.

That summer, Ludwig also spent much time with his aunt, Empress Marie Alexandrovna, who had come to Kissingen with her husband, Alexander II of Russia. She shared one attraction with Elizabeth which made her irresistible to Ludwig, that of being an older, married woman who presented no feminine threat. When Marie Alexandrovna moved on to the spa at Schwalbach, Ludwig followed. He made no secret of his infatuation, much to the chagrin of his suite. One day, his cabinet secretary, Pfistermeister, boldly reproached Ludwig, saying, "But, Your Majesty, the empress might well be your mother." "Oh, I wish she were!" the king replied with a heavy sigh.[9]

Although officially Ludwig was simply making a number of calls on his fellow sovereigns, in reality, he was also making discreet inquiries about the Russian sovereigns' young daughter, Grand Duchess Marie. He appears to have had no particular interest in the grand duchess, who, at only ten years of age, was far too young for marriage. But his questioning appeased a few vocal members of the Munich court, who had begun to hint that the king should marry and provide an heir as soon as possible.

Nothing came of the proposed Russian alliance. Ludwig remained extremely fond of Empress Marie, however, and spent long hours with her, discussing his life and hopes. Sensitive and motherly, she listened to the romantic young man who poured out his heart. When he left Schwalbach, he carried with him a strangely prophetic letter from Marie Alexandrovna: "I am afraid there is in you an urge for loneliness, for separation from the world and the people. I understand that tendency, for it is in my nature, too. But in the position God has put us in, we have no right to it."[10]

9

Wagner

Scarcely a month after ascending the Bavarian throne, Ludwig had a fateful meeting with his cabinet secretary, Franz von Pfistermeister. During the course of their audience, Ludwig first raised the name of Richard Wagner. The city of Munich kept a so-called Stranger's List on which the names of visitors were regularly inscribed. Rumor had it that Wagner had recently been in Munich; but when Ludwig got hold of the list, he could not find the composer's name. He asked Pfistermeister why Wagner's name was not included, to which the Cabinet Secretary questioned, "Which Wagner?"—the name not being an uncommon one. The king replied that for him there was only one Wagner, the composer Richard Wagner. With this, he ordered Pfistermeister to begin an immediate search for the composer and to bring him immediately to Munich.[1]

Pfistermeister first traveled to Penzing, where Wagner was last known to have lived, but he found the composer's rented villa standing empty. One of Wagner's friends told the secretary that he had gone to Russia, and Pfistermeister cabled Ludwig with the news that the composer could not be found. Ludwig, however, would not be put off so easily. He replied: "The contents of your telegram horrify me. My resolution stands firm: go after R. Wagner as swiftly as possible, if you can do so without attracting attention. . . . It is of the utmost importance to me that this long cherished wish of mine shall soon be gratified."[2]

The cabinet secretary finally caught up with Wagner in Stuttgart. On the evening of 2 May 1864, Wagner was visiting some friends when a servant brought a card from a man inquiring at the door which read "Franz von Pfistermeister, Secretary to the King of Bavaria." Wagner immediately suspected one of his numerous creditors and fled back to his hotel, where he began to pack up his belongings. But he was interrupted by the manager, who informed him that the mysterious man had called there earlier in the evening as well. Tired of running, Wagner reluctantly decided to face the stranger the following morning. That night, he slept badly, fearing the worst.

At ten o'clock the next morning, Pfistermeister introduced himself to Wagner with what must have seemed incredible words: "I have the honour to be Private Secretary to His Majesty King Ludwig II of Bavaria. He has charged me, my dear Master, to invite you to his Court, and to beg that you will come without delay."[3] He handed Wagner a photograph of the king in a silver frame and a ruby ring. There was also a message from the king: "As this stone burns, so do I burn with ardour to behold the creator of the words and music of *Lohengrin*."[4] Pfistermeister explained that the king promised to do all within his power to help the composer achieve his goals; if Wagner agreed, then he should be ready to accompany Pfistermeister back to Munich at once.

Wagner was overwhelmed; his salvation was at hand. The fifty-year-old composer immediately sat down and wrote the first of many letters to the young king.

> Beloved, Gracious King!
> I send you these tears of most heavenly emotion, to tell you that now the wonders of poetry have appeared as a divine truth into my wretched, loveless life. That life, its ultimate poetry, its finest music, belongs henceforth to you, my gracious young King, dispense it as your own!
> In utmost rapture, faithful and true,
>   Your subject,
>   Richard Wagner.[5]

The very next day, Wagner pawned a valuable snuffbox which he had received as a gift in Russia and settled his hotel bill. From a friend, he borrowed the money for a first-class railway ticket from Stuttgart to Munich and finished his packing. That afternoon, Pfistermeister at his side, the composer set off for the Bavarian capital.

Richard Wagner was born in Leipzig on 22 May 1813, the son of middle-class parents. He was one of eight children. Six months after his birth, his father, Carl Friedrich Wagner, died, leaving Richard's mother a widow. She soon found comfort in the arms of Ludwig Geyer and quickly married him. Much of Wagner's life is shrouded in controversy, and his parentage has often been called into doubt. Theories that Geyer may have been Wagner's real father have always been popular, but there is little evidence to support the allegation, spread by Wagner's detractors and perhaps feared true by the composer himself, that Geyer—and thus, by implication, Wagner—was Jewish.

If things continue so disastrously bad as they have been hither to, I must cease to expect any good and I have already come to feel that every hope is in vain. Anyone taking my age and past history into consideration would feel that it is extremely doubtful if, in this frame of mind, which naturally sickens me of life, I can possibly delight in artistic creation—My situation is perilous—I balance on the narrowest foothold—one push and all is over—there will be nothing more to be got out of me, then, nothing, nothing more. *Some* light must show itself, *someone must arise* to help me *vigourously now*, and then I shall still have the strength to recompense that help—but later I shall not, I feel it.[7]

This was less than a month before Pfistermeister appeared at his doorstep with the king's letters and gifts. It is no exaggeration to suggest that Ludwig II's timely intervention literally saved Wagner from further ruin. Without the king's support, it is unlikely that the composer would ever have completed his great Ring cycle or *Parsifal*, or lived to see the staging of *Tristan und Isolde*.

Ludwig had already retired for the evening by the time Pfistermeister returned from Stuttgart with Wagner. The cabinet secretary rushed to the king's apartments in the Residenz, where he awakened the sleeping monarch with the news that the composer had arrived with him that evening and was now safely installed at the opulent Bayerischer Hof hotel. Ludwig sat up in his bed and listened while Pfistermeister—who, according to royal etiquette, had to remain standing during the interview—reported on Wagner until well after midnight. The first meeting between king and composer was fixed for the following afternoon. As soon as Pfistermeister left, the king rose from his bed and, filled with emotion, wrote in his diary: "Transports of the highest rapture went through me when he told me that the man I had yearned for was here and would remain here! Oh, blessed evening which brought me this news!"[8]

The following afternoon, at the appointed time, Wagner, dressed in the customary black frock coat and white tie, presented his card at the Residenz and was escorted to the King's Audience Chamber. The scene must have been a curious one: the tall, striking young king, standing in his splendid rococo reception room as he greeted the stooped, fifty-year-old composer, worn out and plagued with worries. Ludwig had poured years of anticipation and hope into this meeting; it was perhaps inevitable that he should feel disappointed that this romantic climax to his dreams took so prosaic a form as the man who now stood before him. And yet, the words which passed between these two men, so utterly different in looks and character, filled the king's soul. Ludwig himself described the event to his cousin Sophie in Bavaria, sister of Empress Elizabeth of Austria.

> If you could but have witnessed how his gratitude shamed me, when I extended my hand to him and gave him my sincere word that his great Nibelungen work would not only be completed but also performed in the manner he intended. He bent low over me, took my hand, and seemed moved by what really was so natural, for he remained in this posture for a long time without speaking a word. I felt we had exchanged roles. I stooped down to him and drew him to my heart with a feeling that I was taking a silent oath to be faithful to him til the end of time.[9]

That same evening, Wagner wrote to a friend:

> You know that the young King of Bavaria has been looking for me. He is, sad to say, so beautiful, so gifted, so full of deep feeling and so wonderful, that I fear his life must vanish like a fleeting god-like dream in this crude world of ours. He loves me with the fire and tenderness of a first love; he knows and understands me like my own soul. He wants me to always be at his side, to work, to relax, to produce my operas. He will give me everything I need to this end. . . . You cannot begin to imagine the magic of his eyes! Oh, may he but live! It is an unbelievable miracle![10]

The following day, blissfully enveloped in his own dreams and romantic ideas, Ludwig wrote to Wagner:

> Believe me, I will do all within my power to make up to you for what you have suffered in the past. I will take from you the everyday cares of life forever; I will secure for you the peace which you have longed for, so that you will be free to spread the mighty wings of your genius in the holy air of your rapturous art. Unconscious though you were of the fact, you have been the sole source of my happiness ever since I was a mere boy, my friend who spoke to my heart as no other did, my best teacher and educator. I will repay to you all that it is within my power. Oh, how I have waited for this moment—the moment when I am able to do this. I hardly dared to indulge my wish of being able to prove my love to you so soon.[11]

On 18 May, Wagner reported to a friend: "I have no other disciple who is so utterly my own. It is scarcely believable. You must hear, see, feel this glorious youth for yourself. . . . He is said to be resolute, strict and most zealous in the business of government. He stands alone, no one influences him and all recognize him as absolutely and verifiably King."[12]

A few days later, Munich buzzed with talk of the newly arrived composer. With an uncanny degree of clairvoyance, the Austrian ambassador reported back to Vienna: "No doubt Wagner will cost the King a good deal of money, but it would be a sad thing if, at his age, he could not do something foolish. Much more serious, it seems to me, is the fact that his entourage has begun telling him how handsome he is, how handsome women find him."[13]

The Austrian official was well-informed: Money soon became the sole subject on Wagner's mind. Along with his luggage, the composer brought with him to Munich enormous debts. From the first, Wagner, encouraged by the king, never hesitated to speak frankly to Ludwig of his financial needs. The king, in turn, always responded swiftly. Scarcely a week after Wagner arrived, for example, Ludwig gave him, as a personal gift, some 4,000 gulden. This accompanied the first of numerous installments of Wagner's official salary of 4,000 gulden a year. Much of this gift, as well as the first installment of his annual salary, went toward paying off his creditors.

He did not, at least, have to worry about the maintenance of his own establishment. Ludwig provided for the composer by renting for his use Villa Pellet on the shores of Lake Starnberg. It had two advantages: First, it removed Wagner from the public eye in Munich, where resentment had already begun to grow over his new position as the king's favorite; and, second, it was only three miles from Castle Berg. Once his friend was safely installed at Pellet, Ludwig summoned Wagner to Berg nearly every day; they spent hours discussing the composer's latest ideas and projects and plans for the future. The king wrote rapturous declarations of undying love and support.

> You cannot believe how supremely happy I am to see, at last and face to face, the man whose sublime nature attracted and captured me with irresistible might from my tenderest youth. I used to long incessantly for the time when I should be able to compensate you in some degree for the many cares and sufferings you have had to endure; now, to my delight, the time has come, now that I am wrapped in the purple mantle, and now that I have the power, I will use it, so far as I am able, to sweeten life for you. You shall wear no bonds; you shall be free

to devote yourself to your magnificent art solely as the spirit moves you. When, as lately, I see you before me, deeply moved, and I can say to myself, "Through you has been made happy and contented," then I am so happy, and more than happy, so borne aloft on exquisite emotions, that I imagine heaven to have come to earth. You often say to me that you owe me so much, but all that is the smallest inconsequence compared with what I may thank you for.[14]

In these early days, with an admiring king worshiping at his altar, Wagner made extravagant plans for the production of his operas. His first instructions were scarcely short of demands: Only Wagner's operas must be produced during any given cycle, so as not to interfere with the poetic atmosphere of his own works. Blinded by his admiration and happiness at having finally achieved his goal, Ludwig agreed.

One final, momentous drama involving Wagner was left to be played out in the dramatic summer of 1864. On 18 June, the king departed for Kissingen, leaving Wagner at Villa Pellet. Depressed and lonely, the composer repeatedly begged his scattered friends to keep him company at Starnberg in the king's absence. In the end, it was the Prussian conductor Hans von Bülow and his wife, Cosima, who eventually accepted Wagner's invitation.

Wagner had known the von Bülows for several years. Hans was a conductor of some repute, a man of undoubted talent but little imagination. In 1857, at the age of twenty, he had married Cosima, daughter of Franz Liszt, a tall, slender, unconventional woman, possessed of a brilliant and artistic mind. The marriage was a disaster from the very beginning; nervous and temperamental, Hans was a poor match for the intellectual, energetic Cosima. In 1863, Wagner stayed with the von Bülows in Berlin. One afternoon, Hans was called away, and Wagner and Cosima found themselves impulsively drawn to each other. Although twenty-four years younger than Wagner, Cosima was captivated by the composer, recognizing the brilliance he possessed, and Wagner returned her passion; with a solemn vow, they parted company. Perhaps neither thought that fate would play so easily into their hands, for at the time of Wagner's invitation to the pair to stay with him at Pellet, Hans was ill. But he insisted that his wife and their two daughters, Daniela and Blandine, precede him, and the trio duly set off for Lake Starnberg. Cosima arrived on 29 June, with Hans following a week later. Over the course of that week, with Ludwig II away and Wagner and Cosima alone at the lakeside villa, the pair became lovers.

10

"The World Will Sing Your Praises"

Throughout the summer of 1864, Wagner was busy at work on a gift for his new royal benefactor: To commemorate Ludwig's nineteenth birthday on 25 August, Wagner composed the *Huldigungsmarsch*, *The March of Homage*. He planned to have it first performed at Hohenschwangau, where the king was in residence. Ludwig eagerly awaited the arrival of the band of eighty players who were to perform the piece when, unexpectedly, his mother arrived at Hohenschwangau. For the king, this was an intolerable intrusion on his privacy: "Unfortunately," he wrote, "my present stay is completely spoilt by Mother, who tortures me with her endless love; she has no idea of the rest and every sparkle of poetry vanishes in her company."[1] Unable to share his emotional experience with his mother, Ludwig ordered the performance canceled. The *Huldigungsmarsch* eventually had its first performance on 5 October, in the courtyard of the Residenz.

Effusive declarations on the parts of both the king and Wagner, in their personal conversations and in the poems and letters they exchanged, eventually led to speculation as to the nature of the relationship. Cosima von Bülow, who later married Wagner, confided, "Richard is writing to the King. . . . He then reads me the letter which really makes my heart ache. I wish he could find a different tone for this correspondence, one which would sound more truthful, without losing its warmth."[2] Even Wagner himself admitted, "Oh, those don't sound very good, but it wasn't I who set the tone."[3]

Much of the voluminous correspondence between the king and his friend can be understood only within the context of the era in which it was composed and in light of the romantic sentiments of the day. Ludwig existed on an exalted plain; he disliked reality, and this was never more true than in his relations with Wagner. Their friendship and the letters they exchanged were thus forced into an idealized conception which often lacked sincerity and significance, replaced with florid sentiment to disguise an utter lack of content.[4] Their relationship had a certain ethereal tone which existed only on paper; indeed, for the king, such letters quickly became reality. On paper, Wagner's age, personal appearance, foibles, debts, and adultery remained hidden among the velvet passages of love and swirling sagas he painted for the king. Nothing so prosaic as truth or imperfect emotion was allowed to interfere with the poetic, rhapsodic nature of their exchange.

Ludwig's latent homosexuality and Wagner's well-known taste for silks, satins, ribbons, and scents added fuel to the indiscreet whisperings at court. Ludwig certainly loved Wagner, and their friendship was a deep one, but the intensity and passion between the two men was spiritual, artistic, and emotional, not physical. The king did not love Wagner the man; rather, he worshiped Wagner the artist, who gave life to his own dreams and spoke to his soul.

The years of letters filled with affection for Wagner, along with the unrestrained financial support from the royal treasury, reflected the king's deep desire and dedication to the composer's art and obsessive need to see his fantasies brought to life. But Ludwig's continued encouragement of Wagner rested almost exclusively with this dual vision of himself as both benefactor and recipient of the composer's undoubted genius. He was a true successor of the chivalrous medieval knights he so admired, only it was not a fair maiden Ludwig sought to protect, but the middle-aged Richard Wagner. His friendship was a product of his sovereign position, a measure of grace extended to Wagner to protect the art which he produced. Ludwig never embraced the composer as his equal but rather looked upon his patronage as the bestowal of royal favor in the Wittelsbach tradition.

From his earliest days, the king had been surrounded by the stories of medieval Germany: in the murals at the Residenz and in Hohenschwangau, in the stories told him by his mother and by his tutors, and in the books which he read. Wagner, through operas such as *Tannhäuser* and *Lohengrin*, brought this childhood world of fantasy to life for Ludwig. The king lost himself in the world which Wagner had created, and, in doing so, escaped, for however brief a period, from the Victorian, bourgeois world which he so hated.

The young king saw himself not only as a patron, but, through the act of patronage itself, as a cocreator along with Wagner. He often referred to "our work" in his letters to Wagner, and this, along with the nature of the operas themselves, is the key to Ludwig's tolerance and generosity where the wayward composer was concerned.

The joint vision of the king and Wagner included several new, extravagantly expensive programs which were to be undertaken. In order to accomplish his schedule, Wagner told Ludwig that he must personally supervise the training of singers dedicated solely to his works and trained to his standards. To this end, Ludwig arranged to offer a temporary post to Leipzig singing instructor Friedrich Schmitt. Worry soon spread in Munich of the prospect of Wagner holding the musical life of the capital hostage to his own works and subjecting its musicians and singers to his demands.

Wagner also let it be known that a new theater, designed specially for the production of his own works, would be an eventual necessity. He presented the idea of a special school to train Wagnerian singers in a piece called "Report to His Majesty King Ludwig II of Bavaria Upon a German Music School to be Founded in Munich." The composer argued that only such a school could ensure the quality and correct performance of his operas. He was aware of the growing hostility toward him in certain Munich quarters and therefore never mentioned the production of his operas as a goal. Instead, he spoke in veiled terms of the need for a national style in the opera world, performed by correctly trained artists.

Sensible though Wagner's ideas might have been, they were considered revolutionary in their own time. When the people of Munich learned of the composer's goals, they feared the total subversion of Bavarian music to Wagner's aims. Musicians, singers, and music teachers all assumed that their own positions were to be sacrificed, replaced with Wagner's candidates at untold cost to Bavarian taxpayers.

Ludwig undoubtedly agreed with the composer's objectives, but, unlike Wagner, he was shrewd enough to recognize the effects of such a program on public opinion. He warned Wagner:

> I grant you that it will be difficult to achieve an improvement in this area; most men of our time, preoccupied as they are with selfish, money-making schemes, have a greatly diminished view of the splendour of true art. I therefore strongly urge you, my dear friend, to proceed with your plan in the manner you propose in your letter, namely with extreme caution.[5]

Although he fully supported the program proposed by Wagner, Ludwig also envisioned a cultural revolution in his capital—one which he himself would champion. On 8 November 1864, the king wrote to the composer: "My intent is to bring the Munich public into a more serious and higher state of mind by the production of such important works as those of Shakespeare, Calderón, Goethe, Schiller, Beethoven, Mozart, Gluck and Weber. By doing so, I hope to eventually free the public from their vulgar and frivolous tastes . . . everyone should be made aware of the seriousness of art."[6]

By October of 1864, Richard Wagner had been in Munich for five months; he was still living at Starnberg in the house Ludwig had rented for him. But Pellet soon proved inconvenient. Ludwig, by the very nature of his position, had to be in Munich on a regular basis and, thus, out of touch with the composer. He found this intolerable; as a result, he rented a new house for his friend at 21 Briennerstrasse, just down the avenue from the Residenz. Ironically, it stood almost directly opposite the mansion on the Barerstrasse formerly occupied by Ludwig I's paramour, Lola Montez.

Wagner's new home was an imposing building adorned with columned balconies and pediments, and set in a large garden. As soon as the composer moved in, he began redecorating: He covered the walls with expensive silks and velvets, hung the windows with heavy brocades, and scented the rooms with lavish fragrances. The newspaper *Allgemeine Zeitung* wrote that "an Oriental Grand *Siegneur* need not hesitate to take up his abode there."[7]

Not that Wagner was content to stop with the decoration of his house. One visitor later recalled: "That day he was in a violet mood. The window was covered with a heavy curtain of violet velvet. He was sitting in a violet armchair, on his head was a violet velvet cap, which he raised ever so slightly when he got up on my entering."[8]

This hedonistic luxury cost money. Wagner felt that only by living in such surroundings could he create his works. To Franz Liszt, he once explained:

> If I am once again to submerge myself in the current of artistic creativity, in order to thrive in a world of my imagination, then this imagination needs a good deal of support, my fancy needs sustenance. I cannot live like a dog when I am working, nor can I sleep on straw and swill cheap liqueur. I must be coaxed one way or another if I am to accomplish the horribly difficult task of creating a non-existent world.[9]

Now, with an adoring, rich young patron and many years of poverty behind him, it would indeed have been incredible had Wagner not taken advantage of his unique situation. But he was shrewd enough to judge the political situation in Munich and tried to hide the facts of his exotic style of life by ordering all of these costly materials from Austrian merchants rather than from the Bavarians.

Money was, in fact, foremost on Wagner's mind. His style of living, combined with huge debts from his past, meant that he was nearly always without funds. The king's first annual grant to his friend had been fixed at 4,000 gulden. In addition, he had given Wagner 4,000 gulden of his own money on 10 May, followed by 20,000 more gulden on 10 June. The state treasury had also paid bills owed to Wagner's creditors at the beginning of his stay in Munich.[10] By the end of the summer, however, nearly all of this money was gone.

Much has been made of the immense fortune the king lavished on Wagner. Although the financial affairs between the king and composer were conducted in private, angry court officials provided a constant stream of leaks to the Munich press, fueling the growing anger over Wagner's royal favor. Over the entire course of their friendship, Ludwig gave the composer a total of approximately 985,099 gulden (562,914 marks); this included the rents for his various houses, personal gifts, salaries, stipends, the value of presents, and his financing of all of Wagner's operas, including his loans which rescued the Bayreuth Festspielhaus and the Ring cycle from disaster.

As King, Ludwig received an annual civil list of 2 million gulden; a quarter of this sum was regularly paid to his grandfather as a form of royal pension. After payment of the various household expenses, salaries, and maintenance of the royal palaces, Ludwig possessed a disposable income of roughly 300,000 gulden a year.[11] From this sum, Ludwig subsidized all of Wagner's projects. Yet the king lavishly spent far larger sums of money on his various projects; his famous gilded wedding coach alone cost more than the total amount of all of these gifts to Wagner. Nor were Wagner's frequent complaints as to the compensation he personally drew from his works empty rhetoric; he was never properly compensated for the production of any of his operas, even though he enjoyed popular status during his lifetime. In contrast to the total amount Wagner received from the king over the course of nineteen years, the composer Giacomo Meyerbeer was paid more, 750,000 marks, for one hundred performances of his work *La Prophète* in Berlin.[12]

At Ludwig's request, Wagner drew up a timetable outlining his future plans. In 1865, according to the composer, his *Tristan und Isolde* would be ready for production; this would be followed by *Die Meistersinger von Nürnberg* and the completed cycle of *Der Ring des Nibelungen* in 1867–68; *Die Sieger* in 1870 and *Parsifal* a year later.[13] In the end, despite the king's generous financial aid, only *Tristan und Isolde* would be produced according to schedule. The timetable was a feeble effort on Wagner's part to silence his growing critics; instead, he was about to plunge headlong into a controversy which nearly ended his relations with his royal benefactor.

11

Growing Troubles

On 1 October 1864, Ludwig granted a raise in Wagner's official salary, at the composer's request, from 4,000 to 5,000 gulden. Although the circumstances and amounts of the stipends were supposed to have been a carefully maintained secret, soon enough, word spread through Munich. Talk of money consumed everyone's attention: Wagner's seemingly insatiable need for it and his incredible talent for dispensing with it. There was growing hostility to the royal support which kept Wagner in the decadent style of life he so relished. The public outcry was fueled by the fact that by the fall of 1864 Wagner had done little except to pay off some of his old debts. Months of laboring on the scores of his operas had produced little, and his affair with Cosima von Bülow seems to have been his most enthusiastic pursuit. That the money paid to Wagner came from the king's personal civil list via the royal treasury and not from public funds mattered not at all. The outcry was all the greater, as a councillor for the Bavarian Supreme Court made 2,800 gulden a year, an administrator in a grammar school 2,200 gulden, and the head of a ministerial department with eighteen years of government service only 3,900 gulden.[1]

Five days after granting Wagner this new salary, Ludwig received a letter in which the composer informed him that, infused with renewed confidence and inspiration, he was prepared to dedicate himself to the completion of the Ring cycle. "I ask for three years of Your Royal Grace, and on the twenty-second birthday of my Noble Lord the work will be produced, and, through him, disclosed to the German Nation."[2] In this case, of course, "royal grace" actually meant further financial support. On 7 October, the king granted his friend an audience; the composer outlined his plans for the completion of the Ring cycle, along with the funds he felt were necessary to sustain him through the work. Ludwig was in complete agreement; before Wagner departed the Residenz, the king had acquiesced to all of his requests.

Ludwig left the details to Julius Hofmann, his court secretary and the head of the royal treasury. Two weeks later, on 18 October, Hofmann presented the composer with a formal contract for the completion of the Ring operas. Ludwig believed that the conditions were binding on the composer: Wagner promised that a copy of the score of each of the four operas would be delivered to the king within three years, the king would be the sole owner of the rights to the works, Wagner would receive 30,000 gulden for the work, and the composer had to bear any and all further expenses associated with the completion and presentation of his operas. Wagner had dictated the terms; if these conditions were granted, he promised his "definite assurance" that he would require no more from the king. In reality, the contract was far from generous, considering the amount of work involved and the costs anticipated for their staging. Ludwig entered into the agreement in good faith; Wagner, however, technically had no rights to the four operas in the Ring cycle as he had, in effect, already sold them to his former patron, Otto Wesendonck. The king would not learn of this duplicity until many years later.[3]

Ludwig was pleased with these developments. He now had a formal contract with the composer, a timetable, and every expectation that Wagner's more vocal critics would thus be silenced. But his ministers were less than joyous. Pfistermeister, who to Ludwig's face played the humble civil servant, had already become, in fact, a dedicated enemy of the composer. He feared that what he saw as Wagner's unabashed rape of the royal treasury would likely result in the ruin of the king. That December, Ludwig relieved Baron von Schrenck, who held the dual cabinet positions of prime minister and minister of foreign affairs, of his posts. In his place, the king appointed Baron Ludwig von der Pfordten, who accepted both portfolios. This was somewhat surprising, considering Pfordten's well-known dislike of Wagner. The composer could scarcely have welcomed the news: Pfordten had been professor of Roman law at Leipzig and minister of education in the Saxony government in 1848. He was well acquainted, therefore, with Wagner's revolutionary activities. During his service under Maximilian II, Pfordten had tried to induce the king not to allow *Tannhäuser* to be performed in Munich, an act which is said to have earned him the everlasting scorn of Ludwig II.[4] The cabinet secretary quickly allied himself with Pfordten, and together, the pair set out to thwart all of Wagner's schemes which involved further funding from the royal treasury. To Ludwig and Wagner, the pair soon became "Pfi" and "Pfo"—both dedicated enemies.

Wagner's enemies, by the winter of 1864, fell into roughly two groups. First, there were those members of the court—including the

king's ministers and most of his personal household—who not only
distrusted the composer but feared that his growing influence over the
king would lead to Ludwig's eventual dereliction of his royal duties.
Already, since Wagner had come to Munich, Ludwig had done his best
to avoid the official and ceremonial sides of court life: There were no
balls, receptions, banquets, inspections, or speeches. When concerned
officials quietly asked the king when he would consent to host the next
event at court, Ludwig inevitably met their polite inquiries with
repeated excuses. At first, his pretense was that he was still in mourning for his late father. This excuse held for only so long, however, and
by the fall of 1864, the six-month period of official mourning had come
to its end. Yet the king refused to resume the court calendar.

Some of the public animosity was directed at the composer's private life. Cosima von Bülow had been living with Wagner since the
previous summer at Villa Pellet, joined only infrequently by her husband, Hans. Late in the summer of 1864, von Bülow had a stroke which
kept him in his rooms in Munich's Europaischer Hof Hotel; during her
husband's illness, Cosima remained with Wagner at Starnberg, an
indiscretion which provided the gossipmongers of Munich with endless speculation.

Wagner repeatedly begged the king to grant von Bülow an official position at court. By the end of the year, Ludwig agreed to appoint
von Bülow, who normally lived in Berlin and worked as a conductor
and teacher at the respected Stern Conservatory, to the position of Vor-
spieler or court pianist. Wagner genuinely valued von Bülow's abilities
and deep understanding of his music, yet this was far from a gracious
act on the part of the composer. With von Bülow safely and firmly
installed in Munich, Wagner also guaranteed the continued presence of
his mistress in the Bavarian capital.

Then again, on a completely different level, there were those who
seized upon Wagner's presence as evidence that the king was under the
counsel of liberals and Protestants. Most of this latter group came from
the clerical circles within the Bavarian government, including the
Jesuits, who still held considerable power. Much of the public animosity which Wagner first encountered in Munich stemmed from the fact
that many Bavarian citizens regarded the composer in precisely this
light: He was a well-known revolutionary, a fugitive from justice after
his participation in the 1848 riots in Dresden, an exile who was just as
likely to cause turmoil in the Alpine capital.

Whatever their fears or fantasies, these two diverse forces, both
court and clerical, drew together and became allies in one common
cause: the removal of Richard Wagner from the king's side. Ludwig's
religious advisor, Ignaz von Döllinger, predicted, "If this continues, the

good Bavarians will hate the foreign musician just as they hated the foreign scholars imported by the King's father."[5] And the king's grandfather, the former King Ludwig I—well aware of the consequences of ignoring public opinion to indulge a private folly—remarked to the Austrian ambassador: "Very sad, that misconduct of my grandson, but in no time at all the people will put an end to it."[6]

In the fall of 1864, Ludwig asked Wagner to begin work on the production of *Tristan und Isolde*. But *Tristan*, which had not yet been staged, proved an impossible task, and Wagner decided to substitute *Der fliegende Holländer* instead. Ludwig was perturbed; he had little concept of the immense amount of work and effort involved in the world premiere of *Tristan und Isolde* and, like a child deprived of immediate gratification, declared that he did not know if he would still be able to attend the first night in December. This news alarmed Wagner. Suspecting that Munich would interpret the king's absence as a royal snub, he managed to convince Ludwig to change his previously arranged schedule. Ludwig duly attended and left the theater overwhelmed. He was so impressed that a week later he ordered the regularly scheduled court play canceled so that excerpts from *Tristan und Isolde, Die Meistersinger von Nürnberg, Die Walküre,* and *Siegfried* could be performed. Ticket holders arriving at the court theater expecting to see the previously scheduled play were unpleasantly surprised to discover this last-minute change, and the theater was half empty for the performance. But Ludwig was perfectly happy, unaware of the growing resentment against his new friend's privileged position.

As long as Wagner restricted himself to the arts, there was little his enemies could do. But at the beginning of 1865, the composer felt confident enough in his relationship with the king to raise the subject of politics. The invasion began innocently enough when the composer presented the king with some of his prose writings. In *Was ist Deutsch?* Wagner suggested that the German people were bound together in a mystical union of faith, common history, and values. In stressing national unity, Wagner aspired to form and found a German arts movement, saying that all people of common ancestry and heritage should embrace the collective ideals which would best promote German superiority.

His next essay, *On State and Religion,* had been composed specially for the king's consumption. It began with an overview of political and social matters in Bavaria and the German nations as Wagner saw them. His examination began in 1848, the year in which Ludwig I had abdicated and he himself had been forced to flee Dresden to escape a prison sentence for revolutionary activity. To please the king, Wagner proceeded to espouse traditional conservative values, which infuriated both Pfistermeister and Pfordten, who were well aware of the composer's egalitarian leanings. In *On State and Religion*, Wagner argued that all of the German nationalistic ideals—cultural aspirations, artistic integrity, and spiritual and political fulfillment—were bound up in the person of the king. The composer went further, stating that since a king was selected by God, his role in the life of his people was spiritual by nature, and thus the person of the king was endowed with divine authority. Such reasoning greatly appealed to Ludwig, who envisioned himself very much in these terms, a political and spiritual leader of not only his own but of all German princes.

Innocent on the surface, these arguements appeared to both Pfistermeister and Pfordten as subtle designs for power on Wagner's part. By convincing Ludwig of the providential nature of his role and encouraging his belief that his authority was absolute, the composer was, in effect, weakening the constitutional position of the cabinet over the king. When certain courtiers learned of this political incursion, the whispering campaign against the increasingly unpopular composer continued unchecked.

Ludwig actually paid little attention to Wagner's political advice. When the composer talked politics, the king stared at the ceiling and whistled softly. And Pfistermeister complained that Ludwig "returned from each meeting with Wagner ill-humoured and moody, conditioned against his duties of office."[7] Ludwig himself was far too absorbed in his own royal prerogatives to subject himself to much political advice, and certainly he never accepted any from Wagner which he did not also agree with. But Munich had no real idea as to the extent of Wagner's influence over the king, and the composer was soon nicknamed Lolus and Lolette by those who feared another Lola Montez affair. But the anger on the part of the cabinet and the general public steadily grew, and Wagner, never before subjected to the close scrutiny a public figure must endure, continued to make mistake after mistake, errors in judgment which reflected badly on Ludwig himself.

The new year opened with an event which seriously threatened relations between the two friends. In 1864, Ludwig had given Wagner a portrait of himself and asked that the composer return the favor and sit for Josef Bernhardt. It was customary that the bill for such a request be sent directly to the royal treasury, as it was the king's wish, and he would then pay the fee. Wagner, however, had taken an interest in another painter, Friedrich Pecht, and sat for him instead. When the painting was finished, Wagner had it delivered to the king, and Pecht duly dispatched a bill to the royal treasury. At a meeting with the composer shortly thereafter, Pfistermeister raised the question of the outstanding fee. Wagner still believed that Ludwig would pay for the portrait; he did not consider that the change in artist might alter this.

Ludwig, however, had unexpectedly changed his mind and elected to look upon the requested painting as a gift. Wagner can scarcely have welcomed this unforeseen expense, but he duly made the arrangements and paid Pecht from his own pocket. Ludwig was too busy to concern himself with the details, and his ignorance provided the anti-Wagnerian forces at court with an opportunity to drive a wedge between the king and his friend. Ludwig was told that Wagner had demanded an inflated sum from the royal treasury; soon afterward, an anonymous source leaked news of the alleged incident to the Munich press.

Worse was yet to come. On 5 February, Wagner asked for, and was granted, an audience with the king on the following day. Later that same afternoon, Pfistermeister called on the composer, and during the course of their conversation over the Pecht portrait, Wagner inadvertently referred to the king as *"mein Junge"*—"my boy." The next day, when Wagner presented himself at the Residenz for his audience, he was turned away at the door.

Undoubtedly, Ludwig's decision to deny Wagner his agreed-to audience came when he learned of the *"mein Junge"* remark. For the king, this was an unforgivable breech of royal etiquette. It has always been assumed that Pfistermeister gleefully informed the king of the composer's unfortunate choice of words, but an entry in the secretary's diary seems to contradict this. On 7 February, he recorded: "The King apparently angry with Wagner, because Leinfelder has been telling him all kinds of things about him."[8] It appears that Pfistermeister, on returning to the Residenz, discussed the incident with his colleague, who then went to the king and repeated the story. Thus, while it may have been Pfistermeister who was indirectly responsible for the king's decision, it was Leinfelder who actually carried the news to Ludwig.

It did not take long for word of Wagner's humiliation to spread. No one knew the true circumstances, and it was widely believed and reported that the incident over the Pecht portrait had been responsible for the king's refusal to receive his friend. Ludwig found the speculation unbearable; to end these rumors, he authorized a public statement on the matter, which was printed in the newspaper *Neueste Nachrichten* on 12 February.

> The report in various quarters that Richard Wagner is in disgrace can be characterized as unfounded. Wagner's position is bound up with the duty of talking to the King about music when leisure and circumstances permit. The preoccupation of

legislative plans for the coming Landtag makes, however, more than normal demands on the King's time just now; moreover, he has entered upon the study of jurisprudence. So that if the composer has not been summoned to the King during the past month for a discussion of music, this is because His Majesty has had even weightier things to occupy him; meanwhile the King did not fail to express his highest praise to the composer after the private performance of some of Wagner's music in the Residenz Theatre on the first of this month.[9]

No one believed this royal denial. On the morning of 14 February, Ludwig scanned the newspapers, only to discover that the Augsburg *Allgemeine Zeitung* had printed a lengthy article on the subject, declaring that relations between the king and composer had cooled considerably.

Richard Wagner has completely fallen out of favour with the King. Our Monarch, so appreciative of the arts, has now decided to make a clear distinction between his love for Wagner's music and the man himself. . . . As for the Royal Favour, Wagner has tried it sorely with his constant, incredibly excessive demands on the generosity of his illustrious protector. To cap it all, Wagner has now had his portrait painted by his friend Friedrich Pecht, without the Court's instructions, and has left the unbidden picture in the Royal Antechamber, together with the bill for one thousand gulden. . . . What we are now asking for is just this, that Richard Wagner should not be so misguided as to overstep the limits now clearly set for his demands, that he and his friends here should understand that they must open their eyes and stop placing themselves between the people of Bavaria and their beloved Monarch. . . . If Wagner disregards our advice, we should have to hail the day when he and his friends will be well and truly overthrown and will turn their backs on our dear, loyal Munich. For however celebrated Wagner and his music may be, we must proclaim something that is a hundred times more important—our love for our King.[10]

Inaccurate though this article was, it did reflect a growing attitude on the part of the Munich public where Wagner was concerned. Because the incident was known only to the king, a few members of his household, and the composer himself, it was obvious to everyone that Ludwig's cabinet had taken the initiative in firing the opening shot in the public war against Wagner. The next day, Wagner—taking advantage of "the rights of a private man to run his private affairs according to his own notions"—answered his critics in the same journal. "Solely to reassure my friend abroad, I characterize as false the communications from a Munich correspondent relative to myself and all my friends in the town which appeared in yesterday's issue of the *Allgemeine Zeitung*."[11] That same afternoon, he formally asked Pfistermeister, as an agent of the Bavarian government, to put an end to the talk of his "shameless demands" on the royal treasury.[12]

But Pfistermeister had no interest in sparing Wagner from the scrutiny of the press and proclaimed that there was nothing he could do. On the very next day, Ludwig was unpleasantly surprised to find that the *Allgemeine Zeitung* had printed a long and scathing attack on his friend.

> That His Majesty knows well, in the Richard Wagner affair, how to distinguish between persons and things, is shown by the latest resolution of the King, notwithstanding all that has happened, to assure the poet-composer, as before, the means to enable him to finish in Munich, free of care, his great work of the Nibelungen. We ought to add, however, that a definite time limit is in view for the completion of the work mentioned. Anyone who knows the firm will of the King will understand that this means that there is now an end not only to the wide-reaching . . . artistic plans cherished, if not by Wagner himself, at any rate by his associates and spread abroad by them, but also to any further relationship—which these people, it appears—have abused, between themselves and the Court.[13]

This infuriated Wagner. On 17 February, he wrote to Pfistermeister:

> There cannot be the least doubt that a simple order from the Cabinet would suffice to refute these offensive statements and to silence them. Since as you well know, they affect in an unpleasant manner His Majesty Himself, I shall have no alternative, if no contradictions follow or these calumnious reports are continued in the press of all countries, but to assume an agreement with them inside the Cabinet itself.[14]

Pfistermeister gave this letter to the king, and Ludwig consented to receive the composer. He listened as Wagner paced back and forth, insisting that the government make some kind of official pronouncement on the statements appearing in the press. Certainly the articles had reached the press by way of the government. Common reporters would have had no access to the private talks between Pfistermeister and Wagner, nor would they have known the details of the king's displeasure with the composer. The only logical explanation is that either Pfistermeister himself or one of his fellow court officials leaked the news to the press in an attempt to discredit the composer. Of this complicity, Ernest Newman wrote: "There can be no question, however, that ammunition for the press campaign against Wagner must have come from Court circles, unfriendly to him, in close touch with the Cabinet."[15]

But Ludwig himself was far from happy over the situation. He therefore forbade Pfistermeister to step in and halt the flow of reports about the composer. With no disavowals forthcoming and given a free hand, the press attacked in a more personal tone. On 19 February, the *Allgemeine Zeitung* printed a devastating article called "Richard Wagner and Public Opinion." It read in part:

> His demands in matters of ordinary life and comfort seem to be of so exquisitely sybaritic a nature that truly an Oriental *Grand Seigneur* need not hesitate to take up his abode in his house near the Propylaen and sit as a guest at his table. The ugly trait of ingratitude for benefits received is evident in Wagner's behaviour towards his former gracious royal Maecenas, the noble Friedrich August of Saxony—in comparison with which, in our opinion, his political aberration is wholly pardonable— this misuse of princely favour and liberality has moved the Bavarian people for months past to suppressed as well as open, and more than justified, displeasure. Or is it perhaps worthy of a really great and noble artist that Wagner, in his luxurious home furnishing here, should spend thousands on carpets alone, for instance—out of the purse of his generous benefactour in the ostentatious role of a modern Croesus? And previously to all this prodigality it happened, as is well known, that his royal protector had terminated the old familiar conflict, in Vienna, between Wagnerian receipts and Wagnerian expenditures by the grant of so incredibly large a sum that Mozart and Beethoven, Wagner's much greater predecessors, would have been heartily grateful to any prince for the gift of the mere interest on this debt capital for any year of their anxious life. . . . We who have so profound a regard for this young and lovable monarch and would gladly protect his head from the smallest shadow, ask ourselves whether . . . we ought not to have rejoiced when we learned that the King, enlightened by all this

abuse of his grace, has now determined to keep his enthusiasm for Wagner's music separate from the personality of the composer and to restrain the unconscionable financial and artistic demands of the latter within reasonable limits, which henceforth he will go beyond only to his own damage. . . . How many a great artist who starved his whole life through would have been supremely happy to have suffered such "disfavour," even if it had brought him only a quarter of what Wagner can still enjoy, thanks to this disfavour. Let us repeat, however, that we are really not so pitifully envious as to grudge Wagner the means to a decent, comfortable, free existence as that term is understood by ordinary people. Nor would any true Bavarian wish to deprive his King, on whose young shoulders so heavy a burden of office has fallen, of his enthusiasm for Wagner's music. . . . We ask only one thing—that Richard Wagner shall not again overstep, in fresh blindness, the limits now set to his demands, and that both he and his "friends here" will learn that they must no longer, by their continual disdain for what our modest opinion tells us is a very wealthy situation, even in matters musical, thrust themselves between us Bavarians and our beloved King, like a false note that pains our piety. Otherwise we shall have to praise the day when Richard Wagner and his friends, this time really and truly "overthrown," will have to turn their backs on our good Munich and on Bavaria itself. For however exalted Wagner and his music may be, our King and our love for him stand, for us, a hundred times higher.[16]

Wagner again appealed to the king, but Ludwig did nothing. He was confused by this sudden burst of animosity against his friend and more than a little angry that his private relationship had become front-page news for Bavaria's journalists. Ludwig refused to receive the composer again and to involve himself in the scandal being played out in the press. He wrote to Wagner:

Some day, my dear one, it will be seen by everyone that the bond between us is pure and holy and eternal. . . . Some day their astonished eyes will behold the wonders that you and I together have dedicated to a better age than this. And so, have courage. Let us have faith in each other; love's work is for all eternity.[17]

This, however, did little to comfort Wagner, who felt, with some justification, that the king had abandoned him to the hostile press. He was still smarting over the incident of 6 February, when the Residenz door was closed to him. On 9 March, he wrote to the king:

> My King,
> My Beloved Friend,
>   So I must take up my pen, that I may end a situation which cannot be allowed to last a moment longer if my very soul is not to be consumed!
>   What this state of mine must be my understanding friend may judge for himself!—
>   On the 6th February this year, at 1 o'clock, a most terrible thing happened to me: I was turned away from the door of my August Friend, having appeared there at his kind invitation, and was led back down to the courtyard. It was not my King's indisposition but his great displeasure with me which was adduced as the reason for this rebuff. Ever since that day, more and more rumours have been circulating concerning this dis-favour which I am said to have suffered. Finally, certain accusa-tions which I have no hesitation in declaring completely false and which—if needs be—I shall denounce as such in public . . . and then proceed to lay the blame on the Court and on the King for believing them.[18]

This thinly veiled threat to take his side of the dispute to the press greatly upset Ludwig. The next day, the king wrote:

> Moved by terrible anguish, I take up my pen today in order to reply to the letter you addressed to me yesterday.
>   I must make a confession which will affect you deeply; how hard it will be for me to do so, you can all too well imag-ine. Recall the love with which I feel drawn to you, remember the warmth of this everlasting love, which, as you have long known, my beloved friend, can never die nor ever shall; and then judge how profound my grief must be! I am bound to inform my unique friend that there are circumstances over which I do not have control at present, and that the iron grip of necessity makes it my sacred duty not to speak to you, at least for the present. That my love for you will remain loyal unto death—this, I know, you will never doubt.
>   Hope will sustain both you and me, and give us strength and courage; what would man be without this precious gift from God? Yes, I firmly hope for happier times, we shall see each other and speak to each other as we did before.

The terrible grip will weaken—courage! All will be well;
O! bitter lot! Who would have thought it, foreseen it! Love is
all-powerful; we shall triumph![19]

Ludwig assumed that his reassuring words would quiet his
friend. But Wagner was as stubborn as the king and took no comfort
in this letter. He finally wrote to the king, threatening to leave Munich.

> Shall I go? Shall I remain?
> Your will is mine.
> If I go it will be to some distant land and I will never
> return to Germany. For my work I will do what I can, but I will
> sever completely the connection between the Man and the
> Thing. If I remain, my Glorious Friend has given me strength to
> be patient, to bear every trial; for my trust is unassailable. So
> the Friend must decide: a single word—and I joyfully accept
> my fate. But the decision must be made—and made this very
> day. My spiritual forces are near a breaking point. I must
> known for certain by which decision I can bring peace to my
> dear one.

This amounted to emotional blackmail on Wagner's part, since he never
had the slightest doubt as to what the king's answer would be. Sure
enough, Ludwig was in a panic when he received Wagner's letter.
Hastily, the king dispatched the following note:

> Dear Friend!
> Stay, oh Stay! Everything will be as glorious as it used to
> be. I am very busy.
> Till death,
> Your Ludwig.

Wagner replied:

> I live again![20]

12

The Triumph of Tristan

In the spring of 1865, Ludwig's thoughts again turned to the production of *Tristan und Isolde*, which Wagner had promised for May. Ludwig's excitement was matched by Wagner's worry. There had been one attempt to stage *Tristan* in Vienna in 1862, and it had been an undisguised disaster. The opera was dismissed as impossible to produce, and no singers could be found anywhere who were up to the heavy demands of playing the two lead characters. The king, however, was adamant. In the end, *Tristan und Isolde* premiered in Munich according to schedule and proved to be the height of Wagner's success during his tenure in the Bavarian capital.

Wagner had composed *Tristan und Isolde* between 1857 and 1859. At the time, he was living in Switzerland under the patronage of Otto Wesendonck, and the story of *Tristan und Isolde*, with its themes of forbidden love and betrayal, remarkably paralleled the composer's own adulterous affair with Wesendonck's wife Mathilde. The composer took his story from the epic thirteenth-century poem by Gottfried von Strassburg, a narrative filled with lust, greed, sin, redemption, passion, and death. The encompassing passion of Tristan and Isolde ended with their deception of her husband King Mark in favor of their illicit relationship. This theme was echoed not only in Wagner's affair with Mathilde Wesendonck but later, also, in his liaison with Cosima von Bülow, a relationship shrouded in secrecy in an attempt to deceive Ludwig II. The story itself was a scandalous one for the conservative nineteenth century, with its blatant adultery and question of free will. In deceiving King Mark, the lovers make a choice which condemns them. Overcome with guilt and longing, they can find fulfillment only in death—the *liebestod* of so many of Wagner's operas—which brought a tragic, surreal quality to the drama. This theme of forbidden love, from *Tristan* onward, became a key element in Wagner's operas: the eternal triangle of life, love, and death, with its unearthly passions and inevitable betrayal and tragic end.

One of the main problems Wagner had previously encountered in the production of the opera was the lack of suitable singers to carry the lead roles. For the Munich premiere, the composer solved this problem by obtaining the services of Ludwig Schnorr von Carolsfeld, a hefty, twenty-nine-year-old court singer at Dresden. For the part of Isolde, Wagner selected Schnorr von Carolsfeld's own wife, Malvina, some ten years her husband's senior. Since the pair were under contract to the king of Saxony, Ludwig had to ask permission to borrow them; in the beginning of April, they were granted a three-month leave of absence. Wagner was somewhat put off by their appearance: Schnorr and his wife were both extremely obese, and their movements were far from graceful. But when they sang, the composer realized that not only were their voices superb but that their very sizable stage presences would help carry the emotion of the story.

Originally, Ludwig had asked Wagner to conduct the opera himself, but the composer, weary and unwilling to endure the long hours of rehearsals, instead asked Hans von Bülow, who took over while Wagner supervised the training of the singers at his home on the Briennerstrasse. On 10 April, the very first day of the rehearsals, Cosima von Bülow gave birth to a daughter. In an effort to prevent the inevitable gossip, Hans accepted the child as his own, but few in Munich were fooled. Wagner's paternity was seemingly confirmed when Cosima named the baby Isolde.

The king told Wagner that he wished to have *Tristan und Isolde* produced in the court theater of the Residenz, which seated two thousand. For artistic reasons, however, the composer pleaded for the smaller Cuvilliés Residenztheater. Ludwig immediately agreed. But once the full-scale rehearsals were underway, with the entire cast and orchestra present, the acoustics made this impossible, and Wagner was forced to return to the larger court theater.

The premiere was scheduled for 15 May, and Wagner extended an open invitation to "friends of his art" to come to Munich.[1] In the months leading up to the premiere, Hans von Bülow nearly crumbled under the strain. Bülow had never been in very good health; now, overcome by the pressures of his personal life and the difficulties presented by conducting *Tristan und Isolde*, he fainted at one of the strenuous rehearsals. However, Bülow completely lost whatever minute sympathy his unfortunate position may have generated among the general public after an indiscreet and offensive remark he made during a rehearsal on the afternoon of 2 May. Bülow, working under Wagner's instructions, needed to add more musicians to the orchestra; this, however, meant the removal of some thirty stalls for the public. When informed of this, Bülow cried, "What difference does that make, whether we have thirty *schweinehunde* [pigs] more or less in the place?"[2]

Bülow had spoken in a dark theater, unaware that anyone might be listening to his devastating words. But a reporter from the *Neueste Nachrichten*, sitting unnoticed in the hall, quickly ran back to his paper, and Bülow's offhand remark became the following day's front-page headline. Deeply embarrassed, Bülow wrote a letter of apology, stating, not very convincingly, that he had not been referring to the "cultured Munich public" but rather to the anti-Wagnerian critics. The *Neueste Nachrichten* printed the letter and accepted the apology, but other papers were quick to seize any opportunity to humiliate Wagner and his supporters. The *Neuer Bayerischer Kurier*, for example, printed the same headline, "Hans von Bülow is Still Here!" every day for a week, in increasingly large letters, in an attempt to drive the conductor from Munich and thus ruin the premiere of *Tristan und Isolde*.[3] The outcry might have died of its own accord had not Bülow been such a close associate of Wagner's but in attacking the conductor, the papers could slander, by implication, the hated composer himself.

Ludwig was unperturbed by the controversy. His anticipation over the production of the opera itself far outweighed any negative publicity. On 10 May, he wrote to Wagner:

> My Heart's rapture gives me no peace; I *must* write to you. Nearer and nearer draws the happy day—*Tristan* will arise! . . . We must break through the barriers of custom, shatter the laws of the base, egotistical world. The ideal must and shall come to life. We will march forward conscious of victory. My loved one, I shall never forget you. Oh, *Tristan, Tristan* shall come to me! The dreams of my boyhood and youth will be realized. You should have nothing to do with the baseness of the world; I shall bear you high above all earthly cares. Complete happiness must be yours. . . . My love for you and for your art grows ever greater and this flame of love shall bring you happiness and salvation.
> > Oh—write to me—I yearn for it!
> > > Until death,
> > > > Your faithful,
> > > > > Ludwig.[4]

On 11 May, the final dress rehearsal took place in the presence of the king and his six hundred invited guests. Ludwig was enchanted, and his feverish anticipation only increased as he awaited the actual premiere, which was set for 15 May. On that morning, the king issued a general amnesty for all military personnel and non-Bavarians who had participated in any revolutionary activities in 1848, a not-so-subtle gift to the composer himself. Ludwig's excitement infused his morning letter to Wagner.

> Day of Rapture! *Tristan*! Oh, how I long for this evening! If only it were here! *When will the torch be extinguished; when will it be night in the house*? Today! Today! How can I realize it? Why praise and humour *me*? The deed is YOURS! YOU are the wonder of the world; what am I without *you*? Why, I implore you, why cannot you find peace, why are you ever in torment? No joy without pain; oh, how can lasting calm, lasting peace on earth, constant joy, be found for you? Why always sad for you? . . . My love for you, I need not repeat, will endure forever. Faithful unto death! I am now well, hoping to soon see my Only One again![5]

But *Tristan* Day proved to be an unqualified disaster. As King Ludwig II sat in the Residenz writing these adoring lines to Wagner, baliffs arrived at 21 Briennerstrasse, demanding that the composer pay them 2,400 gulden immediately. Some years earlier, when suffering from one of his frequent financial crises, the composer had procured a loan from a rich Frenchwoman named Julia Schwabe. When she learned of Wagner's good fortune in Munich, she naturally asked that the loan be repaid. Characteristically, Wagner ignored her. She then engaged Herr von Schauss, a solicitor in Munich, to act on her behalf. He approached Wagner several times, but the composer refused to even discuss the matter of the outstanding debt. The lawyer then obtained a court order allowing him to seize the equivalent amount of the composer's personal property in lieu of payment. And so, on 15 May— *Tristan* Day—court officials informed Wagner that he must immediately pay the debt or that his belongings would be confiscated. Wagner had no money at hand but managed to forestall his creditors for several hours while Cosima rushed to see the king. Sure enough, Ludwig agreed to pay the entire debt at once.

A second caller to Wagner's house brought even worse news: Malvina Schnorr von Carolsfeld had taken a steam bath and lost her voice. She would not be able to appear as Isolde that evening. It was too late to even attempt to find a replacement. Wagner was devastated. Convinced that his career was finally ruined, Wagner reluctantly canceled the gala evening performance.

Rumors exploded in Munich: Wagner's barbaric music, it was said, had ruined Malvina's voice; Wagner was the target of an assassination plot; von Bülow had been threatened due to his now infamous *"schweine-hunde"* remark. No one wanted to believe the truth, and newspapers printed gleeful articles attacking Wagner and rejoicing in the ill fortune which seemed to consume the composer and his luckless circle of friends.

Ludwig Schnorr von Carolsfeld took his wife to Bad Reichenstall near the Austrian border so that she could rest; nearly a month passed before Malvina regained her voice. The date for the premiere of *Tristan und Isolde* had been changed to 10 June, and a great sense of anticipation and curiosity filled the air. No one knew what to expect, and there was the vague suspicion that a riot might erupt at any point during the performance itself.

Ludwig arrived at the court theater shortly before the six o'clock curtain, dressed in a simple black frock coat and striped trousers. A fanfare of trumpets announced his entry into the royal box, and he stepped to the edge to acknowledge the cheers of the crowd. He sat alone; although his grandfather and other Wittelsbach relatives attended the opening night, they were not allowed into the royal box. The king did not wish to disturb Wagner's spell with any idle conversation or share this emotional evening with anyone.

Tristan und Isolde proved a completely new experience for those present. There had never been anything remotely like it before in the opera world. The sets were bare, the stage dominated by the two leads. The music was disturbing as well—somehow unearthly and full of the lovers' despair. The opera was an ordeal for the majority of the audience. Most had never before been required to sit through anything quite as long or demanding. At the end of each act, some of the audience hissed toward Wagner's box. His dedicated enemy, the music critic Eduard Hanslick, declared afterward: "The Prelude to *Tristan und Isolde* reminds me of the old Italian painting of a martyr whose intestines are slowly unwound from his body on a reel."[6] But the majority of those present broke into applause; they realized that history had been made that night.

No one was as moved as Ludwig. At times during the performance, the king was seen to grip the edge of the box, tears streaming down his face. After the opera, overcome with emotion, he returned to his apartments in the Residenz and wrote Wagner a letter of adoration.

> My Unique One! My Holy One!
>   How glorious! Perfect! So full of Rapture! . . . *To drown . . . to sink down—unconscious—supreme joy* !
>   Divine work!
>   Eternally true—to beyond the grave![7]

Three days later, Ludwig attended the second performance, but the third performance was marred for the king by the presence of his hated uncle Otto, the former king of Greece, and so Ludwig reluctantly stayed away. He returned, however, for the evening performance on 1 July, and was, if anything, even more overcome with the effects of the opera. As his gilded train sped through the dark night on its way back to Berg, Ludwig was so overwhelmed that he pulled the emergency cord, and the gently rocking carriage came to a sudden halt. He opened the carriage door and left the plush velvet interior for the surrounding forests, where he wandered alone with his thoughts, strolling through thick groves of trees until the sky was washed with the early morning light. Finally, he returned to the distant lights of the royal train, which stood waiting on the lonely track, and with a burst of steam, the locomotive continued on to Berg as dawn broke over Bavaria.

The Schnorrs took a brief rest, then returned to Munich for further performances. Schnorr von Carolsfeld sang the role of Erik in *Der fliegende Holländer* and gave a private concert composed of excerpts from *Siegfried, Die Meistersinger von Nürnberg, Die Walküre,* and *Das Rheingold.* On 13 July, he and Malvina returned to Dresden. Three days later, Schnorr became ill with rheumatism; his decline was stunningly swift. Nine days later, he died, his last words, "Farewell, Siegfried! Console my Richard!"[8]

Tristan und Isolde had a remarkable impact on Ludwig's life. Although other Wagner operas were to strike more personal chords within the king, it was the production of *Tristan* which proved that through his power and influence he might give vision to his dreams. *Lohengrin* and *Tannhäuser* had both been successes before the king ever met Wagner; but without Ludwig's dedication and support, *Tristan und Isolde* might never have been produced. Now, filled with pride and assurance in his ability to triumph in art against all obstacles, Ludwig set himself to shaping the world of his dreams, the world where he himself could find refuge.

13

Ludwig and Wagner Against the World

Throughout 1865, Ludwig devoted much of his attention to the question of a new theater for Wagner. Gottfried Semper, a well-known architect from Zurich, came to Munich several times and met with both the king and Wagner, discussing details and even preparing models. But as the project progressed, Wagner lost interest due to mounting opposition and tried, unsuccessfully, to convince Ludwig to let the matter drop. The king was determined to see his wishes carried through and, although his government threw increasingly insurmountable obstacles in his way, behaved imperiously. When he himself finally tired of the ordeal and gave up on the theater, he did not even bother to inform the architect he had commissioned to design it. Semper was forced to sue for costs and in 1869 finally won damages against the crown.

The episode over the Festival Theater, and the manner in which it had been handled, was not flattering to either the king or the composer. Although Wagner had declared his opposition to the project after several months, the public continued to believe that it remained his main goal. He was intensely unpopular in Munich. By the summer of 1865, while Ludwig and Wagner celebrated their triumph in *Tristan und Isolde*, three powerful men in the Bavarian government had joined forces as the composer's virulent enemies: in addition to Pfistermeister and Pfordten, the king and Wagner now had to worry over the presence of Baron Sigmund von Pfeufer, the Munich chief of police. Together, these three men eagerly worked toward the composer's downfall.

During the final rehearsals for *Tristan und Isolde*, Ludwig dispatched a letter to Pfordten in which he asked that two official communications be made and published on his behalf. The first was to announce that he could not undertake any journeys that year on account of his ill health, while the second was a request that the true nature of his relations with Wagner were to be set forth and clarified for the Bavarian public. Pfordten agreed to Ludwig's first request, although he knew that nothing was wrong with the king's health. But it was an entirely different matter where the second request was concerned. Without himself knowing the true nature of the king's relations with the composer, Pfordten wrote to Pfistermeister on 28 May that he felt unable to produce any public statement on the matter. Instead, he declared, he felt that it was his duty to

> set forth the misgivings which the Wagner-Bülow situation arouses in everyone who sincerely and faithfully loves the King and would . . . preserve him from a damage that is unhappily drawing only too near. . . . My conviction is that Bülow must be discharged by His Majesty, and the sooner the better. As regards Wagner, all contracts made with him are to be observed, but personal relations between him and the King must be put an end to if His Majesty is not to be prejudiced both at home and abroad.[1]

Such animosity against the composer worried the king greatly. In the beginning, it had been easy for Ludwig to ignore the drift of public opinion; but as time went on and the press and official attacks continued, he grew concerned about the effects of his own position and popularity. He consulted Pfistermeister and Pfordten as to public opinion, and they, handed such a rare opportunity to denounce the composer, asked Chief of Police Pfeufer to draft a report on the situation. The king received this report on 31 May.

In his report, Pfeufer outlined what he believed to be the three principal groups who stood in opposition to Wagner. First, there were those who disliked Wagner simply because they considered him a foreigner. Then, there were those who felt that he had designs on the royal treasury. According to Pfeufer, this second group consisted of those.

> who reckon up the thousands that Wagner has already cost His Majesty and will continue to cost him, and cannot imagine what profit Wagner's music will bring. This view is the least dangerous one, because it is the least justified. The matter of cost is the concern of the King and no one else—an opinion shared by rational people who, although enemies of Wagner, fully recognize the King's right to spend when and how he chooses. The so-called Finance Party, which would like to make political capital out of this matter of expenditure, is therefore not to be taken seriously. It is quite another matter with the third group, however—those who count up the days and hours spent by His Majesty in seclusion and say, "Our King keeps

himself almost entirely to himself; he hardly ever sees anyone
from the official, military, learned or artistic world. And the
man who is to blame for this seclusion is Richard Wagner, who
has brought the King to feel at ease in no society but his, com-
munes with him by the hour (if not orally, at all events by
letter), pays homage to his kind of poetry and music and to
none other and shows no interest in the rest of the world." This
is the point of view that has the largest and most influential following in all sections of society—of the aristocracy and of the
bourgeoisie. And the longer the opinion of this section prevails
the more dangerous becomes the situation of the King, since
there comes a slackening in the love and veneration without
which no ruler can really rule.

You will now ask, "What is to be done? Must the King
drive Wagner away?" This would be asking too much of a
young, novel, poetic, romantically-inclined heart. Therefore, I
reply, "No!" to the question. Richard Wagner can remain if the
King will decide to give up his hermit's life and come into
closer contact with individual officials and personalities. The
Court officials, the Ministers, the upper officials and officers,
savants and artists should be invited oftener to Court; the present etiquette, which rules only in Spain, Austria and Bavaria,
should be abolished or modified; the King should go to the
Odeon concerts, and not confine his visits to the theatre to
Wagner's operas; the higher ranks of society should be diverted
with Court balls and concerts.[2]

In fairness to Wagner, the king withdrew from society largely of
his own accord. But the perception remained that a malevolent influence had placed itself between the Bavarian people and the throne. The
implied message in Pfeufer's report, however, was sound: Unless
Ludwig began to associate with others, unless he was seen in public
more often carrying out his royal duties, the animosity over his friendship with Wagner was likely to continue.

Aware of this growing opposition, Wagner foolishly tried to influence the king to reorganize his cabinet and strip Pfistermeister of much
of his power. Wagner suggested that Ludwig should create a new position, to be called keeper of the royal treasury in matters concerning art,
the holder of which would then assume sole responsibility over royal
funding of the king's artistic projects. The composer asked Ludwig to
name Baron Karl von Moy to this post; the position would encompass
directorship of all theaters and orchestras; the holder would allot and
dispense a yearly budget to such concerns and individuals involved in

artistic productions, and he would supervise the construction of the proposed Festival Theater in accordance with the king's wishes. Upon careful reflection, however, Ludwig refused to consider such a major cabinet reshuffling, knowing that he would face furious opposition from his officials.

Although the king considered his relationship with Wagner to be a private matter, he could not escape the fact that the unpopularity that plagued the composer had also begun to affect the throne. Ludwig made deliberate choices to stay away from important court functions, either to be with Wagner or, increasingly, to retreat into the solitude of the Alps. In the summer of 1865, he had written to his former governess: "I am happy; and I am glad about the profession which God gave me; now I am taking a rest from the most difficult business, and next winter I shall start afresh at my work. I intend to study very seriously and shall do everything within my power to make my dear people happy."[3] Soon enough, however, he was purposely isolating himself. "More than anything else I like to be alone," he confided to his mother.[4] He spent endless hours in the forest, riding at breakneck speed, alone except for a groom who struggled to keep pace with him.

Ludwig flaunted his growing disregard of public opinion and common sense in rather visible ways. When his father's coffin was transferred in state to his tomb in the vault of the Theatinerkirche, Ludwig was absent, pleading ill health. He had never been very fond of the military, and refused to attend the fall army maneuvers, again on the excuse that he was unwell. No one was deceived, however, and the king's refusal prompted one official to note: "If the King can ride for eight to ten hours in mist and darkness without endangering his health, then His Majesty is also able to devote a few hours to his Army."[5] His frequent absences from the capital—to either Hohenschwangau, Castle Berg, or some remote hunting lodge in the Alps—were beginning to cause considerable, and unfavorable, comment in Munich. It was a dark portent of things to come.

14

The Approaching Storm

By the end of the summer of 1865, Wagner was once again short of funds. Ludwig gave him as a gift a new coach and the sum of 1,200 gulden toward its upkeep and, on 1 August, agreed to raise his stipend from 5,000 to 6,000 gulden. Yet even this was not enough. A week after granting this increase, Ludwig received a letter from the composer.

> I have now considered the conditions necessary for my existence on earth. If I am denied them, my will shall have failed me. I can no longer want anything, as such, for myself. If you find it difficult, then deny me; that shall be my fate. But the common people and the world already believe me far better provided for; this much is certain. Perhaps it is therefore not too difficult for you. But, once again: I—desire nothing!—I say this without the least bitterness, with a tender heart, serious and calm.[1]

Simply put, if Ludwig was not forthcoming with more funds, there would be no further operas written. Of Wagner's demands, Ernest Newman wrote: "Once again, then, we observe, he was stoically facing a supreme renunciation. Without the least bitterness, gently, earnestly, calmly, this much enduring man desired nothing at all—except a mere 200,000 gulden more of Bavarian money."[2]

It is not known what Ludwig's immediate reaction to his friend's new proposal might have been. The sum was enormous and, if paid, would almost certainly have resulted in a great public outcry against the composer. The request for 200,000 gulden consisted of two different proposals. Wagner wrote:

> 1. His Majesty the King shall assign to me, rent-free, for the duration of my life, the property which belongs to him at No. 21 Briennerstrasse.

2. Use of assets totalling twice one hundred thousand gulden, also for the duration of my life, the said sum to be made over to me in such a way that 40,000 gulden in cash be transferred to me with immediate effect, to be administered by the Royal Cabinet Exchequer, with only the interest at five percent being made available to me in quarterly installments of 2,000 gulden each, in return for which all the annuities and subventions previously granted me by His Majesty, together with the stipulations thereto relating, shall be regarded as having been revoked and cancelled.[3]

This agreement would have guaranteed Wagner an annual income of 8,000 gulden—certainly a large amount, but only comparable to the sums many of his contemporary musicians and composers received. In addition, Wagner, even a year and a half after his arrival in Munich, still had enormous debts and desperately needed the money to pay off his creditors. Ludwig had recognized this by granting his friend an increase in his stipend only a week earlier; now, it appeared, even this generous sum would not do.

On the surface, Wagner's new demands appeared outrageous; yet his requests were not as frivolous as many cabinet officials believed. At the point the composer made this new request, he was entering the second year of his three-year contract with the king to complete and produce the entire Ring cycle by October 1867. Although the composer had done some work on *Siegfried*, there was no chance that he would complete all four operas in time to meet the deadline. By the terms of the contract Wagner had signed the previous year, if at the end of October 1867 he had not fulfilled all of his obligations and completed and produced the entire Ring cycle, all of the money he had received from the royal treasury would have to be paid back.

Aside from the stipulations of the October 1864 contract, Wagner had good reason to worry over his security. Ludwig II had often expressed his dissatisfaction over his position; if he should abdicate the throne or even unexpectedly die, Wagner would be left with a binding contract and a less-than-likely chance that the king's successor would be as understanding. Although he had received considerable sums of money, in reality, Wagner had little to show for his good fortune: The house on the Briennerstrasse was not legally his, and should the conditions of the October 1864 contract fail to be met, he could theoretically be turned into the street. His official position, his salary, and his future income were all tied to the successful completion of the previous contract. Should anything happen to Ludwig, Wagner would face the prospect not only of losing his position and home but also of being forced to repay thousands of gulden which he no longer possessed. A new contract seemed the only way in which he could secure his future.

It was perhaps inevitable that Ludwig would agree; he had no choice if he wished to keep Wagner in Munich. It was not to be a complete capitulation, however. He told Pfistermeister to inform the composer that he would immediately make available to Wagner the original sum of 40,000 gulden. But he was not to get the remaining 160,000 gulden to invest; rather, the royal treasury would keep it and pay Wagner the same amount which he had expected to earn on the interest, 8,000 gulden a year. Although this arrangement guaranteed that Wagner would still receive the exact amount which his own proposal had intended, the composer was angry when he learned of the details. He had clearly expected the king to acquiesce on all counts.

On 10 October 1865, Ludwig informed Wagner of further conditions: The 40,000 gulden, while being granted to Wagner, was not his to dispose of as he wished. He must use it for current living expenses. Since he had wished to pay off his old debts with most of this sum, Wagner was unhappy and did not hesitate to make this known to the king.

Negotiations continued for a week. Wagner felt that Ludwig had deceived him over the conditions of the new contract, as the king had at first appeared to grant all of his requests. Pfistermeister was so exasperated at the entire affair that he received Ludwig's permission to be relieved of his unofficial duties as intermediary between the king and composer. That unenviable task was left to Pfistermeister's undersecretary, Johann von Lutz. Only four days later, however, Ludwig relented and told Wagner that he could dispose of the 40,000 gulden as he saw fit.[4]

Wagner rejoiced in his partial triumph. But the public was outraged at this new grant from the royal treasury; at least the press had the satisfaction of knowing the humiliation the composer had to endure in order to collect the money. On the appointed day, so the story goes, Wagner sent Cosima von Bülow to the royal treasury to receive the 40,000 gulden. When she arrived and presented the bank with the note, the official in charge informed her, one suspects with a fair measure of glee, that she would have to take half the amount in coin, as they had only enough paper bills on hand for half the sum. Unperturbed, Cosima ordered two carriages and a police escort; she herself helped load the sacks of coin into the carriages, then set off through the streets of Munich to 21 Briennerstrasse.

With these financial difficulties behind them, Ludwig invited Wagner to spend a week with him at Hohenschwangau. The composer arrived at the little castle on 11 November. The Bavarian government was unhappy with the arrangement, and Pfistermeister asked to be relieved from attending the king during that week, so distasteful did he find Wagner's presence. In his place, the cabinet dispatched Lutz, who tried to influence Wagner to raise certain pro-Prussian policies during his meetings with the king; when Wagner refused, Lutz offered him a vast sum of money if he would leave Munich forever. But Wagner, with his seemingly unlimited access to the king and his royal treasury, angrily dismissed Lutz on the spot.

The week at Hohenschwangau passed all too quickly for Ludwig. Each day, he and Wagner took long walks along the Alpsee. Wandering among the fallen leaves and patches of frost skirting the lake, they discussed the composer's latest plans. Back at the castle, they composed florid letters of endless devotion to one another. One cold, snowy morning, Wagner awoke to the sounds of the fanfare from the second act of *Lohengrin*, played at the king's request by a group of oboists perched atop the towers. After Wagner had returned to Munich, there was a strange display on the Alpsee one evening. Ludwig, who delighted in fireworks, had hundreds of them set off on the shore below the castle, attracting the curious attention of the people who lived in the little village of Hohenschwangau. He stood at the edge of the lake, watching the spectacle. Soon, an enormous swan boat appeared from the reeds, with the figure of Lohengrin standing proudly as he journeyed across the chill lake. It was Prince Paul von Thurn und Taxis, dressed in costume as the Swan Knight. While Paul played the part of Lohengrin, a hidden orchestra supplied the appropriate musical passages. Ludwig was delighted with his tableau, but the villagers, attracted by the fireworks, had also witnessed the curious nocturnal spectacle. Soon enough, word spread back to Munich, and the Bavarian capital was consumed with tales of the curious goings-on at the king's retreat.

On 13 November 1865, while the King played host to Wagner at Hohenschwangau, an article appeared in the Nuremberg *Anzeiger* entitled "Plain Words to the King of Bavaria and His People on the Subject of the Cabinet Secretariat." The author of "Plain Words" wrote that the king was isolated from his people, not through any fault of his own, or the influence of any outside person, but owing entirely to the institution of the cabinet secretariat, which forced him to communicate indirectly with all officials. The article called the post of Cabinet Secretary "entirely unconstitutional," and was, in effect, a thinly veiled attack on Pfistermeister.[5]

Although Wagner apparently had nothing to do with the article, everyone assumed that he had been behind it. Ludwig himself was too enraptured at the composer's presence at Hohenschwangau to take too much notice of the press. Two weeks later, however, he was horrified to find that the newspaper *Volksbote* had replied to "Plain Words" in an article which roundly condemned Wagner. It did not openly accuse the composer of having authored the article, "though under the circumstances, there seems to be some reason to suppose that he may not have been wholly unaware of its contents." The newspaper was careful to point out the various grants and gifts which the king had given to Wagner, adding up the figures line by line, in devastating detail, until it stood, inaccurately, at 190,000 gulden. The article ended with a defense of Pfistermeister and Julius Hofmann, the Head of the Royal Treasury: "These two men are to be set aside in order that certain hankerings after the exploitation of the Royal Treasury may be more easily satisfied."[6]

If the intention of the author of "Plain Words" had been to goad Wagner into a public fight, he succeeded admirably. The composer was furious at this attack, and fired off an angry letter to the king, recommending that Maximilian von Neumayr, who had previously held the post of minister of the interior, be appointed as head of the cabinet immediately in place of Pfistermeister. He also sent along a copy of the *Volksbote* article. Ludwig, however, refused to consider the change. He wrote on 27 November:

> I have considered your advice very carefully. Rest assured, my Dear One, that what I now write in answer is not the result of hasty and superficial considerations. . . . I had the best of reasons for letting Neumayr go and for withdrawing the confidence I had long had in him . . . so it would be wholly inconsistent for me now to entrust to this man—with whom I have *every reason* to be dissatisfied—the formation of a new Cabinet. There is no doubt that Pfistermeister is second rate and stupid; I shall not retain him much longer in the Cabinet. But to dismiss him and other members of the Cabinet at this moment does not seem to me to be advisable; the time is not yet developed. This I say most definitely: and believe me, I have the best of reasons for saying it. The article you sent to me is scandalously written. . . . You will be astonished when I tell you that my Cabinet had nothing to do with it, however much it may appear that they had.[7]

On the same day that the *Volksbote* article appeared, Wagner replied with an anonymous piece in the *Neueste Nachrichten*. In it, he attacked the members of the royal cabinet "whom I have no need to mention by name since they are the object of universal and contemptuous indignation in Bavaria." He claimed that they criticized "the

King's unshakeable friendship for Wagner" in order to save themselves. Again, Wagner wrote:

> Of one thing you can be quite certain: it is in no way a question of any principal, any party politician, being attacked by Wagner; it is purely and simply an affair of the lowest personal self-interest, and that on the part of a very small number of individuals; and I dare to assure you that with the removal of two or three persons who do not enjoy the smallest respect among the Bavarian people, both the King and the Bavarian people would once and for all be set free from these annoyances.[8]

Although the article was unattributed, all of Munich knew that Wagner was the author. He was the only person who stood to gain by the removal of his enemies in the cabinet. Wagner had aggrevated the situation by dragging the king's name into the newspapers; the same day as this article appeared, when Ludwig questioned him, the composer lied to the king and pleaded ignorance, denying that he had any knowledge prior to publication. But Wagner must have known the truth.

Pfistermeister himself entered the debate on 30 November with a contemptuous letter published by the official government paper *Bayerische Zeitung*. Pfistermeister denied all of the allegations in the *Nachrichten* article, "the authorship of which is evident enough from the style and the construction."[9] As cabinet secretary, he would hardly have engaged in such a public denial and denunciation of Wagner without the king's full approval.

Wagner wrote:

> If I feel called upon by fate to perform a great and noble service for you and the country it must remain your secret and mine alone. No one must know that it was I who opened your eyes. That is why my advice to you remains the same as before: dismiss Pfistermeister immediately and, at the same time, appoint Neumayr to advise you on the formation of a new Cabinet. The first of these actions will alarm your opponents and paralyze them, the second will show the country what it can expect of you. Prudence and justice come together: their relationship is pure, helpful to the good of the public and to Bavaria. . . . Resist the thought that his appointment will cause you humiliation; the King can never be unjust, especially when he dispenses justice. The injustice was bound up with the whole of this rotten system which, made wise by this tragic turn of events, you now intend to resolve. . . . My King! Act quickly and decisively! As

bold as you are, and as I love you, I almost wish to see you mount your horse, ride merrily into Munich without saying a word to anyone, summon Neumayr to you here and immediately put everything back on the right course, like a true hero![10]

Wagner should have known better than to push the king in the political arena; Ludwig jealously guarded his royal prerogatives and did not take kindly to any unsolicited advice, even if it did come from his beloved friend. His only reply to the composer's letters was curt: "That article in the *Neueste Nachrichten* has contributed not a little to embitter the last days of my stay here. It was unquestionably written by one of your friends who thought he was doing you a service thereby; unfortunately, so far from helping you, it has hurt you."[11]

The debate had entered the arena of public opinion once again, but this time, Wagner lacked the common sense to save himself. The floodgates were opened. The satirical magazine *Punsch* filled its pages with caricatures of Wagner and printed a venomous parody of the Lord's Prayer, titled "The Morning Prayer of a Modest Man":

My Dear God, keep me in good health. Let me continue to enjoy my small house, my garden and my income, and grant to me, please, 100,000 gulden more, if not all at once, then at least in installments. Dear God, bless everyone on this earth, especially those people who have got such a strong tenor voice that they can be of service to me. I Pray Thee, grant strength to all who are sick. Only, please, send an apoplectic stroke or some kind of disease to two or three people who do not enjoy the least amount of respect in the Bavarian Government, so as to put them out of my way upon this earth and allow them to enter into eternal peace. Amen.[12]

It was the Lola Montez scandal all over again: the public animosity, the press attacks on the king's favorite, the king himself dragged into the controversy. The Wagner affair had reached its crescendo; fearing for the continued survival of the throne, those closest to the king, from members of his family and court officials to government ministers and church hierarchy, all prepared to pressure Ludwig to do the inevitable. However, their whispered plans and hasty meetings would be unnecessary: Ludwig, for all of his infatuation with the composer and his music, still retained enough belief in the sanctity of his royal office not to discard it on personal folly. There would be no repeat of the dangerous events of 1848: Wagner would go.

15

Exile

The storm which so abruptly changed the king's mind and drove Wagner from Munich broke on 27 November 1865. On that day, Pfordten had been asked by Lutz about the possible establishment of Wagner's special minister in matters of art. Pfordten received this information with some anxiety. He replied that he hoped the king would give much thought before ordering "a reconstruction of the Cabinet according to Richard Wagner's notions." He continued:

> Loyal Bavaria will, although discontentedly, continue to put up
> with seeing the money that could dry the tears of so many
> people squandered by Wagner and his associates—if that be the
> King's pleasure; but I am afraid that what Bavaria will not put
> up with is its King's "friendship" for a Richard Wagner. Please,
> therefore, beg His Majesty, in my name, not to make any decision
> until he returns to Munich and has heard what I have to say.[1]

The king replied on the same day. Although he understood there was much talk concerning Wagner in Munich, he urged Pfordten not to listen to the rumors of political influence. All of his associations with Wagner, he assured the minister, were confined to questions of music and art.

Pfordten was not convinced. He had been presented with too great an opportunity to drive Wagner from the capital to simply let the matter drop. On 1 December, he wrote to the king:

> Your Majesty now stands at a fateful parting of the ways: you
> have to choose between the love and respect of your faithful
> people and the "friendship" of Richard Wagner. This man, who
> has the audacity to assert that members of the Cabinet who have
> proved their fidelity do not enjoy the smallest respect among the
> Bavarian people, is himself despised by every section of the com-

munity to which alone the Throne can look for support—despised not only for his democratic leanings (in which the democrats themselves do not believe) but for his ingratitude and treachery towards friends and benefactours, his overweening and vicious luxury and extravagance, and the shamelessness with which he exploits the undeserved favour of Your Majesty. This is the opinion not only of the nobility and the clergy but also of the respectable middle class and workers, who painfully earn their bread by the sweat of their brow while arrogant strangers luxuriate in the royal generosity and, by way of thanks for this, vilify and deride the Bavarian People and its condition.[2]

Ludwig was at Hohenschwangau when this letter arrived. For the next five days, he refused to see anyone. He spent restless nights pacing up and down his bedroom, carefully considering his options. Unwilling and unable to continue the dangerous and destructive battle in the press, he reluctantly made his decision. By the time he returned to Munich at the end of the week, if his government continued to push him, the king was prepared to part with his friend.

On the afternoon of 6 December, Ludwig summoned his mother; his uncle, Prince Karl; and the archbishop of Munich to a meeting at the Residenz. Pfistermeister was also present, carefully concealing his joy that it was he who had helped drive the king to his momentous decision. He presented Ludwig with a petition, allegedly on behalf of the entire nation, calling for Wagner's expulsion from Bavaria. Ludwig did not know that the majority of the signatories, whom Pfistermeister referred to as a cross-section of the general public, were actually employed by the court, or minor bureaucrats who worked for the government, or merchants who supplied the king with goods. This petition was followed by a delegation from the Council of Ministers, who presented a bill calling for the composer's immediate exile as the only means of restoring "calm in the country." Ludwig sat in silence, listening to the opinions offered and reading through the various government reports. Finally, his face set in a grim mask, he rose and abruptly terminated the audience.[3]

That same afternoon, the king's physician, Dr. Gietl, found him sitting alone in his room, head bowed. When the doctor entered, Ludwig said brokenly, more to himself than to Gietl, "Yes ... he has transgressed," referring to Wagner.[4] Ludwig reluctantly summoned Pfistermeister and informed him that Wagner was to be expelled at once. The king had previously agreed to attend a performance at the theater that night; he arrived in the royal box, pale and nervous, and the audience, unaware of his decision, turned and greeted him not with

Nymphenburg Palace in the suburbs of Munich, where Ludwig
was born in 1845

The Blue Salon in the apart-
ments of the crown prince in
Nymphenburg Palace
Susanne Meslans collection

*All pictures from the author's
collection unless otherwise noted.*

Lola Montez, painted by Friedrich August von Laulbach for Ludwig I's Gallery of Beauties *Nymphenburg collection*

Princess Marie of Prussia, Ludwig II's mother *Nymphenburg collection*

King Maximillian II, Queen Marie, Crown Prince Ludwig, and Prince Otto before the Lion Fountain on the terrace at Hohenschwangau *Lithograph by E. Correns, 1850*

The *Konigsbau* of the Munich Residenz, built by Leo von Klenze for Ludwig I between 1826 and 1835 and modeled on the Pitti Palace in Florence

The Grotto Court in the Residenz   The Court Chapel in the Residenz

The *Riche Kapelle* in
the Residenz

Hohenschwangau Castle

Crown Prince Ludwig, about 1861
Private collection

Crown Prince Ludwig in military uniform, about 1862   *Private collection*

King Ludwig II riding   *Painting by F.
Dietz, 1864—Nymphenburg collection*

King Ludwig II, 1864

King Ludwig II, about 1864

King Ludwig II, about 1864

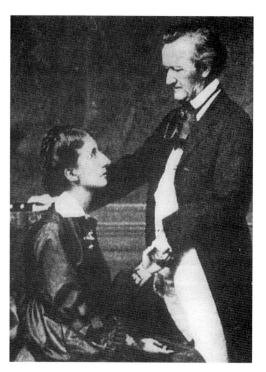

Richard Wagner and Cosima von Bülow
after their marriage *Private collection*

Hans von Bülow *Private collection*

King Ludwig II, dressed in the robes of the Knights of the Order of St. George, 1864

Empress Elizabeth of Austria on horseback at her father's estate of Possenhofen, 1853
Engraving by A. Fleischmann

Emperor Franz-Joseph of Austria during the reign of Ludwig II *Archive Photo*

King Ludwig II and Princess Sophie in Bavaria, an engagement photograph, 1867

King Ludwig II and Princess Sophie, 1867

Ludwig's gilded wedding coach
Susanne Meslans collection

the customary applause but with hisses. The queen mother, standing next to her son, fainted and had to be carried from the box, Ludwig quickly following behind her.

Ludwig's official letter the next day to Pfordten must have torn him apart.

> My Dear Minister:
> My resolution stands firm. Richard Wagner must leave Bavaria. I will show my dear people that its love and confidence are the first things of all to me. You will realize that this has not been easy for me; but I have overcome.[5]

Wagner was still unaware of his fall from grace. The king left it to Johann von Lutz to inform the composer of his forced exile. When the undersecretary arrived at 21 Briennerstrasse, Wagner greeted him with his customary glare. He listened with disbelief while Lutz informed him of the king's request that he leave Bavaria for a period of not less than six months. Then Wagner began to threaten Lutz and called Pfistermeister such names that the undersecretary declared, "Restrain yourself! I am here in my official capacity!"[6]

That same day, Ludwig wrote to Wagner:

> My Dear Friend!
> Much as it grieves me, I must ask you to carry out the request that I made to you yesterday through my secretary. Believe me, I had no choice. My love for you will endure forever, and I beg you to keep for ever your friendship for me; I can say with a clear conscience that I am worthy of it. Sundered, who can part us?
> I know that you feel with me, that you can plumb the whole depths of my grief. I could not act otherwise; rest assured of that. Never doubt the faithfulness of your best friend. It will certainly not be forever.
> Until death,
> Your Faithful,
> Ludwig.[7]

Wagner left Munich for his Swiss exile early on the morning of 10 December 1865. As his train steamed slowly out of the station, Cosima von Bülow stood on the siding watching him go, crying bitterly.

Few people, least of all Ludwig himself, expected the exile to last more than a few months. Six weeks after his friend left Bavaria, Ludwig wrote to Wagner:

I have not given up hope: better times will come, everything
will calm down here, the Friend will return and inspire me with
his dear proximity, we will go on with our art plans, the School
will be founded, the festival theatre will rise in its undreamed-
of pride and splendour. . . . I hope, believe, love. . . . No, no,
what began so divinely shall not end thus! . . . I will do as you
desire, will govern firmly, like a King in the fullest sense of the
word. But why must we remain apart, each living only for
himself? . . . I have a presentiment that you will never find
peace abroad. . . . I implore you, let a few months go by quietly,
and many things will be quite different. . . . Then, I hope and
believe, your return will have no political significance.[8]

However, having escaped the antagonistic press and officials of
the Bavarian capital, Wagner had no wish to come back. He wrote the
king a letter in which he honestly explained that he would not return
to Munich to live.

But such an admission fell on deaf ears where Ludwig was concerned. Three weeks after this exchange, he begged the composer to
return to Munich that spring. Wagner considered this proposal carefully and agreed if the king would grant to him three conditions: His
stipend would have to be granted to him for life, the house at 21
Briennerstrasse was to become his personal property, and he was to be
granted immediate Bavarian citizenship. The king could grant the first
two requests of his own accord, but the third proposition would have
to be approved by both the cabinet and the two legislative chambers
of the Landtag. As such, it was hardly likely to pass. When Ludwig
casually mentioned a grant of naturalization papers, the entire cabinet
threatened to resign. The king could not risk such a move, and Wagner,
without it, would not return to Munich. Ludwig could only be with his
friend if he would abdicate.[9]

Realizing that he would have to make his permanent residence
somewhere other than in Munich, Wagner began his search for a suitable new house. In March of 1866, he found one: Tribschen, on the
shores of Lake Lucerne. The king sent Wagner a gift of 5,000 francs
to cover the rent for a year, and the composer moved in. Tribschen
was a small, three-storey villa high on a slope above the lake, surrounded by orchards and a forest. The composer intended to take the
middle floor for himself, with Hans and Cosima von Bülow on the
ground floor and their children on the top. On taking up residence,
Wagner had its low-ceilinged rooms hung with his favorite pink
satins and rich brocades, lavish materials he deemed necessary to the
creative process.

In the first weeks at Tribschen, Wagner seemed happy enough. His letters conveyed this sense of serenity, and he genuinely accepted his exile as a matter of course.

On 25 January 1866, the composer's wife, Minna, had died of a stroke. Although they had not lived together for many years, Wagner had always been careful to ensure that she received regular funds. Her death removed an obstacle which had prevented the relationship between him and Cosima from progressing. Shortly after Wagner took possession of the little Swiss villa, his mistress duly moved in, bringing her three daughters, Daniela, Blandine, and Isolde, the latter undoubtedly fathered by Wagner himself.

16

The Schleswig-Holstein Crisis

In 1866, the ominous specter of Schleswig-Holstein once again threatened to engulf Germany in the flames of war. The joint Austro-Prussian incursion into the Elbe duchies two years earlier had done nothing to settle their contentious fate. For Chancellor Bismarck, the issue meant more than a new port and northern army encampments: It was a question of realpolitik, and Prussia's role in modern Germany. Finally, forcefully, he was determined to make Prussia not only the dominant German state but also a contender in the European balance of power.

After the military occupation of 1864, Prussia had taken administrative control of Schleswig while Austria governed the neighboring state of Holstein. This arrangement pleased no one, least of all Bismarck, who had no great desire to see the Habsburg army entrenched as a power in northern Germany. He repeatedly declared that Prussia, by her very proximity to the two duchies, enjoyed privileged status and should be granted special rights. For strategic reasons he wished to build a canal from Kiel on the Baltic across Holstein to the North Sea, an impossibility as long as Austria retained military control of the coveted territory.

Hoping to avert a crisis, Emperor Franz Josef summoned diplomats to Vienna to discuss the matter in August of 1864. Beneath the gilded rococo ceilings and crystal chandeliers of Schonbrunn Palace, ministers and monarchs spent endless hours arguing over territorial rights and compensation. Bismarck proposed that Austria cede her interests in Holstein to Prussia; in return, he would support Austrian interests elsewhere in Europe, hinting that the Habsburgs would be free to annex Italy, but Franz Josef proved less than receptive to the idea. Instead, the emperor suggested that Austria might willingly cede Holstein if only Prussia would return several provinces annexed a hundred years earlier by Friedrich the Great. Wilhelm I of Prussia, however, put a stop to this by declaring that he had no interest in trading portions of his kingdom for a questionable claim to Holstein.

But Bismarck would not give up so easily on acquiring the duchies. Convinced that Prussia needed exclusive rights to the duchies, he asserted that she would forgo the idea of annexation only if certain conditions were met: The armies of both duchies would have to swear allegiance to Prussia, Prussian military bases were to be established in both Schleswig and Holstein, and the duchies would be forced to enter the Zollverein, or German customs union.[1] Not surprisingly, Austria rejected the Prussian demands. It took six months of occupation in Holstein before the Austrians realized that Bismarck had simply used their troops to subvert the Danes and lay the groundwork for his own eventual annexation. Austria quietly opened diplomatic talks with the duke of Augustenburg, pretender to the duchies; more strategically, they allowed rebellious demonstrations to take place in the streets of Holstein for the duke's return, a movement which quickly spread to neighboring Schleswig. To Bismarck, it was as good as a renunciation of the mutual treaty which had led to the war against Denmark. From this moment on, the chancellor was determined to use Austrian sympathy for the claims of the duke of Augustenburg as an excuse to drive the Habsburg empire from the German Confederation.

Bismarck ordered his troops into Schleswig to put down the rebellion and expected Austria to follow suit in Holstein. Franz Josef's refusal to crush the revolt led to a new Prussian ultimatum: Either Austria support Bismarck in ending the Augustenburg movement or King Wilhelm I would order his troops to act independently and invade Holstein. Austria had little choice but to agree; at a conference held in Bad Gastein that August, Franz Josef's envoys reluctantly agreed to permit Prussian military bases in Holstein as well as construction of the Kiel Canal for use by the Prussian navy. "Just fancy finding an Austrian diplomat willing to sign a thing like that!" Bismarck exclaimed on learning of the treaty.[2] Austria's capitulation to Prussian demands finally convinced Bismarck that he would face no serious opposition in his eventual annexation of the duchies.

In Bavaria, situated between the two powers, Austria, its neighbor to the south, and Prussia in the north, Ludwig observed these developments with growing apprehension. The nineteen-year-old was suddenly thrust into the military arena, forced to take charge of his country's destiny and play the role of a warrior. The lives of thousands of his soldiers and subjects now rested in Ludwig's uncertain, inexperienced hands.

Modern warfare, with its cannon and rifles, clashed violently with Ludwig's romanticized vision of heroic knights and chivalrous crusades. As crown prince, he had joined the army as expected, participating in military drills and duly appearing in his regimental uniforms, yet he was always ill at ease in the company of his intimidating general staff. He once derisively described his staff officers as "clipped porcupines."[3] Although he enjoyed the pomp and pageantry of the military, Ludwig hated the duties which accompanied his position as Bavarian commander in chief: He found reviews a great bore, and regimental dinners and receptions were an ordeal he only managed to endure by drinking glass upon glass of wine and champagne. At one review, his cousin Empress Elizabeth of Austria saw him walking across a muddy parade ground wearing the full dress uniform of a field marshal. In one hand he carried his plumed helmet, in the other, a large, open umbrella. Elizabeth found the sight so absurd that she immediately burst into fits of laughter, but Ludwig only gave her an angry stare, declaring, "I've no intention of spoiling my coiffure."[4] Once, Ludwig expressed his desire that some weapon might be found which would kill entire regiments of soldiers at a time. "If battles are to be fought by machinery," he explained, "let us do our worst against each other until we are sick of carnage, and come back to the time when nations settled their differences by single combat."[5]

Ludwig wished to remain neutral in any larger German conflict. When he appointed Ludwig von der Pfordten as his prime minister in December of 1864, the king made a clear and conscious choice for isolation. Pfordten, in taking up his office, submitted his program to the throne, and the king wholeheartedly approved of its contents: "Within Germany, it is Bavaria's function to pursue neither an Austrian nor a Prussian but a Bavarian and a German policy; which means, a Greater Germany must not aim at a conflict between Austria and Prussia but at their reconciliation within the laws of the Union."[6]

The question of Bavarian alliances was a complicated one. Ludwig's natural sympathies lay with Austria, Bavaria's neighbor to the south. The Wittelsbachs and the Habsburgs were closely linked through centuries of marriage and also by their Catholicism. In addition, Bavaria and Austria enjoyed strong commercial and industrial ties. However, for all of these real and imagined bonds, the Habsburg empire was an anachronism, her economy struggling and her army antiquated.

Yet, an alliance with Prussia was less conventional; on the surface, Bavaria and her neighbor to the north were unlikely allies, divided, as they were, by religion, by character, and by mutual animosity. Many in the Bavarian government, however, were convinced that only by securing a Prussian alliance would their own country escape future humiliation.

By personal inclination and political sentiment, Ludwig wished to avoid an alliance with Prussia. Although Bismarck often expressed only the fondest thoughts of the king, Ludwig himself felt otherwise, referring to the chancellor as "that Junker from the marshes."[7] He had no false illusions as to Bismarck's eventual goals. When one of his advisers insisted that "Prussia's only ambition just now is supremacy in northern Germany," the king replied, "*Just now*, yes; but presently, she will want more."[8]

Ludwig was torn by the very idea of making a military alliance against a fellow German state, yet he could not avoid the inevitable. In late February 1866, he learned that Prussia had signed an offensive alliance with Italy; the knowledge that Prussia had formed such a union with a non-German state to use in a military conflict against a fellow Deutscher Bund member finally convinced the king that he could wait no longer in making his decision. On 2 March, the Bavarian ambassador in Vienna formally told the Austrian government that "should she be attacked in Germany because of her insistence on the law of the Union," King Ludwig II's troops would support the Habsburgs.[9] Having made the fateful decision, Ludwig was overwhelmed with depression. Throughout April, he watched helplessly as the situation in the duchies escalated, armies went on alert, and diplomats rushed from one capital to another, trying to negotiate a peaceful solution. By the beginning of May, Prussian and Austrian soldiers stood ready to attack each other.

On 9 May, Ludwig presided over an emergency meeting of the Council of Ministers at the Residenz. He listened in stunned silence as minister after minister declared that the king had no choice but to mobilize his army against Prussia. He paced up and down the room in agonized frustration, unwilling to commit his country to a German civil war. The responsibility of the momentous decision proved too great for the tormented young man: To the horror of his government, Ludwig suddenly dismissed the meeting with an announcement that he would rather abdicate the Bavarian throne in favor of his brother, Otto, than order the requested mobilization. As they left the Residenz late that afternoon, the ministers were convinced that their country faced imminent ruin. Ludwig spent a restless night pondering his decision; the fact that he had already given his word to Austria eventually convinced him to change his mind, for on the following day, he ordered his general staff to undertake the full mobilization of the Bavarian army and called for a special session of the Landtag on 22 May to discuss the crisis.

Feeling that his hand had been forced, Ludwig impetuously fled to the solitude of Castle Berg. Although he declared that Berg was close enough to the capital in the event that he was needed, this was not necessarily the case in wartime, when decisions had to be made instantly. Ludwig himself had little concept of the growing emergency or his need to be available and could rarely be found at the castle itself, but instead wandered through the woods or retreated to the small villa on the Roseninsel in the middle of Lake Starnberg. There was no direct communication with the latter, and a messenger from Munich, having spent upward of two hours getting to Berg, was then forced to find a launch to transport him to the king's hideaway. Worse still, the king often escaped from the Roseninsel on his own, rowing himself up and down the lakeshore or sailing on his steamer which he had renamed *Tristan*, so that it was no easy task to locate him.

The king's move to Berg was not popular with the people of Munich, who felt that their sovereign, having made preparations for war, had then abandoned them in a moment of crisis. When Ludwig protested, through Pfistermeister, that his decision to move to Berg inconvenienced no one, Munich chief of police Pfeufer replied in a direct letter, in which he asked

> whether it is possible for a train to be available at any moment it may be wanted, for the King to be found at his villa at any given moment, whether now and then there may not be some sudden decision or other on His Majesty's part that cannot be entrusted to the telegraph, and so must suffer delay until the ministers can arrive at Berg. These and other questions are being asked in all walks of life. . . . His Majesty wants to know whether his retreat to Berg is deplored. I can only reply, "Yes:" what in normal and peaceful times can be regarded as a "negligible distance" is looked upon in extraordinary times as a great distance.[10]

Disillusioned with the coming war and his inability to prevent it, Ludwig sank deeper and deeper into despair. He wandered along the lonely lakeshore as twilight fell, returning to the castle only to pace up and down his apartments, lost in indecision. When he received Pfistermeister for their regular session on the morning of 15 May, his fatigue was obvious: Pale and nervous, Ludwig could scarcely control his emotions. He refused to discuss any official business; instead, he declared that he wished to abdicate in favor of his brother and take up residence in Switzerland. In tears, Ludwig confessed to the startled cabinet secretary that he feared he might be going mad, and he asked Pfistermeister to convey to the court physician, Dr. Gietl, "messages for you which I cannot commit to paper."[11] Pfistermeister left Berg fearing the worst.

Ludwig's anguish at his impotent position, his reluctant assumption of military responsibility, and his horror of war tore at his heart. Forced to face the harsh contemporary reality of Bismarck and German politics, his thoughts turned increasingly to his exiled friend. His desperate longing drove him to consider the unthinkable. When Pfistermeister had gone, Ludwig wrote to Wagner:

> I long more and more for the Dear One. The political horizon grows darker and darker. . . . I beg the Friend for an immediate answer: if it is the Dear One's wish and will, I will gladly resign the Throne and its empty splendour and come to him, never again to part from him. . . . I say it again: to be separated from him and alone is more than I can bear; to be united with him and away from this mundane existence is the only thing that can save me from despair and death.[12]

This letter put Wagner into a panic. If Ludwig abdicated, the most money he would receive was 500,000 gulden, which had been left to Maximilian II by King Ludwig I. Out of this sum, the king could not possibly support himself, a court in exile, and the composer in the completion of his operas. Wagner hastily replied:

> Denounce, I beseech you, during this half year, all concern with art and our plans. . . . Turn your attention with the greatest energy to affairs of state; give up your comfortable solitude in Berg; remain in your Residenz, stay with your people, show yourself to them. If you love me, as I have earnestly hoped, then hear my pleas when I ask you to open Parliament in person on 22 May.[13]

But Ludwig would not be put off so easily, nor was he willing to make such a dramatic choice between his duty and his personal desire. On the morning of 22 May, after informing Pfistermeister that he would not be able to open the special session of the Landtag that afternoon due to a sudden illness, the king mounted his horse for his usual ride. Accompanied only by his favorite groom, Volk, he escaped through the woods from Berg to Biessenhofen, where he boarded a train to Lindau. The journey across Lake Constance was swift, and by early afternoon, the king's carriage pulled up the long drive at Tribschen for a surprise reunion with Wagner.

It happened, not coincidentally, to be Wagner's fifty-third birthday. Ludwig announced himself at the door as Walther von Stolzing, one of the principal characters in Wagner's still unfinished opera *Die Meistersinger von Nürnberg;* a servant conveyed this message to the composer, who quickly guessed the identity of his caller. The two men spent the afternoon discussing *Meistersinger* and the conflict with Prussia, but

Ludwig revealed his real reason for the visit on his second, and last, day, when he once again raised the issue of a possible abdication with Wagner. Although the composer begged the king to abandon such a plan, Ludwig made no commitment and left Tribschen with his future apparently undecided.

Almost immediately upon his return to the capital, rumors of the king's indiscreet and untimely visit to his friend flew across Munich. Empress Elizabeth of Austria, never blind to the faults of her favorite cousin, wrote to her mother: "I hear the King has gone away again. If only he would pay a little more attention to the Government now that times are so ominous."[14] And Pfeufer, when informed of the king's decision to cancel the opening of the Landtag, complained to Pfistermeister: "In the first year, it was the mourning; in the second year, the condition of His Majesty's health in general; in the third year, his hoarseness. What ostensible sickness, people are asking, will the royal physician find for this year?"[15]

Ludwig had delayed the opening of the Landtag until 27 May. The heavier the burden of his royal office became, however, the greater his desire to avoid any responsibility, and he once again declared that he would not be able to attend the opening of the Landtag's special session. His grandfather had to lecture Ludwig on his duties before the king finally agreed to attend. Rumors of the recent visit to Switzerland were widespread; as he drove through the streets of Munich to the Landtag, Ludwig was greeted not with cheers but, to his horror, with hisses. That their king would leave his country, with their army mobilized for war, to pay a social visit to the despised Wagner, was simply too much for most of his subjects.

Ludwig was so outraged at his reception in the streets of Munich that he struck out immediately against the person he held most responsible: Pfeufer, the chief of the Munich police, who he believed had done nothing to contain the rumors of the Swiss visit. Ludwig fired him. One government official wrote:

> Instead of entering a protest against this Sultanic encroachment on the part of the King, the Minister of the Interior, like the thorough old bureaucratic sleepy-head he is, let it pass without a word. So long as the King is encouraged in his caprices by the sycophancy of the Court and the Government officials, so long will he continue to regard himself as a demi-god who can do what he pleases and for whose pleasure the rest of the world—at any rate, Bavaria—was created.[16]

✳   ✳   ✳

On 1 June, Austria formally broke the Treaty of Bad Gastein and submitted the question of the duchies to the federal Bundestag in Frankfurt. Bismarck reacted immediately: He ordered Prussian troops to invade Holstein. Emperor Napoléon III of France, who had no great desire to see Prussia firmly entrenched as the most powerful German state, tried to mediate between the parties, suggesting that a European conference be called to settle the fate of the duchies. But to everyone's surprise, and Bismarck's undisguised joy, Austria declared that a general European commission had no authority to determine German territorial claims. War was now inevitable.

Ludwig was beside himself with agitation. On the same day that the treaty was finally broken, he received a letter from Wagner, in which the composer implored him not to abdicate or make any hasty decision.

Ludwig was not convinced. He dispatched a telegram to Cosima von Bülow at Tribschen in which he once again threatened to abdicate.

For all of his self-serving aims, Wagner was truly concerned that Ludwig would sacrifice his position under the pressure of the threatened war. While he undoubtedly worried about the potential loss of the royal civil list—and the stipends which eminated from it—Wagner believed that members of his own court and government were manipulating the young king.

There were vague rumors in Berlin that Bavaria had signed a secret alliance with Austria, but Bismarck refused to give in so easily. On 10 June, a Prussian envoy delivered a new union proposal to King Ludwig II. Austria, as the chancellor desired, was excluded from the German Confederation, but the remainder of the old Deutscher Bund was to be divided geographically, into northern and southern zones of influence. Prussia, naturally, would occupy the dominant position in the north, but Bismarck was willing to cede and support Bavarian sovereignty over all southern states. As a further incentive, Bismarck slyly suggested that if Austria was defeated in the coming war, Prussia would not stand in the way if Bavaria desired to annex portions of the former Habsburg empire. Pfordten conveyed this information to the king, but both Ludwig and his ministers were unwilling to betray Austria, even with these added incentives.

The day after Bavaria rejected this proposal, Austria formally requested the Deutscher Bund in Frankfurt to mobilize the federal army against Prussia. Ludwig feared that Prussia would naturally interpret this as an act of war by the confederation, and instructed the Bavarian representative to introduce a more conciliatory measure. The Bund eventually adopted the Bavarian proposal on 14 June, but, by this time, it was too late for Ludwig or anyone else to save the peace. Two days later, on 16 June, war between the German Confederation and Prussia finally erupted.

17

The Seven Weeks' War

Ludwig had dreaded the very thought of a German civil war, and now that it had come to pass, he could not bear to face the realities of the crisis. This was not a war which Ludwig understood or supported; there were no chivalrous issues at hand, no rescue of imperiled innocents, but rather questions of territorial annexation, of domination and humiliation—ideals totally alien to the king. He was fully aware that his own troops were no match for the Prussians and feared for the outcome of the conflict. Unwilling to pit German against German, he felt himself maneuvered and coerced into a war he abhorred. This sense of impotence and premonition of impending doom drove the king from Munich to the isolation of Castle Berg.

On the day that Prussia declared war on Bavaria, the minister of war and a delegation of officials from the Landtag left Munich for Lake Starnberg to present the announcement to the king and gain his signature on his counter act. The commission rode the three miles from the lakeside train station at Starnberg to the confines of the royal estate. On arriving at the castle gates, however, they found their entrance barred by a pair of sentries, and no amount of pleading and threatening could induce the guards to let the delegation on the grounds: The king had given strict orders that no one from his government was to be received.

Humiliated and angered, the delegation returned to Starnberg and telegraphed the prime minister, who immediately set off to confront the king. When Pfordten arrived at Berg, he forced his way past the guards and into the castle. No servant would announce him, and no one seemed to know where the king was. Furious, Pfordten began a room-to-room search of the castle himself. Finally, he burst into a darkened chamber only to discover the king and Prince Paul von Thurn und Taxis, dressed in elaborate costumes as Barbarossa and Lohengrin, reciting love poetry to each other beneath an artificial moon.[1]

Ludwig's disillusion increasingly manifested itself in such irresponsible displays. Werner Richter describes his behavior as that of "a humiliated youngster."[2] Until the last minute, he had hoped, however naively, to avert the catastrophe. Ludwig felt that the war had been forced upon him: It had broken out without his consent or cooperation; like a child angered when circumstances prevent what he wants, the king decided that the war could follow its natural course without his participation. His threats of abdication reflected this overwhelming despair. Rather than face up to his royal responsibilities and undertake the traditional role of popular figurehead in this time of national crisis, he chose to simply pretend that the situation did not exist, the first of many times he would do so. He spent the weeks leading up to the conflict sheltered at Castle Berg, setting off hundreds of fireworks on the Roseninsel in Lake Starnberg with Prince Paul von Thurn und Taxis as his soldiers prepared to march off to war. The general mood in the capital was one of disbelief. More than a few highly placed persons, party to the rumors swirling round the king that summer, concurred with the judgment of the Austrian ambassador, who wrote, "One begins to think that the King is demented."[3]

"Oh! lamentable time, Oh! baneful discord that turns Germany's will against Germany!" the king had cabled to Wagner on learning that war had been declared.[4] He had good reason to be concerned because, from the first days of the war, the conflict promised to be uneven: Prussia had spent the last three years diligently preparing for some kind of armed conflict. The brilliant Helmuth von Moltke commanded the youthful, highly trained Prussian soldiers. His troops were equipped with new needle guns, which allowed for rapid firing and reloading; and Prussia's efficient rail system allowed for this extensive deployment of troops, as well as a cut in the time needed for reinforcements to reach any trouble spots. Fighting alongside Prussia were the minor German states of Saxe-Coburg-Gotha and Oldenburg, as well as Italy. The opposing forces were to prove no match for this powerful and impressive coalition.

Bavaria and Austria were the two largest states fighting on the side of the German Federation. But Austria was an old kingdom, her army antiquated and uninspired; her military was unequipped for a modern, extended conflict. The other countries whose troops formed the Union army—Saxony, Hanover, Württemberg, Baden, Hesse, and Nassau—were scarcely better prepared or organized to present a credible challenge to the stronger Prussians. Bavaria possessed the largest standing army of all the allied forces, but this was her only strength. It was to be a contest of men against machines.

The Bavarian soldiers who marched off to war were in poor condition. They were armed with Podewil rifles, antiquated weapons inferior to the needle guns used by the Prussians. The infantry and cavalry regiments were terribly disorganized, with no clear sense of direction or inspiration. Peacetime reserves had been kept to a minimum, and their training was often neglected under the premise that they were not likely to face armed conflict; likewise, the officer corps was inadequate, and entire regiments lacked commanders. Strategic communications were almost nonexistent, and no one seemed to have any clear idea as to the ultimate aims of the Bavarian army.

Members of the Bavarian government pleaded with Ludwig to take over the role of supreme commander of the army, a purely symbolic position which required little other than attendance at reviews and strategy sessions. But they argued in vain: Ludwig positively refused to assume his role as commander in chief or to have anything to do with the German war. Instead, he allowed his elderly and uninspiring uncle, the seventy-one-year-old Prince Karl, to assume the role of commander in chief. Sharing responsibility for deployment of the army was General Ludwig van der Tann. This was scarcely a better move: Van der Tann had spent most of his military career sitting behind a massive desk in the ministry of war, and the general consensus was that he knew nothing about military strategy. Against this ominous background, Bavarians went to war.

Bavarian troops formed the Seventh Union Army Corps, under the command of Prince Alexander of Hesse in Hanover. At the beginning of the war, they were sent off to join the Eighth Union Army Corps to the northeast, which was composed of forces from Württemberg, Hesse, and Baden. Thus the two southern armies—the Union forces and the Austrian troops—were separated, allowing the Prussians to penetrate the inevitable gaps and storm south. Under the confused leadership of Prince Karl and General van der Tann, entire regiments marched to wrong locales, disappeared into the onslaught on Prussian bullets, circled to meet with nonexistent allies, and retreated amid the suicides of their commanders.

The Seventh Union Army Corps received orders to join the forces at Hersfeld, where they were to regroup with the Hanoverian troops retreating from the north. Prince Karl had no idea where the Hanoverian soldiers were encamped, however, and so he waited to dispatch his own troops to assist them. By the time the Bavarians learned the whereabouts of the Hanoverian troops, it was too late; instead, Bavarian troops swept through Thuringia without resistance, establishing themselves at the Meiningen Castle. Here, Prince Karl, ignoring the pleas of the retreating Hanoverians, joined his troops as the first division made their way through more than fifteen hundred barrels of beer in less than three days.[5]

Prince Chlodwig von zu Hohenlohe-Schillingsfürst, a member of the government, kept a diary in which he recorded the events of that June in detail, revealing the public reaction to the war and their growing frustration and dissatisfaction with the king.

16 June: One startling piece of news comes on the heels of another these days. First Prussia's secession from the Confederation because of the mobilization of the Federal forces and now the entry of the Prussians into Saxony, King Johann's departure for Prague, and the retreat of the Saxon troops across the Bohemian frontier. Prussia has sent an ultimatum to Hanover and also to the Electorate of Hesse—to disarm or she will send an army of occupation. And so the scheme for the partition of Germany is well-nigh complete. We, for our part, allow ourselves to be hustled, now by Prussia, now by Austria, and we have no definite plans of any kind. The Bavarian Army is in a most unsatisfactory state. Prince Karl is too old to be Commander-in-Chief. The officers have not sufficient confidence in their own powers. I hardly think we shall win many laurels for all the hearty goodwill of the men and the Bavarians' inborn love of a fight.

19 June: On account of the proposal to mobilize the Army Corps of the Confederation, Prussia has announced her withdrawal and has attacked Saxony, Hanover and Hesse. The Bavarian Government, which up to now has assumed an indecisive attitude of ostensible impartiality, and flattered itself that it could keep it up, has suddenly, to its astonishment, been waked out of its dream and compelled to range itself on the Austrian side. . . .

I met Pfordten at the club tonight. He was lamenting over the war, which will result in the dismemberment of Germany; he said over and over again, "This is the end of Germany!" I almost believe it myself now. Prussia will become a great and compact state in North Germany; we in the south will go on vegetating under French or Austrian protection, until our hour strikes and half of us falls to France, and the other half to Austria. . . . They are arguing in the club about the war. "What quarrel have we with the Prussians, then, that we should go to war for Augustenburg?" the habitues there say. "If Max were alive now," he added, "things would not have come to this."[6]

*   *   *

The situation in the Bavarian capital rapidly deteriorated, as public confidence fell with news of the army's defeats and mistakes. The king himself was roundly criticized for not having taken on the role of supreme commander or even having shown the merest interest in the military proceedings. Members of the government continually urged him to at least visit the troops in the field, but the king repeatedly refused. Writing from Switzerland, Wagner expressed great concern if Ludwig did not at least make some effort, declaring:

> The press told us that you would go with your brother to the army. I beg you to do this! Bavaria's King at the head of his troops in the army of the Confederation—Listen! Listen to me!—such a King would hold the destiny of the world in his hands! Fate calls to you! She desires that you leave your musty Residenz. Go out into your country, make a journey through your Bavaria, comfort our Germany. . . . Fate calls: to the army![7]

On 26 June, the king finally gave in to pressure from his ministers and consented to visit the army at field headquarters in Bamberg. Despite his great reluctance and lack of enthusiasm, Ludwig diligently called on regimental camps and field hospitals; he was stunned at the devastation, the terrible injuries, the constant moans from his soldiers as he passed from cot to cot. He had never seen suffering and death before, and he left these camps deeply traumatized. His presence among the wounded, however, seemed to uplift their spirits, and he made a favorable impression on most of his men. One Hessian officer saw the king as he entered a mess during a tour of inspection. "He was so beautiful that my heart stopped beating," he later recalled. "I was so deeply moved that a terrible thought seized me: this godlike youth is too beautiful for this world. I whispered to my Bavarian neighbour, who, with all the Bavarian officers, had risen when this glorious figure entered, 'Who is he?' 'Our young King,' he answered."[8]

On 3 July, the Prussian army scored a decisive victory over Austria at Königgrätz. The Bavarians considered that the situation was hopeless but continued to fight. Hanoverian troops surrendered to the Prussians at Langensalza, and the Bavarian army was ordered to join forces with the Eighth Union Army Corps, but they offered little resistance to the better-trained Prussians. At Gersfeld, the Bavarian troops heard that the Prussians were marching toward them and fled in a panic: Seven cavalry regiments disappeared into the forests surrounding the town, and the commander, Colonel von Pechman, rode off and shot himself. A few days after the battle of Königgrätz, the Prussians swept down from the forests into the resort town of Kissingen, where the Bavarian troops were entrenched. Fully expecting such an offensive, the Bavarian commanders had ordered all of the bridges leading to the town blown up, but somehow the orders were misinterpreted, and the Bavarians left one approach untouched. Sure enough, the Prussian troops discovered this and marched across it as they stormed into town.

The war was over and everyone knew it. Bismarck, ever crafty and determined to humiliate Austria, directed the Prussian ambassador in Paris, Count Glotz, to approach his Bavarian colleague there and make an offer for a separate peace. The Bavarian ambassador, von Wendland, dutifully communicated the terms to the king. Under the circumstances, Bismarck was being more than generous: He offered Ludwig immediate cessation of all hostilities in return for his signature on the treaty, and once the war was formally over, he would allow Bavaria control over all of the southern German states. Ludwig stood to gain a considerable amount of power and land if he signed, at the same time sparing Bavaria the necessity of having to pay an indemnity and perhaps cede land to the victors. In other words, Bavaria would walk away from the conflicts just as if she had signed a prewar alliance with Prussia, complete with the guarantees which Bismarck had first offered to try to woo her to his side. But Ludwig, with his antiquated notions of chivalry and code of honor, refused to enhance his own position at the expense of his allies. He communicated to von Wendland: "The King has decided that the law of the Union and Our Honour do not permit Us to start peace negotiations without Our Allies."[9]

In the end, Ludwig's decision meant nothing. Almost as soon as he rejected the offer of a separate peace, word reached the king that his army had surrendered to the Prussians. The Austrian government soon sued for a separate peace, as did the other southern German states, abandoning Bavaria to Bismarck. There was nothing Ludwig could do: On 16 July, he authorized his government to begin negotiations for peace. The Seven Weeks' War was finally over.

The Treaty of Nikolsburg, which called a temporary end to the hostilities, was the beginning of Prussian domination. Austria was immediately expelled from the German Union, and all of the northern German states which had sided with the Habsburg troops, including Hesse, Hanover, and Saxony, were forcibly incorporated into the new North German Union, controlled by Prussia. The old German Federation, laid out by Metternich at the Congress of Vienna, had ceased to exist.

The end of the war again raised the question of alliances. Emperor Napoléon III offered a Franco-Bavarian treaty through his envoy, intended to protect the south German kingdom and to frustrate Bismarck's quest for domination. But Ludwig, for all of his expressed dislike of Prussia, had even less interest in a French alliance. Siding with the French might result in renewed hostilities with Prussia, and Napoléon would certainly want some kind of territorial compensation for his offer of protection. In addition, even a defeated Ludwig was still susceptible enough to the voices which spoke of a German empire not to risk fracturing the former confederation with foreign alliances.

Luckily for Bavaria, even though she had sided with Austria in the war, Bismarck still admired Ludwig. The chancellor, in the words of writer Francis Gerard, "treated the young King as if he had been a naughty schoolboy."[10] On 22 August, the Treaty of Prague was formally signed between Bavaria and Prussia. Reparations were minimal under the circumstances: Bavaria lost a small amount of territory and had to pay a 30 million gulden indemnity to Prussia. In addition, certain palaces, as well as the art collection of Wittelsbach ancestor Johann Wilhelm, were to be ceded to the Hohenzollerns. The most important clause was a secret mutual defense treaty between the two countries, which guaranteed Bavarian support for future Prussian military campaigns if Bismarck should meet with resistance.

Despite his frequently expressed indifference to the war, Ludwig was crushed by the outcome. He had witnessed the terrible, devastating effects of modern warfare, an experience which left the sensitive young man shattered. But the war had done more than simply destroy the king's romantic illusions of heroic battles and valiant soldiers. His increasing reluctance to play the role of king in times of national crisis, his selfish visit to his nationally hated friend in Switzerland, and his self-imposed isolation at Berg alienated many of his subjects; he found himself criticized and even hissed by his once adoring public.

The war also forced Ludwig to acknowledge Prussian supremacy. One of the requests from the king of Prussia was that he be given the Hohenzollern Castle, which belonged to Ludwig but had been the ancestral home of the Prussian royal family. On 29 August, Ludwig reluctantly wrote to his uncle, Wilhelm I:

> After the peace between Us has been concluded and a firm and lasting Friendship between Our House and State has been mutually cemented, I feel that I cannot give a better expression to My feelings than by offering Your Most Gracious Majesty a joint right with Myself in the proprietorship of the ancient Castle of Hohenzollern. When from the towers of the Castle which belonged to Our common ancestors shall float the banners of Hohenzollern and Wittelsbach, this truly shall be as a

symbol to show that Prussia and Bavaria are joint guardians over the future of Germany, to which the providence of Your Most Gracious Majesty has given new life.[11]

Ludwig was greatly upset by this letter. It was a final, personal humiliation to the defeated Bavarian king. At the end of the war, he felt betrayed, forced into an alliance which he did not want, made to bow before the triumphant Prussia. In a sad letter to Wagner, he complained bitterly that he had now been reduced to *"ein Schattenkönig ohne Macht,"* "a shadow king without any real power."[12]

18

Scandal at Tribschen

Although Ludwig had tried to keep his May 1866 visit to Wagner at Tribschen a secret, inevitably the news leaked out and caused an uproar when it was printed in the capital's newspapers. And although some of this hostility was directed at the king, Wagner proved the easier target. On 29 May, the *Neuer Bayerischer Kurier* printed a scathing, virulent attack on Wagner and his circle of friends. Worse still, the press wrote of the strange ménage à trois at Tribschen. On 31 May, the newspaper *Volksbote* reported:

> It is not a year since the infamous "Madame Hans de Bülow" got away in the famous two cabs with 40,000 gulden from the Treasury for her "friend" (or what?) . . . Meanwhile the same "Madame Hans de Bülow" who has been known to the public since last December by the descriptive title of "the Carrier Pigeon" is with her "friend" (or what?) in Lucerne, where she was also during the visit of an exalted person.[1]

When Bülow read this, he was understandably outraged. It was bad enough to know that his wife lived openly as Wagner's mistress, but to have the allegations printed for all of Germany to see was akin to a personal attack. Feeling that his own honor was at stake, Bülow rushed to the editor of the *Volksbote*, demanding, somewhat theatrically, that he either print an apology or agree to fight a duel. He then hurried to Tribschen to confront his wife and Wagner with this latest scandal. All three agreed that the only possible response was a public denial of the *Volksbote* allegations, and the best possible source for this denial seemed to be King Ludwig II himself. A royal confirmation of Cosima's honor would silence the press attacks. With this duplicitous aim in mind, Wagner himself wrote a plea to the king begging, on Bülow's behalf, for his intervention.

His noble wife, who, with the most sympathetic devotion and helpful encouragement, has consoled, supported and sacrificed herself to the friend of her father, the mentor of her husband, and the highly regarded protege of a King whom she reveres with such deep feeling—this woman is now, as a reward for the love which a kind-hearted monarch has shown to his friends, who, for that same reason are now being persecuted—this woman, I say, is being dragged publicly through the mud and heaped with a shame which, were it inflicted upon the angel of innocence himself, would stain him with its taint. And all of this—has gone unpunished! . . .

To you, My King and Beloved Friend, I address but a single request at this time of such great need: break your royal silence, at least on this single occasion: write a letter expressing your sovereign satisfaction with my friend Hans von Bülow and, at the same time, give vent to your royal indignation at the horrible treatment which he and his wife have suffered at the hands of the newspapers in your capital city of Munich. . . . Since I am bound to assume that my kind friend is so far removed from the lowly concerns to which the rest of us are exposed that he will be unable to discover which are the best means by which to express himself in the letter which we are requesting of him, I have been bold enough to enclose, by way of suggestion, a draft which I myself have composed![2]

There was also a letter from Cosima, drafted by Wagner.

On my knees, I humbly beg my King to write the letter for my husband so that he may not be forced to leave the country in disgrace and shame. Only Your Royal Word can re-establish our insulted honour. . . . How would it be possible for my husband to work in a town where the honour of his wife has been doubted? My Royal Master, I have three children to whom I must transfer the honourable name of their father without blemish. . . .[3]

A proposed outline of the king's letter to Bülow, written by Wagner himself, accompanied Cosima's plea. Wagner suggested that Ludwig write an open letter to Bülow.

As I have been in a position to obtain the most intimate knowledge of the noble character of your honoured lady . . . it only remains for me to discover the inexplicable reason for these criminal insults, so that, having obtained the clearest insight into this outrageous conduct, I may see that the strictest justice is meted out to the offenders.[4]

The *Volksbote* affair showed both Wagner and Cosima at their worst; through deliberate lies and deception, they used the honor of the king to protect their reputations. It is doubtful if Ludwig believed in the protested innocence of the situation at Tribschen, but he was still unfailingly loyal to the composer. He duly signed the letter and sent it to Bülow, who then published it in the Munich papers. When it appeared, no one believed it; nevertheless, the letter silenced press speculation over the scandalous goings-on at Tribschen.

By signing Wagner's ugly, self-serving letter to Bülow, Ludwig confirmed what everyone suspected: that the young king remained besotted with his friend and determined, against all odds, to support the man who had breathed life into the world of his dreams. More than anything else, the Bülow letter indicated Ludwig's growing irresponsibility and his shocking disregard of public opinion, traits which would worsen with the passing years.

Even with circumstances throwing obstacles between the king and Wagner, Ludwig refused to abandon his friend. Wagner had already been sacrificed once, to the demands of both public opinion and members of the court; the king would not repeat what he now regarded as a fatal mistake. He was never blind to Wagner's faults, though he was undoubtedly guilty of a youthful naïveté where the composer's sexual relations with Cosima von Bülow were concerned. But, for Ludwig, the loss of the hedonistic, scandalous man also meant the loss of the brilliant artist who had touched his soul and spirit as no other had before. The king reflected on this need in a letter to Cosima.

> Let us two take a solemn vow to do all it is in our power to preserve for Wagner the peace he has won, to banish from him, to take upon ourselves, whenever possible, every grief of his, to love him, love him with all the strength that God has put into the human heart. . . . Oh, he is godlike, godlike! My mission is to live for Him, to suffer for Him, if that be necessary for his full salvation.[5]

Inevitably, the effusive nature of the relationship suffered with time. In February of 1867, Ludwig learned that Cosima von Bülow had given birth to a fourth child, a daughter called Eva. As she had been living with Wagner at Tribschen for nearly a year, with only infrequent visits with her husband, no one believed that Hans von Bülow was the father.

On learning of the birth, Hans rushed to his wife's side, aware that they could no longer hope to conceal the truth of the affair. They reached a final understanding, and Cosima formally left Hans for Wagner. She took Isolde and Eva into her sole custody and moved to Tribschen for good. Ludwig, along with the rest of the world, finally had confirmation of the years of gossip which he had always tried to ignore.

In May of 1867, Ludwig invited Wagner to come to Munich to oversee a new production of *Lohengrin*. In anticipation, he made arrangements to rent the Villa Prestele on Lake Starnberg for the composer's use and ordered, as a special present, a large piano–writing desk of polished maple. It was intended as a gift to mark the third anniversary of the meeting between the king and composer. But things did not go as Ludwig had planned. Wagner was in no mood for an extended stay at Starnberg, nor did he care to submit himself and his relationship with Cosima von Bülow to the scrutiny of the Munich press. The composer tried to forestall the visit, but Ludwig continued to insist, and Cosima, aware that Wagner's refusal to appear might result in a permanent break with the king, urged her lover to accept. Wagner duly arrived, but by this time, Ludwig had grown disillusioned over his obvious lack of enthusiasm at the reunion. The very day after Wagner arrived, Ludwig, without having received his friend, set out with his brother and an aide-de-camp to visit Eisenach. A few days later, the king returned to Berg, but the very next day, he left again, this time on a trip to the Zillerthal and Achensee. It was obvious that Ludwig was irritated with his friend: He ordered the maple piano delivered instead to Hohenschwangau, where it remains to this day.

Unaware of his disfavor, Wagner plunged himself into the new production of *Lohengrin*. The obvious choice for the title character was tenor Albert Niemann, whom Ludwig had previously seen in the role. But Niemann demanded that certain cuts be made in the libretto, and Wagner refused to cast him. Instead, he proposed Josef Tichatschek, the tenor who had created the role of Tannhäuser. Ludwig had his doubts: Tichatschek was sixty years old, fat, and ungraceful—hardly his image of the heroic Swan Knight. His voice, however, was strong and clear, and Wagner felt certain that he had made the correct choice.

On 11 June, Ludwig attended the final dress rehearsal of *Lohengrin*. Ernest Newman wrote:

> Through his opera glasses he saw not the poetic King of the Grail of his boyhood's dream but a sagging face painted and plastered into a simulacrum of youth, and an ancient body maintaining its uncertain equilibrium in the boat only by clinging to a pole let into the deck for that charitable purpose.

He saw nothing he could call acting, only a succession of "grimaces" as he complained afterwards.[6]

Sadly disappointed in the performance, Ludwig stormed back to Berg, declaring that he never wanted to see Tichatschek on the Munich stage again. In an effort to save the production, Wagner wrote:

> When I spoke to you about Tichatschek as Lohengrin and said that his singing was like a painting by Dürer but his outward appearance was more like a picture by Holbein, I ought to have been explicit and begged you to listen to the singer with your ears open but not to observe him too keenly. . . . You ignored my warning: you stared at him with redoubled intensity; it was impossible for him to withstand this scrutiny; the vital illusion was lost.[7]

But Ludwig did not appreciate Wagner's subtle rebuke. He flatly told the composer that both Tichatschek and the soprano who had portrayed Ortrud were to be dismissed and replaced with other singers. When Wagner got wind of this, he angrily left Munich and returned to Tribschen.

Performances of the opera were still scheduled, and it was left to Hans von Bülow to salvage the production. Only five days after the disastrous final dress rehearsal, Heinrich Vogl, a young tenor who had been the king's first choice for the role, took the stage as Lohengrin. He succeeded in a nearly impossible task, and Ludwig was so impressed that after the opera had ended, he wrote a letter of thanks to the tenor. But relations between the king and Wagner remained strained over the incident, and Ludwig refused to attend a performance of *Tannhäuser* that August.

A few letters passed between king and composer before the next incident occured. This time, the trouble came from a series of articles called "German Art and Politics" published in the fall of 1867 by the *Süddeutsche Presse;* although they were published anonymously, everyone knew that Wagner was the author. At first, Ludwig supported the articles; being highly nationalistic in tone, they struck a patriotic chord in him. Prior to their publication, he had written to Wagner: "In Germany, we must raise the banner of pure and holy art so that it flies from the battlements, summoning our German youth to rally round it."[8]

The *Süddeutsche Presse* articles began with flattering portraits of Ludwig I and Maximilian II, praising their patronage of artists, architects, and musicians. Wagner wrote of the "universal mission of the German People since its entry into history" to lead the way in culture and thought.[9] He argued that the role of the monarch was to unify the artistic and political elements of the country and thus combine in his royal person the ideals of German achievement. But, as the series continued, the tone changed; soon, the articles were devoted to scathing attacks on the Jesuits in the Bavarian government, the Catholic Church, Jews, and the French and their culture. Because the *Süddeutsche Presse* was a semiofficial organ of the Bavarian government and Wagner was known to be the author, many readers assumed that these articles carried the approval of the king himself. Even worse, Wagner's scandalous words were being printed at the expense of Bavarian taxpayers. After thirteen installments, Ludwig abruptly stepped in and ordered that publication of "German Art and Politics" be stopped immediately.

Ludwig's decision to terminate the series of articles may have reflected the growing public furor over their publication. But by November of 1867, when he issued his order, he had virtually severed his ties with the composer. The break had been slowly building, fueled not only by the frequent artistic clashes between king and composer but also by Wagner's increasingly notorious private life.

Malvina Schnorr von Carolsfeld, widow of Wagner's first Tristan, had been making numerous allegations against the composer and Cosima for some time. In November of the previous year, she and a female friend, Isidore von Reutter, had visited Wagner at Tribschen to convey what Malvina described as a psychic message from her late husband. According to Malvina, Ludwig Schnorr von Carolsfeld had directed Isidore von Reutter, who received the messages, to marry King Ludwig II, while Malvina herself was to be Wagner's companion. Wagner received this information without comment; when Malvina persisted, he threw her and Isidore out of Tribschen. But Malvina had seen enough of the illicit goings-on at Tribschen to confirm rumors of the ménage à trois, and returned to Munich to spread malicious gossip about the composer and Cosima to anyone willing to listen.

Eventually, of course, news of this visit reached Ludwig. Malvina Schnorr von Carolsfeld wrote a scathing letter to one of the king's aides-de-camp, Lieutenant von Sauer, asking him to relay her late husband's directions regarding Ludwig and her friend Isidore. Sauer passed the letter along to the king, and Ludwig, in turn, sent it to Cosima von Bülow at Tribschen. According to the king, he found the letter "outrageous," but "as your sincere and eternally faithful friend I regard it as my duty to send it to you."[10]

Wagner was horrified that Malvina had carried her tales to the Bavarian throne. From Tribschen, he denounced Malvina and her friend Isidore, urging Ludwig to cut off her pension and exile her from Munich. But things had gone too far for the king to be appeased

so easily. Malvina Schnorr von Carolsfeld's accusations had reached
the highest court circles, and Ludwig's court secretary, Lorenz von
Düfflipp, urged the king to distance himself from his exiled friend. On
13 December, Ludwig responded:

> I am surprised that you believe the situation as regards Wagner,
> Frau von Bülow and Frau Schnorr is not quite kosher. If that
> should turn out that this miserable rumour is true—which I
> was never really able to bring myself to believe—should it
> really be a case of adultery after all—then, alas![11]

From 30 November 1867 until March of the following year, not
one letter passed between the king and the composer. Ludwig, confronted with incontrovertible evidence of Wagner's adultery, for the
first and only time made a clear and conscious attempt to cut him out
of his life. More important than the actual issue of adultery for the king
was the unconscionable abuse of his royal trust in the matter of the
public letter he had written to Hans von Bülow—the contents of which
he knew to be false. Before, he had always vowed never to abandon his
friend; now he felt that he had finally been betrayed and that the relationship was beyond redemption.

Those hundred days of silence were torture for the king. In the
end, he could not bring himself to keep his resolve of silence. Wagner
had betrayed him and abused his trust, but a complete break with the
composer threatened the very basis of Ludwig's dreams, his hopes for
Die Meistersinger von Nürnberg, Der Ring des Nibelungen, Parsifal, and
Die Sieger. This he could not bring himself to do. On 9 March, he wrote:
"I can no longer endure being without news of you. If you want me
soon to be whole and well again, I beg you to delay no longer, dearest
man, and let me have without delay a long letter." He invited Wagner
to Hohenschwangau where, he hoped, they would be able to discuss
plans for future operas. He ended by calling Wagner, in a quote from
the libretto of *Die Walküre*, the "spring which I have longed for in the
frosty depths of winter."[12]

Wagner's answer was coldly calculated. Rather than accepting the
blame for the scandalous situation which had led to the break, he
shamelessly tried to make the king believe that all of the problems
between them were of Ludwig's making. "I know," he wrote, "that I am
only welcome to you when I am silent. So why disturb the silence and
reawaken the old hopeful echoes of my soul, that should by now have
died of your silence."[13]

But to Wagner's surprise, the king did not capitulate. He was as
sly as Wagner when pushed into a corner. He needed, for his own rea-

sons, to renew the friendship with Wagner the artist, but Wagner the man had repeatedly failed him and could never be forgiven for his duplicitous behavior and abuse of the royal trust. In his reply, Ludwig was humble but gently told the composer that it was *he* who had not faithfully understood the situation.

> Oh! My Friend! Once the world seemed rosy to me and the man noble; since then I have suffered unspeakably bitter experiences . . . so that my feeling of hate and misanthropy was fully justified—only in myself, and, above all, in the pursuit of our ideal, was I able to find comfort and strength. I shut myself away forever, in myself, for I was gripped with abhorrence and humiliation in the face of the world. Now, that phase is past; it was a process of purification, an episode in my life; I am strengthened, I will forget and forgive the dreadful things that have been done to me and will throw myself bravely into life, devote myself to my sacred obligations . . . for I clearly realize my great task and I will, believe me, fulfill it faithfully and conscientiously.[14]

By the time the king sent this letter, Cosima was once again pregnant. This time, there was no pretense that anyone other than Wagner was the father. On 6 June 1869, Cosima gave birth to Wagner's son, Siegfried. Barely a week later, she finally asked von Bülow for a divorce. Throughout the ordeal, he had behaved admirably; now, with Cosima's prior knowledge and consent, he lodged a formal complaint in a Berlin court against his wife, charging her with desertion. On 18 July 1870, the divorce was granted and Cosima was free. A month later, in a Protestant church in Lucerne, she and Wagner were married. To soften the blow, they selected 25 August for the ceremony, Ludwig's twenty-fifth birthday.

19

Meistersinger, Rheingold, *and* Walküre

On 24 October, 1867, Wagner presented the king with the completed score of his great comic opera *Die Meistersinger von Nürnberg*. Originally, Wagner had declared that the opera would be ready for production in 1865. But *Meistersinger* suffered from the tumult of the composer's increasingly unstable life, and Ludwig received the opera nearly two and a half years after it had first been promised him.

Meistersinger was Wagner's lightest opera, featuring a cast filled not with gods and dwarfs but with common workers and medieval artisans. It told the story of Walther von Stolzing, a young Nuremberg knight who, through a song contest, is able to win the hand of the lovely Eva Pogner. Wagner wrote a grand spectacle, filled with rousing choruses and marches; musically, it contained some of his finest and most popular work, including the prize song of Walther von Stolzing and the final, triumphant chorus. It also encompassed the idea of the Volk or the German national identity, containing physical, spiritual, and artistic aspirations. According to *Meistersinger*, in German art, the Teutonic peoples could be unified and, with their culture, triumph over other races. These sentiments, along with the final words of the character Hans Sachs in praise of German art and a chorus trumpeting holy German ideals, made *Meistersinger* not only a call to national unity but also a denunciation of foreign influence and culture.

Wagner first wished to have *Meistersinger* staged in Nuremberg itself. Ludwig, however, insisted on Munich. Once rehearsals began, the composer faced a number of difficulties. The opera was four and a half hours in length, Wagner's longest to date, and called for three major set changes which involved the re-creation of medieval Nuremberg. In addition, the opera needed a chorus of more than a hundred members, all of whom Wagner wished to personally train himself. Again, Wagner asked Hans von Bülow to conduct; however, relations between him and the composer were so strained over the latter's affair with Cosima that the pair avoided each other even at rehearsals.

Ludwig himself initially felt little enthusiasm for *Meistersinger;* an opera composed of artisans and medieval villagers seemed to lack the same kind of romantic aura and fantasy as *Tannhäuser* or *Lohengrin*. However, when he finally heard the music and read the libretto, the king quickly changed his mind. He relished the religious sentiments, the calls for national unity, and the praise of German ideals and culture. After attending the final dress rehearsal, he wrote: "I was so moved and carried away that it was impossible for me to join in with the profane expression of praise by hand-clapping."[1]

The premiere of *Die Meistersinger von Nürnberg* took place on 21 June 1868, at the court theater in Munich. Hundreds of Wagner's friends from across Europe filled the stalls and boxes, whispering with anticipation. Just before the performance was scheduled to begin, Ludwig II entered the royal box. The king wore evening dress and bowed to the audience when they rose from their seats. As custom dictated, Wagner duly presented himself in the royal box just before the curtain rose, but to his surprise, Ludwig made him take a seat in the loge beside him, an unprecedented honor which he customarily denied even to members of his own family.

Finally, the heavy curtains rose on Wagner's latest masterpiece. At the end of the first act, there were a great many ovations for the composer, but Wagner refused to acknowledge them. At the end of the second act, however, the king bade him to answer the cheers, and the composer dutifully rose from his seat and bowed to the crowd from the edge of the royal box. Such action on the part of a commoner, taking ovations from the royal nox, deeply shocked the prim Munich public.

Nothing, however, could dampen the triumph of *Die Meistersinger von Nürnberg*. Five more performances had been scheduled, and these were duly given, although without the presence of the composer. After the premiere, Wagner returned to Tribschen, exhausted by the staging of the opera and the continued battles waged against him in the Munich press. Shortly after, Ludwig received a letter in which his friend informed him that henceforth he would remain in Switzerland and devote himself solely to his work. This time, Wagner was true to his word: It was to be eight years before the king and the composer met again.

On 27 September 1869, the king attended the premiere of *Das Rheingold*, the first of the four operas in Wagner's great tetralogy, *Der Ring des Nibelungen*. This proved to be anything but a triumph for Wagner, however, as the king had it staged against the composer's own wishes. Wagner had completed *Das Rheingold* in 1854; it had not yet been performed, though portions of the score had been played before the public. The composer wished, rather naturally, to wait until the other three

Ring operas were completed and could be performed together in the same cycle. But in 1864, he had promised Ludwig that, given favorable circumstances—which, to Wagner, meant a royal allowance—the entire Ring cycle would be ready for production in 1867. Wagner himself, after much thought, agreed that he would not object to separate stagings of the Ring operas.

According to the formal contract signed between the king and Wagner several years earlier, Ludwig actually owned the rights to the four operas as soon as each was completed. The king waited for two years beyond this date before acting on what he considered to be his right to have the completed opera staged. Realizing the importance of Wagner's cooperation, Ludwig attempted to soften the blow.

> I *implore* you, dear friend, to do what you can to make this performance possible: oh, I need such joys if I am not to perish in the trivial whirlpool of everyday life. Yet I do not withdraw myself from this; I even take pleasure now in the fulfilling of my kingly duties, which I formerly hated; I am interested in the affairs of government; even with the dry ministerial communications and reports of debates in Parliament I have been able to acquire as much of a taste as possible; it is a sad necessity. It is the hope of the accomplishment of what I yearn for, the realization of our ideals, that gives me strength for *everything:* we shall not go under, Dear Friend! We shall accomplish everything, everything: I know it, I am as sure of it as I am that I live and breathe.[2]

As preparations for the performance began, Bülow resigned his post as kapellmeister. He had worked himself into a state of nervous exhaustion with worry over the affair between Cosima and Wagner, and the thought of again appearing before the public to conduct his wife's lover's opera was simply too much for him to contemplate. Wagner, although he did not approve of the plan to stage *Das Rheingold* independently from the rest of the cycle, realized that his cooperation would at least ensure that he maintained some degree of control over the situation in Munich. He therefore suggested to the king that Hans Richter, a headstrong but devoted young conductor, take Bülow's place. Ludwig duly approved of this plan, and with Richter in place, Wagner knew that his directions would be followed. Through Richter, the composer was kept informed of the latest developments and problems, and over the course of the summer, many of those in the cast of *Rheingold* made their way to Tribschen to personally rehearse under Wagner's instruction.

There were problems from the outset. First and foremost were the technical difficulties. The opera called for Alberich to transform himself into a serpent and a toad; there was the rainbow bridge to Valhalla to be worked out and the question of the swimming Rhine maidens. To solve these issues, Richter hired Karl Brandt, a man of immense technical genius. The scene with the three Rhine maidens caused untold hours of frustration. At first, the singers were strapped to tall iron braces attached to small carts, which stagehands then pushed behind the scenery to create the impression that the maidens were swimming. But this method quickly proved too considerable a strain on the cast; when one of the maidens became sick during a rehearsal and vomited on the stagehands wheeling her about, Brandt decided to seek an alternative solution. Eventually, it was agreed that three dancers—ladies with apparently stronger constitutions and stomachs—could take the place of the singers, who would then be offstage in the wings as they sang their chorus.

Richter caused a good deal of bad feeling during the rehearsals. Relations between himself and the administrator of the Munich Theater, Karl von Perfall, were strained from the very beginning. When the young conductor insisted on following Wagner's instructions, no matter how much trouble the arrangement caused, Perfall protested directly to the king. Amid these troubles, the final dress rehearsal took place on 27 August, in the presence of the king and some five hundred invited guests, including Cosima's father, Franz Liszt. Things went badly. Musically, the performance was perfect, and Richter did an admirable job under the circumstances. But the technical effects, which formed such a crucial element in the drama, proved disastrous. Immediately after the performance, Richter sent a telegram to Wagner, informing him of the problems and suggesting that the premiere, which was set for 29 August, be postponed until they could be solved. Wagner immediately asked Ludwig to agree to this and recommended that some other work of his could temporarily be given in place of *Rheingold*.

Ludwig, in deference to Wagner, would most likely have agreed to this request had it not been for the imperious behavior of Hans Richter. The day after the fatal dress rehearsal, Richter informed Perfall that he refused to conduct at the premiere, which was still scheduled for the following evening. Not only were the effects unsatisfactory, but Richter believed, perhaps correctly, that the press would rip Wagner to pieces in their reviews, turning the premiere into a personal attack. Richter then made the mistake of declaring in front of Lorenz von Düfflipp, the king's court secretary, that he took orders from no one except Wagner.

Richter responded in this manner with Wagner's full approval. The composer had been certain that, knowing his wishes and faced with the refusal of Richter to conduct, the king would accede to his request and cancel the performances. And, indeed, the premiere was postponed. But he had not taken Ludwig's notoriously difficult and mercurial temperament into account. The king took Richter's threat and remark to Düfflipp as a direct insult to his sovereign authority. He reacted like a true autocrat: On 30 August, Ludwig wrote to Düfflipp:

> The behaviour of Wagner and the theatre rabble is absolutely criminal and impudent; it is an open revolt against My Orders, and this I will not allow! Under no circumstances is Richter to conduct and he is to be dismissed forthwith. The theatre people will obey My Orders and not Wagner's whims! In many of the papers it is stated that it was I who cancelled the performance. I saw this coming. It is easy enough to spread false rumours, and it is My Will that they give the true story and do everything in their power to make the performance possible; for if these dreadful intrigues of Wagner's succeed, then the whole crowd will get steadily more brazen and more shameless and finally completely beyond control. Therefore, this evil must be torn out by the roots: Richter must go. . . . Never before have I met with such impertinence! I repeat how satisfied I am with the way you are handling the situation. . . . *Vivat* Düfflipp! *Perat* the theatre rabble! With kindest regards and all best wishes to yourself, but with curses on that vulgar and impudent pack![3]

The king was so agitated that on the very next day he dispatched another angry letter to Düfflipp.

> An end must be put immediately to the quite unforgivable intrigues by Wagner and his fellows! I herewith give distinct orders for the performance to take place on Sunday. Richter is to be dismissed instantaneously. If Wagner dares to object once again, his grant is to be revoked for good, and his works are never again to be performed on any Munich stage![4]

Richter was summarily dismissed on the king's orders. Even with this disgrace, Wagner continued to appeal to Ludwig to stop the production. His concern was genuine enough, and he feared the effect which a bad public performance was likely to have not only on his reputation but also on his future efforts to raise funds for his Festival Theater. Realizing that Ludwig's mind was set, he asked that the king make the premiere a royal command performance, with an audience restricted to those personally invited by Ludwig himself. Ludwig, however, was so angry over the entire incident that even this reasonable request fell on deaf ears. On 30 August, Wagner wrote to the king, offering to come to Munich to supervise the production and oversee the problems. But Ludwig feared that Wagner, once installed in the capital, would somehow manage to cancel the performances entirely. For the first time in their relationship, the king actually conspired, along with his court officials, to keep Wagner out of Bavaria. To this end, Düfflipp was given instructions to prevent Wagner's entry into the kingdom should the composer be bold enough to try.

To Wagner, it appeared that Ludwig was simply being obstinate and unreasonable. Both he and Richter had failed to understand that the one thing the king valued even more than his friendship with the composer was his own sovereign authority; any threat to this power, whether real or perceived, was inevitably met with a streak of autocratic imperiousness. Still, he was willing to indulge the composer's wishes as long as they did not conflict with his own. He wrote to the cabinet secretary: "Wagner's wishes should be accomodated as far as possible; on the whole they are justified. Peruse his letter to Me and do everything in your power to deter him from coming to Munich. But there is no need for him to know that this is My Wish, otherwise all hell will break loose!"[5]

In place of Richter, Perfall, with the king's blessing, appointed Franz Wüllner, the conductor of the Munich Theater. On learning of this commission, an angry Wagner wrote to Wüllner:

> Look out and keep your hands off my score, Sir, or go to hell! Run along and beat time in glee clubs and choral societies, or if you really must handle opera scores, get yourself one composed by your friend Perfall. You can tell that fine gentleman to go to the King and make a clean breast of his incompetence, as far as producing my work is concerned. Otherwise I shall light him a bonfire which all his newshound scandal-mongers whom he pays from the ill-gotten *Rheingold* profits, will not be able to quench! The two of you need plenty of lessons from me, before you will understand that you understand nothing.[6]

Finally, on 22 September, with Wüllner conducting, *Das Rheingold* had its public premiere. Ironically, on that same day, Gottfried Semper's Court Theater in Dresden, which had witnessed the premieres of Wagner's *Rienzi* and *Der fliegende Holländer*, burned to the ground. Wagner, of course, was not present, but the king, along with a number of his specially invited guests, was, and he considered the evening a triumph. On the whole, the press was favorable to the production, although the *Bayerischer Vaterland* referred to the opening scene with the three Rhine maidens as "that aquarium of whores."[7] The majority of the technical difficulties had been successfully solved by Brandt; despite Wagner's attempts to portray the premiere as an unmitigated disaster, he later commissioned Brandt to apply his technical experience for the first production of the Ring cycle in Bayreuth. The only sour note came from Wagner himself. He had somehow managed to circumvent Düfflipp and made his way to Munich, where he requested an immediate audience with the king. Ludwig refused him, writing to the cabinet secretary: "This wretched development of the *Rheingold* affair, which has now become intolerable to Me, has reached its climax in R. Wagner's coming to Munich entirely against My Will! It would serve him perfectly right if there is a nasty demonstration against him, now that the Bülow scandal is *au combe. J'en ai assez.*"[8]

The scandal over the staging of *Das Rheingold* showed once and for all that for Ludwig the composer's art came first, before the man himself. The king had triumphed, but, inevitably, he could not maintain the silence between himself and the composer. On 22 October, he wrote to Wagner:

> I despise lying, have no desire to make excuses, and tell you quite openly that I realize my mistake and regret it; I should have conveyed my wishes to you personally . . . and I felt in my soul deep anger—which is not without some justification—against those people who claimed for themselves the right—surely against your instructions—of carrying out your instructions in no very tactful way (to put it mildly). . . . I think (if I may say so) that you imagine my post to be easier than it is. To stand alone, absolutely alone in this harsh and dreary world, alone with my ideas, misunderstood and distrusted, that is not an easy task. In the first years after my ascension, it was to some extent the charm of novelty that was responsible for my pleasing people—oh, woe to those who have to deal with individuals! I have learnt, believe me, to know human beings; I approached them with genuine love and felt myself rejected, and such wounds heal very, very slowly. . . . My feelings of love and friendship for you are stronger than ever, your ideals are mine, and to be of service to you is my mission on earth. The man does not exist who is capable of wounding me, but when *you* are displeased with me, you deal me a death blow. Oh, write to me and forgive your friend, for he is aware of his guilt. No, oh no! We shall never separate! It would cut me to the quick and I would surrender myself to endless despair. Thoughts of suicide would haunt me.[9]

In spite of this letter and its conciliatory tone, difficulties did not end with the production of *Rheingold*. Two months after the first opera in the Ring cycle had its premiere, Ludwig declared his intention of staging the second opera, *Die Walküre*. Wagner, having gone through the recent struggle with the king over *Das Rheingold*, realized that Ludwig would no doubt see his plans through, and offered to come to Munich to oversee the premiere. The only caveat to the composer's generosity was that he asked the king to wait a full year before commanding the production. But Ludwig had grown tired of Wagner's evasions. "Forgive my youthful impetuosity," he wrote to Wagner, "but I cannot wait until next year for the performance of *Walküre*. Oh! My longing for it is so irresistible! . . . Very well, find me guilty, condemn me, if you have the heart!"[10]

When Wagner learned of this latest development, he was beside himself with anger. Only weeks before, the king had seemingly confessed that the production of *Das Rheingold* had been an error. Now Wagner felt that his rights as an artist were being violated. To the king, he wrote:

> Then you hold me at a distance, avoid me even—when there are difficulties which we could quite easily resolve together— ally yourself against me, so that I, completely despised, begin to wonder whether I only dreamed that I had a King for a Friend. . . . And now, only one question remains, the answer to which will determine our entire future: Do you wish to have my work done in the way I want it, or do you not? . . . Or do you wish, my Gracious King, to just add to my difficulties? You will do this if you continue to give your theatre director instructions to provide further performances of my Nibelungen works.[11]

If Wagner hoped that this blunt letter would change the king's mind, he was sadly mistaken. Ludwig was so furious at the tone of the note that he did not even bother to respond to it.

Eventually, Wagner realized that the king would stage *Die Walküre* with or without his assistance. He therefore wrote to his friend Hermann Levi, urging him to cooperate.

The premiere of *Die Walküre* took place on 26 June 1870. Ludwig did not attend the opening night, wishing to see a repeat performance of *Das Rheingold* and then *Die Walküre* in their proper sequence. Up until the very day of the premiere, Wagner had begged the king to cancel the production or, at the very least, to restrict the audience solely to himself and a handful of invited guests. Ludwig refused to give in, and Wagner wrote angrily of the "deep pain caused by this unheard of treatment of my works!"[12] But Ludwig, insulted by the behavior of the composer and his circle of friends, considered the matter settled.

From the heights of royal devotion, Wagner had now fallen into abysmal disgrace. De la Rosée had warned Ludwig to trust no one; he had extended his royal grace and benevolence to the artist who had allowed him access to a world of ancient sagas and inspiring dreams. But Wagner, through indifference, deception, and greed, had proved himself unworthy of such exalted attention. Ludwig could not bring himself to entirely sever his ties with the composer, but their relationship, for all practical purposes, had come to an end.

20

Romantic Entanglements

In 1867, Ludwig was twenty-one years old. His first three years on the throne had been marked with troubles: the scandal of his friendship with Wagner, uncertainty over the Schleswig-Holstein crisis, and Bavaria's humiliating defeat in the Seven Weeks' War. Although there had been some negative public gossip attached to Ludwig's more visible foibles and isolated criticism of his behavior during the military crisis, he remained, to most of his subjects, an immensely popular king.

As time passed, however, concerned rumblings grew over Ludwig's dislike of Munich, his dereliction of his royal duties, and his fondness for the theater. Many hoped that he would marry and settle down, devoting himself to the business of ruling and producing an heir. He was still young and handsome and cut a sleek figure in his military uniform. His beauty continued to inspire romantic devotion: Women clipped locks of hair from the horse which he rode, and giggling girls quickly snatched flowers that he had trampled underfoot during a walk as keepsakes.[1] But there had never been any real gossip connecting Ludwig to a feminine interest or, indeed, even the slightest public hint that he was susceptible to feminine charms. The idea of a Russian alliance with the daughter of Emperor Alexander II passed into oblivion, and discreet overtures made by Queen Victoria on behalf of her daughter Princess Louise were likewise met with polite but firm rejections. The Austrian ambassador went so far as to report that "only the scenery of the ballet has penetrated into the royal apartments, for His Majesty does not find any pleasure in associating with the opposite sex."[2]

Ludwig's most intimate relationship until this time had undoubtedly been with his aide-de-camp Prince Paul von Thurn und Taxis. At first, the two young men were lost in a rush of romantic enthusiasm. Alone in the silent countryside, they rode through the dark Alpine forests, racing from one hunting lodge to the next to curl before roaring fires and recite poetry to each other. Together, they sat hidden in the shadowy recesses of the Residenztheatre's royal box, watching

Ludwig's beloved operas and historical plays. When separated, they wrote to each other daily, filling page after page with florid sentiments and pledges of eternal devotion.

At first, Ludwig had been enraptured with the handsome aide-de-camp. His obsessive, almost overwhelming love was total; in return, he expected the same kind of complete devotion, body and soul. Paul inevitably failed to live up to such high standards, and Ludwig quickly grew disillusioned. Hearing rumors that Paul was spending his evenings in the company of several unknown women, Ludwig severed all but the most formal of ties with his friend. He could not understand that someone he loved so greatly might harbor similiar feelings for another, whether man or woman. To Ludwig, loyalty was all-important: The merest hint of betrayal—real or imagined—was enough to alienate even the most intimate of friends from his affections.

Ludwig brooded in his isolation until he could stand it no longer; lonely, missing his friend, he finally broke down and dispatched a letter asking Paul to renew the friendship. For the next few weeks, Paul was in rapturous delight, writing romantic, emotional letters to his royal friend.

> Dear and Beloved Ludwig!
>
> I am just finishing my diary with the thought of the beautiful hours which we spent together that evening a week ago which made me the happiest man on earth . . . and I recalled the days of the past week, revelled in the happiest and most rapturous memory, pressed you in thought close to my heart, and so tried to overcome the sadness of being alone today. Then your dear letter was brought to me—balsam, heavenly balsam for my heart.
>
> A thousand thanks for it! The reason why the dearest friend seemed to be sad is because, at the end of the wonderful symphony which impressed me extremely, I saw you getting up and leaving the box whereupon your last words after dinner came back to my mind: "When shall we see each other again?" Tears came to my eyes when I saw you leaving! Oh, Ludwig, Ludwig, I am devoted to you! I couldn't stand the people around me; I sat still and in my thought I was with you. I had to go home; I knew that I would hear from you! How my heart beat when, as I passed the Residenz, I saw a light in your window! But now I am calm and shall sleep quietly and shall be with you in my dreams.[3]
>
> After I finished writing my diary, I looked through the books which I had ordered for you and which arrived during my

absence. While I was reading, the bell suddenly rang. My heart rejoiced! . . . your dear letter was brought to me and I hurried to my desk in order to thank you. By your lines you have given me the most divine end of this day and have delighted me anew. Oh, my beloved friend! I shall also dream sweetly of you. You shall appear in my dreams, your gracious face, your beautiful dear eyes shall look at me. Oh, I shall be wonderfully happy! Farewell, dear friend, sleep well; dream sweetly and think of your loving Paul.[4]

But for all the protestations of undying love, the relationship was doomed. Ludwig's feelings for his friend grew deeper and developed into love; the friendship was so precariously balanced that the slightest tremor of reality threatened to send it plummeting to oblivion. Paul, whom Ludwig had re-christened "Friedrich," again faltered, making a wrong choice, saying the wrong word, displaying too much familiarity on one occasion and not enough affection on another. Trivial in themselves, such incidents preyed upon Ludwig's mind until they became unbearable. Once and for all, he cut Paul out of his life. Apparently the final indiscretion was so trivial that even Paul himself was unaware of it. When he learned of his fall from grace, he sent an agonized letter to the king, but there was to be no response from Ludwig; he had made up his mind and stubbornly would not bow to his friend's pleas. Somewhat callously, he wrote to a friend that Paul had become "too haughty, and so I had to remove him."[5]

Although he himself had made the decision, the final break with Paul devastated Ludwig. A growing awareness of his homosexual desires left him plagued with self-doubt; officials and members of the court found him high-strung, emotional, and nervous. His thoughts repeatedly turned to marriage, as if he felt the need to prove to himself that he was capable of sustaining an intimate relationship with a member of the opposite sex. Once, he had exclaimed to his old religious tutor Ignaz von Döllinger, "Oh, women! Even the most intelligent argue with logic!"[6] Now, he seemed uncertain. During an audience with Bomhard, his minister of justice, Ludwig asked suddenly, "Do you think I ought to get married soon?" Bomhard was surprised at the suggestion but immediately recommended a prompt marriage to a suitable Protestant princess, in the interest of religious harmony. But just as suddenly as he had raised the issue, the king closed it. "No—I haven't time to get married—Otto can see to that," he declared.[7] It is surprising, therefore, with this reckless attitude toward marriage and his growing awareness of his own homosexuality, that Ludwig should plunge himself into an engagement with a woman he did not love.

Of all the women in his life, none was more important to Ludwig than Empress Elizabeth of Austria. The king certainly loved his cousin, but he was not in love with her. Instead, he worshiped the empress as a feminine ideal, beautiful, refined, and sensitive; most important, as a married woman, she held no threat to Ludwig's fragile sexual identity. The empress shared her cousin's dislike of court life, his passion for nature and poetry, his quest for beauty. Whereas many gossiped, she tolerated Ludwig's peculiar behavior, made no effort to rebuke or condemn him, and granted him a sympathetic understanding denied by others.

Elizabeth had undoubtedly made the grandest marriage within her family. Duke Max in Bavaria and his ambitious wife Ludovica had four other daughters, including Hélène, who eventually married a Thurn und Taxis prince; Marie, who married Francis II, king of Naples; and Mathilde, who married Louis de Bourbon, count of Trani. But it was the youngest daughter, Sophie, whom Duchess Ludovica enthusiastically promoted as a perfect queen consort for Ludwig II of Bavaria.

Ludwig had known Sophie from childhood, but relations between his parents and the family of Duke Max had been distant and formal. Only after he came to the throne and renewed his acquaintance with her elder sister Elizabeth did Ludwig encounter Sophie. She was no longer the giggling schoolgirl he remembered but a beautiful seventeen-year-old woman, tall and slender. Like her sister, Sophie possessed deep-set blue eyes, but her thick mane of hair was golden. She had a lovely voice and, more important to Ludwig, loved Wagner nearly as much as he did. It was this mutual admiration for the composer which initially drew the cousins together. In the fall of 1866, Ludwig began visiting Sophie at her father's house, Possenhofen, just across Lake Starnberg from his own castle at Berg. Frequently, he would ride to Possenhofen to ask his cousin to play and sing arias from *Tannhäuser* and *Lohengrin*.

Grateful for the apparent attraction between their two children, both Queen Marie and Duchess Ludovica did all they could to propel the pair together. The king wrote frequent letters to his cousin, addressing Sophie as "Elsa" and signing himself as "Heinrich," two of the principal characters from *Lohengrin*. Yet he was reluctant to allow the friendship with Sophie to progress any deeper. Not only was Ludwig plagued with doubts about his own sexuality, but he also suffered from an abnormal degree of self-conscious dignity. As sovereign, he carefully hid his emotions from prying eyes behind an impenetrable reserve. This shyness extended even to Ludwig's own family: He never forgot that he was king, and could not break down the emotional barriers which separated the romantic, ritualistic, and regal from the harsher realities of the world. He found it nearly impossible to honestly share his own feelings or emotions, or treat his relatives as equals.

Although Ludwig was fond of Sophie, he did not love her. Nevertheless, Sophie's mother, Ludovica, had already placed two daughters on European thrones and was determined to see Sophie and Ludwig marry. She therefore dispatched one of her sons, Karl Theodor, to ask the king of his intentions. When confronted, Ludwig declared that although he found Sophie charming, he was not yet ready to marry. Karl Theodor conveyed this message to his mother, who then informed the king that, as he had no intention of marrying Sophie, he must cease his frequent visits to Possenhofen and halt the voluminous correspondence. Ludwig was genuinely saddened at this request but, feeling that he must honor a mother's wish, wrote his cousin a farewell letter.

Before long, however, word began to filter back to Ludwig that Sophie was desperately unhappy. She declared to everyone that she was in love with her crowned cousin, and created a terrible fuss at Possenhofen over his apparent lack of feeling for her. This was certainly news to the naive Ludwig; until this time, he had not the slightest idea that Sophie felt anything for him beyond friendship. Although he had many lovesick admirers vying for his attentions, Ludwig was extremely flattered by his cousin's desire. Quietly, he informed Sophie that at some future date it might be possible for him to return her feelings. He made no promise or proposal, but Ludovica, given this slight hope, relented and allowed the relationship to continue.

Still, Ludwig was careful to point out to Sophie his own view of their friendship. On 19 January 1867, he wrote to his cousin:

You know the nature of my destiny. I once wrote to you from Berg about my mission in the world. You also know that I do not have many years to live, that I shall leave this earth when the unthinkable happens, when my star no longer shines, when He has gone, the Truly Beloved friend; yes, then my time will also be up, for then shall I no longer be able to live. You have always taken such a true, sincere and devoted interest in my fate, dear Sophie, that I shall deeply thank you for it for the rest of my life. The main basis of our interchange, as you will confirm, has always been the remarkable, sweeping destiny of Richard Wagner.[8]

This letter, full of affection for Wagner, can hardly have reassured Sophie of the king's affections. Nevertheless, she let it pass without comment.

Inexplicably, the King suddenly changed his mind. On the evening of 21 January 1867, he and the queen mother gave a state ball at the Residenz. Ordinarily, Ludwig despised such occasions, but this night proved to be a happy exception. On that cold, snowy night, the Residenz blazed with light; the lavish halls were banked with exotic, out-of-season roses, orchids, and lilacs, their powerful scent and the heat from the roaring fires creating an atmosphere akin to a hothouse's. A fanfare of trumpets announced the arrival of the king and his mother; Ludwig entered the Throne Room dressed in a sleek, dark blue military uniform, a slight smile on his lips. He slowly escorted the queen across the room, receiving the low bows and deep curtsies of the aristocracy and members of the court. Amid the crowd of officers and crush of admiring ladies, he spotted Sophie. She wore a beautiful satin-and-velvet gown, cut low to show off her lovely neck and shoulders; her golden hair was swept up and coiled atop her head, framing the becoming flush caused by the chill night outside. Ludwig was enchanted. "There are many beautiful women here tonight," he declared to one of his aides, "but my cousin Sophie is the most beautiful of all."[9] He immediately set out across the throne room to ask his cousin to dance. For the next three hours, he never left her side, whispering to her, nodding and smiling as they swirled around the gleaming parquet floor to the music of a concealed orchestra. At the end of the ball, he accompanied Sophie to her carriage, watching as its flickering lamps disappeared into the snowy night.

Long after silence reigned in the marble halls of the Residenz, the lights in the king's private apartments burned. Pacing restlessly through the gilded chambers, Ludwig worked himself into a romantic fervor, convinced that he must marry Sophie. He may have believed that in committing himself to his cousin he would forever banish his homosexual desires, feelings he had only begun to recognize. His engagement with Sophie offered a reprieve from his own sexual desires. Having reached this momentous decision, Ludwig was overcome with an almost childish excitement: Perhaps he feared that if he postponed his proposal, he would lose his confidence. Early the next morning, unable to wait any longer, he burst into his mother's bedroom, waking her and announcing his news. He immediately ordered a carriage and, just after dawn, set off with the queen on the royal train for Lake Starnberg.

Ludwig and his mother arrived at Possenhofen just as Duke Max's family was sitting down to breakfast. Queen Marie and Duchess Ludovica disappeared, leaving Ludwig and Sophie alone. The king asked his cousin to accept his proposal: Sophie, somewhat startled at this sudden declaration of love, nevertheless saw her opportunity and quickly agreed. By nine o'clock that morning, King Ludwig II and Princess Sophie in Bavaria were formally engaged to be married.

21

A Disastrous Engagement

The urgent and impetuous engagement of King Ludwig II of Bavaria to Princess Sophie in Bavaria remained a state secret for nearly a week. On 22 January, the night of the engagement itself, Ludwig attended a performance at the court theater with his mother. At the intermission for the first act, he and Queen Marie walked to Duke Max in Bavaria's box and brought Sophie back with them to the royal loge. She walked on Ludwig's arm and bowed to the stunned audience before taking her seat between mother and son. Those who witnessed the scene quickly guessed its symbolic significance. But this ambiguous declaration had to wait another week to receive official confirmation: On 29 January 1867, the news of the engagement was announced to both houses of the Landtag, to cheers and congratulations from members of the government.

To Wagner, Ludwig immediately reported: "Walther confirms to the dear Sachs that he has found his faithful Eva—Siegfried his Brünnhilde."[1] And to Cosima von Bülow, he wrote: "My love for her is deep and loyal; but the Friend will never cease to be dear to me beyond all others."[2] Wagner himself was pleased at the news. Only a year before, he had found himself having to persuade the king to remain on the throne; surely, he reasoned, a marriage would settled him down and further dedicate him to his role. For Wagner, a king without a royal treasury was of no use at all.

The Wittelsbach family, as stunned as the future bride at the proposal, responded with great enthusiasm and much relief. Although Ludwig was only twenty-one years old, he had, up until the time of his sudden engagement, shown absolutely no interest in the possibility of a marriage. Without an heir, the throne would pass, after Ludwig's death, to his brother, Otto, and any children whom he might have if he married. With the king's engagement, therefore, the succession seemed assured. Old King Ludwig I, writing his congratulations to his grandson, summed up what many in the family must have felt: "May God's blessing, dear Ludwig, rest upon your marriage! I have for some time read in the looks of beautiful Sophie that you are deep-rooted in her heart . . . happiness at home is the greatest blessing on earth. How happy I shall be to carry your first son, my great-grandson, in my arms!"[3]

Bavarians, on the whole, reacted favorably to the engagement. It is true that some factions complained that the king should have made a more political match in order to cement alliances, and there were those who had hoped for a Protestant princess. But most Bavarians were happy that their beautiful young monarch had found such a charming companion. Those who were associated with the court had heard the malicious rumors already beginning to circulate about the King's private life, and his marriage seemed to promise an end to the uncertainty over the stability of the throne. Commemorative vases, plates, medals, and coins flooded the shops. Postcards of the official engagement photographs showed Ludwig standing arm in arm with his fiancée, the king looking somewhat distant and preoccupied, while Sophie appeared positively triumphant. Only Robert von Mohl, the Baden ambassador, expressed doubts: "One felt unavoidably that the Princess had not an amiable nor pliant character. Her beautiful face held a suggestion of hardness and coldness which remained even when the King approached her in a friendly manner and talked to her."[4]

Empress Elizabeth of Austria happened, by coincidence, to be passing through Munich on her way to Zurich when her sister's engagement was announced. She arranged for her train to stop in the Bavarian capital so that she might present her personal congratulations to the couple. Ludwig had secluded himself in his bedroom at the Residenz, saying that he was ill with a bad cold, but when he heard that Elizabeth was at the train station, he hurriedly dressed, collected Sophie from her father's palace in the city, and drove to meet the empress. Once there, Ludwig, in front of his fiancée, undiplomatically declared to Elizabeth that the thing he found most attractive about Sophie was her resemblance to her elder sister.[5]

This can hardly have been comforting to Sophie. Even after his engagement was announced, Ludwig still maintained his façade of kingly dignity, and any affection which he may have felt for Sophie he kept strictly to himself. He continued the lengthy correspondence between "Elsa" and "Heinrich," occasionally punctuating his thoughts with a word or two of devotion, and this long-distance affection seemed all that he was capable of expressing.

Wagner paid a private visit to Munich in March, and Ludwig arranged for him to meet Sophie at her father's palace. Afterward, the composer wrote to the king: "I was profoundly stirred by your dear chosen one! My Gracious King! For the first time since your fate was joined to mine, I looked into a human eye from which blessed but anxious love for Your Majesty spoke deeply and eloquently to my soul. Oh, if only you could be united, soon, soon!"[6]

Although Ludwig's letters opened and closed with affectionate terms, Sophie found little solace in them. Still, the worship of Wagner must have seemed inconsequential compared to the manner in which he carried on about his love for Sophie's brother, Karl Theodor. Karl Theodor, the "Gackl" of Ludwig's youth, had just suffered the death of his wife when, on 13 March 1867, the king wrote the following very disturbing letter:

> My Dear Elsa:
> Please forgive me for bothering you at this late hour. To nobody but you will I tell what I suffer. I am so truly happy about our engagement . . . and, at the same time I am so utterly unhappy and miserable. Oh, God, my dear Elsa, in spite of all my happiness my heart aches. Gackl, who is so close to my heart that I would gladly go through fire for him without trembling for my own life, is wounded. Oh, should I come near him in danger; I would bear every pain in the world with pleasure for him. How it hurts my heart. There is nobody in the world whom I acknowledge to be above me; nobody can order me; but if he would resign I would leave the throne, yes, even transfer the crown to him. I would serve him gladly, be obedient to him whatever he might want—to him, but to no one else on the whole earth. I entreat you, do make it possible for me to talk to him quietly and cosily as soon as he comes back; he shall see how faithfully this friend's heart beats for him unto the end. . . .
> O, God! To nobody on earth could he possibly be more precious than to me—not even to his own mother. To think of the possibility of his death is unbearable—I would go mad.[7]

Sophie's reaction to this letter is not known. Ludwig could scarcely bring himself to express any emotion toward his own fiancée, yet he did not hesitate to confide his love for her brother in this indiscreet letter. For all of his kind words, it was becoming increasingly obvious that Ludwig's heart was not in the marriage. The very tone of their correspondence, too, did not suggest a passionate romance: As a fellow Wagner enthusiast, Sophie must have found it odd that Ludwig continued to sign himself as "Heinrich" rather than as "Lohengrin" himself. But when Sophie complained to her mother about the cold treatment from her fiancé, Ludovica only replied that "no one could be more tiresome and eccentric than her husband, and he did not even have the excuse of being a king."[8]

Still, Ludwig showed no outward sign that he was dissatisfied with the engagement. He immediately set about decorating rooms in the Residenz for his bride, selecting a handful of chambers a floor below his own. Sophie's apartments, like Ludwig's, overlooked the Hofgarten. He had wall coverings for these rooms faithfully copied from the set designs of the latest Munich productions of *Lohengrin*, and a small staircase was built to link his study with Sophie's future boudoir. Wagner's great, and as yet unfinished, opera, *Die Meistersinger von Nürnberg*, was to form the centerpiece of the festivities, intended as the composer's personal gift to the royal couple on their wedding. And Ludwig ordered a new coach for the wedding, an ornate, bristling mass of carved and gilded foliage, with cherubs and painted side panels depicting events from the life of Louis XV, and surmounted by a replica of the Bavarian state crown. This piece of fantasy was rumored to have cost the king more than a million gulden.[9]

In the early months of the engagement, Sophie and her family were often subjected to Ludwig's curious nocturnal fancies. In the middle of the night, he might suddenly decide that he wished to see his fiancée and dispatch an equerry to Possenhofen. While the rest of Lake Starnberg slept, Ludwig climbed into a carriage and set off into the dark night, riding from Berg to Duke Max's house on the opposite side of the lake. Forewarned by an equerry, the entire ducal household roused themselves from their sleep and dressed, for Ludwig always insisted on being properly received as sovereign, no matter how late the hour. Sophie and her parents stood on the steps, listening for the sounds of Ludwig's carriage and outriders' horses crunching on the gravel drive, Possenhofen blazing with light behind them. Ludwig did not always remain after creating this disturbance: Sometimes, he would leave a bunch of flowers or a letter for Sophie and then disappear once again into the darkness of the night just as suddenly as he had come.

When Ludwig did remain, he would often demand to see Sophie alone, and a lady-in-waiting would be hidden discreetly behind a screen of potted palms. He would slump into an armchair while Sophie played the piano and sang for him. After several hours of this, she would sit before him doing her needlework, their embarrassing silence only occasionally punctuated by Ludwig's remark that she had pretty eyes. Their conversation was always strained, and Ludwig soon found that when they spoke, Sophie was not quite as intelligent or as entertaining as he had first thought. Her slightly uneducated, girlish talk at first bored, then, more ominously, irritated him. The nights wore on in this uncomfortable fashion until Ludwig, wearied, took his leave. Only occasionally would he drop the wall of reserve and allow himself to show any emotion, but even this was limited to a few carefully placed kisses on Sophie's forehead. Once, she grew tired of this game and dared to kiss Ludwig on the lips; he was so upset that he nearly called off the engagement on the spot. Sophie never complained to Ludwig, never let on that she was anything less than satisfied with the arrangement. On one occasion, however, the strain proved too much. During one of his midnight visits, he brought the consort's crown with him for Sophie to try on. It proved too big, and this seemed to amuse Ludwig, who collapsed in laughter at seeing his bride-to-be in her crown. To heighten his amusement, he made Sophie take the crown off and put it back on again several times so that he might observe how it hung over her brow. When he left, Sophie burst into tears, crying, "He does not love me! He is merely playing with me!"[10]

As long as Ludwig's peculiar behavior remained hidden within Possenhofen's silent walls, only he and Sophie knew the intricate steps of the dance in which they were both engaged. This deceit could only last so long, however; when Prince Chlodwig von zu Hohenlohe-Schillingfurst gave a ball for the couple, the delicate balance gave way and exposed Ludwig's true feelings. Bomhard explained:

> Towards ten o'clock the King came up to me in the middle of a throng of guests and asked what time it was and whether he would still be able to reach the theatre before the end of a Schiller drama which was playing there. I pointed out to the King that it would be taken amiss if I were seen looking at my watch. I asked the King to stand before me, and, as he did so, I pulled out my watch and informed him that he would still be able to see a part of the play. But I warned him that it would certainly not be proper behaviour toward his future bride if he were to leave the ball so soon. He thanked me and very soon word went round: "The King has gone." The astonished guests believed that he had left without even saying goodbye to his bride, although I myself do not know if that was true. Having witnessed this scene, I was forced to conclude that the King was not in love with his bride.[11]

Soon, all of Munich learned of this incident, and serious questions about the wedding began to surface.

The wedding had been planned for Ludwig's twenty-second birthday, 25 August 1867. Sophie was busy with her trousseau, while Ludwig worried over the elaborate ceremonial that a state wedding demanded: the wedding itself, the reception, the state dinner, and the ball, not to mention the great triumph of the premiere of Wagner's *Die Meistersinger von Nürnberg*. Although he ordinarily hated public ceremony, Ludwig was caught up in the moment, poring over the lengthy Wittelsbach etiquette for the most impressive details. When he gazed out from the windows of his study in the Residenz, he could watch as the eight black horses which were to draw the golden wedding coach through the streets in the state procession were run through their paces. Once, though, the thought of it all overwhelmed him, and he wrote to Sophie: "How much more beautiful it would be if we could have it all in a little church on Lake Starnberg."[12]

But this was not mere romantic sentiment. Ludwig was increasingly terrified at the thought of the thousands of prying eyes which would gaze upon him at his own wedding, at being paraded through the streets of his capital like an exhibit. Soon, he regretted the impetuous way in which he had asked for Sophie's hand, and the sudden enthusiasm which had pushed him into the wedding now coalesced against it. His anxiety over the festivities, coupled with a growing realization that Sophie was not a replacement for Empress Elizabeth, led Ludwig to a fateful decision to call off the wedding.

More important, Ludwig grew to dread the very idea of marriage, whether to Sophie or to anyone else. The homosexual thoughts and feelings, which had done so much to push him toward this public expression of romantic love, now resurfaced to plunge him into despair. It was not only a desire to call off the marriage; Ludwig, having repeatedly ignored his own sexual inclinations, found that he could not banish them by simply contracting a marriage with a suitable princess. He went so far as to ask his own physician, Dr. Gietl, for a certificate declaring that he was unfit to marry. To one official, he announced that he would sooner drown himself in the Alpsee than go through with the marriage.[13] He was increasingly agitated and nervous, pacing alone through his rooms at all hours of the night or bursting into his mother's bedroom as she lay asleep to fling himself upon the bed and cry for help. Once, he was found sitting before his dressing table mirror, making faces at his own reflection and saying, "At times, I would not swear that I am not mad."[14]

Ludwig's first decisive step was to formally postpone the wedding. Instead of 25 August, he informed Sophie that their marriage would now take place on 12 October, the date on which both his own parents and grandparents had been married. Sophie was not overly alarmed at this news: The delay seemed reasonable enough, as the ceremonial was behind schedule and the date selected was something of a family tradition. Then, at a performance of *Tannhäuser* that August, the engaged couple were seen to occupy separate boxes in the court theater, Sophie in her father's box and Ludwig alone in the royal loge. By the end of the evening, the gossip over the state of the king's engagement had spread. After the *Tannhäuser* performance, Franz Liszt commented slyly, "His Majesty does not appear to be a very ardent suitor."[15]

To the public, however, the engagement continued, with the wedding simply delayed. Ludwig alone knew that this was simply a ruse, intended to pacify both the public and his fiancée until he could gather enough courage to formally break off the engagement. That he had made up his own mind to do just this is confirmed in the letter which he wrote to Baroness Leonrod. On 25 August, his own birthday and the day upon which the royal nuptials were originally to have taken place, he declared:

> The happy feeling which inspires me now that I have shaken off the burdensome bonds—which I knew would turn out unfortunate for me—can only be compared with the rapture of a convalescent who at last breathes again with the fresh air after a dangerous illness. Sophie was always dear and precious to me as a friend and darling sister, but she would not have done for my wife; the nearer the date of the wedding came the more I dreaded my intended step. I felt very, very unhappy and so resolved to free myself from the self-imposed bonds and chains: for Sophie also it was not too difficult to give back her word because she saw herself the unsuitability to each other; so we avoided misfortune and now we both have the possibility of making an engagement which promises to make us happy; I am sure that she will pick a happy party in the near future and, so far as I am concerned, I am not in any hurry. I am still young and marriage would have been premature anyhow.[16]

This letter foreshadowed what was to come; although Ludwig declared that his fiancée understood the reasons for the reversal, she did not, in fact, know any more than that it had been postponed. With the approach of the new date set for the wedding, 12 October, all of his old anxiety and terror resurfaced. When he could bear it no longer, Ludwig declared that the wedding would again have to be postponed, this time until 28 November. He could not bring himself to go through with the marriage nor could he face up to the responsibility of having to break off the engagement.

On 4 October, Ludwig received a letter from Duke Max in Bavaria, demanding that the king either set a definite date for the wedding and stick to it or cancel the engagement. Ludwig was beside himself with anger at having been addressed in this manner by a "subject."

But the letter also provided him with the very excuse which he had been seeking. To his intended, he wrote with abrupt callousness: "Beloved Elsa, Your Parents desire to break our engagement. I accept their proposal."[17] It was in this manner that Sophie first learned of her fiancé's decision. A few days later, she received a long letter in which he tried to explain as honestly as discretion permitted his reasons for breaking their relationship.

My Beloved Elsa:

As the wedding day was forced upon me like a hothouse plant, just as the day of the engagement was, I consider it my sacred duty to tell you something now when it is not too late. Always, you have been precious to me, and dear to me, I love you with true and sincere affection, I love you like a dear sister; and this feeling, which is deeply rooted in my heart, shall never leave me, and so I would like to beg for a continuance of your precious and amiable affections; should you remember me with sorrow and bitterness it would cause me deep grief.

When we wrote to each other a great deal the summer before last, and when I gave you proofs of my friendship and trust, your mother pressed me to make a decision; she thought I had infatuated you, because she did not believe in the existence of a friendship without "real" love. You will remember the answer which I gave to you and to your mother through Gackl. When I then heard how unhappy it had made you, and that you would have to go away and that we should not see each other again, it gave me great sorrow; I was deeply touched by the proofs of true love which you gave; my affection for you grew deeper so that I was carried away into asking for your hand. The reason I ordered all the preparations for the wedding, talked and wrote to you about it, put it off, and, at the same time, did not want to give it up, was not in order to cheat you or, as you may think, to go back slowly and step by step, oh no! I certainly did not want to deceive you. That was quite beside the question. I acted in the firm belief that everything would lead to a satisfactory conclusion. Now I have had time to test myself and think the whole matter over, and I see that my true and faithful brotherly love is now, and will always be, deeply rooted in my soul. But I also see that there is not the love which is necessary for a matrimonial union.

I owe you this, dear Elsa, and I beg for the continuance of your friendship when you give me back your word; and when we part from each other, please let us do so without illness and bitterness and please—I ask you heartily for this—do keep all souvenirs which I gave you and allow me to keep yours. They will always remind me of a time which will never cease to be precious to me and of a dear friend and relation for the happiness of whom—who is so close to my heart—I will pray to God daily. Should you within a year's time not have found somebody with whom you think you could be happy and should it be the same with me (which I think is altogether not impossible) then we could join ourselves together for-ever—that is to say, of course, if you still felt like it; but now it is better to part and not tie ourselves for the future. I must say again that the interference of your mother in our affairs as they were last winter was very unfortunate. Should there be ill-will or bitterness—which are the fiancés of hatred—in your soul may a good God give your heart mercy so that you may recog-nize in this, my sincere confession, the proof of the most pure and faithful friendship. May the Father—and that is my deep-est wish—who is above Us guide you to the way of true hap-piness, my faithful, beloved Elsa, you do deserve it. And now, farewell, do not forget,

Your heartily affectionate and faithful,
Heinrich.[18]

After writing this letter, Ludwig was filled with relief. To his diary, he confided: "Sophie written off. The gloomy picture fades. I longed for freedom, thirsted for freedom, to awake from this terrible nightmare!"[19] At the same time, it was said, he picked up a marble bust of Sophie which had sat upon his desk and flung it out of the window to the court-yard below, shattering it into hundreds of pieces. He did everything pos-sible to destroy the traces of his intended union. The commemorative coins were withdrawn from circulation, the crown purchased the plates and vases en masse and officials smashed them, all prints describing Sophie as queen of Bavaria were burned in Ludwig's presence, and acid was poured on the copper plates and lithographic blocks.[20]

After he had time to consider the situation, he wrote: "Sophie, who was in fact in love with me, was infinitely sad when she learned that I did not feel the same way. Moved by her unhappiness and feel-ing genuine sympathy for her, I allowed myself to be lured into the ill-conceived step of becoming engaged."[21] And on 28 November, the date that the wedding was finally to have taken place, he wrote: "Thanks be to God that the fearful thing was not realized."[23]

Public reaction was mixed. A simple, terse announcement declared that the engagement was broken "by mutual agreement, after realizing the non-existence of that true attachment necessary for happy married life."[23] All manner of rumors surrounded the collapse of the engagement, and most of the blame seemed to be directed at Sophie. One of the ugliest allegations made against her was that she had been having an affair with Edgar Hansfstaengal, the court photographer.

Knowing Ludwig, many of his royal aunts, uncles, and cousins across Europe simply dismissed this scandalous affair as another of his foibles. Empress Marie Alexandrovna of Russia, in an unusually frank letter, wrote:

> Talking of weddings reminds me of the King of Bavaria. I give him up, he really cannot be quite right in the head! I should like to hear what his mother has to say about it! Some people say he is impotent, but I don't see what reason there is to suppose so. His grandfather told Mary Hamilton in Paris that he [Ludwig] thought you could have children by lying in the same bed with a woman! I had a letter from him last summer, in which he spoke so mournfully of his loneliness. In reply, I sent him a warm dissertation upon wedded love. And this now is the result![24]

Not surprisingly, Sophie's family was furious at the cancellation and the rumors which cast aspersions upon their daughter's character. Even Ludwig's beloved cousin Empress Elizabeth felt that he had wronged her sister. She wrote:

> You can well imagine how angry I am about the King, and so is the Emperor. There are no words for such behaviour. I cannot understand how he can show his face in Munich after all that has happened. I am glad that Sophie has taken it as well as she has. God knows that she could never have been happy with such a husband.[25]

The following year, on 28 September, Sophie married the Duc d'Alençon, Prince Ferdinand d'Orléans, a grandson of King Louis Philippe of France. The wedding took place at Possenhofen, and Sophie walked down the aisle on the arm of her father to the wedding march from *Lohengrin*. Ludwig did not attend, although he was in residence at Castle Berg, just across the lake. Instead, he spent the wedding night alone on the Roseninsel in the middle of Lake Starnberg, setting off hundreds of fireworks.

22

Retreat into Solitude

The failure of his engagement to Sophie had a profound effect on Ludwig. Until 1867, he had made at least minimal efforts to be a conscientious monarch, sitting through the hundreds of audiences which bored him, and submitting to the public ceremony which he hated. In November of 1866, he had undertaken a great tour of the battlefields and war-ravaged cities in Franconia, including Würzburg and Nuremberg; although the tour was a success and Ludwig was warmly received, he could not bring himself to continue this kind of public duty. Increasingly, he came to regard the crown as a burden and sought to relieve himself of its bonds through his own fantasies. His disastrous attempt at marriage left him with no doubt as to his homosexuality, and his answer to all of it—the duties, the ceremonies, the private feelings—was to flee into a world where there were no doubts, where he faced no dilemma. Since such a world did not exist in reality, Ludwig created his own, living a closeted, eccentric existence. According to the Bavarian constitution, the reigning monarch had, by law, to spend twenty-one nights each year in his capital. From 1867 onward, Ludwig would confine his stays in Munich to the required period of time and rarely longer. He virtually abandoned his duties as king and retreated into solitude.

When he had to stay in Munich, he did all he could to lessen the ordeal. Even during his engagement to Sophie, Ludwig had already begun to live a nocturnal existence. For the king, night became day. One of the most famous of his eccentricities was his habit of nocturnal "rides." In the evening, when most of his subjects had retired for the night, Ludwig left the Residenz and drove to the *manège* of the Royal Riding Pavilion. He looked over maps and charts and decided upon the night's "destination." He then worked out how far it was from Munich to his goal and how long it would take to get there. For the rest of the night, Ludwig then rode round and round the perimeter of the ring, accompanied by a groom, using a stopwatch to calculate how much farther Innsbruck, for example, might be. He changed horses when necessary and dismounted around two or three in the morning to have a picnic lunch on blankets spread over the chipped bark on the floor of the Riding Pavilion. This strange activity went on night after night, throughout Ludwig's stay in his capital.[1]

Three tumultuous years on the Bavarian throne had taken their toll on the fragile young man. Ludwig's celebrated beauty had begun to fade. The shy youth who had so entranced his subjects was gone; his once lean figure was fuller now, the angular lines on his face hidden behind a dark imperial. The romantic expression in his eyes had grown darker, more troubled, a reflection of the devastation of the war he had witnessed and the personal turmoils he had experienced. Ludwig's careless passion for sweets affected his teeth, and several had already begun to fall out. His fear of dentists and doctors prevented him from seeking treatment, and as a result, he suffered violent toothaches and headaches. Increasingly, he turned to chloral hydrate and other narcotics in an attempt to ease his suffering.

His dislike of strangers, pervasive shyness, and growing disillusion caused Ludwig to purposely isolate himself from his court. Despite his lavish and sometimes theatrical surroundings, he disliked ceremony, and his style of life was at times distinctly unroyal.

The company that Ludwig now kept was just as artificial as the world in which he lived. He confined his intimacies to two kinds of people: those with whom he could be completely honest and in whose presence he could temporarily throw off the bonds of the crown, and those people who brought into his life the dramatic, theatrical world which he relished. Empress Elizabeth, Prince Paul von Thurn und Taxis, and later, Richard Hornig, largely comprised the first group, though by 1867, Paul had fallen from favor. In the second group, Wagner, actors, actresses, and singers predominated. One such lady was the soprano Josefine Scheffsky, a singer of some repute who later went on to play Sieglinde in the first performance of the Ring operas.

Josefine had a charming and powerful voice. Unfortunately, she also possessed the typical Wagnerian girth, which made her aesthetically unpleasant to the image-conscious king. Ludwig did not want the perfect illusion of Wagner's poetic works shattered by her somewhat ungainly presence, and whenever she sang for him, Josefine was carefully hidden behind a screen of potted palms or some other shield. She was frequently summoned to the winter garden in the Residenz for these private performances, and there is a story that, tired of being ignored by the king, she "accidentally" fell into the lake, hoping that Ludwig would valiantly come to her rescue. But on finding her splashing about, he merely rang a bell and watched as servants pulled the bulky and indignant singer from the water.[2]

Scheffsky also tried to manipulate Ludwig through exaggerated demands on the royal treasury. It was usual for those in the king's favor to present him with gifts as return presents for those which they inevitably received from him. They then submitted a bill to the royal treasury for payment. Scheffsky gave the king an Oriental rug and then turned in a receipt with an amount altered to reflect five times what she had actually paid. An official soon discovered the fraud and Ludwig was furious. He ordered that the singer be denounced on-stage before the entire opera company and then had her temporarily banished from Munich.[3]

In May of 1866, Ludwig attended a performance of Schiller's *Maria Stuart*. Lila von Bulyowsky, a Hungarian actress some ten years older than the king, played the title role. Along with Marie Antoinette, the doomed Mary, Queen of Scots, had always been one of Ludwig's greatest tragic heroines. Lila von Bulyowsky's performance captivated him; he was so moved by the play that on leaving the theater just before midnight, he ordered that a church be specially opened so that he could say prayers for the martyred queen's soul.

Ludwig appears to have been quite taken with Lila. But his interest lay in Mary, Queen of Scots, not a Hungarian actress. Soon, he began writing her long, intimate letters filled with entire passages from *Maria Stuart* and *Romeo and Juliet*. Flattered by such royal attention, Lila became convinced that he intended to follow in the tradition of taking a mistress from the stage. She did not understand that Ludwig's only interest lay in her as the personification of his heroine, not as a woman.

Lila was understandably infatuated. She admitted to several of her friends that she was in love with the king, and even kept a large framed photograph of him before her bed.[4] Ludwig knew nothing of her impressionable character and, indeed, did not care to know. But one of her many friends later recalled her as "a real woman of the world. She was not without small faults; somewhat avaricious, somewhat snobbish, somewhat pretty, but amusing, even scintillating, and a kind, devoted friend. As she was a very pretty woman with many admirers and occasionally adopted a rather free manner, nobody credited her with much virtue, but I would wager my right arm that not many had ever been shown the inside of her charming blue bedroom in the Maximilianstrasse."[5]

If Lila was not the ideal, Ludwig saw none of it. He had discovered the incarnation of one of his heroines, and Lila was crafty enough to respond. She frequently found herself called in the middle of the night to the Residenz or to Castle Berg, where she would be asked to read Schiller or Shakespeare for hours while Ludwig listened with contentment.

One weekend, though, the romantic illusion came to a stunning and tragic end. Ludwig had invited Lila to visit him at Hohenschwangau; when she arrived, he conducted her on an evening tour, wandering from room to room and explaining the murals and their legends. When they entered the king's bedroom, Lila expressed great shock at the paintings of Armida's seduction at the hands of Rinaldo. This seemed to amuse Ludwig; from his jacket, he pulled out a miniature portrait of Lila as Mary, Queen of Scots, saying with a smile, "I have a protection against them." He lay on his bed, closing his eyes as he sank against the cushions. Lila perched on the edge of the bed and began to read aloud from a book of poetry; as he listened, Ludwig was overcome with emotion. He sat up and turned to the actress, confessing in a whisper that he had never slept with a woman. Saying that he often thought of her at night and covered his pillow with kisses, Ludwig gently lay his head in Lila's lap and closed his eyes.[6]

Suddenly, Lila leaned forward and tried to kiss him. Horrified, Ludwig jumped from the bed, pushing her away as he ran to a corner of the room. Confused, Lila attempted to follow him, declaring her love. Ludwig fled through the double doors of the bedroom with Lila in hot pursuit, chasing him from room to room. After several minutes of this chase, however, the actress finally gave up and stormed out of the castle, leaving the young king cowering beneath the romantic murals. "He is as cold-blooded as a fish!" she angrily declared on returning to Munich.[7] Ludwig was shocked at her behavior, saying, "That brazen Bulyowsky tramp can go to the devil!"[8]

At Ludwig's request, Queen Marie summoned Lila to a private audience and asked her to leave Bavaria. Reluctantly, she agreed, and promised the king that when her contract with the theater expired, she would not renew it. True to her word, Lila did indeed leave Munich. But Ludwig wrote, "I only wish her to leave Munich for a short time, not for ever. I am quite willing to treat her as before, provided that she does not forget again the respect due to the King. Try to put her into good humour and to pacify her; for women who have been scorned are like hyenas."[9]

Through sheer determination, Elizabeth Ney became one of Ludwig's confidants. Ney was a famous sculptress, a great-niece of Marshal Michel Ney, Napoléon's famous military commander. In 1867, at the Paris International Exposition, she exhibited busts of Bismarck and Giuseppe Garibaldi to much acclaim. Like hundreds of other women, she was fascinated by the young king's beauty and was determined to meet him. By now, Ludwig was used to this sort of seige on the part of his female admirers, and he ignored her constant letters and requests for an audience. After much pleading and months of letters, however, he relented and graciously granted Ney funds to build a new studio in Munich; he refused, though, to sit for her.

For reasons which remain a mystery, Ludwig eventually did give in and grant the sculptress an audience, followed by a formal sitting for a proposed life-size statue. He placed two conditions on this, however: She must agree not to speak to him during her work, and she must not touch him or take any measurements. The sitting bored Ludwig, and he posed staring vacantly into the distance. With a stroke of genius, Ney grabbed a nearby copy of Johann Wolfgang von Goethe's *Iphigenia in Taurus* and began to read aloud to him. As she continued, Ludwig's mood began to change; Ney propped the book up where she could see it, continuing to read aloud as she resumed her work. The result of these sittings is the only surviving contemporary life-size statue of the king, showing him in the robes of the Order of St. Hubertus.

Ludwig's clear disillusion with life had led him to misanthropic despair. He felt no one understood him, and disliked and distrusted the world. No matter how much he tried, Ludwig could not bring himself to face the harsher realities of the nineteenth-century or his own personal desires. His homosexuality continued to weigh heavily upon him during this time, for in one of Ney's letters, she indicates that he confessed as much to her. But she did not judge him; rather, she wrote: "God has made you as you are. You did not create yourself. Therefore you may freely admit what you are."[10]

With each passing week and month, each reception and court ball canceled, each public appearance delayed, and each military review postponed, it became harder and harder for Ludwig to resume his ceremonial duties as sovereign. He had purposely isolated himself in his gilded rooms in the Munich Residenz, in remote hunting lodges, and in distant Alpine castles; now, having avoided them for so long, he found it nearly impossible to face his ministers, his court, or his subjects. Every political setback made him recoil from affairs of state; every infringement against the throne seemed a deliberate humiliation; every personal failure and homosexual thought drove him further inward. As the modern world became increasingly distasteful, unfriendly, less receptive to his own dreams of knights and art and beauty, Ludwig simply avoided reality. Further and further, he drove himself into a world of isolation.

23

Overtures and Alliances

T he aftermath of the Seven Weeks' War found Bavaria in a state of turmoil, with uncertain alliances and military threats casting a dark shadow across the horizon. Prussia's continued use of force, coupled with Bismarck's escalating rhetoric, thrust Bavaria and her king into an uncomfortable diplomatic corner. The chancellor's looming political dominance struck at the heart of Ludwig's sovereign authority; fearing for the future independence of his own kingdom, his thoughts turned increasingly to the idealized concept of the Triad, in which Bavaria, Prussia, and Austria would be equal partners in a new German Confederation. Ludwig envisioned Bavaria leading a loose organization composed of itself, Württemberg, and Saxony, the southernmost German states. By proposing himself as head of the Triad, however, Ludwig had planted the seeds of its destruction. As one statesman, Prince Chlodwig von zu Hohenlohe-Schillingfurst, wrote: "I hardly think that either the King of Saxony or of Württemberg would care to hand over any of their rights to our youthful monarch."[1]

Ludwig's political naïveté and persistent distrust of his own officials, particularly in light of the ominous rumblings from Berlin, led him to appoint Prince Hohenlohe as both prime minister and foreign minister in December of 1866.

Hohenlohe proved something of an unusual choice as prime minister. His Prussian heritage drew him naturally toward support of Bismarck's aims, and his liberal views contrasted strongly with the nationalistic, conservative beliefs Ludwig harbored. In addition, one of the king's biographers, Gottfried von Bohm, described Hohenlohe as "a good diplomat, but no statesman, and lacking in any productive ideas of his own. He always knew the short cuts and side alleys, but was not able to follow a straight path with a firm step."[2] In the cobbled squares of Munich and the quiet corners of the capital shops, gossips attributed Hohenlohe's good fortune less to his questionable abilities than to the rumor that Wagner had supported his candidacy.

At first, relations between Ludwig and Hohenlohe were friendly. He found the king agreeable, though distant. "He looks well," the minister noted in his diary, "but I could not help thinking that he is beginning to take on his father's distrustful expression."[3] He continued:

Yesterday at half-past twelve, I received a telegram . . . informing me that the King wished to see me at Schloss Berg between two and three, and would send a carriage. At first I thought this last sentence must be a mistake, but a carriage actually came and took us to Berg through the Fürstenrieder Park. We arrived at three. The King received me first. He gave me his hand, which he seldom does, and was very amicable. I spoke to him first of my report of the discussion with Bismarck and enlarged on the reasons why a further threat to Bavaria through Prussia is now to be thought of. The King is always distrustful, which is due to his extremely sceptical nature. We could give up the Treaty of Alliance at any moment, he maintains, as there is a passage in it which makes this possible for us. I, of course, disputed this, but on the other hand I conceded that one can give notice to withdraw from any treaty if one finds it in one's interests to do so. This, however, is not the case here. I pointed out the danger into which this could bring us. It would be better to conclude an alliance with Prussia on the lines of the old Germanic Confederation. Those ministers who maintained that such an alliance would be too little for the Progressives and too much for the Ultramontanes would certainly be against this. The King answered very pertinently that it would be all the same, and that too much must not be left to public opinion.[4]

The old alliances which bonded Germany together in a confederation of states had been torn asunder as a result of the Seven Weeks' War. The Treaty of Prague had established the North German Union under Prussian leadership; Bavaria also had the same power to formulate a southern confederation or to unite herself with either Prussia or Austria.

Thus far, negotiations over Bavarian alliances had served only to emphasize Ludwig's impotence before Prussia. Although the Treaty of Prague had left the country free to pursue any diplomatic or political unions she wished, it also excluded an understanding with the Habsburg empire. Should Bavaria break these conditions, according to the treaty, she would forfit not only any future position in the German Confederation but also run the risk of seeing her land overrun with eager Prussian soldiers. Attempting to combat Bismarck's threat, Ludwig first proposed an alliance between Bavaria, Baden, Württemberg, and Southern Hesse. He vacillated over his options, but Hohenlohe worried that this delay threatened the position not only of Bavaria but also of the monarchy. At the same time, the prime minister saw no solution other than some form of Prussian alliance. He advised the king:

> The danger which threatens the Kingdom through the continuance of the present state of affairs is a double one:
>
> 1. Any European complication, however favourably it might result for one or other of the great powers, might prove the greatest danger to the existence and independence of Bavaria, should Germany be involved in it.
> 2. The aspiration of the German People to realize their national ideal, even against the will of their governments, may lead to internal struggles which would threaten the Dynasty.
>
> It must, therefore, be the task of the Government:
>
> 1. To conclude alliances by which the danger of European complications would be averted.
> 2. To strive for the formulation of a national union of Germany which would satisfy the legitimate demands of the nation, without infringing the Sovereign Rights of Your Majesty of the integrity of Bavaria.[5]

Ludwig found this unacceptable; although Hohenlohe favored a Prussian alliance, the king instructed him to continue his negotiations with the southern German states, explaining:

> In assenting to the negotiations undertaken between Bavaria and Württemberg as well as to the documents addressed to Karlsruhe and Darmstadt, I have started from the supposition, repeatedly put forward by you, that the introduction of negotiations between South Germany and Prussia, as to a reconstitution of the confederation, is not to be urged and will in no case be urged by Bavaria. It seems to me, however, that caution is now duly necessary, as it concerns not merely the preservation of Bavaria's independence but also the safeguarding of European peace in view of the excited feeling in France and in Austria against Prussia, on account of the former's existing and determined interpretation, no matter whether justified or not justified, of the Peace of Prague.[6]

Bismarck had already expelled Austria from the German Confederation; now the only other threat to Prussian dominance on the continent was France. When France declared its intention of acquiring the Grand Duchy of Luxembourg, Bismarck demanded to know how the Bavarian government would respond. Under the circumstances, all of Ludwig's negotiations were for nothing: Hohenlohe met with the king, reminding him of the secret mutual defense treaty which compelled Bavaria to come to the aid of Prussia in times of war. Eventually, France backed down from its threat of annexation, but Ludwig realized that sooner or later Bismarck would call on Bavaria to fight alongside Prussia and that the war, when it came, would be directed against France. The urgency of the negotiations to form a confederation separate from Prussia therefore increased.

But Prussian domination could not easily be ignored. In July, Bismarck forced Bavaria to sign an agreement in Berlin which established the Zollverein, a German customs union with its own legislative powers. Ludwig's personal opposition to Prussia's political maneuvering was fierce, but there was little he could do. Undaunted by the continual displays of Prussian might over the Bavarian political machine, Ludwig still pressed for a strong, independent confederation of southern German states. His intentions were obvious: Seeing the inevitability of a confrontation between Prussia and France, he fervently sought diminished ties with both Prussia and Austria, hoping to maintain the autonomy which Bavaria had enjoyed since the end of the Seven Weeks' War, an autonomy which rested solely upon Bismarck's continued benevolence.

Hoping to avert the looming crisis, Grand Duke Friedrich of Baden suggested a meeting between himself, Ludwig, the king of Prussia, and the king of Württemberg, to take place on the island of Mainau in Lake Constance. The agenda was to have dealt exclusively with the question of confederation and north-south German relations. The grand duke of Baden wrote to Prince Hohenlohe:

> It is needless to say how gratifying it would be if the King of Bavaria could make up his mind to take this opportunity of likewise paying a visit to the King of Prussia on the Lake of Constance. On the other hand, I will not delay in submitting this question for your earnest consideration and thereby give you the assurance that I should consider myself fortunate in affording the King from the requisite opportunity at Schloss Mainau. The distance from Hohenschwangau and Lindau is not great and from Lindau the King could pay a visit to the Schloss Mainau and return in one day. I need not say that, should the King be pleased to stay longer with us, it would be a great pleasure.[7]

But Ludwig, aware of the grand duke's pro-Prussian leanings, had little enthusiasm for the proposed meeting. Fearing that Ludwig might attempt to use one of his well-known convenient "illnesses" as an excuse to stay away from Mainau, Hohenlohe urged the king to attend.

> If it is permitted to the undersigned to express an opinion, he ventures to remark with the greatest respect that the meeting with the King of Prussia and the visit on the Island of Mainau, in the company of the King of Württemberg, offers many advantages. Apart from the object of maintaining the friendly relations of Your Majesty with the Court of Prussia, the presence of Your Majesty at the meeting of the south German monarchs would prevent the inception of biased schemes, which are in opposition to the intentions and the interests of Your Majesty.[8]

Ludwig was not impressed with this subtle arguement. He believed that a meeting at Mainau would lead to political denunciation and isolation of both Austria and France, further alienating them from friendly relations and pushing Bavaria toward a formal alliance with Prussia. Instead, he suggested a meeting with the king of Prussia at a later date, in some other location.

Hohenlohe was horrified at this idea. On receiving this alternate proposal, he wrote to the king:

> Great dissatisfaction would be aroused by the omission of this visit, for the Grand Duke of Baden and the King of Prussia have reckoned positively on Your Majesty's visit, as is obvious from the Grand Duke's lette. . . . and Your Majesty's most obedient servant does not conceal from Your Majesty his fear that, in view of the position which Prussia now occupies in Germany and of the means which are at the disposal of the Prussian Government, this dissatisfaction on the part of the Prussian Monarch might be fraught with the most serious consequences for Your Majesty and also for Bavaria. Occasions and circumstances may arise when Your Majesty may stand in need of the friendly sentiments of the King of Prussia, and these occasions may arise so soon that a delay in re-establishing friendly relations seems very much to be depricated.[9]

Ludwig's eventual refusal to attend the conference may have had more to do with his political fears than with his well-known dislike of such occasions. Over and over again, in the course of the negotiations, he demonstrated a remarkable grasp of the threatening conflict and stuck faithfully and stubbornly to his belief that any agreement with Prussia would almost certainly undermine his own sovereignty. Although the king dismissed Hohenlohe's pleas for his attendance at the Mainau conference, he was wise enough to meet with the king of Prussia, though as he had wished it—at a later date and alone, in a railway carriage at a siding in Augsburg.

Negotiations continued, and by the fall of 1867, an agreement in principle had been reached. Under the terms of this charter, Bavaria, Baden, Württemberg, and Southern Hesse were to be united in a confederation called the United States of Southern Germany. A special executive body would control policy, and in this union, Bavaria, as the principal state, would have six votes to Württemberg's four, Baden's three, and Hesse's two, and the executive power would rotate year by year. At a military academy in Munich, the army of this confederation was to be trained. In times of conflict, however, the army, by the terms of the Treaty of Prague, automatically came under the command of Prussia.

The plans for this United States of Southern Germany came to nothing. In the spring of 1868, negotiations among the four southern states collapsed. Hohenlohe unhappily reported to the king:

> The foundation of a Southern German Confederation of States, which was to be accomplished . . . had, from the outset, only a prospect of success if the idea obtained Your Majesty's entire approval, and if hope was thereby afforded that Your Majesty would accord your most unconditional concurrence in the diplomatic action proposed. . . . [I] gathered that Your Majesty by no means entirely approved the proposed conclusion of the treaty, and that Your Majesty entertained scruples concerning it. This had the effect of awakening fears . . . that the success of the proposed measures would be doubtful from the outset.

Hohenlohe went on to explain that, nevertheless, he had presented copies of the proposal to all of the cabinet ministers in the Bavarian government. "No sympathy," he continued, "was shown the proposal by the Cabinet. During the discussions objection was raised by nearly all the Ministers, and only the Minister of War expressed himself in favour of a mutual understanding between the south German states."[10] With the ministers in complete disagreement over the future of southern Germany, the possibility of Ludwig's beloved Triad was lost. Bavaria's fate was sealed: Nothing could now be done to halt growing Prussian dominance.

24

The Franco-Prussian War

On 3 July 1870, Europe awoke to the news that the Spanish Cortes had voted to offer the vacant throne of their country to Prince Leopold of Hohenzollern-Sigmaringen. Although Spain's marshal Juan Prim had been in secret negotiations with Bismarck over the offer for nearly a year, the proposal had originated not in Berlin but in Madrid. Leopold's nomination was clearly calculated to avoid antagonizing France: He shared the same Catholic faith, and he was also a distant relative of Emperor Napoléon III. As such, Spain believed him to be the ideal candidate, offensive to no one.

When France learned of the Spanish decision, however, there was an immediate outcry: The idea of being surrounded by the Hohenzollern dynasty was too much for Napoléon III and his government. Unless Spain rescinded its offer to Leopold, the emperor warned, France would invade Madrid. Such a bold move caught Spain off guard; unwilling to face the possible onslaught of the superior French troops, they agreed to revoke their offer, and Leopold's father withdrew his son's name from further consideration. The volatile issue appeared resolved. But France went further: Through diplomatic channels, Napoleon III's government declared that under no circumstances would they tolerate the accession of any member of the Hohenzollern dynasty to the Spanish throne. Reaction was swift. Spain was furious at this nationalistic threat against her own sovereign authority, and Prussia was equally offended at the slight to her ruling family

Napoléon III was still not satisfied, and he dispatched the French chargé d'affaires in Berlin, Count Vincente Benedetti, to meet with Wilhelm I. The old king was on holiday at Ems when Benedetti arrived on 11 July 1870. On behalf of the French government, he formally requested that Wilhelm publicly issue an order to Leopold himself to withdraw his name from consideration for the Spanish throne; this was a mere formality, but one which France greatly desired. The king saw no harm in the request and duly issued a statement to this effect, which was published in Paris the following day. The tension seemed averted; twice Prussia had publicly submitted to French demands.

Bismarck was not happy at this weakness, particularly as France made no effort to conceal her glee at what they believed to be Prussia's humiliation. But there was little the chancellor could do; King Wilhelm I had acquiesced. Then, in an unimaginable move, France handed Bismarck the war for which he had so long been preparing.

On 13 July, the day after King Wilhelm I submitted to all of France's requests, Count Benedetti once again approached him as he took his afternoon stroll along the promenade at Ems. With the full approval and prior knowledge of Napoléon III, the count demanded an audience with the king, saying that France required a new guarantee that Prussia would allow no member of the Hohenzollern family to ascend the Spanish throne. Wilhelm I was angry at Benedetti's arrogance and refused to grant him a second meeting. The king then dispatched a cable to Bismarck in Berlin, telling the chancellor of his refusal to receive the French envoy. The cable itself was innocuous, but in Bismarck's hands, it soon became a powerful weapon in this diplomatic war. The chancellor carefully edited the king's telegram, removing the polite, diplomatic language to make the cable as insulting to the French as possible, and then released his edited version to the German press. When it was published in this abbreviated form on 14 July, there were riots in the streets of Paris. Patriotic outrage swept across the French capital: Their country had been publicly humiliated, and now Napoléon's subjects demanded satisfaction. Two days later, France declared war on Prussia.

Under the terms of the secret mutual defense agreement, signed in 1866 as a codicil to the Treaty of Prague, Bavaria was honor bound to come to the aid of Prussia. The defense treaty had been imposed upon an unwilling Bavaria as part of their indemnity after the Seven Weeks' War, but no one in Bavaria, least of all Ludwig, had any idea that their country would be called upon to put the agreement into force. Even in the midst of the diplomatic crisis between France and Prussia, he naively believed that he could not possibly have to implement the despised codicil, refusing to acknowledge the possibility of a war or the necessity of mobilizing his troops against France.

Five days before the French declaration of war, the king decided to set off for one of his remote hunting lodges in the Alps. It was only with the greatest difficulty that he could be persuaded to abandon this plan; tensions were high, and no one knew what might happen. Still, Ludwig refused to go to Munich; instead, as he had done during the Seven Weeks' War, he took up residence at Castle Berg, which was only just a little less inconvenient in times of crisis than his shooting boxes in the mountains. Here, on 15 July, he summoned his new cabinet secretary, August von Eisenhart, to deliver a full report on the crisis.

Eisenhart received his summons just as he was preparing to leave his office for the day. He hurried to Starnberg and from there took a carriage to the castle, arriving at midnight. The king, according to Eisenhart, was "very nervous and excited." Ludwig paced back and forth, smoking one cigarette after another. "Is there no way," he repeatedly asked, "no possibility of avoiding war?" Eisenhart, who was kept standing for the duration of the four-hour audience, replied that all efforts to maintain the peace had been exhausted. Bavaria, he declared, now had no choice but to come to the aid of Prussia: the king must order the mobilization of his troops. On hearing this, Ludwig flung himself into a nearby chair, burying his face in his hands, torn with indecision. The formal recommendation of his cabinet was expected early that morning; informing Eisenhart that he intended to wait for word from Munich, Ludwig retired to bed.[1]

Two hours later, at five in the morning, Ludwig was awoken with the news that Count Berchem, an official from the Ministry of Foreign Affairs, had arrived with the decision of the government. By this time, Ludwig had also made up his mind: He would honor the secret defense treaty with Prussia. In reality, he had little choice; had he ignored the pledge, Prussia would undoubtedly have commenced hostilities against Bavaria, and Ludwig had no enthusiasm for an alliance with Napoléon III. The king hated contemporary France; his love for the Bourbons did not extend to either Paris, which he regarded as a city filled with evil influences, or to the nouveau emperor, whom he made no secret of despising.

The king's decision to comply with the treaty was a recognition not only of the political realities faced by Bavaria but also of the opportunities which the Franco-Prussian conflict presented. There was every expectation that war against France would end with internal German reorganization, with alliances solidified and the position of Prussia strengthened as the dominant northern state. But if Germany united to form a new empire, or so Ludwig earnestly believed, there was reason to hope that the imperial crown might be offered to the Wittelsbach dynasty. Certainly, the Wittelsbachs were older, more distinguished, and better connected than their Hohenzollern cousins, and the question of a united empire would of necessity involve all German states, not just Prussia.

Ludwig's Imperial aspirations, however well thought out, were based only on his assumption that his own ruling house would enjoy popular support over that of Prussia. He failed to realize that Bismarck's only aim all along had been the unification of Germany under Prussian control. The chancellor was careful to cloak his plans in a veil of nationalism and repeatedly flattery for Ludwig, but no one else—not the diplomats in their offices on Berlin's Wilhelmstrasse or the king's own ministers in the Landtag—had any doubts as to Bismarck's ultimate aims.

Although Ludwig was easily seduced by thoughts concerning assumption of an imperial crown, his reasoning in undertaking the mobilization was sound. If the war was successful, there was the tempting promise of territorial gains as well as a reduction in the still unsettled indemnity from the Seven Weeks' War. Clearly, a quick and affirmative response to the Prussian request would weigh heavily in Bavaria's favor during peace negotiations, and her decision would grant preeminent status among the victors.

Thus, when Berchem presented Ludwig with the decision of the cabinet regarding the mobilization request, he cut him short, announcing that he had already decided to honor the secret defense treaty. He grabbed a pen and signed the order. Berchem carried the Bavarian order of mobilization against France—a document written, ironically, in French—back to Munich, and the king retired to bed. Later that day, Ludwig received his new prime minister, Count Otto von Bray-Steinburg, and the minister of war, Lieutenant General Sigmund von Pranckh. To these two gentlemen, he appeared quite animated and content. Indeed, to one of his aides-de-camp, Ludwig remarked, "I have the feeling of having done a good deed."[2]

The following day, Ludwig returned to Munich. It was a sweltering summer day, and the streets around the Residenz were filled with crowds celebrating the announcement of war against France. Through the open windows in his Writing Room, he could hear the cheers of his subjects, repeatedly calling for their sovereign to show himself. Ludwig hated crowds and had no taste for public display, but on this occasion, the enthusiasm of the moment seemingly overwhelmed him, and he duly appeared at his window, bowing and waving to the crowd below. When they caught sight of their elusive monarch, they erupted with shouts of "God save the King!" and spontaneous renditions of the national anthem. "Shall I go to the window again?" Ludwig asked an aide-de-camp with obvious pleasure; he had not realized how popular he remained with his subjects, and for this one moment, he basked in their affection and in his position as king.[3]

Crown Prince Friedrich Wilhelm of Prussia had been appointed commander in chief of the southern German armies. He arrived in Munich on 27 July to assume formal command. Ludwig had always disliked his pompous cousin Fritz, as the crown prince was called in the family, and the visit proved an ordeal. It was the first time that the royal standards of both Bavaria and Prussia flew side by side as allies, a sight which made many in the crowd, Ludwig included, uneasy. Prince Hohenlohe was one of many who reluctantly observed the ominous spectacle of the Prussians' arrival in the capital.

> The Schutzenstrasse, the square in front of the station and the neighbouring squares were all full of people. Scarcely had we taken up our position before the Sterngarten when in the station gateway appeared an escort of Cuirassiers followed by the carriages in which was seated the King, with the Crown Prince of Prussia and Prince Otto. The public gave them a good welcome, and cried "Hurrah!" but not too warmly. The lower classes, workers and so on, were principally represented, and these in Munich are not particularly enthusiastic about the war, nor very inclined to shout *"Hoch!"* to a Prussian Prince.[4]

If the good citizens of Munich were less than enthusiastic in their welcome of the crown prince, Friedrich reciprocated this discomfort in the presence of Ludwig. The two royal cousins had not met for several years, and Fritz was quick to record his less-than-flattering impressions in his diary.

> I find him strikingly changed. His good looks have largely vanished, he has lost his front teeth, looks pale and has something nervous and agitated in his way of speaking, so that he never wants to hear the answer to his own question, but while his interlocutor is speaking is putting fresh questions relating to other matters. He appears to be heart and soul in the business and to be eagerly following the national bent. His swift decision to sign the order for mobilization presented him by the War Minister, Lieutenant General von Pranckh, without the cognizance of the Minister of Foreign Affairs, Count Bray, is universally commended.[5]

On the first evening of the visit, Ludwig arranged for a gala performance of Schiller's *Wallensteins Lager*. Friedrich Wilhelm, a tall, imposing figure in his smart Prussian uniform, was still dwarfed by his Bavarian cousin as the pair met at the front of the royal box. Political differences were momentarily put aside as they embraced, a symbolic gesture which neither man much enjoyed. But the king's quickly found the ceremonies which followed a terrible ordeal.

Before the crown prince left Munich, Ludwig gave him a personal letter for his father, the king of Prussia. In it, Ludwig stressed his country's immediate cooperation with the war effort and expressed his hope that this loyalty would not go unrewarded. King Wilhelm was less than enthusiastic about the contents of the note, but Bismarck warned that if he did not reassure Ludwig, Bavaria might very well withdraw her troops from the conflict. Bowing to his chancellor's wishes, Wilhelm duly, though begrudgingly, informed his nephew that Bavaria would retain a unique and secure position in the new Germany.

In spite of the pleas of both his family and members of the government, Ludwig once again refused to take command of the Bavarian army. Instead, control of the troops rested with two elderly generals, the seventy-five-year-old C. F. Hartmann and the equally feeble and inefficient von der Tann from the Seven Weeks' War. The poor condition of the Bavarian army had not improved since the previous conflict. Crown Prince Friedrich Wilhelm wrote in his diary:

> I visited a Bavarian Infantry and Cavalry Regiment, taking this opportunity to make acquaintance with the Bavarian soldier. True, the Prussian point of view must be entirely abandoned, for here everything is quite different from what it is with us; clumsiness of build and startling corpulence prevail even in the younger class of men. Still, the soldier shows quite a smart bearing, only he does not seem accustomed to being addressed by superiors.[6]

Despite his initial enthusiasm for the war and his dreams of an imperial crown, Ludwig took little interest in the conduct of his soldiers. On the day of the Battle of Worth, he was starting out for his daily carriage ride when Eisenhart ran after him, saying that reports on the battle were just beginning to come in and that he must wait to hear the news. "A King never *must*!" Ludwig cried angrily, and set off, ordering his driver to stay out one hour later than usual.[7]

The war lasted for just over a month. The Prussian army, once again under the brilliant command of Helmuth von Moltke, lost no time in marching toward the frontier, while the French troops fumbled and argued about their deployment. On 4 August, the French were defeated at Weissenburg and, two days later, at Worth; the great battle of the war occurred at Sedan on 1 September. On the following day, realizing that the conflict was as good as over, Napoléon III, together with 83,000 French troops, surrendered.

Ludwig rejoiced in the laurels won by his soldiers. To Baroness Leonrod, he wrote: "You can imagine how pleased I am at the brilliant victories of my brave troops; who could have dreamt of such extraordinary, rapid results. Those quick and decisive victories of the Germans

over the famous indefeatable French Army. . . . All the same, with all
my strength, I am longing for an early peace which shall be lasting and
blessed for the whole of Germany, but especially for my beloved
Bavaria."[8] Even as he wrote this letter, however, Ludwig had begun to
realize that each successfully prosecuted offensive brought Prussia
closer to German domination. After the battle of Sedan, he refused to
come to the capital or to allow any German flags to be flown in celebration. "As there exists neither a German Empire nor a German
Republic, nor yet even a German Federation," he wrote, "it is My Wish
that only Bavarian flags, or, better still, no flags at all, should be flown
from Government buildings."[9]

The siege of Paris began on 9 September. The atrocities committed by the surrounding German troops filled Ludwig with shame and
contempt, so much so that on one occasion, he declared that he would
not receive his mother on the grounds that she was "a Prussian
Princess."[10] He had entered the war hopefully, if naively, comforted by
thoughts of a united Germany and an imperial crown under Wittelsbach rule. With the war virtually over, it became clear that such a crown
would be worn only by a member of the Hohenzollern dynasty. As
much as Ludwig dreaded the idea, he was still in favor of a united
German Empire, but he was equally concerned that his royal sovereignty not be reduced to accomodate a new Reich. This naive hope was
soon to be shattered.

25

The Kaiserbrief

At the conclusion of the Franco-Prussian War, Bismarck lodged himself at Versailles, a humiliation that the French would later vindictively repay at the end of the World War I. Directing the destinies of the German states from the palace of the Sun King, the chancellor moved swiftly to incorporate them all under Prussian rule and form a new empire. In order to achieve this goal, however, Bavarian power and prestige first had to be undermined; with this objective, Bismarck invited representatives of Baden, Hesse, and Württemberg to Versailles to open confederation negotiations. Ludwig desperately tried to intervene with the delegates from the southern german states, asking that they not make any concessions at the negotiations until they consulted with Bavaria; by preserving a unified front, he hoped to avoid any great Bavarian losses. Although none of these states wished to be incorporated, each felt that they had no choice and could not resist the military might of their Prussian neighbor. This left Bavaria alone. If she did not wish to find herself isolated—or worse, involved in a greater Germanic conflict—she had no alternative but to enter into the negotiations at Versailles.

Under this threat, the Bavarian government began deliberations on a formal alliance with Prussia. While they had supported the war effort by honoring the secret defense treaty, Bavaria felt less inclined to tie herself to the Hohenzollern dynasty at the end of the conflict. Prime Minister Bray presided over a cabinet meeting on 9 September to discuss the issue, and three days later, they voted to recommend that the king order formal negotiations with Prussia.

To this end, a delegate from Bismarck was dispatched to meet with Ludwig. The representative, Rudolf von Delbrück, the president of the North German Federal Chancellor's Office, had the unenviable and nearly impossible task of convincing Ludwig to enter into the negotiations over the fate of the German states at Versailles. This was no easy task, for it was obvious that the only possible outcome of these talks would be the loss of Bavarian sovereignty and autonomy within a new German Empire. Delbrück found the king less than receptive: At his first audience, Ludwig refused to discuss the matter. As soon as Delbrück left, Ludwig met with Mittnacht, the Württemberg envoy, and flatly declared, "Of course we shall not enter the North German Union."[1]

Ludwig had asked both Delbrück and Mittnacht to remain at Berg for dinner, but he then abruptly changed his mind and declared that he was unwell. As the two delegates sat dining with some aides-de-camp in a ground-floor room, however, they were startled to see the king ride by the open windows on horseback. By protocol, everyone had to rise and bow as he passed, and Ludwig seemed to delight in their discomfort, riding back and forth before the windows several times.[2]

The Versailles Conference opened on 20 October, but without any delegates from Bavaria; Ludwig began to play a careful waiting game. Prussian soldiers were engaged in a drawn-out battle at Metz, as well as encircling Paris, a preoccupation which allowed the king some room to manuever. As long as Bismarck's troops were thus committed, the chancellor could not afford to push Ludwig and risk the possible withdrawal of Bavarian soldiers from Orléans. But, when Metz fell, the balance of power once again shifted back to Bismarck, and the Bavarian position was visibly weakened.

Eventually the other German states, through fear, foresight, or intimidation, all lined up squarely behind Prussia. Even Ludwig realized that delay could prove fatal; with each passing day, his negotiating position was weakened. He therefore reluctantly sent a delegation, composed of Bray, von Pranckh, and Lutz, to participate in the conference. At Versailles, Bray proposed in the king's name that once the empire was declared the imperial crown of Germany should alternate jointly between the Hohenzollern and Wittelsbach dynasties. This idea, however, was clearly unacceptable to Bismarck, who had not fought for Prussian supremacy for many years only to share it with Bavaria. He was too crafty, however, to reject the idea outright; instead, he worked on his own series of proposals.

The most difficult question Bismarck faced was that of Ludwig II's position within the new Reich. Clearly, the king of Bavaria was loath to grant any reduction in his sovereign authority, but such a concession was necessary before the empire could be formed. King Wilhelm I of Prussia himself seemed unconcerned about such details, but his son, Crown Prince Friedrich, made no secret of his desire to humiliate Bavaria and his hated cousin. According to Bismarck, "The Crown Prince is as stupid and vain as anybody else. All this Emperor Madness has gone to his head again."[3] The chancellor, however, would not tolerate this petty revenge and helped to win for Ludwig a position second only to that of the new emperor.

Under Bismarck's direction, Bavaria received a series of guarantees which, if not actually assuring the autonomy of the country, certainly gave the impression of more independence than any other German state would enjoy in the newly created German Empire. Bismarck was willing to grant Bavaria the same status as a partner in the confederation of the Second Reich alongside Prussia: the Bavarian army would remain independent from the imperial army except in times of war, when it would fall under Prussian control. Money for military matters had to be approved by the Reichstag in Berlin, but Bavaria could spend the grant in any way she thought fit. Bavaria would be allowed to keep her own railway and postal systems, and to set up independent diplomatic missions and embassies. Finally, in the unlikely event of the extinction of the eligible male line of the house of Hohenzollern, the Wittelsbachs would then be entitled to assume the imperial crown. On 23 November, on behalf of the Bavarian government, Bray signed this agreement with Bismarck. "This is the beginning of the new Germany and, if our plans are approved, the end of the old Bavaria," Bray wrote to his wife. "It would be useless to deceive oneself about this."[4]

The chancellor had one more goal: To help legitimize the new empire under the Prussian crown, Bismarck wanted Ludwig, as the reigning head of the next largest German state, to offer King Wilhelm I the imperial title. There was a good deal of arguement over the arrangement, and it took some time before the title of emperor or kaiser could be agreed upon. Wilhelm I had declared that he would assume no title greater than that of king, and expressed the wish that he simply be crowned king of Germany. This, however, created immense problems. If Wilhelm was proclaimed king of Germany, this then precluded the use of the title by any of the other monarchs in the new Reich. In other words, Ludwig II's status, as well as that of the kings of Saxony and Württemberg, would have to be constitutionally reduced to that of a mere duke, and all other ranks in the German peerage likewise downgraded accordingly. Eventually, Wilhelm I agreed to accept the title of emperor, but only if it was offered to him not by a parliament but by royal assent.

The very idea of his hated Prussian uncle assuming the title emperor of Germany was abhorrent to Ludwig. Bismarck, however, repeatedly offered the king invitations to come to Versailles. Delbrück is reported to have said, "Let us give him one of the famous historical suites, possibly the bedroom of Louis XIV, and he will be so enraptured that he won't notice the absence of all normal conveniences," and the crown prince noted in his diary that the Trianon was being put in readiness for the king's arrival.[5] But Ludwig could not be bought off so easily. He wrote to Dürflipp: "His Majesty is more and more convinced that it will be impossible for Him to undertake the planned journey to France. His Majesty therefore thinks that it is necessary to pretend an illness such as a sprain; will *Herr* Dürflipp please let this be known to the general public and to the Army?"[6]

Instead, Ludwig first dispatched his brother, Prince Otto, to Versailles. Otto was on his journey to France when Ludwig, overcome with humiliation at his position, once again decided to abandon his crown: He would abdicate in favor of his brother. But Ludwig's hopes were soon dashed. At Versailles, Otto began to show the first serious signs of an unmistakable illness; he rarely spoke at the meetings but instead sat shivering, staring vacantly into space. Reports of his brother's decline reached Ludwig, and he bowed to fate: He had no choice but to continue his reign.

Still, Ludwig recognized that some effort would have to be made toward the negotiations at Versailles. His government, of course, was already represented at the conference by Bray, Pranckh, and Lutz, but he decided that his interests should be represented in a more personal manner. Rather than undertake the journey himself, he sent Count Maximilian von Holnstein, his Oberstallmeister, the master of the royal horse. Contrary to his title, Holnstein held a position of great importance and respect at Ludwig II's court. The post of Oberstallmeister was more in the nature of that of the lord chamberlain at the Court of St. James's, and Holnstein had been a man of great influence in Ludwig's household for some years. Ludwig knew him to be unscrupulous and hungry for power, but there was no one else whom he trusted to send to Versailles.

Holnstein was an enigmatic man; thought to be the illegitimate son of a royal duke, he married a granddaughter of Ludwig II's uncle, Prince Karl. He was also related by marriage to the family of Duke Max in Bavaria. His ambition and questionable honor were well-known. The Prussian ambassador in Munich, Prince Philip Eulenburg, described him as "a political adventurer in the manner of the eighteenth century who is dissatisfied with the orderly conditions of modern government. . . . He comes from a family that abounds with adventurers. Suicides, duels, abductions, etc., are their routine."[7] And one of the king's biographers declared that he was "a man of true Bavarian type and manners, powerful and intelligent enough to accomplish just about anything he wanted."[8]

Holnstein arrived at Versailles on 25 November. As soon as possible he met Bismarck, who immediately seized upon the man's pliable loyalty and convinced him that it was in the best interest of Germany if Ludwig could be induced to offer the crown and imperial title to the Hohenzollern king. It was, in fact, Holnstein who first suggested to Bismarck that he draft a letter which he wanted Ludwig to write to the king of Prussia offering him the imperial crown. Accordingly, Bismarck wrote the first letter, the famous Kaiserbrief as it was later to be known, which was to serve as a guide for Ludwig. Along with it, the chancellor dispatched a second, personal letter to the Bavarian king, in which he emphasized the importance of a German emperor and the role which the Wittelsbach dynasty had always played at great and decisive moments throughout centuries of German history. Holnstein also received assurances of a great financial reward for both himself and for the king in the event that the offer to Wilhelm I was made and that the treaties were concluded.

After this meeting, Holnstein hurried back to Bavaria to present these requests to the king in person. He went straight to Hohenschwangau, where Ludwig was in residence, but was at first refused admittance and then left to wait in an anteroom from ten in the morning until four in the afternoon. At last, he declared that he had made arrangements to return to Versailles at six and that he must therefore see the king at once. An aide conveyed this message to Ludwig, who reluctantly relented.

Holnstein found Ludwig propped up in his bed on a mountain of pillows, an enormous bandage tied around his head and mouth. He told Holnstein that he had a terrible toothache, and the entire bedroom smelled of chloroform. Holnstein handed over both of Bismarck's letters and waited while the king read through them carefully. Ludwig at first declared that he could not possibly sign the document; then, after listening to Holnstein's pleadings, he finally agreed. He rose and went to his desk to copy out the draft in his own hand but declared that he could not find any suitable paper and that the letter would therefore have to wait. Not to be put off by this delaying tactic, Holnstein rang for a servant and directed him to find the correct writing paper for the king. Once it was delivered, Ludwig could not continue to stall, and he duly copied out the Kaiserbrief, inviting his hated Prussian uncle to assume the imperial throne of Germany.

Most Serene Highness, High and Mighty Prince, Brother, Friend and Cousin!
After the entry of South Germany to the German Confederation, the presidial law ceded to Your Majesty stretches of land throughout the German Territories.

I have already declared Myself wholeheartedly to the Union, that through it, the combined interests of the German Fatherland and all the Princes are united in the belief that they will be true to the vested rights of the General Presidium, according to the formation of which Your Majesty works towards unified agreement between the Princes.

I have therefore turned to the German Princes with the suggestion that the Presidial Rights of the Union should be bound together under the leadership of one who holds the title of German Emperor. As soon as Your Majesty states His intention to all the Princes, I shall instruct My Government to carry through the further details of the attainment of the same in accordance with this.

With the assurance of deep respect and friendship, I remain Your Majesty's friendly Cousin, Brother and Nephew, Ludwig.[9]

At the same time, Ludwig wrote to Bismarck:

My letter to Your King, My loved and honoured Uncle, will reach His hand tomorrow. I wish with My whole heart, that the proposal I have set before the King may meet with the fullest response from the other members of the Federation to whom I have written, as well as of the nation. It is satisfactory to Me to be conscious that at the beginning of this glorious war, as at the conclusion, I was, in virtue of My Rank in Germany, in the position to make a decisive step in favour of the national cause. But I hope, and with much assurance, that Bavaria will in the future preserve her position, for it is surely consistent with a loyal, unreserved federal policy, and will be most safe to obviate a pernicious centralization.[10]

In acting to offer the imperial crown to his uncle, Ludwig, tortured though he was by the gesture, also saw himself in the role of his medieval ancestors, helping to form the shape and destiny of the new German empire. As naive a view as this was, it became his only consolation. In some way he managed to convince himself that it had been his divine mission to offer the title to the king of Prussia.

Ludwig had made his decision without the knowledge or consent of any of his government ministers, the most important of whom remained cloistered at Versailles. In an attempt to reassure himself, he asked Holnstein to consult his secretary, Eisenhart. Holnstein duly hurried to Munich, where he found the cabinet secretary attending a performance at the Residenztheatre. The count called him out of his box and handed him the Kaiserbrief, along with a note from Ludwig: "Should a differently composed letter be deemed better and more appropriate, should the sacrifices . . . asked of me be too great—all right, in that case, this thing is called off and I authorize you to tear up the letter to the King of Prussia."[11] Eisenhart, however, could find no fault with the king's proposal, nor could Lutz, the minister of justice, who was also consulted.

Holnstein arrived at Versailles and went straight to Bismarck with both of the king's letters. On 3 December, Prince Luitpold, on behalf of the delegation of Bavarian representatives, formally turned them over to Bismarck. Bismarck himself was overjoyed. "It was Holnstein who did most in this matter," he wrote. "He played his part very cleverly. . . . What Order can we give him?"[12] There was a sense of general amazement at his willingness to give in to Bismarck's request so easily. In his diary, the crown prince recorded, in obvious disbelief, "The King of Bavaria has really and truly written our King the letter suggested by Bismarck."[13] Bray, Ludwig's own prime minister, had not even been consulted on the matter, and Ruggenbach, the Baden delegate, said with obvious irony, "There was not likely to be another King of Bavaria who would offer the Imperial Crown to someone because he had a toothache."[14]

On 18 January 1871, Wilhelm I was proclaimed emperor of Germany in the Hall of Mirrors at Versailles. Ludwig refused to attend the glittering ceremony; instead, he sent his brother, Otto. He wrote: "Alas, Ludwig! I cannot describe to you how unhappy and wretched I felt during the ceremony, how every fibre of my being revolted at what I saw! Everything was so cold, so brilliant, so ostentatious and showy, so empty and unfeeling. I felt so oppressed, so stale in that great hall!"[15]

After the proclamation at Versailles, Ludwig wrote defensively to Baroness Leonrod: "It is in Bavaria's interests that I acted as I did. If I had not sacrificed for the Crown and the Country what I did we should have been forced before long to sacrifice much bigger and more important things. Moreover, it is clearly foreseeable that by then we could not have even pretended that we did it voluntarily, and that would injure our whole political future, and our position in the new Reich."[16] And scarcely a month later, he confided:

That this last war, which in many respects ended so gloriously for Bavaria, should have forced myself and my country into the iron clutches of that damned German Reich with its Prussian colouring—that just this unhappy war which is enthusiastically loved by so many of my people should have done it—is a most deplorable dispensation of Providence. The popularity which, thanks to the quickness of my resolution and my political sacrifices, I enjoy especially in Northern Germany does not at all make up for what I have lost.[17]

Paris eventually capitulated and the peace was signed at Frankfurt on 10 May. On 16 July, the victorious Bavarian army returned to Munich. Much as he hated the ceremony, Ludwig had to attend the review at the side of his cousin the crown prince of the new empire. At a large inspection at Nymphenburg Palace outside of Munich, Ludwig sat atop his horse in the hot sun, watching in silence as his hated Prussian cousin distributed Iron Crosses in the name of the new emperor. Eventually, this spectacle became too much, and Ludwig put spurs to his horse and galloped off the field in the middle of the review. In his diary, he confided that he found "the presence of the Crown Prince of Pr. *very* disturbing and disagreeable!"[18]

Ludwig had to await the arrival of his troops in the city itself. They were led, not by their Bavarian commanders, but by the crown prince himself, down the Ludwigstrasse to the Odeonplatz. "This is my first ride as a vassal," Ludwig commented bitterly to an aide-de-camp.[19] That night, there was a gala performance of Paul Johann Ludwig von Heyse's play *Peace*. The royal cousins walked to the front of their box together and embraced in a gesture designed to demonstrate the goodwill and strong ties uniting Bavaria and Prussia. But Ludwig, who could barely tolerate the presence of Friedrich Wilhelm and the political charade accompanying his visit, was in agony.

The next day, there was a family luncheon on the Roseninsel on Lake Starnberg which ended in a disastrous scene between the two cousins. Ludwig invited the crown prince to become honorary commander in chief of a regiment of Bavarian lancers. Instead of expressing gratitude at the gesture, Fritz declared that he would have to ask his father for permission, and, in any case, he did not like the cut of the lancer uniform and thought it would not suit his large frame. Ludwig was furious. He rose from the table and stormed out of the luncheon. He declared that he would not attend the great celebratory dinner that evening which was being held in the Glaspalast in Munich. Some nine hundred guests were expected, and it was generally regarded as the centerpiece of the entire victory ceremonies. No amount of pleading would convince him to change his mind. The king announced that he was too ill, but no one believed this news. Early the next morning, without saying farewell to either his family or his Prussian cousin, the king departed Munich for one of his remote hunting lodges, high in the lonely Bavarian Alps.

26

Bavaria in Turmoil

Wilhelm I's great acclamation as German emperor in the magnificent Hall of Mirrors at Versailles represented the height of Bismarck's triumph, but to Ludwig II, news of the momentuous event outside Paris signaled the end of his own sovereignty. The threat of war, the question of alliances, and the future position of Bavaria in the new Reich had been internal dilemmas for the king, demanding his full concentration in an effort to preserve Bavarian autonomy. But the end of the war did not bring Bavaria the peace Ludwig so desired, for chaos soon erupted in the Catholic Church. The increasing politicization of the Catholic Church and Bismarck's resulting *Kulturkampf*, helped set the scene for the coup which would overthrow the king of Bavaria fifteen years later.

In 1846, Pope Pius IX had acceded to the throne of St. Peter; he soon forgot his reputation as an enlightened and liberal leader amid the pomp and splendor of the Vatican. Pius issued a number of decrees which restricted personal freedom within the Catholic Church, and vehemently promoted the idea of a papal cult. His obsession with power and authority reached its despotic climax with his declaration of papal infallibility in 1870. The issue caused a good deal of worry to both Ludwig and his government. Hohenlohe, who opposed the consideration, wrote that "this goes far beyond the domain of purely religious questions, and has a highly political character, because the power of the Papacy over all princes and peoples, even those in schism with Rome, would thereby be defined in secular affairs and elevated into an article of faith."[1]

Ludwig consulted a number of senior church officials on the question of infallibility; all expressed great fear for Bavarian sovereignty if the issue was approved. Previous papal pronouncements on matters of faith and morals, they warned, would automatically become dogma for the church.

Until this time, the Bavarian government had largely managed to steer a moderate course, working with coalitions to form responsible ministries; now, however, the question of papal infallability became a political issue, slowly seeping its way into the inner workings of the Bavarian Landtag and dividing the faithful into disjointed factions. The May 1869 general election had ended the primacy of liberal power in Bavaria, and in its place, came the new Patriots' Party: an ultraconservative Catholic group composed chiefly of ambitious Jesuits and other clerics. Like the king, the Patriot's Party opposed closer ties with Prussia, but they had campaigned and come to power largely on the strength of their opposition to an education reform bill, supported by both Ludwig and Hohenlohe. Their solid, unquestioned support of the Catholic Church flew violently in the face of everything which Ludwig believed, and he could never support any political party which expressed itself in terms of claiming to have a legitimate parliamentary right to exist.

Hoping to turn one of the king's rare public appearances into a visible display of royal support, Hohenlohe requested that he personally open the new legislative session of the Landtag in autumn of 1869. Ludwig reluctantly agreed, though he was filled with dread at the thought of hundreds of staring eyes during the ceremony. However, as things transpired, he was not called upon to perform before the public. The legislature failed to produce a working majority, and on 6 October 1869, Ludwig dissolved the lower chamber on Hohenlohe's advice. The liberals in the government were delighted, but the Patriot's Party immediately protested and attempted unsuccessfully to call a no-confidence vote against the prime minister.

The Patriot's Party had their revenge only weeks later. In the fall elections, they won eighty seats in the Landtag, compared to sixty-three for the Progressive Party and eleven independents. When Hohenlohe learned of this humiliating defeat, he immediately offered his resignation, but Ludwig refused to accept it. Hohenlohe's detractors now outnumbered his supporters; the upper house of the Landtag introduced a resolution calling for a vote of no confidence in his government. In an effort to save his prime minister, the king asked members of the Wittelsbach family who held seats in the chamber to refrain from casting their ballots. But, contrary to the king's wishes, they almost all voted in favor of the resolution; it was clear that Hohenlohe would have to go.

Hohenlohe resigned his post as prime minister on 8 March 1870 and was replaced with Count Otto von Bray-Steinburg, who had served as Bavarian ambassador to Vienna. Bray inherited all of the problems Hohenlohe had left, including the Catholic schism and the continuing crisis over closer ties with Prussia. Hohenlohe's departure marked the beginning of a tumultuous period in Bavarian politics whose instability would eventually reach to the throne itself.

The doctrine of papal infallability was successfully proclaimed dogma on 18 July 1870, barely passing on a second vote. Dissenting bishops angrily stormed out of the Vatican, and a new schism between those who supported the declaration and those who did not—now to be known as the Old Catholics—erupted. The king's former religious tutor, theologian Ignaz von Döllinger, had violently opposed the declaration and was excommunicated for his public stance. Ludwig tried until the very end to intercede on his behalf with the church; even after Döllinger's excommunication the king repeatedly urged him to continue in his priestly functions, in open defiance of Rome.

On 9 August 1870, Johann von Lutz, minister of justice and culture, forbade Catholic bishops to announce the new dogma of papal infallability without special royal permission. The bishops ignored the order, and Lutz, in return, immediately granted the Old Catholics legal status as an independent church in Bavaria, thus sanctioning the schismatics as an officially recognized faith. The Jesuits in the Landtag protested and intrigued for the king's abdication; but Ludwig, who never responded well to threats against his authority, simply retaliated by ordering all Jesuits expelled from the kingdom.

The anarchy rent the government asunder. Within the space of five short years, Ludwig II had six prime ministers: Hohenlohe was succeeded by Bray, who in turn was followed by Count Friedrich von Hegenberg-Dux, Baron Rudolf von Gesser, Baron Adolf von Pfretzschner, and Baron von und zu Franckenstein. It soon became apparent that the king would never be able to form a government to his liking. His disgust with the political situation led to his pronounced and permanent withdrawal from affairs of state. He had tried, naively, to shape Bavarian politics to reflect his own inclinations; having failed, he bowed to the will of the politicians and absented himself from all but the most necessary of political functions.

While the top post in the Bavarian government frequently changed hands in the 1870s, one politician remained dominant. This was Johann von Lutz, who held several important positions in the government, including under-cabinet secretary and minister of justice. Between 1875 and 1880, Lutz had worked behind the scenes as a powerful liberal protégé, shaping Bavarian policy. As an acknowledgment of this influence and authority, Ludwig finally appointed him prime minister in 1880.

Lutz was born in 1826, the son of a Franconian schoolmaster. From these humble beginnings, he rose through the ranks of the Bavarian government, aided by his undeniable skill as a lawyer. Lutz scarcely looked the part of the most important politician in Bavaria: Short, and balding, his round face framed by gold-rimmed glasses, Lutz bore a striking likeness to the caricatures of bureaucrats which filled the cartoons of the satirical magazine *Punsch*. But this uninspiring appearance masked a brilliant if somewhat ruthless mind and consuming ambition. In this, Lutz closely resembled Bismarck, whom he greatly admired: Both men were intelligent politicians dedicated to the promotion of reactionary agendas. Indeed, Lutz's crucial role in the negotiations over the Kaiserbrief helped secure his position among the liberal elements of the Bavarian government, who continued their support once he assumed the office of prime minister.

Bismarck apparently thought little of Lutz, even though he became one of the most ardent supporters of the chancellor's *Kulturkampf*. While Ludwig II himself opposed this reactionary policy, he recognized that Lutz was the only man in his government capable of drawing together both the liberals and the conservatives to form a working majority. Much more important to Ludwig, Lutz knew how to deal with the king. Very early on, he realized that the king's only concern in the political arena was that he be left alone.

By 1880, the king had almost completely isolated himself from the day-to-day workings of the government, leaving affairs of state to the various cabinet heads. He had come to the throne preoccupied with his own sovereign authority, filled with vague notions of royal power. Yet over and over again, his illusions had been shattered: The Schleswig-Holstein crisis had escaped his control, erupting in a German war, his sovereignty had been threatened with enforced alliances and treaties, his friendship with Wagner had been sacrificed on the altar of public opinion, his imperial aspirations had resulted in the promotion not of his own family but of his hated Hohenzollern cousins, and he had repeatedly seen his efforts to influence the character of the Bavarian government end in failure. By the time of Lutz's promotion to prime minister, Ludwig had no wish to involve himself in the political life of his country. He ignored affairs of state, leaving such concerns to the bureaucrats who peopled the offices along the Maximilianstrasse.

Lutz, himself hungry for power and filled with personal ambition, seized upon the king's hatred of politics as an excuse to isolate Ludwig II from important decisions. This became the hallmark of the Lutz regime, which remained in power in Bavaria even after the king's death. The king appointed Lutz on the strength of the coalition which he promised to deliver; yet in six years it was Johann von Lutz, proud, arrogant, and ambitious, who would topple Ludwig II from the Bavarian throne. Once positioned, the new prime minister, well aware of the king's difficult attitude regarding governmental cooperation and the execution of his duties, simply left Ludwig to his own devices. The Bavarian government, a constitutional monarchy which required the active participation of the sovereign, became a dictatorship under the prime minister. Government decisions which ordinarily would have required royal assent were, as a matter of course, undertaken without the king's knowledge. This circumvention of his sovereign rights suited the king perfectly. Only too late would he realize that his failure to insist on his rights paved the way for his eventual downfall.

27

Twilight

In 1874, Ludwig marked his tenth anniversary on the Bavarian throne. The decade had not been kind to him. Although he was only twenty-nine years old, he looked much older; instead of the youthful Adonis who had captivated Munich at his father's funeral, the king was now a bloated giant, weighing nearly two hundred and fifty pounds. The finely chiseled lines of his face had disappeared behind a dark imperial, and he frequently bore a strange, almost maniacal look. Several of his teeth had already fallen out, a result of the king's penchant for sweets, and hours of reading by candlelight had left his eyesight failing; in consequence, he suffered from repeated and violent headaches. His entire bearing, too, had changed: He no longer moved with the grace of a young man but walked in an almost studied and theatrical manner, sweeping his arms across his path, nodding his head from left to right, throwing each leg out in front of him with a jerk and bringing his foot down with great force, "as though with each step he was trying to crush a scorpion."[1]

Gossip about the king was rampant. In 1871, Count Maximilian Holnstein wrote to Bismarck: "He drinks before every audience and court ceremony large quantities of the strongest wines, and then says the most extraordinary things."[2] Holnstein's report was true enough, for Ludwig had become increasingly dependent on the soothing effects of alcohol. His favorite drink was a somewhat lethal combination of Rhine wine and champagne, mixed together in a silver bowl with flower petals floated on top.[3] He could drink this in considerable quantities, though he rarely appears to have been drunk as a result.

Ludwig found the world around him increasingly cold and unfriendly. The wars, political struggles, and personal demons had torn at his soul. He felt himself a victim, not only of the grim circumstances sweeping across Bavaria but of his own homosexual desires and physical disintegration. After the end of the Franco-Prussian War, photographs of the king became rare. Vain and so conscious of beauty in those around him, Ludwig found his deterioration hard to bear. To escape the harsh, revealing light of day, he closeted himself in his gilded rooms; increasingly, he saw the world only in the rarefied light from hundreds of flickering candles, in the glow from the Munich stage, and in the soft moonlight which accompanied him on his nocturnal rides through the Alps.

In the last decade of his life, Ludwig virtually abandoned day for night. As the doors in the government chancelleries closed in Munich and hundreds of clerks filtered out into the descending night, Bavaria's king rose from his bed to begin his day. He rarely woke before six in the evening; wrapping himself in a silk dressing gown, he rang for a servant who appeared with a cup of strong black coffee. By the time Ludwig had finished, his bathtub had been filled and its top sprinkled with perfume, and he sank himself into its warm, scented waters. When he was done, a servant armed with a silver pitcher rinsed him first with warm then with cold water while Lorenz Mayr, his valet, helped him into his dressing gown again. After bathing, Ludwig covered himself in his favorite scents, selected from an extensive collection of crystal bottles lined up on his dressing table, while Hoppe, his barber, arranged his hair. On most days, Mayr selected simple trousers, shirt, waistcoat, and jacket; Ludwig never wore a military uniform in his later years unless it was absolutely necessary. He rarely ate a large breakfast, preferring just coffee and butter croissants before he began his night in earnest.[4]

Ludwig's nights were banal; most of his time was spent reading his favorite classics and French literature, and studying plans and schemes for his architectural projects. Only occasionally did he open the dispatches from Munich, allowing state papers to pile up until the burden became so great that he was forced to spend hours at his desk. He was a diligent correspondent, writing volumes of letters to his royal cousins, aunts, and uncles. After lunch, which Ludwig had at midnight, he left the warmth of his castles to walk or ride in the night air. In the summer, he used open landaus or phaetons; in the winter, elaborately carved and gilded sleighs decorated with cherubs.

In the early hours, the king's carriages or sleighs sped through the Bavarian Alps, his outriders attired as footmen from the court of Louis XIV. Through fog and mist, rain and snow, Ludwig flew through the dark forests, safely huddled beneath a thick, fur rug and wrapped in a heavy coat, the carriage lanterns flickering and sleigh bells ringing out into the frosty air. When the pounding gusts of snow proved too much for the indefatigable king, he sought refuge among the isolated farms and remote villages scattered across the lonely mountains, the clanging bells and shouts of the grooms waking the inhabitants from their peaceful sleep. Opening their doors, they saw before them a magical, unreal scene: white horses, their breath steaming in the cold air, ostrich plumes waving as they bobbed their heads; grooms in velvet knee breeches, tricorn hats, and powdered wigs illuminated by the flickering shadows from the glowing lanterns; and their mysterious, rarely seen king climbing out of a gilded fantasy of rococo cherubs and humbly asking for a few hours' shelter until the weather permitted him to return home, to retire as the sun rose over his kingdom.

While Ludwig the king became a distant figure to the people of Munich, these peasants in the Alps were delighted: The fairy-tale appearance, the splendid carriages, the riders in elaborate costume, the king with his diamond brooches, fitted perfectly the peasants' conceptions of what a king should be. To them, he became all the more real the further he retreated into his fantasy world. In the evenings, he would often stop at village fairs or festivals, greeting his smiling subjects and moving about them with an ease which he could never display at the Munich court. He knew many of the farmers in the Allgau region by name and sent inquiries after the state of their crops, sometimes personally stopping by to discuss the harvest. He always left something of himself behind when he made these visits, a tangible reminder of his royal presence: small jeweled pins or watches, elegant and refined pieces, and certainly of no use to these practical farmers. Yet these common people loved Ludwig all the more for this contradiction; the king who could not bear to mix with his subjects at court mingled freely with them in the country, showering them with precious trinkets and happily playing with their children.

In his lonely, self-imposed isolation, Ludwig frequently sought the company of his cousin Empress Elizabeth either at Possenhofen or at some remote lodge in the Alps. Together, they rode through the dark forests or stood on the deck of his steamer *Tristan* as it cruised across the smooth, moonlit waters of Lake Starnberg, reciting poetry and reading Schiller or Shakespeare to each other. One of the empress's ladies-in-waiting recorded the details of such a meeting:

> Quickly he replaced the cap, which rode precariously atop the beautiful, wavy hair. . . . He was wearing Austrian uniform and sported aslant across his breast the ribbon of the Great Cross of the Order of St. Stephen and over it, going in the opposite direction, the field ribbon. He alighted from the carriage—a handsome man with the mannerisms of a strange king or like Lohengrin in the wedding processions. . . . [He] had wonderful dark eyes which quickly changed expressions; dreamily soft, then again, like lightning, a flash of spiteful amusement—and to say it all—the glowing, sparkling eyes grow cold, and a

glance, a glow more like cruelty flashes in them. Then again, he looks melancholy and gentle.[5]

The close family ties with Elizabeth and her family helped in part to compensate Ludwig for his strained relations with his own mother and brother. In time, he became greatly attached to Elizabeth's son, Crown Prince Rudolf, a sensitive, high-strung young man disillusioned with his life and position. He admired Ludwig's determined efforts to create for himself a world of escape, a continuous stage play in which he was the only principal actor.

On nights when he did not venture into the Alps, Ludwig immersed himself in the study of French history and culture. He often ordered his cabinet secretary, Friedrich Ziegler, to find the books for him. The secretary's son-in-law later recalled:

> King Ludwig read . . . a great deal and on all manner of subjects. All of this reading material had to be obtained by Ziegler, whether it had to do with medieval or modern German literature or with long forgotten French works. The main requirement was for books of the seventeenth and eighteenth centuries with the time of Louis XIV and XV. As the King did not want to read everything himself, Ziegler was required to give detailed expositions of these works and to make extracts. . . . All the French Louis: the Fourteenth, the Fifteenth and Sixteenth, their wives and mistresses, the Dauphine, the Prince de Conde, the Duc de Berry, the Comtess D'Artois and Provence, were woken out of their sleep. The whole glittering court life of the period at Versailles and Fountainbleau was conjured up—the *fêtes gallantes*, cavalcades, tournaments, jousting, high masses, parades, illuminations, fireworks, concerts, allegories and pastoral picnics. Then the theatre: the thousand tragedies and comedies both lyrical and heroical, the divertissements, heroic ballet, fairy-heroic comedies, pantomine ballets, dramatized proverbs, tragi-pantomine ballets and pastorals. Not merely the name and title of these works, but also the plot and full contents, had to be discussed in detail. . . . He alone could not manage this task. His wife sprang to his aid and made extract after extract. Even just the titles of these countless works filled whole volumes.[6]

So intense was this passion for the ancien régime that Ludwig began to order performances of some of these dramatic works for his private consumption. These private performances, known as the Separatvorstellungen, began in 1872 and continued until 1885. There were

209 of these performances, 47 of which took place in the Residenztheatre and 162 in the larger court theater. There were 154 dramatic works, 44 operas and 11 ballets which were performed for the king's pleasure.[7] The majority of the dramatic works were plays which dealt with the lives of the French kings: *A Minister Under Louis XIV*, *The Boyhood of Louis XV*, and *Madame Dubarry* were some that Ludwig particularly enjoyed. Once, Düfflipp, after looking over a schedule of the performances, commented to the king, "I cannot understand how Your Majesty can enjoy such stuff!" But, instead of expressing annoyance, Ludwig merely smiled and answered, "I also think the play is bad—but still, it breathes the odor of Versailles!"[8]

But the private performances were not tasteless indulgences on the part of the king. In addition to the minor French works, Ludwig also had major works by Schiller, Shakespeare, Victor-Marie Hugo, and Henrik Ibsen staged. These performances kept members of the Munich Theater busy for months, with new set designs, costumes, scenery, and musical scores. Ludwig always paid for the costs of these performances, but the dividends remained the property of the Munich Theater, to be utilized again and again in their public works.

In time, world of these private performances spread, and they were regarded as another sign of the king's mental instability. But Ludwig had always disliked being on public display when at the theater, and at these private performances, he could concentrate on the stage without the nagging thought that he himself was being stared at. "I go to look myself," he once declared, "not to provide a spectacle for others."[9]

28

The Government Disintegrates

By the beginning of the 1880s, Ludwig's peculiar lifestyle and his overwhelming desire for seclusion had begun to seriously disturb the efficient running of the government. At any given time, no one could say with certainty precisely where in the mountains he might be found. Ludwig's distaste for government business led him to ignore important documents until the dispatches reached into the hundreds of pages; by putting off what he might reasonably have dealt with in an hour, he made his duty far worse, ensuring that when he did sit down to business it would take an entire day to read through the papers. Weeks passed before he could bring himself to attend to official business or meet with any member of the government. Eventually, he solved this problem by combining his Alpine excursions with government audiences. A member of the cabinet might find himself summoned to some remote mountain lodge at any time of the day or night in order to conduct official business. Louise von Kobell, wife of Cabinet Secretary August von Eisenhart, described one such meeting at Altach near the Walchensee.

> The ranger . . . had brought a table and chairs out on to the meadow, spread a red woollen cloth over the table and on it placed an enormous bunch of flowers, and banished the daschunds to the kennels. . . . The King and his equipage arrived, then Eisenhart with his portfolio, and the session took place in the open. The setting was unconventional. Further off on the meadow the grooms had encamped and drawn up the vehicles in a row. The King, wearing traveling clothes and a glengarry, seated himself at the table. Behind him, stiff as ramrods, stood two lackeys, while in front of him, standing also, was the head of the Cabinet in a black morning coat, his opera hat under his arm, loudly declaiming the proposals and suggestions of the various ministers. Now and then there intruded the

sound of a cow bell or the barking of a dog, angry at being shut up. As soon as the King had come to his last decision and signed the documents, he politely took his leave of his secretary and made a sign, whereupon as if by magic the whole company vanished.[1]

It was Ludwig's great misfortune that he had no close friends, no circle of intimates from which to draw support; the most constant and influential of his companions was Richard Hornig, who held the position of chief horsemaster. Hornig was born in Mecklenburg in 1840, the son of an official who served as chief horsemaster to Maximilian II. Although he has often been painted as a lower-class, glorified stableboy, Hornig was landed gentry, had attended private schools, and had been commissioned as an artillery officer in the Bavarian army. His manner was polished and elegant, and he impressed those around him with his unassuming character and intelligence.

Ludwig and Hornig first met in May of 1867, when the king was twenty-one. Ludwig was immediately attracted to the tall, blond-haired and blue-eyed Hornig, and after some discreet inquiries, asked the young man to join the royal household; in time, Hornig became chief horsemaster, a position roughly equivalent to that of crown equerry at the Court of St. James's. On the king's midnight drives, Hornig followed the gilded carriages and sleighs on horseback, dismounting frequently to adjust the king's lap rug or peel an orange for him; as a result, Hornig often suffered frostbite and throat inflammations. Only in 1878 did he finally receive permission to follow Ludwig in a carriage of his own. Their tumultuous relationship, often the subject of malicious innuendo and gossip, finally came to an end in 1886, a few months before Ludwig's death.

The chaos surrounding the Bavarian government had begun to creep into the king's personal household. In 1876 Ludwig dismissed August von Eisenhart as his cabinet secretary. Eisenhart's downfall was abrupt: One day Ludwig simply decided that he would change his cabinet secretary without informing the current officeholder. Eisenhart only learned of his fall when he went to Castle Berg to accompany the king and found that no carriage had been prepared for his use. Düfflipp later tried to influence the king to change his mind, but all Ludwig would say was "Leave me alone! I can't think how I put up with that idiotic face for so long!"[2]

Eisenhart's replacement, Friedrich Ziegler, became the only official to see Ludwig on a regular basis. To facilitate the competent running of the Bavarian government, the six chief ministers all had to seek out audiences with Ziegler, who then acted as intermediary; they made their Cabinet reports to him, and he then submitted this information to the king. Thus, Ziegler was the most powerful man in the kingdom. It was he who decided what the king should see, where his attention should be directed. Ziegler's comments, cleverly stated, could influence the king's decisions. His position was unconstitutional, as Richard Wagner had repeatedly tried to point out to the king with Pfistermeister, yet Ludwig had no desire to remove an official whose very presence eased the burdens of the throne. Nor did the prime minister protest, even though he had been deprived of his constitutional right to consult with the king. When Lutz became prime minister in 1880, this method utterly suited his own ends, as it removed the king from all real decisions undertaken by the cabinet.

Even though he enjoyed his position as an authority, Ziegler took second place to Hornig. Ludwig's regular orders were frequently channeled through Hornig, a slight made all the more humiliating for Ziegler by the very nature of his wishes. For instance, Hornig wrote to Ziegler: "Dear Friend, Owing to shortness of time, it was impossible to send you the enclosed directions with the first lot, so I am forwarding them now." What followed were twenty-four routine errands of absolutely no importance, among them, to write to certain newspapers, reprimanding them "for not printing the pronouns He and His with a capital letter when referring to His Majesty," to "express His Majesty's thanks" to a number of ladies who had written him, and to write to Kaiser Wilhelm I for "not having sent congratulations on the anniversary of the King's Birthday; the Emperor is to be informed," Ziegler was told, "that His Majesty was unpleasantly surprised."[3]

Despite Ludwig's occasional tendency to burden his cabinet secretary with such unimportant tasks, he genuinely liked Ziegler. The new cabinet secretary was a poet and painter in his spare time, and relations between the two men were warm and friendly on a personal level. In his privileged position, the cabinet secretary was able to witness the king's increasingly peculiar behavior. For example, Ludwig once angrily denounced Ziegler for using the words "already mentioned" in a government report. To a king, Ludwig declared, things were never "mentioned" but rather "announced." "Mentioned" was a "reprehensible" word, and Ziegler was forbidden to use it again on threat of dismissal.[4] More disturbing, he seemed to enjoy playing elaborate and ominous games with his cabinet secretary. Once, as the cabinet secretary stood reading aloud from a government report, the king grabbed a small silver revolver from his desk and pointed it directly at Ziegler's head. The cabinet secretary, not surprisingly, stopped reading, shocked and fearing for his life. Ludwig remained silent but waved the gun in the air as a signal for Ziegler to continue his report; nervously, the cabinet secretary turned his eyes back to the pages before him. As soon as he did so, the king again took aim at his head. This continued, with the king aiming and then waving the gun about in the air, for the remainder of the report. Finally, apparently frustrated at his attempts to unnerve Ziegler, Ludwig put the revolver down, saying, "Amazing the sort of things they make nowadays. See how convincingly this has been made to look like a revolver, and it is only a thermometer."[5]

Word of such incidents soon spread through the court and government, eventually giving the king's growing number of enemies ample ammunition to question his sanity. The episode with Ziegler seems more indicative of Ludwig's rather bizarre sense of humor than anything else, a trait he shared with his cousin Empress Elizabeth. Like the empress, Ludwig enjoyed such situations, amusing himself by tormenting those around him. He often said the most indiscreet or scandalous things simply to watch the horrified faces as his courtiers reacted, but no one knew him well enough to understand that this behavior was, in and of itself, innocent enough. Ziegler himself found this level of stress, which remained fairly constant during his term of office, too much, and on 6 September 1879, he resigned his post as cabinet secretary. In May of 1880, Ludwig asked him to take up the position again, emphasizing his personal fondness for him. Ziegler reluctantly agreed, but after three years, he finally left the king's employ, physically worn out and suffering from nervous exhaustion.

Ziegler was only one of a growing number of men in the king's household who were replaced or simply quit during the last half of his reign. In 1877, Court Secretary Düfflipp resigned over a financial disagreement with Ludwig and was replaced with Ludwig von Burkel; Burkel held the post for five years before he was replaced with Philipp Pfister, himself soon supplanted by Hermann Gresser. This game of musical chairs in the king's household, which accelerated in the last years of his reign, reflected not only the strain of working for the demanding and impetuous monarch but also the chaotic state of affairs surrounding the government.

In 1883, Count Maximilian von Holnstein finally fell from power. In his powerful position, Holnstein was exposed to all of the gossip circulating about the king, and this knowledge allowed him to retain his authority. He knew of Ludwig's relationships with various stableboys, grooms, and soldiers, and given Holnstein's duplicitous character, he may have used this damaging material to blackmail the king. His continued presence at the Bavarian court, along with the secret payments from Bismarck over the signing of the Kaiserbrief, raise the possibility that he may have acted as a Prussian spy. On leaving his post in the king's household, Holnstein was discreetly placed on Bismarck's payroll, even though he remained in Munich. It would have been incomprehensible had the Iron Chancellor not utilized Holnstein's intimate position and contacts at the Wittelsbach court. Holnstein maintained a trusted network of spies who worked as members of Ludwig's personal staff, and later relied upon these intimates to help collect the evidence which would eventually be used to declare the king insane.

There was one man in this group of retainers who stood above all others in his loyalty and devotion to the king: Count Alfred Dürckheim-Montmartin. Ludwig first met the twenty-five-year-old Dürckheim in the fall of 1874. Dürckheim was a tall, handsome man, intelligent and appropriately humble to suit the king's tastes; he had previously served as a personal adjutant to Ludwig's cousin Prince Arnulf. Ludwig eventually appointed Dürckheim as a personal aide-de-camp. He remained in this post, at the side of the king, until the very end. He was the only member of the king's household to witness Ludwig's last days at Neuschwanstein and undoubtedly would have accompanied his master on the fateful journey to Berg had he not been forced, under threat of court martial, to abandon his post and return to Munich.

Ludwig admired Dürckheim's reverential character and quiet manner and showered him with personal letters and small gifts. Overwhelmed at this royal attention, Dürckheim wrote:

> I have just received Your Majesty's most gracious letter and the wonderful album of Linderhof which will be a precious souvenir for all time of those days which live in my soul like a fairy dream. . . . Every pulsation of my heart belongs to the Monarchial principle which for me is embodied in the Person of Your Majesty. I am always prepared to shed the last drop of my blood for the triumph of Kingship and the Person of the Sovereign.[6]

Two years later, in 1876, Ludwig appointed Dürckheim a chamberlain of the royal court. The young man responded: "As I stood before Your Majesty I felt a magic power over me, and all the excitement of the last two days, all the worries and troubles which had made my loyal soul restless—all vanished in the magic moment when I saw Your Majesty."[7] Ludwig clearly cherished such sentiments, and he came to regard Dürckheim as an invaluable member of his court. His reward finally came on 30 March 1883, when Ludwig appointed him as his personal aide-de-camp.

By the beginning of the 1880s, Ludwig's dissatisfaction with his life led him to ponder abdication once again. In 1880 the house of Wittelsbach celebrated seven hundred years of rule, but no amount of pleading would convince the king to appear at the festivities. Burkel tried to influence Ludwig, telling him that it was his duty and responsibility to attend and represent his family.

> Naturally he refused. I pressed it on him, and said how much his
> people loved him and with what rejoicing he would be greeted
> in Munich after all this time. "I cannot," he replied, rubbing his
> forehead. "It is frightful, but I can no longer bear to be stared at
> by thousands of people, to smile and to extend greetings a thou
> sand times, to ask questions of people who mean nothing to me
> and to listen to answers that do not interest me. No, no! There is
> no longer any escape from my solitude." Then, softly and sadly,
> he added to me in a whisper, "Sometimes, when I have read
> myself to exhaustion and everything is quiet, I have an irre
> sistible urge to hear a human voice. Then I call one of the domes
> tic servants or postillions and ask him to tell me about his home
> and his family." And, with a sadness which tore at my heart, he
> concluded: "Otherwise I would completely forget the art of
> speech." There was no other explanation; a terrible demon in him
> held him back from returning to the world; he wrestled with this
> dark power and was overcome by it.[8]

Ludwig had clearly lost interest in his kingly duties; the idea of noblesse oblige had, for him at least, died a long time before—in the unpopularity of his friendship with Wagner, in the devious workings and manipulations of his government ministers, in the wars which had stolen his sovereign authority, and in the half-empty, shadow-filled halls of his castles. He no longer seemed to care if he exercised his sovereign powers, and by continuing to act in such a manner, he did much harm to both himself and to the prestige of the throne.

Ludwig grew so disillusioned that he eventually dispatched an official from his court to search the world for a new kingdom. In March of 1873, Franz von Loher, director of the State Archives, was sent with these instructions on a voyage around the world: Ludwig wanted a strip of land upon which he could impose his idea of kingship, where he could be autocratic master, unhampered by the confines of a parliament or alliances. This trip took Loher to the Canary Islands, northern Africa, and the Greek and Turkish islands. The first trip ended without result, and two years later, Loher was again dispatched in search of a new kingdom, this time to Cyprus and Crete. Other locations were considered, including South America, the Pacific islands, and Scandinavia, but none was deemed suitable, and Ludwig eventually gave up on the idea.[9]

29

The Triumph of Bayreuth

Some sixty miles to the north of Nuremberg, in the northern-most part of Bavaria, stood the town of Bayreuth. Until 1822, it had been Prussian. In the eighteenth century, it was the residence of the Margrave Friedrich, whose wife, Wilhelmina, was a sister of Friedrich the Great; the Margraves of Brandenburg-Kulmbach lavished much attention on the town, building several important rococo buildings, including the New Palace, the Hermitage, and the Margrave's Opera House. It was to Bayreuth that Wagner turned his attentions in the spring of 1872 as a possible site for his new opera house.

The abandonment of the proposed Festival Theater in Munich, designed by Semper some years before, meant that Wagner was still without a proper stage for his production of the Ring operas. He had long ago rejected Munich as the center for his new theater. The previous difficulties with the government, as well as the open hostility which his presence seemed to arouse, convinced him that the Bavarian capital would never do for his base. He did not, however, relay this decision to Ludwig; he thought it best to keep the king ignorant of the news, hoping to maintain royal favor. Instead, he and Cosima began making regular, discreet visits to Bayreuth before finally deciding that it was to be chosen as the site of his new Festival Theater.

There were immediate problems with Wagner's wish to have his Ring operas performed in Bayreuth. For one thing, Ludwig owned the rights to all four of the operas, not Wagner. In February of 1871, Wagner had finished the score of the third opera, *Siegfried*. According to the contract signed with the king in 1864, he was obliged to hand it over at once, but Wagner feared that Ludwig would then have the opera produced in Munich—with or without the approval of the composer, as he had done in the cases of *Das Rheingold* and *Die Walküre*. Wagner wished to avoid this at all costs. He therefore deliberately deceived Ludwig, telling him that *Siegfried* remained unfinished, while he was actually working on the fourth and final opera of the cycle, *Götterdäm-*

merung. Ludwig pressed for *Siegfried* but Wagner continued his eva-
sion, wishing to save these last two operas for the first performance of
the festival cycle.

Eventually the composer told Ludwig that he was abandoning
Munich in favor of Bayreuth and that the performances would take
place in the new (and, as yet, unbuilt) theater the following summer.
But the king must have realized that this was wishful thinking on the
composer's part, writing to Düfflipp: "It will be a pure impossibility to
produce the whole Nibelung cycle in Bayreuth next year."[1] Nevertheless, within a few weeks, Wagner had won the king over to his vision
of a new theater in Bayreuth.

Wagner's original decision in favor of Bayreuth had been based
on the fact that the town could lay claim to the largest opera stage in
all of Germany, the Margrave's Opera House. But once he had time to
sit within the fussy rococo interior, with its extravagant decorations
and plush details, Wagner's hopes diminished: Not only was the stage
too small but the lavish interior would never suit the saga of the gods.
It was impossible to remodel the theater; therefore, a new theatre
would have to be constructed. The town of Bayreuth, pleased at the
attention, immediately granted Wagner a choice piece of land on
which to erect the new theater. The composer himself purchased an
adjoining plot of land where he intended to build a house, and Ludwig
gave Wagner and Cosima some 25,000 gulden with which to erect their
new residence.

Wagner's quest to inhabit his new theater began in earnest on 22
May, 1872, his fifty-ninth birthday, when he laid the foundation stone
of his Festspielhaus. Ludwig was absent, although he sent Wagner a
telegram of support: "From the depths of my soul, my Dear Friend, I
send my warmest and most sincere good wishes on this day so full of
import for Germany. May success and prosperity attend the great
undertaking of next year. Today I am more than ever united with you
in spirit."[2] Rain poured down incessantly on the proceedings in
Bayreuth, an inauspicious start to Wagner's dream.

To raise money for the new theater, Wagner traveled all over
Europe, giving lectures about Bayreuth and inaugurating a series of
Wagner societies whose aim was to raise money by public subscrip-
tion. Each contribution guaranteed the donor a certain number of seats
in the theater for the Ring cycle. Some money was raised in this
manner, but scarcely enough to finance the construction; even with the
gifts of several monarchs—including such unlikely Wagnerites as the
sultan of Turkey and the khedive of Egypt—the composer did not have
enough money, and he was forced to embark on a series of European
concert tours.

Otto von Bismarck

Crown Prince Friedrich of Prussia, later
Emperor Friedrich Wilhelm III of
Germany

King Ludwig II,
about 1872

Neuschwanstein Castle from Pollat Gorge to the south, showing the Füssen plain beyond

Neuschwanstein Castle viewed from the northern approach road
Nils Hanson collection

The *Ritterhaus* and main stair tower on the northern façade of Neuschwanstein Castle

The palace block seen from the lower courtyard

Linderhof

The pediment at Linderhof

The terraced garden and Temple of Venus at Linderhof
Susanne Meslans collection

The Moorish kiosk
at Linderhof

The state bedroom at the Palace of Herrenchiemsee

King Ludwig II's gilded carriage and outriders attired in Louis XIV livery, waiting to take the king on one of his Alpine rides at Linderhof. Photo around 1880. *Private collection*

King Ludwig II, about 1878

King Ludwig II and Josef Kainz, 1881 *Private collection*

King Ludwig II,
about 1884

The cross in Lake Starnberg

The Votive Chapel at Berg

St. Michael's Church in Munich,
where King Ludwig II is interred
Susanne Meslans collection

King Ludwig II
lying in state
Private collection

Although Wagner had optimistically promised August of 1873 as the date of the premiere, by early summer of that year, it was apparent to everyone that the theater would not be finished in time for the proposed cycle. Wagner inevitably turned to Ludwig but only received a curt reply from Düfflipp saying that, as the king had already given 25,000 gulden for the Festspielhaus and was now himself occupied with his own building projects, he would not be able to contribute further toward the Bayreuth project. Desperate, Wagner decided to approach the Prussians through the grand duke of Baden. The grand duke refused to act as intermediary, but by this time, it was academic: Ludwig had once again changed his mind and given in to pressure from the composer. Somehow, he had learned of the overtures to Prussia, a thought which was abhorrent to Ludwig. A contract was once again drawn up between king and composer. Wagner was to be given the sum of 100,000 gulden for the purpose of finishing the interior of the Festspielhaus, installing the gas fixtures, and creating the scenery. But it was only a loan. The contract was legally binding on Wagner: Half the proceeds of any concert by which the composer raised funds for the production of the Ring and all future income from the sale of patronage certificates were to be given to the king, and the full loan had to be repaid within an eighteen-month period. The payment schedule, like all other dealings with Wagner, was highly optimistic. At the turn of the century, long after both Wagner and Ludwig were dead, the composer's family was still making regular payments to the Bavarian crown.

By the summer of 1876 the Festspielhaus in Bayreuth was complete. The wooden structure, designed by Leipzig architect Otto Bruckwald, was never intended as Wagner's permanent theater; as a result, it was built quickly, with little attention devoted to such niceties as decoration. But, over the years, the plans to build a stone theater came to nothing, and today, the Festspielhaus in Bayreuth is very much the same as it was at the time of the first festival (with the addition of the Konigsbau, built at a later date to accomodate Ludwig II). The interior was, and is, without ornament, so as not to distract from the music and action on stage, with uncomfortable wooden seats and Wagner's revolutionary sunken orchestra pit.

Adjoining the Festspielhaus, at the edge of the New Palace of the Margraves, stood Wagner's own villa, built at the same time as the theater and christened by the composer as Wahnfried, or Dream Fulfilled. In typical Wagnerian fashion, he filled the interior with silks, brocades, velvets, fringed draperies, potted palms, and marble busts of his friends and fellow artists. At the front of the house stood a gift from Ludwig, a bronze bust of the king by Munich sculptor Kasper von Zumbusch.

The first performance of *Der Ring des Nibelungen* was scheduled for August. Ludwig declared that he would not attend the public performances. Instead, he told Wagner, he would watch the final dress rehearsals, which were to run from August sixth through ninth and would amount to private performances. There was no keeping his presence a secret, however, and the elders of the town of Bayreuth planned an elaborate welcoming ceremony: The railway siding was decorated with flags and bunting, and a brass band lined the platform to greet the king with the Bavarian national anthem. But Ludwig, who got wind of this plan when still some distance from Bayreuth, simply ordered his train to delay his arrival by six hours. When the lights of the royal train finally did appear in the Bayreuth station, it was 1:30 A.M., and only the most determined of royalists remained. But Ludwig thwarted even their hopes by continuing on past Bayreuth, to the small country siding at Rollwenzel, where Wagner waited to greet him. It had been eight years since the pair had last met, and both had changed dramatically. Wagner was older, tired, and more stooped than Ludwig had recalled, while the king, heavier and bearded, was no longer the young Adonis who had so captivated the composer a decade earlier. They climbed into a waiting carriage and drove through the dark forest to the Hermitage, a rococo villa on the outskirts of Bayreuth, where the king was to stay.

Last-minute preparations were underway at the Festspielhaus up until the day of the performance. Hans Richter, who only seven years before had been banned by the king from ever again appearing on the Munich stage after the struggle with *Das Rheingold*, conducted the 115-piece orchestra. There were the usual scenic problems with the effects: The Rhine could not be properly controlled, and the dragon for *Siegfried* did not arrive in one piece, the head having been sent by mistake to Beirut instead of Bayreuth. In truth, the effects at the Bayreuth premiere were no more successful than in the Munich performances of *Das Rhein-gold* and *Die Walküre*, but at Bayreuth, Ludwig could at least see and hear all four of the operas in sequence. However impressed the king might have been with the Munich performances, the full impact of the works could only be appreciated in the context in which they were meant to be seen and heard, over the course of four consecutive nights and in sequence, as Wagner had wished.

On 6 August 1876, Ludwig drove in an open carriage to the Fest-spielhaus to attend the final dress rehearsal of *Das Rheingold*. He had asked that the theater be empty so that he might avoid the inquisitive stares of the audience, and to accomodate the king's wish, only a few specially invited guests were present. Wagner led him to the royal box, where the two men sat together for the performance. For the following performances, however, the king asked that an audience be present, so that he might hear the operas performed with the proper acoustics.

On the last two nights, Ludwig finally saw the third and fourth operas, *Siegfried* and *Götterdämmerung*. Thus, Wagner's four nights of murder, intrigue, love, fear, incest, and hatred reached their climax as the flames engulfed Valhalla. Ludwig was overwhelmed; he sat in the darkened theater, shaking, crying, gripping the arms of his chair in agitation. On returning to Hohenschwangau, he wrote to Wagner:

> I came with great expectations; and, high though these were, they were far, far exceeded. I was so deeply moved that I might well have seemed taciturn to you. . . . Ah, now I recognize again the beautiful world from which I have fled aloof; the sky looks down on me once again, the fields are resplendent with colour, the spring enters my soul with a thousand sweet sounds. . . .
> You are a god-man, the true artist by God's grace who brought the sacred fire down from Heaven to Earth, to purify, to sanctify and to redeem. The god-man who truly cannot fail and cannot err.[3]

So taken was the king with the festival that he declared he would return to attend the second performance of the cycle later that month. He hoped that by that time most of the foreign royal guests would have gone. He returned to Bayreuth on 26 August and attended the four operas once again. At the end of *Götterdämmerung*, Ludwig overcame his fear of crowds and almost joyously stepped to the front of the royal box to acknowledge the cheers of the audience and to join with them in saluting the composer when Wagner took the stage. In his speech before the audience, Wagner declared that the festival had been "embarked upon in trust in the German spirit and completed for the glory of the King of Bavaria," and called Ludwig "not only a benefactor and protector" but also a "co-creator" of the Ring.[4] Ludwig was deeply touched at this tribute. For once, he did not shun the crowds which lined the route his carriage took from the Festspielhaus to the Hermitage but actually seemed to bask in the adulation. His determined belief in, and support of, Wagner, had played not a little part in the triumph of Bayreuth, and he must have believed that he was truly a cocreator of the Ring. Without Ludwig, it is unlikely that Wagner would ever have finished it.

Following the Bayreuth Festival, Wagner returned to the writing of what was to be his last opera, *Parsifal*. Originally based on the twelfth-century tale by Wolfram von Eschenbach, Wagner's opera of redemption and renewal incorporated elements of Arthurian legend, religious mysticism, and the tale of Lohengrin. It was the most traditionally religious of all Wagner's operas, dealing with the concepts of free will, sin, and salvation. There were many similiarities between the character of Parsifal as written by Wagner and the real-life character of the king, and it is almost certain that his association with Ludwig prompted this. Thus, for Ludwig, *Parsifal* became an extremely personal opera, and he was able to recognize himself and his struggles in Parsifal's quest for the Holy Grail. Ludwig, too, regarded his position as monarch as divinely inspired and, like Parsifal, believed that he had to fight against adversity and temptation to attain his higher, preordained destiny.

In the autumn of 1879, Wagner's ill health forced him to abandon Wahnfried in Bayreuth for the warmer climate of Italy. He returned to Germany a year later, and Ludwig received him in Munich, where the composer was to supervise a production of *Lohengrin*. The actual performance on 10 November 1880, proved to be their last face-to-face meeting; two days later, an incident occured between the king and the composer which greatly angered both men. Wagner was to conduct the prelude to *Parsifal* for the king. The evening began badly: Ludwig arrived a quarter hour late, upsetting Wagner, then was so enamored of the prelude that he asked the composer to repeat it. Wagner complied, but when the King asked to hear the prelude of *Lohengrin* so that he might compare the two, the composer angrily handed his baton to his assistant, Hermann Levi, and stormed out of the theater. There is no doubt that the incident was extremely disturbing to both men; however, the flow of letters between king and composer continued unabated, and, on the surface at least, their relationship retained all of its former depth and feeling.

On 26 July 1882, *Parsifal* finally premiered in Bayreuth. Ludwig, however, was absent. To Wagner, he wrote that he was ill and would not be able to attend the performance, but the real reasons may have been political. By this time, the king was a virtual recluse, and a journey to Bayreuth, in the face of his undoubted dereliction of his royal duties, would be bound to upset a good many members of his government. He eventually saw *Parsifal* two years later, but only when it came to Munich. "The first time I saw and heard this extraordinary work was in Spring, and it moved me in an extraordinary way," he wrote. "Truly it is uniquely beautiful. It has a purifying effect and one is carried away in wonder and admiration."[5]

Wagner died on 13 February 1883 in Venice. His body was carried down the Grand Canal from the house where he had lived and died, the Villa Vendramin, to the railway station to begin its long journey back to Bayreuth. On the way, the train came to a halt at Munich. The station was decorated with black crepe, and hundreds of mourners waited along the siding. As the train pulled into the station, a band played Siegfried's funeral march from *Götterdämmerung*, and one of the king's aides-de-camp, Lerchenfeld, stepped forward with a large wreath of laurels in Ludwig's name, inscribed, "To the Composer of Words and Music, the Maestro Richard Wagner, from Ludwig II of Bavaria." But the king himself was nowhere to be seen. Finally, on 18 February, Wagner's body was buried in the garden at Wahnfried.

A servant brought Ludwig the telegram which announced his friend's death. Ludwig tore it open and read it several times before it slipped from his shaking hands. "Wagner's body belongs to me!" he shouted.[6] He was so overwhelmed with grief that he stomped his foot through one of the floorboards in his castle. Rather than attend the funeral in Bayreuth, he closeted himself at Hohenschwangau, giving orders that every piano in his castles was henceforth to be covered in black crepe, as a mark of respect for the beloved Friend. Eighteen years earlier, when their friendship was fresh and both men were filled with hopes for future, the king had predicted: "When we two have long been dead, our work will still be a shining example to distant posterity, a delight to the centuries; and hearts will glow with enthusiasm for art, the God-given, the eternally living."[7]

30

The King's Friendships

In December of 1869, King Ludwig II began to keep a secret diary in which he recorded his thoughts and activities intermittently until his death in 1886. After his death, the Wittelsbach family carefully hid the journal from prying eyes, buried in the house archives. It was eventually destroyed when one of many Allied bombs fell on the Munich Residenz in World War II, but not before extensive portions had been published by several authors. In 1926, a volume called *Tagebuch Aufzeichnungen von Ludwig II, König von Bayern* appeared in Liechtenstein. It was edited by "Edir Grein"—an anagram of Erwin Riedinger, the stepson of Bavarian prime minister Johann von Lutz. The reliability of this version has frequently been called into question. A far better translation was offered by British author Major Desmond Chapman-Huston, who had complete access to the original manuscripts before their destruction in the war.

Ludwig was haunted by his homosexuality. As a Catholic king, he had sworn to uphold the moral principles of the church, and his forbidden desires filled him with guilt. His sexuality, carefully repressed, struggled against and pleadingly repented of, was the greatest tragedy of Ludwig's private life. If he hated the crowds and the bourgeois world of the Munich court, he could isolate himself from them; if he found the nineteenth century distasteful, he could build romantic castles which spoke of the ages of chivalry and absolutism. Yet he could not escape from his own longings, and this knowledge crushed his spirit.

Disheartened and ashamed, Ludwig hid himself in an artificial world, desperately attempting, until the last, to fight against his passions. He turned to the pages of his secret diary for comfort, confiding his emotional and spiritual turmoil and futile efforts to "conquer the evil," resist the "sensual kisses," and "subdue the senses" which ravaged him.[1] Through repeated pledges, vows and seals, numerology, and symbolic appeals to the spirits of Louis XIV and King Charles I of England, he tried to appease his tormented mind and redeem his troubled soul. Above all else, the diary became a heartbreaking record of oaths to remain chaste, followed by admissions of failure and overwhelming shame.

Ludwig's diary eventually spilled over into dozens of volumes, each filled with his nearly indecipherable passages and incomprehensible references to what he termed his sexual "falls."

> 29 June, 1871
> Sworn in memory of the oath in the Pagodenburg on 21 April. . . . Soon I will be a Spirit; heavenly airs are all around me. . . . I repeat it, and as truly as I AM THE KING, I will keep it, not again until the 21st of September. Then to try it otherwise; at the third time it succeeds. Remember the 9th of May 3 times 3—Febr.—April—June—Septemb. Fragrance of the Lilies. The King's delight. This oath has its binding power, as well as its potency, by
> > *De Par Le Roy*
> > LR
> > D P L R
> Solemn oath before the picture of the Great King. "Refrain for 3 months from all excitement." "It is not permitted to approach nearer than one and a half paces."
> > Louis.[2]

The initials "LR" stand for Ludwig and Richard Hornig, who evidently had access to the diary. Hornig figures prominently in many entries:

> Reconciliation with Richard, Beloved of My Soul. . . . On the 21st, the anniversary of the death of the pure and exalted King Louis XVI. Symbolically and allegorically the last sin. Sanctified through this expiatory death, and that catastrophe of the 15th of this month, washed of all mine, a pure and noble vessel for Richard's love and friendship—The Ring, consecrated and sanctified in water, gives the wearer the strength of a giant, and the power of reconciliation—Kiss, pure and Holy, only once. I THE KING. The 21st Jan. 1872: *Vivat Rex et Ricardus in aeternum.*[3]

> 3 February, 1872
> Hands not once more down on penalty of severe punishment. In Jan. Richard was with me here three times . . . ! On the 31 Court Ball Ride with R. in Nymphenburg (Amalienburg). *De Par Le Roy.* It is sworn by our friendship, on no account again before 3rd June.[4]

*   *   *

Ludwig faithfully recorded his every caress, kiss, and sexual thought, along with his heartfelt declarations that he would never again yield to temptation.

> 21st January, 1877
>   In the King's name I swear today—the 21st of January of terrible memory, the anniversary of the assassination of the King of France and of Navarre, Louis XVI by name—that what took place yesterday night was the last time forever; atoned for by the Royal Blood—the Holy Grail. Absolutely the last time under penalty of ceasing to be King.[5]

Often, members of the king's household unwittingly found themselves the object of his affections. Ludwig's favor often fell on the handsome stableboys and young soldiers who were posted to do guard duty at one of his castles. The new favorite would find himself showered with expensive gifts or granted privileged appointments, taken on midnight sleigh rides and nocturnal visits to remote hunting lodges high in the Alps. Flattered by such royal attention, few of these ambitious young men resisted Ludwig's affections, submitting themselves to his "sensual kisses" and sexual passions. But the king's tastes were subject to quick change, and he became easily bored with these new friends. "Many a Bavarian cavalry officer," wrote Richter, "was thus subsequently amazed to see his horse washed by a newly assigned stable boy who was wearing a diamond ring he had gotten from the King."[6]

Ludwig was twenty-eight years old when he first met Baron von Varicourt, a handsome former officer in the Chevaux-Legers Regiment; entranced with the baron's name and its associations with the Bourbons, the king asked him to provide a family genealogy. Varicourt complied, slyly writing the document in French; Ludwig was delighted and immediately appointed the baron as a personal aide-de-camp. Within a few weeks of their meeting and Varicourt's meteoric rise, the king wrote: "You know that you owe the appointment as aide-de-camp to my interest in the history of France in the past centuries, and to my unlimited confidence in you and my true and sincere friendship. . . . I firmly believe you because the word of a Varicourt is as sacred to me as the Bible."[7] Two days later, Ludwig sent along another letter and a photograph of himself.

Ludwig was enraptured with Varicourt, believing that he had at last discovered his true friend, "destined by Providence," as he confided in his diary. Even in this blissful state, however, the king apparently feared that this new friendship would follow the paths of his other failed relationships, for he wrote, "High over all power of doubt my friendship shall remain."[8]

Although Ludwig, with the baron's implicit silence, had firmly convinced himself that Varicourt was a descendant of a member of the court of Louis XIV, there was no such connection. Ludwig still enthused over his new friend and continued to pour out page after page of glowing admiration for Varicourt and his imagined heritage: "Your character is noble and exalted all through; every word you said to me yesterday proved that afresh. The most beautiful and most longed for death for me would be to die for you. Oh, could that happen soon, soon! That death would be more desirable for me than anything else the world can offer."[9]

Ludwig was infatuated with the handsome young officer, but Varicourt did not share his feelings. He was not averse to the royal friendship, but he continually tried to direct it along platonic lines. Despite Ludwig's protests of love until death, the inevitable break came soon enough, as it always did in his liaisons. In one of his last letters to Varicourt, he revealed that the relationship was disintegrating.

> There is something in your letter I keep wondering about. You write that you appreciate most highly—as you express yourself—my favours of a purely spiritual nature. Please explain to me why you emphasize that particularly, as it is a matter of course that they were of a purely spiritual nature. But you emphasize it specially; please write to me the reason why. It is an enigma to me the reason why. I absolutely cannot understand; that is why I ask for an explanation of this curious and completely incomprehensible phrase. It would hurt me deeply if only the shadow of a doubt were to come between us.[10]

As long as the Baron maintained his silence and accepted the king's behavior, Ludwig's romantic illusions remained intact, but Varicourt raised an issue so painful that Ludwig's only defense was to cut him off completely. As he had with Prince Paul von Thurn und Taxis before, he simply severed all of his ties with the Baron, however painful he may have found his decision.

Ludwig's relationship with Varicourt was brief; far more serious was his friendship with Josef Kainz. He first met the twenty-three-year-old Hungarian actor during a private performance at the court theater in Munich. Although not particularly handsome, Kainz had a certain presence onstage and he was brought to the king's attention by Ernest von Possert, the director of the Court theater in Munich. On Possert's recommendation, Ludwig asked that Kainz be given the role of Didier in the upcoming production of Hugo's *Marion de Lorne.*

The king first saw Kainz perform on 30 April 1881. "Didier deep impression," Ludwig recorded in his diary that evening, and he immediately sent Kainz an expensive ring for his work.[11]

The king was so taken with Kainz that he ordered the play to be performed again on 4 and 10 May. Like the first, each of these productions was followed by an expensive gift from the king to the actor: a gold chain with a swan, a diamond watch, a jeweled ring. Ludwig followed this by inviting Kainz to attend two of the private performances given for him in the court theater, although he did not receive the Hungarian actor, who sat in a box below that of the king, a tangible reminder of the distance which still separated them. The third performance of the Hugo play took place at the king's command in place of a scheduled presentation of *Die Meistersinger von Nürnberg*—in the words of Chapman-Huston, "Kainz had dethroned Wagner."[12] Realizing his extraordinary good luck, Kainz wrote to the king:

Joy, happiness and enchantment threaten to burst my bosom! Oh, could I but do a great deed in order to give Your Most Gracious Majesty a proof of how profoundly I am penetrated by feelings of gratitude towards Your Most Gracious Majesty—oh, could I but die for Your Majesty![13]

Such sentiments struck a deep chord within the king. On 30 May, Kainz was rehearsing *Richard II* at the court theater when he received a summons to the director's office. Karl Hesselschwerdt, the king's quartermaster of the royal stable, waited with an order from the king that Kainz was to be brought to him immediately at his new palace at Linderhof to spend three days as his guest. The visit had to remain a secret, and it took most of the day before Kainz could get away from Munich. He arrived on a train at the Murnau station at seven that evening, only to find that the royal coach had been waiting for him since ten that morning. The drive to Linderhof took several hours. Finally, Kainz saw the bobbing lanterns of the approaching outriders, and the carriage quickly sped with its escort through a deep forest, arriving well after two in the morning. A servant led the actor to Maximilian II's old hunting lodge, where he was to stay for the duration of the visit, and told Kainz that he was allowed half an hour to change into a tailcoat and white tie.

At the appointed time, a servant, bearing a flaming torch to light the way, came to collect the actor and take him to the king. It was a beautiful summer night, the silver light of the moon shining upon the white façade of Linderhof. But they did not stop at the palace; instead, the servant escorted Kainz along a dark garden path and began the steep ascent into the forest above. Near the top of the hill, they came to a small clearing where the servant had stopped beneath an immense boulder. With a short push, it swung open, Kainz's introduction to the Grotto of Venus and to the king's world of fantasy.

Ludwig waited at the edge of an artificial lake, also attired in evening dress. He gestured toward a table, composed of artificial coral and seashells, on which a midnight supper had been laid. Kainz, exhausted, could barely stumble through a conversation with the king. He seemed to be a participant in a stage drama, an effect heightened by the changing red and blue lights bathing the grotto. The actor was clearly ill at ease in these curious surroundings. Ludwig himself was disappointed. Instead of the passionate, powerful actor who had commanded his attention, there now stood before him in the dark grotto a tired, shy young man. Kainz could say nothing more than "Yes, Most Gracious Majesty," and "No, Most Serene and Noble Master." This uninspiring farce continued until four in the morning, when the king finally dismissed Kainz. He had expected Didier, not the uncertain young man who quivered before him. With resignation, Ludwig retired.

Later that morning, in a conversation with Burkel, Ludwig said, "Herr Kainz is a pleasant and well-mannered young man, and I was much amused by his amazement, but I was utterly disappointed with his voice. He speaks quite differently off the stage. I find him completely uninteresting and you must take him back to Munich at once."[14] Burkel persuaded the king to give Kainz another chance; if Kainz was sent back to Munich, the appearance of dismissal would almost certainly harm his burgeoning career. Ludwig agreed to this, on the condition that the actor simply be kept out of his sight for the next three days. Burkel then explained the situation to the actor. It was Didier whom the king had invited to Linderhof, not Kainz, and it was Didier he expected to see. A second meeting between the king and the actor was set for the second day, and before Kainz set off to meet Ludwig, Burkel whispered in his ear, "Act, man, act!"[15]

Kainz followed this advice, and when he appeared before the king he was once again the booming, strutting Didier. Ludwig was enchanted and suggested that they address each other by the familiar *du* although at times Kainz apparently forgot himself and overstepped the bounds, much to the king's anger. Still, Ludwig was happy enough, and the three days at Linderhof extended into three weeks. When Kainz eventually returned to Munich, he was deluged with expensive gifts from the king: three gold watches, an ivory cigar case engraved with a scene from *Parsifal*, four pieces of jewelry, clocks, jeweled buttons, and works of art illustrating the story of Wilhelm Tell.[16]

Kainz returned to Munich still glowing from such unprecedented royal favor. The actor prepared to take on his next role, Richard II; this, however, upset the king. He asked Kainz to accept a clause in his contract with the Munich stage that he would "only act beautiful characters." Kainz was taken aback at this odd request; surely, he told the king, such an agreement would make him the object of ridicule among his fellow actors. The king seemed not to sympathize. "A noble character must only play noble parts," he declared shortly.[17]

Ludwig wished to travel to Spain with Kainz; this proved impossible, and instead they set out for Switzerland to visit the sites associated with the Tell legend. They carried passports in the names of Didier for Kainz and the Marquis de Saverny (another character from the Hugo play) for Ludwig. From the very beginning, the journey was a disaster. The train trip proved a fright, as Ludwig had something of a paranoia when it came to traveling through tunnels.

A ship was supposed to have been waiting at dock to take Ludwig and Kainz up the lake on their arrival, but it had been delayed, and the pair had no choice but to sit on the dock and wait. Somehow, word got round that the king of Bavaria was there, and soon enough a small group of curious spectators gathered. After nearly an hour of this intolerable situation, the boat finally arrived: It had been decorated with blue-and-white Bavarian flags and the royal Wittelsbach standard. As the king embarked, the captain bowed and bid welcome to "Your Majesty." Ludwig was distressed, but he had no other choice; reluctantly, he and Kainz set out for Brunnen. When they approached the quay, however, Ludwig saw that it, too, had been decorated with bunting and flags, and that another large crowd stood waiting to catch a glimpse of him. He ordered that the boat continue on until they could finally disembark privately and quietly. On their way to the hotel, the carriage they were riding in broke down, and once again the king was surrounded by a group of curious locals. At the hotel, the entire staff waited at the door, bowing as the king approached, and the manager rushed forward to greet "Your Majesty." This proved too much for Ludwig; he declared that they would leave the very next day, and after some searching, a small, private villa was rented so that the pair might be alone. It was not an auspicious beginning to the trip.

Each day of the visit was spent at the various Tell sites, where Kainz had to read the appropriate section of the Tell saga to the king. Ludwig himself knew these favorite passages by heart, and Kainz was likely to be interrupted with a royal correction if he skipped a line or missed a word. This went on day after day, at all hours of the morning and night. One evening, the king decided that he wished to hear a serenade of alpine horns, and so a group of sleepy players were summoned at midnight and placed atop selected mountains above the king's villa. Ludwig was perfectly happy, but no one in the valley was able to sleep that night.

Kainz, worn out by this schedule of performing day and night, was close to exhaustion when Ludwig suddenly decided that the young man should make the journey over the Suvenen Mountains, as Melchthal had done in the Tell saga. The actor was accompanied by a dozen bottles of Moselle and a half-dozen bottles of champagne to fortify his spirits, along with four sturdy guides, while Ludwig would wait on the other side to hear of his friend's adventure. Kainz had a terrible time of it, not being used to walking miles over mountaintops, and after an arduous twelve-hour hike through the snow, he could go no further and spent the night at a small hotel on the pass. The next day, he refused to continue and returned to the king by carriage. When Ludwig eagerly asked him to describe the journey, Kainz bluntly and undiplomatically referred to it as a "horror."[18] Ludwig was disappointed in his friend's lack of enthusiasm, but that evening, he decided that Kainz could redeem himself by climbing the Rutli and reciting the Melchthal scenes by moonlight.

Kainz had little choice but to agree in the matter. Not surprisingly, he was exhausted and kept falling asleep on the journey up the mountain. Once, he awoke to find the king standing over him, staring in silence. "You were snoring," Ludwig said angrily, and walked away.[19]

A week later, Ludwig tried again. At two in the morning, he asked Kainz to recite poetry to him. The actor complained that he was too tired. Ludwig begged him to recite; again, Kainz refused. The king then commanded him to recite; Kainz refused a third time. "Very well," Ludwig finally said. "If you are too tired, go and rest."[20] By this time, Kainz was already asleep.

When Kainz awoke, the king was gone. Ludwig had proceeded without him to Ebikon, leaving instructions for his friend to follow. Although Ludwig appeared to forget the incident, his illusions about Kainz had been shattered. Kainz sensed the change in the relationship, writing to the king: "I wish I could destroy the memory of that unhappy day with all its roots, because my guilty conscience tortures me like hell."[21] Before they left Switzerland, the king had himself and Kainz photographed together. Kainz, in a rather ordinary gray suit, looked uncomfortable and completely worn out; the king, in black overcoat, with a bowler hat in his hand, sadly uninterested and disappointed in his friend.

31

Architectural Aspirations

Since his earliest days, Ludwig II had nourished a love of architecture. The building blocks and scale models of Munich's arches and monuments given Ludwig by his grandfather quickly became his favorite toys. Such interest formed part of the Wittelsbach tradition; for centuries, dukes, electors, and kings had built the palaces, museums, theaters, and monuments which adorned Bavaria. His grandfather had virtually transformed Munich with his classical buildings and sweeping avenues, and even his own father had built the broad Maximilianstrasse and Maximilianeum. The architecture of both Ludwig I and Maximilian II was, however, almost exclusively public, to be seen and used by their subjects. It provided a visible expression of their sovereign authority, an extension of the proud Wittelsbach tradition. Ludwig II's only attempt at public building had been the proposed Festival Theater by Gottfried Semper on Gasteig Hill; opposed by the government, the king eventually dropped the plans. Thereafter, all of Ludwig's building projects were to be private, for his own personal use.

As a boy, Ludwig had spent endless hours wandering alone through his father's vast palaces and castles. His first introduction to the glittering world of Bourbon France came in the richly decorated Cuvilliés state apartments of the Munich Residenz, with their gilding and brocades and cut crystal and silk; below, the Nibelungen Apartments brought to life the enthralling saga of the gods. Nymphenburg and its pavilions captivated him with their rococo excesses, while the fantastic murals at Hohenschwangau summoned the romantic young man to a world of dreams where Parsifal and Lohengrin still lived. These impressions and experiences influenced Ludwig once he himself began to build, and he was to faithfully duplicate entire themes, if not suites of rooms, in his own castles.

For the first few years of his reign, Ludwig was too preoccupied with Wagner and the conflict with Prussia to concern himself with elaborate architectural pursuits. He confined his interests to the redecoration of his apartments in the Munich Residenz and Hohenschwangau, as well as the construction of the fabled winter garden. He had no need of any new castle or palace; when he finally did embark on his building projects, it was not to satisfy the needs of the court but rather his own imagination.

Ludwig's early disillusion drove him to build. His naive hopes to control Bavarian politics had been shattered: Ludwig watched helplessly as his country was plunged into two unwanted wars, and he himself had been forced to relinquish his sovereignty to the hated new German emperor. His private life had also failed him: Wagner had turned to Cosima for comfort and abandoned Munich, Ludwig's engagement with Sophie ended disastrously, his romantic friendships all collapsed, and his homosexuality broke his spirit. Lonely and isolated, Ludwig sought refuge in his incessant building schemes.

Ludwig built to realize his dreams, to see in brick and stone the themes which dominated his life. He wished to capture images, to re-create atmospheres, to provide real-life stage settings for the dreams of Teutonic lore and the splendors of the Bourbons. Wagner's operas allowed Ludwig to enter the world of his medieval heroes, but the experience was limited to the Munich stage. Furthermore, he could read accounts of Louis XIV and life at his court for hours, but these pleasures were confined to the pages of his favorite books. By building his castles, Ludwig allowed himself entrée to these two diverse worlds, not as a powerless observer but as an active participant. At Neuschwanstein, Linderhof, and Herrenchiemsee, he created a universe which for the rest of nineteenth-century Europe existed only in the pages of history books.

Although Ludwig's castles and pavilions represented an eclectic mixture of medieval, French rococo, Bavarian baroque, and Oriental styles, he did not embark on his building schemes with any clear architectural agenda. His first projects mingled the themes of Bourbon France with Teutonic influences. His private apartments in the Munich Residenz and plans for Linderhof existed at the same time that his more dramatic longings for the world of German lore were realized in his rooms at Hohenschwangau and in Neuschwanstein Castle. As his reign progressed, Ludwig turned from the world of the medieval toward more symbolic depictions of his fleeting sovereign authority. When the obsessive splendors of the ancien régime, embodied in Herrenchiemsee, failed to alleviate his growing sense of impotence, he finally seized upon the exotic tastes and excesses of the Orient and the Byzantine Empire as an overt expression of his autocratic views.

Ludwig was heavily influenced by the romantic movement in nineteenth-century Europe, whose taste for historicism had captured the imaginations of his fellow monarchs across the continent. From Russia, where Catherine the Great and her grandson Alexander I introduced the clean lines of the classical style, to France and England, where the Gothic, Romanesque, and Oriental styles were in fashion, romanticism dominated European architecture and decoration for a hundred years. When Ludwig built a mock-Romanesque castle or a neorococo palace modeled after Bourbon France, he only followed the convention of his own age. While the styles of the king's various projects were frequently criticized by the public, his tastes were no more eclectic than those his grandfather Ludwig I had displayed in building his classical Greek temples in Munich or even those of his own father Maximilian in the Gothic restoration of Hohenschwangau.

Ludwig's finances were never as large or as unlimited as both the public and he himself believed. Of the 2 million gulden he received each year from the Bavarian civil list, three-quarters went toward salaries for personal servants, personal expenses, and stipends for relatives, including some 500,000 gulden given his grandfather Ludwig I as a pension. When Ludwig I died on 29 February 1869, this sum devolved on the king and, together with the remaining 800,000 gulden from the civil list, formed the nucleus of his building fund. Contrary to popular belief, Ludwig never used public money to pay for the construction of his castles; in the last years of his life, he did borrow money against his personal civil list, but he did not touch any other funds from the royal treasury. Additional money was saved by cutting court ceremonial, money which rapidly accrued due to his frugal style of life.

Ludwig's first architectural project was the redecoration of his private apartments in the Munich Residenz. As crown prince, he had occupied a third-floor suite in the northwest corner of the palace, overlooking both the Hofgarten and the Odeonplatz. Soon after he came to the throne, Ludwig decided to enlarge the suite to more suitably royal proportions. Court officials protested the great expense and warned that his wish to extend the apartments to the top of the palace would disturb the chambermaids who resided there. But Ludwig was furious at this opposition; he ordered the project to proceed at once and, in a characteristic show of will, had the rooms decorated in an even more elaborate manner than originally planned.[1]

Ludwig's apartments were connected to the rest of the palace by a long corridor painted by Michael Echter with murals representing the Nibelung saga. Architect Eduard Riedel directed the enlargement of the suite, while in a bow to the element of theatricality which distinguished his life, Ludwig commissioned Munich stage designer Franz Seitz to decorate the rooms in the style of Louis XVI. Here, on his increasingly rare visits to his capital, Ludwig presided over his shadow court from a succession of ostentatious, archaically grand chambers.

Ministers and court officials summoned by the king were ushered through the Nibelungen corridor and into a world of anachronistic, gilded luxury. Ludwig received visitors in his Audience Chamber, a large room hung with rich crimson watered silk and decorated in elaborately carved and gilded moldings. Between the two windows overlooking the Odeonplatz sat the king's throne, a heavily carved and gilded chair surmounted by cherubs holding aloft a golden crown, nearly hidden beneath the ermine folds and plumed ostrich feathers of a brocaded canopy. Ludwig filled his Writing Room with bronzes and marble busts of Wagner, Marie Antoinette, Louis XIV, and St. George; his desk, adorned with ormolu mounts, rested on two large gilded swans, and his writing set was decorated with scenes from *Lohengrin*. In the French manner, his bed was enclosed behind a gilded balustrade; when he slept, a canopy of cloth of gold, embroidered with Wittelsbach insignia and topped with gathered ostrich plumes, hung above his head.[2] It was all as Ludwig had commanded: rooms which could have been taken directly from Versailles itself. Ludwig's first hesitant steps as king were taken within the oppressive, autocratic decorative style which would dominate his last building projects.

With his great love of nature, Ludwig begrudged time spent in his capital. Although the Residenz adjoined the Hofgarten, it lacked a truly private garden; to solve this dilemma, he built his fabled winter garden. The Residenz already possessed a sizable winter garden, constructed by Maximilian II, but his son's creation was something altogether different. Ludwig began his winter garden in 1867, enlarging the space to massive proportions over the following three years. Built on the roof of the Residenz's Festsaalbau, the winter garden was a great cast-iron-and-glass conservatory influenced by Joseph Paxton's designs for London's Crystal Palace and laid out by Bavarian court gardener Karl von Effner. Here, in this exotic fantasy, Ludwig could wander meandering paths which cut across lush lawns, feed the live swans which swam on the placid waters of the artificial lake, read in his Moorish kiosk, and dine in an Indian hut.[3] An immense mural of the Himalayan Mountains by Christian Jank formed a backdrop to this garden, where peacocks roamed free and hummingbirds flew among the foliage. Ludwig frequently entertained amid these startling surroundings. Visitors were surprised to leave the cold, snowy streets of Munich, ascend marble staircases, and pass through a door to find themselves atop the palace in this lavish jungle. The Spanish infanta de la Paz left a vivid description of her visit to the winter garden.

We came to a door hidden by a curtain. With a smile the King drew aside the curtain. I could not believe my eyes. There, before us, was an enourmous garden, illuminated in Venetian style, with palms, a lake, bridges, huts and castellated buildings. "Come in," said the King and I followed him, fascinated. . . . A parrot swinging on his golden perch cried *"Guten Abend!"* to me while a peacock proudly strutted by. We crossed a primitive wooden bridge over a small, illuminated pond, and saw before us an Indian village. . . . We came to a blue silk tent decorated with roses, inside of which was a chair of two carved elephants, resting on a lion skin. The King took us further, down a narrow path to the lake, in which an artificial moon shone, softly lighting up the water lilies and other aquatic plants. A boat was fastened to a tree. We reached an Indian hut; fans and weapons of the country hung from the ceiling. . . . The King moved on again. Suddenly I thought I had been magically spirited to the Alhambra. We entered a little Moorish room, with a splashing fountain in the middle surrounded by flowers. . . . In an adjoining circular pavilion divided from us by a Moorish arch supper was laid out. The King motioned to me to take the place in the middle and rang a little hand bell softly. As if from nowhere a lackey appeared and bowed low. He only came to fetch and carry away dishes and when the King rang the bell. I could see from where I was sitting, behind the arch, a massed bank of flowers lit up by hidden lights. An unseen choir sang softly. Suddenly, a rainbow appeared. "Oh!" I cried involuntarily, "this must be a dream!"[4]

The winter garden soon caught the imagination of the Munich public. One of the most popular stories concerned Queen Marie. One night, according to this tale, the queen was in bed in her rooms in the Residenz when she was awakened by a great deluge of water pouring through her ceiling. Her apartments were located just beneath the winter garden, and it seems that Ludwig's artificial moon had fallen into his lake, causing it to overflow.[5]

This thirst for illusion, for escape from the drab, everyday life at the Munich court, drove Ludwig further and further into a world of fantasy. At Hohenschwangau, where he actually spent the majority of his reign, he completely redecorated his father's former bedroom to suit this quest for the romantic. The room already featured dramatic murals showing the enchanted garden of Armida, but Ludwig wished to heighten the effect. He filled the room with potted palms and orange trees, creating a lush jungle which seemed to blend into the painted garden on the walls, and a small fountain in one corner provided him with the soothing sounds of splashing water at night. When Ludwig retired in the early morning, servants drew the heavy curtains across the windows, closing out all light; then, in the darkness, a magical transformation occured as hundreds of flickering stars burst forth across the ceiling, a twinkling artificial galaxy the king had created by drilling holes in the floor of the room above and filling it with burning oil lamps. Finally, he commissioned Franz Seitz to build an artificial moon, which, through a clockwork device, shone brightly as it crossed the painted sky, complete with all the regular cycles of the real item.

Standing on Hohenschwangau's Italian terrace in the quiet twilight of the Alpine summer, Ludwig could temporarily escape the pressures of his high office and immerse himself in the world of Teutonic legends and the romantic saga of Lohengrin. Inevitably, though, the constant presence of Queen Marie did much to dampen the king's enthusiasm for his childhood home. From the sunken rose garden, he had a magnificent view northwest to the Sauling and Tegelberg Mountains, with their dark forests and cascading waterfalls; it was against this rugged backdrop that he decided to erect his first new architectural commission, Neuschwanstein Castle.

High above the sparkling blue-green waters of the Forggensee and the great expanse of the Füssen plain, the ruined watchtower and crumbling battlements of the old Castle of Vorderhohenschwangau stood guard over the peaks of Jugend Mountain. As a boy, Ludwig II had often hiked up the mountain from Hohenschwangau below. From the top of Jugend, he had a magnificent view: The high crags of the Tannheim Mountains and the Austrian Alps rose to the west, with the clear Alpsee and ochre-colored walls of Maximilian II's castle below them; the Schwangau valley with its rolling hills to the north; the Pollat Gorge and its crashing waterfall to the south; and the sheer walls of the Sauling and Tegelberg Mountains to the east. The natural beauty of the spot enchanted Ludwig. On learning that his father had commissioned plans for the restoration of Vorderhohenschwangau, he decided to undertake the project himself.[6]

Ludwig eventually abandoned his father's plans for restoration in favor of more substantial construction. A visit to Wartburg Castle in Thuringia, where Wagner had set many of the scenes in *Tannhäuser*, inspired Ludwig to commission a new building to house his own recreations. On 13 May 1868, he wrote to Wagner:

> I intend to rebuild the old castle ruins of Hohenschwangau by the Pollat Falls, in the genuine style of the old German knights'

castles, and I must tell you how excited I am at the idea of living there in three years' time. There will be a number of guest rooms, comfortable and homelike, affording splendid views of the magnificent Sauling, the mountains of the Tyrol and the distant plains. . . . The spot is one of the loveliest that can be found, inviolate and inaccessible, a temple worthy of the godlike Friend through whom alone can flower the salvation and true blessedness of the world. There will be reminders of *Tannhäuser* (Singer's Hall with a view of the castle beyond) and of *Lohengrin* (courtyard, arcaded passage and approach to the chapel); in every respect, this castle will be more beautiful and more comfortable than the lower lying Hohenschwangau, which is profaned each year by the presence of my prosaic mother. The outraged gods will always avenge themselves and take refuge with us on the lofty heights of the summit, fanned there by the celestial breezes.[7]

It was no coincidence that Ludwig's new castle was to tower above the battlements of his father's castle at Hohenschwangau below. From the very beginning he conceived Neuschwanstein as an unearthly paradise, where the romantic dreams inspired by Wagner's operas and the ancient German sagas would find life.

In 1868, workers cut a new road from the village of Hohenschwangau through the forest to the top of Jugend Mountain; using dynamite, they blasted the ruins of the old watchtower of Vorderhohenschwangau from the summit, leveling the peak on which the new castle was to stand. Every brick, stone, and piece of wood had to be loaded on a cart and dragged by horses up the long, steep roadway to the top of the mountain, a task which undoubtedly added to the construction time. Work began on the gatehouse in February of 1879; Ludwig laid the cornerstone of the main block that September.

Construction on the castle continued throughout Ludwig's reign, a process made all the more lengthy by his indecision and frequent changes of mind. He poured over his architects' beautiful sketches and paintings, scribbling notes and suggestions on the ground plans, demanding alterations and approving schemes one day, only to ask for new versions in a completely different style the next. Ludwig thought nothing of having construction halted halfway through a project and ordering everything torn out in favor of a new idea, only to later change his mind again and have it all replaced as it had been before.

Ludwig commissioned stage artist Christian Jank to design his new castle, while architect Eduard Riedel translated the drawings into a set of working plans. As the king studied the various concepts, he changed the style from Gothic to Romanesque; the end result pleased no one except the designer and Ludwig himself.

It was Jank's final version which the king erected on the summit of Jugend Mountain. First came a redbrick gatehouse flanked by twin towers; in the middle, an arch led to a courtyard designed after the stage set for the Munich production of *Lohengrin*. At its center, Ludwig planned to have a keep, containing the chapel, built on the ruins of the old watchtower. The upper courtyard was surrounded on three sides by the Kremenate, or Women's Apartments; the Ritterhaus, or Knights' Apartments; and, at the western end, by the five-storey palace block, angled slightly at the middle to follow the shape of the summit and punctuated with two tall towers. Throughout the construction, the king had three architects: Eduard Riedel retired in 1874, succeeded by Georg Dollmann, who himself was replaced ten years later by Julius Hofmann. With the passing years, the increasingly desperate state of the king's finances meant that entire portions of Jank's design, notably the central keep with its chapel, were simply abandoned; by the time of Ludwig's death in 1886, Neuschwanstein was only half completed.

Against the lush green of the forest walls, a white jewel rose from the mountain shadows, a gleaming confection bristling with gables and balconies, arches and crenelated towers which pierced the sky. Although from a distance the castle looked enormous, its true size became apparent the nearer one got to it. At the top of the hill, the roadway curved beneath the arch of the gatehouse, opening into the lower courtyard and a world of medieval fantasy. Turrets and Romanesque windows looked down from the looming palace block, whose white limestone gable was emblazoned with two large frescoes of St. George and Patrona Bavariae, the patron goddess of Ludwig's kingdom.

The interior of the castle stood in complete contrast to the simple exterior. Hyacinth Holland and Peter Herwegen carried out the Gothic schemes, while Eduard Ille, Dollmann, and Hofmann produced Byzantine variations. Ludwig concerned himself with the most minute details of the decoration, from murals and furnishings to chandeliers and porcelain, because this was, for the king, a piece of fantasy, a set upon which to enact his dreams. He was stubborn in his determination to see things carried out as he wished. When Eduard Ille began a canvas of Lohengrin for the new castle, Ludwig saw the painting and had his private secretary immediately write:

> The King orders me to tell you that he would like the attitude of the Emperor to be altered. Then again, if it be technically possible, he would wish either the morning or the evening sun to light the figure of the Archangel Michael and he asks you

also to consider whether the head of the swan is not too large and his breast, as it rests on the water, not too small. The King has seen swans swimming at Hohenschwangau from his earliest childhood and thinks yours is not drawn quite in accord with nature.[8]

As he grew older, Ludwig's eyesight failed him. He was far too vain to regularly wear glasses, and so the decoration in his castles became more excessive with the passing years, the gilding made to shine brighter, the colors more vibrant, the richness of fabrics more oppressive until, in the work undertaken at Herrenchiemsee, the effect of assuaging his vanity was nearly overwhelming.

The majority of both the ground and first floors of the palace block were given over to service and staff. The main kitchen, located on the ground floor, was a masterpiece of the latest nineteenth-century technology. Two automatic roasting spits, powered by the heat rising through the chimney, crowded a large hearth, while the built-in ovens boasted plate warmers, and a large aquarium in the adjoining larder ensured that the king could be served fresh fish on request. Mechanical lifts carried his food from these rooms to his Dining Room on the third floor.[9]

In the tall octagonal tower on the north side of the palace block, the grand staircase, of Untersberg marble, wound its way round a central column carved with scenes of a medieval hunt. Stained-glass windows, decorated with the Wittelsbach coat of arms, swan motifs, and fleurs-de-lis lit the way, along with hanging wrought-iron lanterns carved with dragons' heads.[10] The top of the marble column burst into green palm fronds reaching up to the dark blue ceiling sprinkled with golden stars.

Ludwig's private apartments on the third floor contained only a half-dozen rooms. These were small, intimate chambers, their walls paneled in dark, richly carved oak and hung with murals painted on canvas to give the illusion of tapestry. Ceilings were arched, coffered, or painted to represent scenes from Wagner's operas; massive oak doors, inlaid with brass traceries, opened one after the other to give sweeping vistas through the rooms, with their medieval-style furniture, stained-glass windows, and wrought-iron chandeliers. As Ludwig had wished, Wagnerian themes predominated: the Dining Room murals showed scenes from the Wartburg Singers' Festival and portraits of the writers and poets who had inspired the composer's operas; the life of minnesinger Walther von der Vogelweide filled the walls of the King's Dressing Room, while the story of Tannhäuser formed the decoration of Ludwig's Study. And everywhere within these rooms were reminders of Ludwig's hero, Lohengrin, and his swans, painted on walls, carved into ceilings and arches, cast in porcelain, and exquisitely embroidered in silver thread on richly colored and brocaded silks.

The king lavished his full attention on his Bedroom, a large chamber carried out in High Gothic style. The lower walls were paneled with carved monks' stalls of oak, while the murals above depicted the doomed love affair of Tristan and Isolde. The Bedroom was a superb jewel, from its silver-and-gilt-bronze washstand in the shape of a swan to the elaborate sanctuary which formed Ludwig's bed, a magnificent creation of carved walnut, intricately decorated with spires and arches, pillars and niches. At night, the rich glow of the hand-polished walnut and oak and the vibrant colors of the wall murals shimmered in the flickering light from the ormolu chandelier. In the long winters, fires burned incessantly in the medieval-style porcelain stove, filled from an adjoining room by unseen servants so as not to disturb the king. When he rose from his bed and pulled aside the deep blue curtains embroidered with silver thread, Ludwig could look beyond the stained glass of the room's oriel window and onto an exquisite winter scene as heavy mountain snows thundered against his new fortress.

Beyond this room, Ludwig constructed a curiosity: an artificial grotto, lined with plaster stalactites, a splashing fountain, and a clockwork moon. As he wandered through this elaborate stage set, he was washed with the reds and blues and yellows from a series of hidden lights; through a second door was another surprise, a hanging winter garden overlooking the Füssen plain below. Potted palms, orange trees, and bowers of jasmine and ivy lent their exotic perfume to this enchanted garden, where hummingbirds flew freely through the scented air.

Above his own suite of rooms, occupying half of the fourth floor and reaching into the heights of the gables, stood Ludwig's Festsaal, or Singers' Hall, modeled on the Wartburg room where Wagner had set his famous song contest in *Tannhäuser*. High, arched windows allowed the brilliant mountain light to flood the room, washing the intricate paintings in the arches and walls in the soft shades of the Alpine sky. The arched and vaulted coffered ceiling was richly painted with bright, medieval-style floral designs. Murals depicted not only the legend of Tannhäuser but also the story of Parsifal and the saga of the Holy Grail; above one of the doorways, hidden among the other paintings, a small portrait depicted Ludwig II's coat of arms, the only reference to the creator to be found in this glorious castle perched on the cusp of Jugend Mountain.

The real center of Neuschwanstein, however, was the Throne Room. It stood as a glorious celebration of the divine right of kings, the only room in the castle carried out in the Byzantine style. Ludwig approved designs which drew their inspiration from the churches of St. Sophia in Constantinople and from the Allerheiligen Hofkirche in Munich.[11] Columns of plaster scagliola, painted to resemble porphyry and lapis lazuli, all with gilded Corinthian capitals, supported two-story arcades which circled the room. More than two million colored tiles composed the intricate floor, whose mosaic depicted the animals of the forest. From a cerulean blue central dome, dotted with golden stars surrounding a sunburst, hung an immense ormolu chandelier, shaped like a Byzantine crown and holding ninety-six candles.[12] At the northern end of the room stood an apse, approached by wide marble stairs, dominated by an allegorical painting depicting six holy, canonized kings and crowned with a mural showing Christ in majesty. Ludwig approved plans for a large throne of solid gold, silver, and ivory surmounted by a gilded canopy with four angels holding the heraldic shields of Bavaria and the Wittelsbach dynasty, but he died before the scheme could be executed.[13]

Neuschwanstein, inspired by Wagner's operas and paintings of sagas from Ludwig's childhood, remained a magical place for the king, allowing him to escape into a romantic world which existed only within his new castle. It was, for him, like some gigantic plaything, to be viewed and admired. He frequently left it in the middle of the night, walking through the dark forests to Pollat Gorge where an iron bridge crossed directly above the crashing falls. Standing on this bridge, with the roar of the falls filling the empty forest, Ludwig could see the glow of his castle looming in the distance, its brightly lit windows sparkling like jewels against the black Alpine sky above him.

32

Linderhof and Herrenchiemsee

In the heart of the Graswang Valley, some fifteen miles from Neuschwanstein, stood the royal hunting estate of Linderhof. The land, in the Ammergau hills near the village of Garmisch-Partenkirchen, had once belonged to the nearby monastery of Ettal; a branch of the royal stud was here, and Maximilian II had built a small wooden hunting lodge, which Ludwig often visited as a young man. He loved the peace and solitude of the valley, with its tall, sheltering mountains and meandering river. In January of 1869, he wrote to Baroness Leonrod: "Near the Linderhof, not far from Ettal, I am going to build a little palace with a formal garden in the Renaissance style; the whole will breathe the magnificence and imposing grandeur of the Royal Palace at Versailles. Oh, how necessary it is to create for oneself such poetic places of refuge, where one can forget for a little while the dreadful times in which we live."[1]

The idea for Linderhof originated from a visit to Paris in 1867 to see the International Exposition. For the king, this was clearly less of an opportunity to see an industrial exhibition than it was a chance to see the palaces associated with the Bourbons. Napoleon III arranged for the king to tour Compiègne, the Louvre, the Tuileries, and Versailles; the latter so overwhelmed the impressionable Ludwig that when he returned to Bavaria he decided to create his own palace dedicated to the idea of absolute monarchy.

Although Ludwig at first conceived Linderhof as a representation of Versailles, he eventually abandoned the grandiose idea of reproducing the palace of the Sun King in the Graswang Valley. The landscape did not lend itself to the flat, horizontal gardens which, for the king, formed such an integral part of Versailles. Maximilian II had built a small wooden villa, the Königshauschen, or Royal Cottage, in the picturesque style for use as a hunting lodge, and Ludwig, having abandoned the idea of creating a Bavarian Versailles, at first simply ordered his father's building enlarged to include a new bedroom suite for himself. By the time this construction ended in 1872, however, Ludwig had expanded his demands to include a large reception room and four smaller anterooms, joined to his father's lodge by a small gallery; when it was finished, the whole structure was faced in weather boarding, in keeping with the rustic character of the old lodge.[2]

But Ludwig soon disliked the contrast between the older, chalet-style structure and his more permanent stone suite of rooms; almost as soon as his new addition was completed, he ordered his father's shooting box pulled down, reerected in an adjoining field, and replaced with rooms more in keeping with his new addition. By 1880, the reconstruction was finished, and the entire structure was faced in white ashlar stone; thereafter, the only changes were to the King's Bedroom, which he ordered enlarged twiced.

The very name which Ludwig gave the project, Meicost Ettal, was itself an anagram of l'état, c'est moi. Although Linderhof was intended as a kind of Petit Trianon, erected in the spirit of Versailles, it bore no resemblance to the architecture of either Louis XIV or Louis XV; rather, it stood as a perfect example of Bavarian rococo architecture in the style of Zimmermann and Cuvilliés.

Linderhof's main façade seemed to strain under its exuberant decoration: a rusticated basement supported a first floor ornamented with banded columns, niches filled with allegorical statues, and a central bay crowned with a pediment of swags, cherubs, and, on top, a statue of Atlas holding aloft the world. Despite its heavy decoration, Linderhof was not oppressive, a fact owing in no small part to the little white villa's nearly perfect, jewel-like setting against a dark backdrop of ascending firs.

The relatively ornate façade seemed restrained when compared to the rooms within. There was little hint of this in the Entrance Hall, a classically cool room adorned with red marble columns and dominated by a large equestrian statue of Louis XIV Ludwig had copied from one which had formerly stood in the Place Vendôme in Paris. Above, a gilded sunburst spread across the white ceiling, emblazoned with the motto of the Bourbons: "*Nec Pluribus Impar.*" It was a deliberately impersonal space; the effect of the upper storey was therefore all the more dramatic when a visitor mounted the double staircase and ascended into a world of absolute luxury.

Linderhof's main floor contained only a half-dozen rooms, separated by four oval cabinets hung with yellow, rose, mauve, and blue silk. For the king, his new palace became a visible expression of royal splendor: With this thought, he ordered such symbolic rooms as a Presence Chamber and Hall of Mirrors introduced into what essentially remained an elaborately clad hunting lodge. It was the appearance of power and magnificence which concerned the king, and Linderhof's extravagant decor overwhelmed the senses: colorful tapestries and vibrant paintings of life at the Bourbon court hung upon the walls, surrounded by heavily carved frames and crowned with gilded rocailles, cherubs, and foliage; thick Oriental carpets lay across the intricate geometric designs of the inlaid wooden floors, muffling the careful tread of servants; and endless mirrors in carved gilt frames reflected the fiery prisms of light flashing from the hand-carved ivory, Meissen porcelain, and cut crystal chandeliers floating below the trompe l'oeil ceilings. In winter, fires burned below mantles of lapis lazuli and rare marbles, while lavishly bullioned draperies fell in soft folds from silver pelmets above the double windows. Across the tops of the malachite, rosewood, ebony, and mahogany consoles and bureaus, busts of Wagner, Marie Antoinette, and Teutonic heroes stood next to Chinese vases filled with freshly cut flowers whose overpowering scents mingled with the roaring fires. Everything possessed a surreal, magical quality. When Ludwig dined, he did so without the intrusive presence of servants: his famous *Tischlein Deck Dich*, or magic table, sank through the floor to a pantry below, to be set with each new course and then raised once again through the floor to the waiting king.

The largest and most important room at Linderhof was the King's Bedroom, overlooking a cascade tumbling down Hennenkopf Mountain on the north side of the garden. Ludwig was never entirely satisfied with this room, ordering it completely redesigned and enlarged twice in an attempt to surround himself in the grandeur which he believed his position demanded. An immense gilded bed stood beneath a carved baldachin draped with rich blue velvet sewn with the Bavarian coat of arms in gold thread; above, on a ceiling surrounded by gilded cherubs, swags, and stucco reliefs, a painting depicted the apotheosis of Louis XIV, pierced in the center by a four-tiered crystal chandelier set with 108 candles.

From the windows of his bedroom, Ludwig could look down onto the small, exquisite formal garden surrounding Linderhof. Built on the lower slopes of Hennenkopf Mountain, the garden spread over a series of terraces, descending to a pool in front of the palace. From the center of the pool, a spray of water shot nearly a hundred feet into the sky from out of a gilded group of statuary. Parterres of golden box, fountains, pergolas, and gilded statuary decorated the terraces; at the far end of the pool, twin flights of stairs rose up to a small mound, crowned by a columned Temple of Venus. The formal gardens surrounding the palace merged into avenues of pleached limes and groves of pine and fir that led into an expansive, English-style park.

Ludwig's stays at Linderhof were enhanced by visits to a number of pavilions and follies he had constructed in the park. At night, bored with reading or grown tired of initialing the seemingly endless bunches of official papers dispatched from Munich, he left his elaborate villa and, accompanied by a servant bearing a flaming torch, set off into the dark forest. His destination might be Hunding's Hut, a replica from Wagner's *Die Walküre;* here, in this simple wooden cabin, Ludwig wrapped himself in animal skins, lounging on rustic chairs covered with fur blankets to read or drink mead by the light of a blazing fire. Or he might climb to his Moorish kiosk, a cast-iron building topped with a golden dome which the king had purchased from the owner of a castle in Bohemia. The Moorish kiosk was an elaborate mixture of stained glass, intricately decorated walls and arches, Turkish rugs, a marble fountain, tables inlaid with mother-of-pearl, and ostrich plumes, all illuminated by the rainbow of light cast from a red, green, and blue glass chandelier. Here, in an alcove lit by artificially illuminated stained-glass windows, there stood an enameled cast-metal throne in the form of three peacocks. With its long, divan-style seat covered with rich Oriental silks, and birds with spread tail feathers made of colored Bohemian glass, it was magnificent.[3]

Ludwig had wished to build a small theater in the French style opposite the palace where the Temple of Venus was eventually erected, but the plans were abandoned after 1876 when it became obvious that the proposed structure would completely overshadow Linderhof. In addition to Hunding's Hut, Ludwig built a second Wagnerian set piece, the Hermitage of Gurnemanz, reproduced from *Parsifal.* In the opera, the meadow before the hermitage magically bloomed with spring flowers on Good Friday; to duplicate this magical scene, each year the Linderhof gardeners trudged through the thick Alpine snow and cleared the meadow before Ludwig's replica, filling the space with thousands of fresh flowers shipped from the royal conservatories in Munich.[4]

From the formal garden at Linderhof, a narrow path climbed the slope of Hennenkopf Mountain, twisting through the woods to a small clearing before a rocky ledge of the mountainside where a hidden door-way opened to a subterranean corridor hung with artificial stalactites and stalagmites, the entrance to Ludwig's fabled Grotto of Venus. This sunken cavern, several hundred feet long and fifty feet high, was con-structed of cement over iron girders; a waterfall emptied into the lake, its surface rippled with waves created by an underwater machine. Across the lake, stalactites framed a stage set with a backdrop depict-ing the first scene from *Lohengrin.* Ludwig floated on his artificial lake in a boat designed as a cockleshell, listening to singers brought to the grotto from Munich and feeding the live swans which he kept in this fantastic world, washed by the blue and red lights hidden behind the ledges. All of this mechanical wonder, which so enchanted the king and eased him into his world of dreams, was made possible by twenty-five dynamos run from the first electrical plant in Bavaria. But Ludwig had no interest in the technical details. "I don't wish to know how it is made," he once declared, "I only wish to see the effects."[5]

On the early fall evening of 7 September 1885, as twilight settled over the Alps and the low-lying marshes and farms of southern Bavaria, the railway siding at Stock bustled with activity. Crisply uniformed soldiers scurried back and forth, guarding the platform as officials watched the slow arrival of a steam engine pulling a string of dark blue carriages emblazoned with golden crowns. With a last burst of steam and a shrill whistle, the locomotive came to a halt and King Ludwig II descended the few steps from his compartment to the siding. He hurried past the inquisitive stares of the rail officials, climbed into a gilded coach awaiting him at the station, and drove at breakneck speed across the flat countryside, passing hamlets whose lights glowed against the black of the night. At the edge of the Chiemsee, Bavaria's largest lake, he boarded an elaborately carved and decorated gondola, settling himself against its plush velvet cushions as two sailors dressed in Venetian costume took up the oars. Slowly, the boat sliced through the placid water to a pair of distant torches, their bright orange flames marking a lonely dock. Here, on an isolated island, Ludwig had constructed his last and most magnificent castle, the Palace of Herrenchiemsee.

The Chiemsee lay some fifty miles southeast of Munich, bordered by reed-filled marshes which spread to the foot of the Bavarian mountains. Two large islands dotted the lake: the Herrenworth, where a Benedictine monastery had once stood, and the Frauenworth, which housed an order of nuns. In 1873, a timber company announced that it intended to buy the rights to the deserted Herrenworth and fell its magnificent trees. Hearing this, Ludwig immediately bought the island for himself; only later did it occur to him that it would be the perfect setting for his third castle, a re-creation of the Palace of Versailles.

Ludwig did not set out to copy the entire Palace of Versailles; in fact, he conceived Herrenchiemsee as something of a shell, in which only two rooms were of consequence—the State Bedroom and the Hall of Mirrors. He commissioned architect Georg Dollmann and, later, Julius Hofmann, to faithfully duplicate the center block and side wings. He eventually wished to include the longer auxiliary wings containing the chapel and court theater, but money ran short before these schemes could be executed. The king never intended that all the rooms should be completed: From the beginning, Herrenchiemsee was to be a set piece into which certain rooms were to be introduced. Their bare plaster walls, bricked-up windows, and vaulted stone ceilings only served to fill out the space behind palace's façade, providing an eerie contrast to the extravagant rooms of the *piano nobile*. By the fall of 1885, the palace was ready for a royal visit.

By the time the king's gondola reached the island, the still water of the lake reflected the stars already shining in the sapphire sky above. Ludwig was handed out of his Venetian craft and then slowly made his way across a verdant lawn toward the distant glow of the palace lights. He followed the hand-smoothed, graveled paths which skirted the long canal before the palace, its clear waters emptying into the lake at the edge of the island. The gentle mist from distant fountains shone in the subtle illuminations which lit his way, while borders of fragrant flowers perfumed the night air. Once in front of his miniature Versailles, Ludwig crossed the Cour de Marbre, stepping through arched French doors and into the most lavish of all his extraordinary creations.

The state apartments, grouped on the first floor, all faced the garden. Ludwig climbed to them by the grand staircase, copied from Levau's Escalier des Ambassadeurs at Versailles, a classical ascent from the black-and-white marble squares of the entrance-hall floor below. Banks of orchids and lilies lined the balustrade on one side of the wide, white marble steps, while walls of blue, gray, and white marble lined the other. On the first-floor gallery, tall agate-colored pilasters with gilded Doric capitals supported a heavily carved frieze of cherubs, foliage, garlands, and statuary beneath the high, pane-glassed roof. From this luminous covering hung two splendid ormolu-and-crystal chandeliers, their tall white candles burning to light the king on his way to the neorococo-style parade rooms running *en enfilade* the length of the palace.[6]

The parade rooms had been modeled on existing chambers at Versailles. Ludwig first entered the Guard Room, its pink-and-gray marble walls hung with paintings of French military battles; the First Antechamber followed, with its magnificent painted ceiling, *The Triumph of Bacchus and Ceres*, and furniture embellished with ormolu and tortoiseshell. Next was the Second Antechamber, copied from the Salon de l'Oeil de Boeuf at Versailles, dominated by a painting of the Sun King. The last room in the suite, the Salon de la Paix, afforded Ludwig, as had its counterpart at Versailles, a view through a high doorway to the pièce de résistance: the magnificent Hall of Mirrors.[7]

Ludwig had conceived Herrenchiemsee as a monument to the age of absolutism, and no room better expressed this sentiment than his Hall of Mirrors. But he did not merely copy the existing chamber; Ludwig's Hall of Mirrors was, at 300 feet, nearly a third longer than Jules-Hardouin Mansart's original. It was also far more grand. Twenty-seven arched windows in the long outer wall were reflected in corresponding mirrors on the opposite wall. Above them, an ornate frieze of carved garlands, cherubs, and statuary, all covered with gold leaf, ran beneath a vaulted ceiling decorated with allegorical paintings and gilded carving. On either side of every window and mirror stood an elaborate, tall, two-tiered candelabrum, and down the length of the ceiling hung three rows of equally elaborate chandeliers. As Ludwig walked down the room, the light from more than eighteen hundred candles flashed and sparkled, endlessly reflected in the gleaming mirrors and glass windows.

Beyond the Hall of Mirrors lay the sanctum sanctorum: the State Bedroom. Ludwig never intended to sleep there; it was Louis XIV's Bedroom, and the Bavarian king regarded himself only as a guest of the dead French monarch. Every inch of the wall panels, frames, cornices, and pilasters was intricately carved and gilded, far surpassing the grandeur of the original at Versailles. The deep red velvet canopy and hangings of cloth of gold above the bed were so elaborate that it had taken thirty women seven years just to embroider them.

Facing the Cour de Marbre and in the same position as the rooms of Louis XV at Versailles, were Ludwig's private apartments: a Study in white and gold; an oval Dining Room, with its Magic Table above which hung the world's largest Meissen porcelain chandelier; a Porcelain Cabinet; a Small Hall of Mirrors; and, below, an oval Bathroom and Dressing Room. At the end of the suite lay Ludwig's Bedroom, a decadently splendid chamber of carved and gilded woodwork, blue silk hangings embroidered with a scene depicting the triumph of Louis XIV over Sin, and an immense bed decorated with reliefs of Venus and Adonis. At the foot of the bed stood a blue globe atop an elaborately carved and gilded column, which bathed the room in its soft glow as Ludwig slept.

Ludwig was enchanted with his new palace, but his stay was to be brief. One night, as he wandered among the banked flowers and flickering candles lining the halls of this fantastic illusion, he rapped one of the statues with his walking stick and it shattered into hundreds of pieces: When money ran short, plaster had been substituted for marble. "Everything is false!" he cried in outrage, and he left that same evening for one of his hunting lodges, having spent a total of nine nights amid Herrenchiemsee's rococo isolation. He would never see his last creation again.[8]

Work on Herrenchiemsee proceeded slowly, and Ludwig's thoughts once again turned to further architectural projects. He had plans for three additional castles: a Byzantine palace, a Chinese palace, and a Gothic castle. Two plans were commissioned for the Byzantine structure, which was to have been built near Linderhof. The first, drawn by Dollmann in 1869, depicted a very large complex of buildings of various Byzantine and Moorish influences. From the main palace block, long wings extended to enclose the courtyard, which included a service wing and a large private chapel. Julius Hofmann's design of 1885 was more disturbing, indicating the rapidly deteriorating state of the king's mind, a brooding, darker, highly symbolic depiction of Ludwig's retreat from reality and his growing isolation.

Hofmann also designed the Chinese palace, which was to have been built on the shores of the Plansee, between Linderhof and Neuschwanstein. Closely modeled on the Winter Palace in Peking, it contained a small principal building holding a throne room and bedroom set at the center of a larger, enclosed complex. Here, the king planned to dress his courtiers and servants in Chinese costume and live according to the intricate etiquette of the Chinese imperial court.

The final project called for the construction of a Gothic castle at Falkenstein, a high crag at the Allgau between Lindau and Füssen. Christian Jank produced the first sketches for the project in 1883, and his design was clearly inspired by a drawing he had done twenty years earlier of a ruin on the Rhine.[9] Jank's watercolor for Falkenstein showed a fantastic castle perched perilously on the crest of the mountain, complete with mock ruins tumbling down the slopes and towers covered with ivy. The king charged Dollmann with executing the technical details, but the architect knew that the king could little afford a new building and proposed plans which called for a smaller, less picturesque castle which bore no resemblance to the romantic piece of whimsy Jank had originally conceived. Not surprisingly, Ludwig fired Dollmann on the spot.

To complete the scheme, Ludwig hired Max Schultze. Schultze modified Jank's original design somewhat, toning down the exuberant details but retaining the dramatic spirit of the fantastic scheme. Nevertheless, he lasted barely a year before he, too, was replaced, this time by Hofmann, who brought with him an assistant named Eugen Drollinger. Together, these two men dealt with the king's ever changing ideas. The bedroom at Falkenstein, which was intended to be the largest room in the castle, went through many changes in design, from Gothic and Byzantine to Romanesque. The bed was to stand beneath a gilded baldachin, in an apse, and off to each side were to be smaller apses, one of which would contain a Byzantine altar. Above, an enormous dome was painted blue with golden stars, supported by arches decorated with religious frescoes.[10] For the king, this room was thus a combination bedroom and chapel, and this desire to enshrine it soon became his obsession; he ordered other rooms deleted from the plans in order to add more space to this one chamber.

By 1886, building on Falkenstein had not yet begun, owing to a shortage of money, and the king was growing restless. To pacify him, Drollinger began work on a new series of sketches for the king's bedroom. Ludwig's demands now became more and more excessive, more disturbed: He wanted an enormous mosaic dome, three-story stained-glass windows, murals of the Apostles, and a gilt candelabrum which would stand some thirty feet tall. Momentarily placated, the king commissioned further views and plans of this massive room, now grown to equal in size the entire floor space of Linderhof. Drollinger was at work on an overall view of the room when, on 13 June 1886, he was told that the king was dead.

The cost of Ludwig's building schemes was enormous. He spent 6,180,047 marks on Neuschwanstein and 8,460,937 marks for Linderhof; Herrenchiemsee, his most lavish and expensive project, cost 16,579,674 marks. In one year alone, 1883, Ludwig spent 5,865,607 marks—nearly as much as the entire cost of Neuschwanstein—on work at Herrenchiemsee. The grand total of his three castles, the amount of money which he spent, stood at 32,220,658 marks at the time of his death.[11] After his death, the Bavarian government threw open the doors of the king's castles, and the first tourists paid to walk through the splendors of the romantic world he had created.

33

Financial Troubles

By the spring of 1884, Ludwig's personal debt stood at 7.5 million marks. According to Bavarian law, the monarch could be sued in open court by his creditors, and as the king continued to spend on a steadily increasingly scale, this became a very real possibility. Various court officials were dispatched across Europe in search of funds. Baring Brothers Bank of London offered a loan of 6 million marks, but the conditions were deemed unsuitable by the king. Ludwig discovered that some considerable funds remained in trust from his father's estate, and asked the officials in charge for access. But the lawyers administering the trust refused to grant him control. Philipp Pfister, the court secretary, went to Berlin to obtain a loan from Bismarck; the Iron Chancellor was willing enough, but before a deal could be reached, Emil von Riedel, the Bavarian minister of finance, managed to arrange a loan of 7.5 million marks—the precise amount owed by the king to his creditors—from a group of south German banks. This loan was to be repaid in installments over a period of fifteen years and called for great economies on Ludwig's part.

These financial woes drove members of the king's household to distraction; often, they only managed to hold on to their positions by lying to him. In 1884, Hermann Gresser, Ludwig's court secretary, ingratiated himself with the king by assuring him that there was no need to worry over financial matters, and that "the sanitary conveniences in all of the rooms of His Majesty will from now on be perfect"—apparently some reference having been made as to the condition of the plumbing in his castles.[1] A few months later, Gresser was dispatched, on the king's orders, to the royal treasury to collect all of the loose jewels and to strip the Bavarian state crown of its diamonds, presumably so that the stones could then be sold and the proceeds used to finance Ludwig's building projects. But the official in charge refused to allow this pilfering to take place; when Gresser returned empty-handed, Ludwig fired him on the spot.

Gresser was replaced with von Klug, a man who knew nothing of the king's financial difficulties. Ludwig was so desperate that he even ordered an approach to the hated Hohenzollerns of Prussia; Kaiser Wilhelm I met with his nephew's emissaries and was willing to loan the king 10 million marks. But, once again, Ludwig found the conditions unacceptable: The money was to be used only to pay off his old debts and not for any further building projects. In December, Klug informed the king that a certain banker named Schulein was prepared to loan him 400,000 marks at once, provided that the king reward him with a title. Although at first reluctant to engage in this distasteful business, Ludwig soon accepted and Schulein was duly ennobled.

But this sum barely made a dent in the king's enormous debts; by the end of 1885, Ludwig's debt had nearly doubled, having gone from 7.5 million marks to the staggering sum of 14 million marks. But, for all of his extravagance, Ludwig had known that things could not continue. On 29 August 1885, he had ordered Riedel to look into the "unsatisfactory state" of the privy purse and do whatever he thought necessary "to improve the financial situation." Riedel consulted with the other ministers and, on 3 September, informed the king that his cabinet recommended great economies and a complete halt to his building projects. Riedel also pointed out that the press had already begun to hint at the king's sorry financial state and that any further expenditure might result in permanent damage to the prestige of the Bavarian crown. Hearing this, Ludwig worked himself into such a frenzy that he threatened to fire Riedel, but the minister's position was saved when the rest of the cabinet declared that they would resign as well. In turn, this would lead to the collapse of the Bavarian government. The king was thus forced to retain Riedel.

It was this unsavory business with Riedel which first alerted the Bavarian government to the serious crisis regarding the king's finances. The matter of his debt was technically the king's own business, but when Ludwig threatened to fire ministers for failing to obtain loans for him, it shook the very foundation of the government. The survival of the carefully contrived coalition which held power in Bavaria thus turned on the state of the king's finances. Unwittingly, Ludwig had made his personal debt into a political crisis. He placed his own ministers in the position of opposing him, not because they necessarily disagreed with his building schemes but because his actions threatened their power.

The possibility that Ludwig might be sued by his creditors was very real, and Lutz suggested that the king draw up a list of his debts and immediately cease his building projects. The thought that he might somehow lose his precious castles preyed upon the king's mind. He

asked the minister of the interior whether he could transfer his castles
to the Bavarian government and thus make of them crown estates,
which would protect their status under the law, but this suggestion
was declined. Ludwig was growing desperate. On 28 January 1886, he
wrote to his aide-de-camp Dürckheim:

> If a certain sum is not obtained (in about four weeks) Linderhof
> and Herrenchiemsee, my property, will be legally confiscated. If
> this is not forestalled in good time, I shall either kill myself
> promptly or else depart immediately and forever the cursed
> land where such an abominable thing could happen. I ask you,
> my dear Court, I urgently beg of you, to mobilize a body of
> people who are loyal to me, who will not be intimidated by
> anything and who, if the worst comes and the necessary money
> cannot be found, will throw out the rebellious rabble or traitors.
> I rely upon your going about this discreetly and secretly, for
> ministers and police (whom one cannot trust in this matter) and
> secretaries (Klug, Schneider) must know nothing of it. These are
> officials who are frightened of the Chamber, the law and public
> opinion; they are just a lot of old women, not the loyal subjects
> they ought to be.[2]

In despair, the king again sent Klug to Berlin to implore Bismarck
for funds. The secretary reported to Ludwig on 25 February 1886:

> I have just come back from Berlin—one day earlier than I
> expected because Bleichroeder had an opportunity of talking to
> Prince Bismarck yesterday. According to Bleichroeder, he (Prince
> Bismarck) said: "Without any guarantee it is impossible to raise
> one million in Germany. Even if His Majesty the King of Bavaria
> wrote to me personally I should not be able to give any other
> advice than this: stop the building and go to the Ministers."
> Bleichroeder added that under such circumstances His Bavarian
> Majesty would get the money cheaper in Berlin than anywhere
> else in Europe. All my hopes of being able to get the money
> which is necessary for the continuation of the buildings have
> gone since my return from Berlin. I am deeply grieved that Des-
> tiny has chosen me to break this sad news to His Majesty.[3]

Ludwig was on dangerous political ground. The Patriots' Party,
composed, for the most part, of former Ultramontanes and Jesuits, held
a majority of seats in the Landtag, and one of its members had publicly
discussed the king's financial problems, saying that if the matter came

before the assembly for consideration, his comrades would all side against the monarch. Worse still was the king's quite careless obsession with raising the sum of 20 million marks. Various court officials were dispatched to the king of Sweden, the shah of Persia, and the sultan of Turkey, all in quest of money. A group of servants was allegedly ordered to Frankfurt, Paris, Berlin, and London to rob all of the banks there. This, of course, came to nothing, although the men were careful to humor the king. Dürckheim later recalled a meeting he had with Karl Hesselschwerdt, the king's quartermaster: "In January or February of 1886, Hesselschwerdt came to me with an oral command from the King to go to England and raise ten million marks from the Duke of West-minster." Dürckheim realized the futility of the mission. Nonetheless, he told Hesselschwerdt to inform the king that he had received the order and would report on his efforts as soon as there was any news. But Hesselschwerdt told Dürckheim that he could not convey the message in person, saying, "You see, I'm in Naples at the moment."

"What ever can you mean?" asked the puzzled aide-de-camp.

"Exactly that. The King sent me to Naples; but there was no point in going, so I stayed here. But I said I was going and that I would not be back until Wednesday, so I cannot announce my return before that."[4]

Queen Marie, hearing of her son's financial troubles, wrote to Ludwig, offering him all of the money in her personal accounts. She also offered to sell her personal jewels. He replied: "I feel urged to send you my warmest thanks for your charming offer, which is too kind of you; but I would like to ask you to allow me to decline. Through some sort of manipulation, the Head of the secretariat must succeed in adjusting this matter in time."[5]

Matters came to a head on 11 April 1886, when the king was formally served with legal papers on behalf of the company which supplied his castles with water and gas. By this time, Ludwig owed them well over 100,000 marks. There was a great fear that other creditors would follow suit, and public knowledge of the action would certainly damage the king's prestige. Ludwig, after consulting once again with Bismarck, informed Lutz of his intention to lay the matter before the Landtag.

Lutz presented this information to the rest of the cabinet and once again advised the king that a parliamentary vote would most likely result in defeat. In a letter of 5 May, the prime minister and the cabinet flatly informed the king that they would not introduce a special measure into the legislature calling for additional funds, and refused to discuss the matter any further. Ludwig was furious at this refusal. His solution to this dilemma was simple: He decided to dismiss his entire government. The former cabinet secretary Ziegler was asked to oversee this operation, while Hesselschwerdt and Ludwig's barber, Hoppe, were charged with the task of selecting the new cabinet ministers.

Hesselschwerdt quickly took this news to court Holnstein. Although no longer in the king's employ, Holnstein was in close contact with both his household and with members of the government. He informed Lutz of the king's plan; thus, the Bavarian government learned that Ludwig was actively plotting their downfall.

The king's aide-de-camp, Count Dürckheim, later recalled:

> It was a great misfortune for the King that in the fall of 1885 he did not go to Munich as he normally did at that time of year. On the evening of 10 November, he was already on his way when he suddenly gave the order to turn back and proceed instead to Linderhof. After a few days there he went to Hohenschwangau. . . . This not coming to Munich in the late fall of 1885 was the decisive turning point—the beginning of the end. In consequence of this action the King was also not in residence in Munich in the winter. Had he come then the whole course of the crisis might have been different . . . the catastrophe of 1886 would not have occured. . . .
>
> During the winter and into the spring of 1886 there was a sudden absence of the loyalty and discretion which had hitherto been shown when the King's private affairs were spoken of. Newspaper articles began to appear with increasing regularity—at first only abroad but then also in Bavarian papers. There was public discussion and criticism in the beer halls, and no longer just concerning the financial disasters of the Privy Purse and the King's building projects but all about His Majesty's manner of living, his habits and the like. There were insinuations of the worst kind about the soldiers who for some time had been acting as lackeys, and the most exaggerated stories were told in the press about presents to people, about His Majesty's supposed maltreatment of servants, and so on. Remarkably enough, the police never intervened, although in public hostelries the crudest kind of lèse majesté was continually being heard. As always in these cases, very few people were the actual instigators. The majority listened, agreed or disagreed, went home and repeated what they had heard. It is very easy to create a crisis when no obstacle is placed in the way!
>
> It must occur to impartial observers that there was a deliberate attempt to create hostility against the person of the King. This would never have gone quite as far had the King been in

residence in Munich as was usual during the winter between February and May.

But he stayed away, alone and isolated at Hohenschwan-gau. Who could have thus proven or disproven the kinds of things which were being said as to his mental state?[6]

Dürckheim was aware that something was wrong and understood that Ludwig was in danger. He did not know that as the king pondered his financial situation and the construction of his castles, the royal family and the Bavarian government were actively engaged in a plot to remove him from the throne.

34

The King's Illness

"He is not mad enough to be locked up, but too abnormal to manage comfortably in the world with reasonable people."[1] So said Empress Elizabeth of her cousin Ludwig. Throughout his life, Ludwig demonstrated a marked eccentricity. In the last decade of the king's reign, he appeared to suffer from a disturbing decline in his mental health, referred to by one servant as "a swamp of unfathomable darkness," coupled with a growing eccentricity, which led to the conclusion that he was insane.[2] In its final report, the Bavarian government used the family history of the Wittelsbachs, the mental illness of Prince Otto, and the king's behavior in the last years of his life as evidence that he was incurably mad.

The Wittelsbachs had a long history of eccentricity. On Ludwig's father's side, there was a formidable record of inbreeding and dangerously close liaisons with cousins, which may have undermined the family's already fragile psyche. Maximilian had two sisters afflicted with mental illness. Princess Marie always dressed in white so that she might see any spot or stain of dirt on her, and changed her clothing four or five times a day. His other sister, Princess Alexandra, suffered throughout her life from the belief that she had once swallowed an entire grand piano made of glass. She spent many years locked away in a convent.

On Queen Marie's side, too, there was a history of peculiar behavior. Two of the queen's ancestors, Landgrave Ludwig IX of Hesse and his daughter Caroline, were both prone to fits of paranoia. Marie's family was also terribly inbred: Her parents were first cousins, her grandmothers were sisters, and her great-grandparents were first cousins as well.[3] Her uncle, King Friedrich Wilhelm IV of Prussia, was also believed to be insane.

Maximilian and Marie kept their young sons away from these eccentric relatives, but both Ludwig and Otto learned of their peculiar aunts and uncles through court gossip. The thought that he might be also be predisposed to mental illness preyed upon Ludwig's mind as he grew older. His own worst fears were seemingly confirmed when the disease overtook his brother; Otto's insanity terrified Ludwig, providing him with a glimpse of his own dark family heritage.

Otto first began to exhibit signs of his illness during the Franco-Prussian War; he seemed unable to concentrate, suffering from nervous exhaustion and insomnia. On 6 January 1871, Ludwig wrote to Baroness Leonrod:

> It is really painful to see Otto in such a suffering state which seems to become worse and worse daily. In some respects he is more excitable and nervous than Aunt Alexandra—and that is saying a great deal. He often does not go to bed for forty-eight hours; he did not take off his boots for eight weeks, behaves like a madman, makes terrible faces, barks like a dog, and, at times, says the most indecorous things; and then again, he is quite normal for a while. Gietl and Solbrig examined him and if he does not follow their advice *soon* it will be for ever too late![4]

The twenty-six-year-old prince's behavior eventually grew so erratic that Ludwig asked a commission of four doctors, headed by Dr. Gietl, the royal physician, to examine him. After their preliminary investigation, Gietl wrote to the king:

> The four doctors unanimously consider it necessary that the seriousness of the situation, as well as the serious consequences of his behaviour, should be explained to His Royal Highness. Unless Your Majesty gives other orders, I think I shall myself have to undertake the task because I have known His Royal Highness since he was born, and because I have observed him longer than anyone else.[5]

Ludwig received regular reports on his brother's condition, but the doctors readily admitted that there was little they could do. At first, Otto was treated for nervous exhaustion; none of the physicians appointed to look after him were specialists in mental disorders, and they were reluctant to admit that the prince could be suffering from any hereditary illness. On 16 June, Ludwig wrote to his mother: "I am very upset about Otto's health; it is such a pity that Gietl's warnings did not help at all. If Otto does not do something now it will be for ever too late; then nothing can be done and he will go towards his own ruin."[6] Ludwig himself knew nothing about his brother's illness; he read through the various reports but naively believed that Otto was capable of curing himself if only he altered his behavior. To his mother, he wrote: "I told Gietl to go and see Otto at Hohenschwangau because it is absolutely necessary that he should begin to lead another life, and that he should follow the advice of the doctors; already it is almost too late, because he simply won't listen to the doctors."[7] By October, Otto's behavior had become completely unpredictable, and Ludwig was forced to accept that his illness was mental rather than physical. He reported to his aunt Amalie, queen of Greece: "Otto's state is deplorable. He is in the best way of becoming just like Aunt Alexandra; he suffers from a morbid over-excitement of the whole nervous system which is quite terrible."[8]

Otto's decline was rapid; by 1872, he had been placed under nominal observation. Although Ludwig continued to see his brother regularly, these occasions soon became an ordeal. He often found him sitting alone in the dark, refusing to leave his rooms. Otto avoided bathing for weeks, his hair hung in dirty strands around his gaunt face, and he could not bring himself to dress. He refused to speak with his brother but often imagined that he heard voices calling to him, crying and shouting as Ludwig looked on helplessly. Each visit with Otto left him shaken, terrified that he might fall victim to the disease.[9]

By the end of 1872, the situation had become so bad that Ludwig ordered his brother confined at Nymphenburg, far away from the prying eyes of the Munich court. Otto was indignant that he should be restrained, writing: "You have no right, seeing that I have done no wrong, to treat me thus. I have submitted to duress and I am a prisoner; my treatment has been disgraceful."[10] But Ludwig, constantly advised by the doctors, continued to keep his brother confined. His visits became increasingly rare. After one such occasion, he wrote to his mother: "Fortunately I found Otto less excitable than I expected. He still does not like to go out, and still pretends to have boils on his feet. As we drove along he continually buried his head in his hands—did not look at me, and always saluted much too late when the people had already passed by."[11]

In 1873, Dr. Gietl was replaced with a trained psychiatrist, Dr. Bernhard von Gudden, who presided over his own asylum near Munich. That August, Otto joined his brother and mother at Hohenschwangau to celebrate the king's birthday, and Dr. Gudden was tactless enough to arrive in the midst of the celebrations to present the king with his report on the prince's health. Upon reading it, Ludwig had little doubt that his brother was incurable; Otto was hastily dispatched back to Nymphenburg.

But as much as the King tried to keep his brother's illness a secret, Otto's own behavior made this impossible. In 1875, the British chargé d'affaires in Munich, Sir Robert Morier, reported to the Foreign Office in London on the reasons for the cancellation of a proposed visit by Prince Otto to Queen Victoria:

> His whole state has much worsened during the last month and the whole town is talking of an *esclandre* . . . on the occasion of the Corpus Christi Festival three days ago. The King, who is very cross with the Church, would not attend, or allow the Princes to take part in it. This seems to have worked on Prince Otto's mind (whose hallucinations have of late taken a religious turn) and, just as the procession was entering the Cathedral, he burst through the cordon of soldiers lining the streets, rushed in (dressed in a shooting jacket and wide-awake) and threw himself on the steps of the altar before the officiating Archbishop and began in a loud voice a general confession of his sins. It was with the greatest difficulty that he was conveyed into the vestry and got into a quieter state of mind.[12]

Nymphenburg had not proved remote enough to prevent such displays, and Ludwig was forced to take more drastic measures. On the advice of Dr. Gudden, the prince was confined to Furstenreid, a secluded castle far away from the Munich court. On 15 June 1876, Otto was gazetted out of the Bavarian army; at the end of 1878, he was finally declared insane.

Otto's behavior deteriorated with the passing years. His life in exile at Furstenreid was a nightmare: Long, high-pitched screams came from his rooms at all hours of the day and night, and eventually, the walls had to be padded as he repeatedly bashed his head against them. In quieter moments, he sat playing with the toys sent by Ludwig and, later, by the Bavarian government. When he ate, he ripped his food apart with his fingers like a wild animal. He passed the rest of his days there, smashing flies against the windows and descending further into the depths of madness.[13]

Ludwig was devastated by his brother's illness. Although the pair had never been particularly close, Otto's accelerating madness terrified the king. The fear that he, too, was subject to the same hereditary insanity, began to torment him. On the rare occasions when he appeared at court or before his subjects, he felt himself stared at, whispered about, and compared to his insane brother.

The king first began to exhibit what were later diagnosed as signs of a serious mental disturbance shortly after his thirtieth birthday in 1875. During the government's investigation into the king's sanity, tales of his excesses and eccentricities, carefully collected and related by his servants and staff, slowly built into a seemingly irrefutable dossier of madness. Stories of his strange habits became legendary. One of Ludwig's servants declared that the king in his final years

> would have no one present while he ate. Nevertheless, dinners and suppers had always to be prepared for three or four persons, so that though the King always ate alone he did not feel lonely. He believed himself in the company of Louis XIV and Louis XV and their friends Madame de Pompadour and Madame de Maintenon, and from time to time even made conversation with them as if they were really guests at his table.[14]

Ludwig's table manners apparently left something to be desired. Servants later told of his "slovenly, un-appetizing and revolting manner of eating. . . . His Majesty splashes the gravy and vegetables all over his clothes."[15]

Ludwig seemed to have had a strange love and indulgence for animals. Once, he invited his favorite mare, Cosa Rara, to join him in a complete dinner, with wine, of soup, fish, and roast, served on priceless Wittelsbach china. Cosa Rara, not surprisingly, responded by smashing the table and its place settings. On another occasion, a wild goat burst into the Moorish kiosk at Linderhof and proceeded to smash against the mirrors. When the servants tried to clear the animal out, Ludwig shouted, "Leave him alone! At least he is no liar!"[16]

His obsessive worship of the Bourbons took peculiar forms: In addition to imaginary dinner guests, Ludwig made a cult of Marie Antoinette. At Linderhof, he erected a statue of the french queen, and each time he passed it, Ludwig removed his hat, bowed, and stroked the cheeks. Another column at Linderhof apparently held some special significance, for, on passing, he invariably stopped and kissed it.[17]

Worse was Ludwig's alleged treatment of his servants. If one of them happened upon the king in one of his castles, he had immediately to divert his eyes and bow to the ground. Once, Ludwig caught his valet, Mayr, accidently gazing at him; thereafter, he had to wear a black mask over his head for more than a year. "He has to wear a mask so that I don't see his criminal countenance," Ludwig explained.[18] Servants who offended him were often at the receiving end of incredible orders. In a rage, Ludwig would declare that the servant be flogged, skinned alive, or executed. One of the many examples, collected by the government, read:

> The wretch doesn't deserve to be allowed to live. Besides other misdemeanours he had the impertinence (and has long known it to be forbidden) to look up and to leave the room still looking up. He must be held down for a few seconds (it won't do him

any harm) and have his head roughly banged against the wall. For three days, whenever he comes into My Presence (except while serving at table) he must kneel with his head on the floor . . . and must remain kneeling until I give him permission to rise; this must be firmly drilled into him. For three hours of each of the three days when he is shut up, you must yourself tie his hands in order to bring him into submission, humbly, otherwise it is all up with him and his life will be made a misery for him.[19]

Aside from their peculiarity, however, Ludwig's eccentric orders concerning his servants and others seem more indicative of his autocratic nature and his need to exert absolute control rather than of madness. Ludwig was prone to exaggerate, and never more than when he was irritated. Increasingly, his tempestuous manner expressed itself in such angry declarations. His various orders that servants be thrown in dungeons or skinned alive, all of which figured in the official government declaration of insanity, certainly cannot be taken literally, for Ludwig himself never tried to carry them out, and, in any case, he apparently never seemed disturbed to discover that the offending valet or footman was, the day after receiving such an outrageous sentence, quietly going about his usual business.

At times, though, Ludwig may have been guilty of physical abuse of his servants. For the most part this seems to have amounted to kicks and blows, but there is in fact evidence that in one case he may have gone too far. One young outrider named Rothenanger committed some minor indiscretion and was so badly beaten and kicked by the king that one of his fellows had to come to his aid. Within a year, Rothenanger was dead, and it was suspected that the numerous internal injuries he received from the king may have contributed to his premature death.[20]

Ludwig allegedly suffered from frequent hallucinations. Servants would often enter a room to find him in conversation with no one but himself. He often believed he heard people in other rooms when actually there was no one there. During one dinner, he ordered Mayr to put away a knife. But Mayr objected, saying there was no such knife on the table. "But there should be one there!" Ludwig protested. "Where have you put it? Why have you taken it away? Put it back at once!"[21]

Mayr later gave testimony as to the king's deteriorating mental state. He said:

His Majesty loses control of his limbs at times, being capable in anger of dancing a demonical dislocated kind of dance, ghastly to see, beating the air with his arms like a wild man. For want of anything better to do he sometimes sits for hours twirling a lock of his hair between his fingers or passing the comb through it.[22]

In addition to the rough treatment ordered for his servants, Ludwig's thoughts were also concentrated on removing those whom he considered his enemies. Once he ordered Hesselschwerdt, his stable quartermaster, to travel to Italy and recruit several thugs, who were then to kidnap the Prussian crown prince. The prisoner, according to Ludwig, was then to be kept chained in a cave and fed nothing but bread and water, tortured "but not really killed."[23]

Ludwig's violent headaches and toothaches often tore him from his bed, and his sleep, when it eventually came, was often drug-induced. He suffered terrible nightmares. To Hornig, he once confessed: "I dreamed I was breaking a large jug of water over the Queen's head, dragging her about on the ground by her hair and stomping on her breasts with my heels." And to Ziegler, he related: "I dreamed I was in the crypt of the Theatinerkirche, that I pulled King Max out of his coffin and boxed his ears."[24]

Fantastic stories were told of Ludwig's famous midnight drives. Servants later declared that he would often insist on stopping and eating in the middle of a blizzard, telling them that they were actually at an ocean resort beneath the warm sun. On these rides, he sometimes dressed as Louis XIV and would wear the state crown and carry the sceptre as he crossed through the dark forest, items which he had ordered brought from the treasury in Munich. While the Bavarian government chose to view such incidents as signs of the king's alleged madness, they seem more indicative of his attempts to live out his own vision of reality; like the all-night rides round the perimeter of the manège of the Royal Riding School in Munich, they demonstrate not his insanity but his immense imagination. It seems highly unlikely that the king ever believed himself, as a literal interpretation would suggest, to be in the midst of a summer resort. His utter delight, too, in seeing the bemused and puzzled faces of his courtiers when confronted with such declarations should not be underestimated when examining such behavior.

The great majority of these charges came from servants whose veracity is open to question. Most were paid to testify or bribed by agents acting on behalf of the Lutz regime, their testimony given to bolster a predetermined judgment of insanity. As such, they must be treated skeptically, but few have been questioned by the king's biographers.

Against such allegations, the testimony of other servants must also be considered, and there were many who saw nothing unusual.

Alfonso Welcker, who served in the king's household for many years as a valet, later declared: "I could observe no signs of the alleged mental illness of the King. Nor could I perceive any abnormal changes. I always stayed close to the King. I dressed him and served him. He often talked to me. Never did the King show any sign of mental illness."[25] And Fritz Schwegler, another servant and outrider, testified:

> In the last days of his life, I was often assigned to the King's personal service, and I can only say that he was a good and just master. Although he sometimes scolded and stormed, when someone had done something wrong, his anger usually blew over quickly. I myself never heard about or saw any crazy orders being given, such as scratching at doors for admittance, lying down and having to crawl on the floor, wearing masks and so on. My fellow servant Mayr, who later told so many bad things of the King, often talked to me about the King. If the things he declared had really happened, he would surely have told me about them sooner. On the contrary! I was often surprised of how calm and composed the King was in the last days of his life, when he had to recognize the vastness of the betrayal.[26]

Certainly, Ludwig exhibited a latent eccentricity, which seemed to be a feature of some members of the inbred Wittelsbach family. But eccentricity is not insanity. There is no doubt that Ludwig's eccentricity existed; however, the degrees to which it manifested itself differed greatly during the last ten years of his reign. For example, even during the darkest days of the government coup against him, when Ludwig had virtually given himself over to his fantasy world where he could order his minions flogged and civil servants skinned alive, he was capable of holding extremely lucid conversations and composing very ordinary letters in defense of his position.

Although the government commission's board of physicians later declared the king insane, they did so without ever personally examining him. Only one trained psychiatrist did so. In 1884, the royal family, concerned by rumors of the king's peculiar behavior, dispatched Dr. Franz Karl, a specialist trained in mental disorders, to examine Ludwig. Karl posed as an ordinary physician and spent several hours with the king; he found him perfectly normal and fully in charge of his senses.[27] It would seem that Ludwig, predisposed to hereditary illness, may have been influenced by his family heritage but remained, until the end, competent enough to function normally under pressure. The question of his alleged insanity, therefore, should be one of degrees of eccentricity rather than complete mental illness.

Some of Ludwig's symptoms have been described as manifesta-
tions of drug use. Ludwig suffered from headaches and toothaches all
of his life, and the royal physicians regularly treated such ailments with
doses of chloral hydrate. The king, in his position, also undoubtedly
had access to other drugs, such as opium and laudanum, and it is not
beyond reason to speculate that he may have made use of them to
relieve his pain. Frequent use of these substances could result in hallucinations, sudden euphoria and unexplained rage, the very symptoms which were later described as insanity.[28]

The board of physicians and alienists employed by the Bavarian
government to determine Ludwig's illness declared that he was suffering from inherited insanity. But was this correct? Ninety years after
the king's death, a German physician, Dr. Christoph Biermann, proposed a startling new theory. In an article published in the medical
journal *Deutsches Arzteblatt*, Biermann argued that "the post mortem
findings point without any doubt to an organic brain disease," and
concluded that this was, in fact, syphilis.[29] At the time of the king's
death, syphilis was known as a disease of the nervous system and was
often treated with doses of mercury and potassium. Even so, the disease was surrounded by a stigma which, in the prudish Victorian era,
prevented its frank and open discussion. There is no mention of
syphilis in the king's autopsy report, but this in itself is hardly surprising. If Ludwig actually suffered from syphilis, the very nature of the
disease alone would account for it remaining a medical secret. There is
some evidence for this in a statement made by Bohm, who wrote:

> Things that were long kept secret were one day duly related by
> the Court Secretary Klug at a shooting party given by Baron K.
> I do not myself feel compelled to repeat here the details, which
> really belong to the King's medical history. They do form the
> historical basis for the malicious jokes which could be heard
> about this matter, and proved to justify the request of the
> Master of the Horse that an investigation of the King's illness
> should not include his sexual relations.[30]

This seems to indicate that the nature of the king's illness was related
directly to his sexual history. The unavoidable conclusion, therefore, is
that the king must have been suffering from some form of sexual disease which affected his brain, most likely syphilis.

If Ludwig suffered from syphilis, it is likely that he contracted
the disease sometime before his thirtieth birthday in 1875. The trans-
mission was probably through homosexual contact. All of the evidence
indicates that Ludwig only began to engage in intimate relations after

the failure of his engagement with his cousin Sophie in 1867. This is supported by the entries in his secret diary, begun two years later, in December 1869. Assuming that the infection first occurred shortly after this, the disease would likely have remained dormant for some time after the initial appearance of the first symptoms. But the passage of time allows for the full scope of the disease to have manifested itself in the king, from infection to the beginnings of the third stage, general paralysis of the insane.

The syphilis theory, supported by some evidence in the king's autopsy report and by secondary evidence including Ludwig's own diary admissions, answers many of the troubling questions surrounding the king's last years. First of all, it helps account for Ludwig's own withdrawal from society and his horror of court life. The tremendous social stigma attached to the disease, coupled with the shame the king must have felt, would have naturally preyed upon his mind and joined with his well-known predisposition to solitude to increasingly isolate him. It also addresses the intense secrecy surrounding his final years and, particularly, the area of his sexuality. The damage that such a revelation might have done to the prestige of the Wittelsbach family and their throne in conservative, Catholic Bavaria, whether real or perceived, may have been enough to result in a cover-up of massive proportions, designed both to protect the memory of the king after his death and the stability of the crown. Joined with his marked eccentricity and possible drug use, such symptoms might well have passed for insanity. In the end, the infamous Mad King may simply have fallen victim to a series of unfortunate coincidences which he was powerless to fight against.

Shortly before his death in 1886, Ludwig received an American author, Lew Vanderpoole, and answered the charges which had been directed against him, haunting words which admirably serve as the last word on the subject of the king's madness.

> Insults wound me so deeply that they disarm me, they force me to the ground, and I am sure that they will one day destroy me. . . . If not, everything I've read and seen myself has deceived me, then a great part of what is taken for madness is really hyper-sensitiveness. It has often been maliciously hinted and even openly declared that I am a fool. Maybe I am, but I doubt it. . . . A real madman is, as a rule, the only person who doesn't recognize his madness. . . . If I were a poet, I might be able to reap praise by putting these things to verse. But the talent of expression was not given to me, and so I must bear being laughed at, scorned at, and slandered. I am called a fool. Will God call me a fool when I am summoned before Him?[31]

35

The Plot

One sweltering summer day in 1885, Prince Luitpold of Bavaria issued an urgent summons to Johann von Lutz, imploring the prime minister to come at once to his Munich palace to discuss his nephew the king. A shy, retiring man, Luitpold had never expressed much interest in the political questions of the day, although his conservative views made him popular with members of the influential Patriots' Party. But Luitpold occupied a powerful position: Otto's insanity meant that the elderly prince stood second in line to the Bavarian throne, and members of the Wittelsbach family looked to him to restore some degree of order amid Ludwig II's turbulent and unpredictable reign.

Lutz's carriage brought him to a door where a footman in livery waited to usher him to the prince's study. Once the prime minister had arrived, Luitpold wasted no time. As Lutz listened in silence, the prince repeated the scandalous tales which had reached him concerning the king: his financial excesses, his volatile and unstable personality, and his questionable private life. Why, Luitpold asked, did the Bavarian government continue to allow such dangerous behavior? The welfare of the country and the prestige of the house of Wittelsbach, he declared, increasingly suffered from the folly of the king. For the sake of the royal family, Prince Luitpold implored Lutz to finally take official action against the monarch.[1]

The prime minister had awaited such a summons; already, he had spent a considerable amount of time pondering the king's position and what, if anything, the Bavarian government might do to halt his erratic behavior. There was no shortage of ammunition at the government's disposal, for Ludwig was vulnerable to attack in three areas: his private finances, his personal health, and his public duties. Lutz believed that each of these three aspects afforded ample evidence on which the Bavarian government could act.

Ludwig's tangled finances were his private concern, but when he ordered government officials to secure extravagant loans, then threatened them with dismissal if they failed, he imperiled the continued operation of the state. The spectacle of a reigning monarch being sued in open court by his creditors exposed the royal family to scorn, and if Lutz aided in the passage of a special bill to provide additional finances for the king, he feared the establishment of a dangerous precedent. The prime minister had no guarantee that Ludwig would not simply use the sum for further building projects and place himself in the same financial position in another year or two. Nor did Lutz wish to play the role of villain where the king's finances were concerned; if Ludwig were to be sued by his creditors, questions would almost certainly be raised as to why the government had done nothing to prevent the scandal. The only way for Lutz to avoid either complication was to remove the king from the throne before the scandal broke.

According to the Bavarian constitution of 1818, a regency could be established should a sitting monarch be deemed mentally unstable. From the prime minister's information, filtered back to his office through a network of spies within Ludwig's household, he believed a strong circumstantial case could be made that the king was no longer fit to rule. Whether or not Ludwig was actually insane mattered little to the prime minister; all Lutz needed to move against the king was the appearance of insanity and a medical declaration to back this conclusion.

But the prime minister's strongest ammunition against the king concerned Ludwig's constitutional status. Ludwig had been guilty of ignoring his royal duties for years; after the Franco-Prussian War, he had all but abandoned his political prerogatives in favor of seclusion. He no longer functioned as a constitutional monarch, refusing his prime minister the right to regular face-to-face consultations on important questions of the day. State papers, delivered to the royal castles, were left to sit unattended on the king's desk for weeks at a time. With this evidence, the Bavarian government believed it faced no shortage of reasons on which they could act to remove the king.

Prince Luitpold's urgent meeting with the prime minister convinced Lutz that he would face no opposition from the Wittelsbach family if he rid the country of the troublesome king. The royal family appeared less concerned with Ludwig's questionable political practices than with the perceived damage they felt his continued presence on the throne did to the prestige of the monarchy. By abandoning the capital and his ceremonial duties as sovereign, Ludwig had succeeded in alienating many influential members of the court and Munich society. He made no attempt to disguise his disdain for the aristocracy, and they, in turn, felt little loyalty toward the king. Such sentiments clearly harmed the dynasty, and as long as Ludwig II continued to sit on the throne, there seemed little chance that this animosity would disappear.

While the majority of the Bavarian population, including peasants and inhabitants of smaller cities, held the king in high esteem, such provincial support mattered little in Munich, particularly at a time when the country itself faced an uncertain future in its relations with the new German Empire.

The king's expenditures also troubled his family. Although Ludwig did not use any state funds in the building of his castles, he nevertheless repeatedly borrowed money against his personal civil list, until his debt stood at 14 million marks. Unable to secure any further grants from the Bavarian government, he had approached other monarchs for personal loans; the possibility that his successor on the throne would spend his entire reign making regular payments to the hated kaiser or the sultan of Turkey was very real. No one in the royal family had any wish to see the monarchy driven bankrupt by the unchecked extravagance of its sovereign.

Lutz and Luitpold made an odd pair; the conservative prince had made no secret of his distaste for closer ties with Prussia, a matter which formed the central policy of the Lutz regime. Yet it was Lutz who held real power in the Bavarian government; Luitpold entered into the plot to save the dynasty from financial ruin and public scorn, and not with any political agenda. He and the prime minister held long talks, during the course of which the two men agreed as to their ultimate aims: Luitpold would take the regency and restore the prestige of the house of Wittelsbach; in return, he would guarantee Lutz his position as prime minister and the continued survival of his government. His power thus solidified, Lutz assured Luitpold that the Bavarian Government would settle Ludwig II's debts and restore the civil list to order.

Plans for the coup d'état moved slowly. Secrecy was vital; there was no shortage of danger, and there existed the very real possibility of a civil war should the affair not reach a quick and satisfactory conclusion. Despite his financial difficulties and peculiar personal life, Ludwig II remained enormously popular among his common subjects. Members of the government and the Munich court might not have much loyalty to the monarch, but they could not afford to alienate those millions of Bavarians who did.

One non-Bavarian had to be told of the plot: Bismarck. Despite Bavaria's preeminent position within the Second Reich, she was not independent enough to remove her king without first consulting with Prussia. To this end, Lutz directed Count Lerchenfeld, the Bavarian ambassador in Berlin, to seek an audience with Bismarck and inform him of the government's decision. Lerchenfeld reported back to Munich:

I explained briefly to the Imperial Chancellor that the mental condition of the King did not permit that the ruling of the country should be left in his hands any further. I pointed out that, although it was the financial question which had given the impetus toward undertaking a quick solution, this was by itself a secondary consideration when compared with other sad things. I described the mood in the country and the impossibility of an orderly regime under the King. I told the Prince that the person next in line for the Throne, in agreement with the ministers of the Government, had decided that the country could no longer be exposed to the incalculable dangers. Things had come to a limit in Bavaria.[2]

Bismarck listened as Lerchenfeld outlined the planned coup. The chancellor declared that the forced deposition of the king was a matter of internal Bavarian politics, and, as such, Prussia would not intervene in any way once the action began. Thus reassured, Lutz stepped up his efforts to overthrow Ludwig II.

On 23 March 1886, the prime minister met with Dr. Bernhard von Gudden, a sixty-one-year-old professor of psychiatry and distinguished expert on insanity at the University of Munich. He had been one of the commissioners charged with the care of Ludwig's brother, Otto, and in this capacity had previously consulted with the king through reports and in personal meetings. Prime Minister Lutz formally asked Gudden to weigh the evidence of the king's insanity—evidence which Lutz would provide.

The question of the king's state of mind thus became the formal raison d'être for his deposition, the easiest and most convenient manner in which Ludwig could be removed from the throne. For all of the king's negligence of his duty and his financial woes, neither of these two factors was a permanent conditions. Threatened with deposition on these grounds, it was always possible that the king would reform his errant ways. This the Bavarian government and the Wittelsbach family would not risk; once the plan for the coup d'état swung into motion, it was imperative to Lutz and Luitpold that it reach a successful conclusion. A declaration of insanity, therefore, neatly resolved the dilemma: There was no possible appeal available to the king once such a declaration had been made.

Gudden was to draft a formal medical appraisal of Ludwig II's mental condition, upon which the Bavarian government could then legally act to remove him from the throne. This document, the Arzliches Gutachten, contained all of the evidence which Lutz and his men were able to muster against the king. The very nature of the document, and

the conclusions it reached, was inherently flawed, written only to satisfy a preconceived notion of the king's mental health. Any evidence
which did not support this conclusion was simply ignored. Gudden
was employed by the prime minister expressly to draw up a medical
document which proclaimed Ludwig insane; he could hardly have
been expected to include any findings contrary to this idea or to reach
any other conclusion.

The most serious problem with the document was that it was a
medical assessment of the king's mental health, yet Gudden and his
colleagues never were able to examine the patient in person. Ludwig
was declared insane without benefit of a personal diagnosis. Such
Machiavellian tactics were clearly necessary for the Bavarian government to obtain its declaration, for Ludwig was hardly likely to cooperate with a commission whose sole charge was to find him insane.
The lack of ethical standards employed by both the government and by
Gudden and his colleagues undermined any fragment of truth which
the Arzliches Gutachten might have contained.

The document was largely composed of the testimony of former
servants and stableboys who had witnessed the king's behavior on a
personal basis over an extended period of time. At the time the
Gutachten was composed, Ludwig II was surrounded by spies working for the Bavarian government and possibly Prussia; many of these
servants happily pilfered from the king's wastebaskets in search of
damning notes or scraps of letters which they then smuggled to Lutz
in Munich. Some of the testimony in the Arzliches Gutachten may have
been coerced; certainly a great majority of it only came after Count
Maximilian von Holnstein, working on behalf of the prime minister,
offered members of the king's household large sums of money for
depositions which helped to build the government's case. Thus, witness
by witness, the allegations of the king's insanity filtered back to Lutz:
tales of Ludwig's midnight sleigh rides, financial extravagance, nocturnal existence, his peculiar dining habits, and imaginary conversations as well as accounts of his harsh treatment of servants, and
autocratic orders for their punishment. Undoubtedly some of these
tales were true, or at least contained some element of the truth. But the
bulk of the evidence, obtained through bribes and other illicit methods
from men of questionable character, seems to have been either deliberately manufactured or highly exaggerated to bolster the government's case.

No attempt was made to interview those members of the king's
household who disputed the conclusion that he was mentally ill. His
aide-de-camp Count Dürckheim and Ludwig von Burkel refused to
cooperate with the commission on the grounds that the king was per-

fectly sane and that the government was acting in a duplicitous and treacherous manner. Ludwig's last cabinet secretary, N. Schneider, had made a dossier of some three hundred notes and letters from the king, none of which exhibited symptoms of any illness. He contacted both Holnstein and Lutz once he learned that the commission was taking evidence, and waited to present his case, but Schneider was never called to testify on the king's behalf.[3] Baron von und zu Franckenstein likewise had a meeting with several members of the government, at which he protested the prime minister's decision. Ludwig II, he declared, was not mad but rather possessed an imagination which he described as infinitely sensitive. Not surprisingly, Franckenstein was not called as a witness.[4]

On 1 June, Prince Luitpold sent the following letter to Ziegler:

> The obvious illness of His Majesty the King has, as you know, put the country in a very sad predicament so that I consider it my duty to consider taking measures within the constitution which would guarantee the continuity of the Government. For that purpose it is absolutely necessary to get as exact a picture as possible of the mental state of His Majesty the King. As you have been in the immediate surroundings of His Majesty for a long time, you should be in a position to give trustworthy facts which would be valuable as psychological evidence and I therefore request you to let me have a memorandum with the observations which you have in that direction.[5]

With such royal prompting, work speeded up on the document. On Monday, 7 June, Gudden examined Welcker and Hesselschwerdt. The next morning, the four doctors—Gudden, his son-in-law Dr. Hubert Grashey, and Drs. I. Hagen and J. Hubrich—met and reviewed all of the evidence collected. They agreed that on the basis of this evidence it was not necessary to make a personal examination of their subject. Their conclusions were written into the Gutachten.

> The mental powers of His Majesty are disrupted to such an extent that all judgement is lacking, and his thinking is in total contradiction with reality. . . . Gripped by the illusion that he holds absolute power in abundance and made lonely by self-isolation, he stands like a blind man without a guide at the edge of a precipice.[6]

Following this highly melodramatic wording, the Gutachten ended with the last three points:

1. His Majesty is in a very advanced state of mental disturbance, suffering from that form of mental illness well known to alienists by the name of paranoia (insanity).

2. Due to the form of this illness, which has been developing gradually and continuously over a number of years, His Majesty must be declared incurable, and a further decay of his mental facilities is almost certain.

3. Because of the nature of this disease, free volition on the part of His Majesty is impossible. His Majesty must therefore be regarded as incapable of exercising government; and this incapacity will last, not only longer than a year, but for the whole of the rest of his life.[7]

This last point concerning the period over which the king could expect to be ill addressed a specific clause in the Bavarian constitution which provided for the removal of a monarch in the event of incapacitation for a period of over a year. Without having had the benefit of personal examination, it is difficult to say how Gudden and his associates arrived at such a damning, anticipatory conclusion. The document left no doubt that, according to the Bavarian government, the king would thus never recover. With the completed document in hand, the Lutz government and Prince Luitpold finally had the evidence with which to depose Ludwig II.

36

The Coup

Late on the morning of Monday, 7 June 1886, Prince Luitpold presided over an emergency meeting of the Bavarian government. He and Prime Minister Lutz had summoned the cabinet ministers to discuss the deposition of the king. Nothing was left to chance; prior to the session, Lutz had personally consulted with the ministers, ensuring their cooperation. Not one dissenting voice threatened the secret meeting. Having previously discussed the situation with Lutz, the cabinet ministers, declaring that they felt incapable of governing any further, now expressed their intention to tender a joint resignation if Ludwig remained on the throne. However, should the Bavarian government see fit to remove the king on the grounds of his mental state, the officials would consider it their "bounden duty" to remain in their positions of power. This was no surprise to either Luitpold or Lutz, who for six months had maneuvered to reach this ominous moment. Nevertheless, the ministers' melodramatic threat was all the official ammunition the prime minister needed. Together with Prince Luitpold, he ordered that the constitutional process to establish a regency begin immediately.[1]

Despite the care taken to ensure that the medical opinion of the king's health appear devastating, none of the conspirators had any illusions that the actual coup would be without danger. Special provisions were made to prevent any popular uprising in favor of Ludwig II. The deposition of the king on medical grounds was to be followed immediately by an announcement of the regency by Prince Luitpold. The minister of war proposed that members of the army be given a special order on the day the actual coup occurred, to ensure their continued loyalty to the Lutz regime. Finally, the Bavarian Landtag was to be called in a special session on 15 June to deal with any trouble, should it arise.

According to the plan worked out by the conspirators, Ludwig was to be informed of the government's decision in a letter written by his uncle Luitpold. The prince's letter was careful to emphasize that the king's "present" state of health was injurious to the continuance of the safe administration of Bavaria. In consideration of this illness, and the state of the king's brother, Prince Otto, Luitpold declared that it had been his duty to establish a regency. Luitpold also informed his nephew that his affairs were now to come under the control of a special commission, established by the government, who would look after his finances and personal needs. It was "with all respect and humility," wrote the new prince regent, that he informed the king of this sad development. He prayed that the king would bear this distressing news and forced deposition with royal dignity and accept the consequences of the illness which God had seen fit to inflict upon him. Luitpold wrote that he hoped "God in His Infinite wisdom" would grant "an early recovery as a prerequisite for the recision" of the government's decision. He ended by declaring that he remained "in unyielding affection and loyalty to Your Royal and August Person, Your Most Excellent Majesty's humble and obedient servant and uncle, Prince Luitpold."[2]

Luitpold's letter was a masterpiece of dissimulation. Although he was careful to suggest the possibility of a cure, he himself made attempt to assist in such rehabilitation. The very day after he had written this letter, Luitpold urged the cabinet ministers to accept the conclusions of the Gutachten, which held that the king was incurable, and to make a final decision on a permanent regency according to the Bavarian constitution. The ministers duly acquiesced, and the plan, given final, official approval, was set in motion. On 10 June, the Regency was officially proclaimed in Munich. Within a week, Ludwig II would be dead.

The morning of 8 June dawned cold and cloudy in the Bavarian Alps. The gray sky above Neuschwanstein poured forth torrents of rain upon the still unfinished castle, its ivory towers shrouded in mist. Through the dismal fog, lights burned in the arched windows spread along the third floor, a sign that the king was in residence. Ludwig, unusually restless, awoke at two that afternoon, an early start to his nocturnal existence. He had his customary bath, breakfasted, and spent the afternoon reading in his study. At midnight, he ate luncheon and afterward prepared for his usual carriage ride at one o'clock. He knew nothing of the events in Munich.

That afternoon a delegation from Munich had arrived at Hohenschwangau to take the king into custody. It was headed by the minister of the royal house and of foreign affairs, Baron Krafft von Crailsheim, and included Count Maximilian von Holnstein; Baron R. von Malsen, grand master of the king's household; Count Clemens von Toerring-Jettenbach, who, along with Holnstein, had been appointed as joint legal guardian for the king; Lieutenant-Colonel Baron von Washington, an aide-de-camp; Karl von Rumpler, who acted as secretary to the delegation; and Dr. Bernhard von Gudden. As they climbed the steep driveway from the village to the little yellow castle, the commission believed that the king was in residence. They were surprised to discover that he had unexpectedly moved to his new castle the previous day. Rather than immediately proceeding, the commission spent the evening resting and arguing over their next move.

At midnight, the commission members sat down to a meal which had been prepared for the king before he moved to Neuschwanstein. The menu card bore the ironic title *"Souper de Sa Majesté le Roi,"* and the meal consisted of seven courses, which the commission members washed down with more than forty quarts of beer and ten bottles of champagne ordered from the king's cellars. Once this somewhat tactless meal had concluded, Holnstein wandered off down the hill to the edge of the Alpsee where the royal stables were housed. He had hoped to arrange for some form of transportation for the commission members to Neuschwanstein; instead, he found Ludwig's chief coachman, Franz Osterholzer, harnessing the horses for the king's one o'clock drive. Holnstein asked what he was doing and Osterholzer explained. The count then told the startled coachman that a commission had come from Munich to take the king into custody and that he was to prepare suitable transportation for their use. Osterholzer refused, saying that he took orders from no one but the king. He was surprised to hear the count exclaim, "The King no longer commands! His Royal Highness Prince Luitpold is master!"[3] Osterholzer immediately understood the implication of this talk and left Holnstein in the stables. The coachman hurried back to Neuschwanstein by way of the steep mountain service drive.

Ludwig had finished his lunch and was just wrapping himself in his heavy greatcoat when Osterholzer unexpectedly burst into his room. He listened in disbelief as the coachman told him of Holnstein's ominous conversation. At first, Ludwig was stunned, saying, "It cannot be; Hesselschwerdt would have warned me."[4] He did not know that Hesselschwerdt had already defected to the other side. Finally, however, he agreed that the entrance gates to the castle courtyard should be closed. He also dispatched a sentry named Bruckner to ride the two miles to the nearby town of Füssen to inform the local officials that a coup d'état was underway. Bruckner returned to Neuschwanstein with Police Sergeant Boppeler, who brought with him an entire unit of guards to supplement those sentries already on duty at the castle.

Below the fir-clad slopes of Neuschwanstein's rocky perch, meanwhile, Count Holnstein waited at the royal stables for Osterholzer to return. When the coachman failed to appear, Holnstein finally realized that the commission had been betrayed. He ran back up the hill to Hohenschwangau and urged his fellow conspirators to act at once.

Shortly after three in the morning, the group changed their clothes and climbed into a group of carriages which Holnstein had finally managed to arrange. Just before dawn, they set off through the rain and mist to the distant shadow of Neuschwanstein.

It was already light when the string of carriages rounded the curve of the new driveway to Neuschwanstein and pulled up before the redbrick gatehouse. They found their way barred, the massive wooden gates closed and guarded. One by one, the commission members climbed out of their carriages. They made a curious group: Crailsheim, Toerring, and Holnstein wore their gold court uniforms, with rows of medals and tricorn hats; Rumpler sported red tails; and Gudden and his colleagues wore formal morning coats and top hats. One of the carriages they had brought with them had been designed so that the doors could only be opened from the exterior, and there were facilities for its passenger to be strapped into the seat.[5]

Buried deep in a pocket of his gold uniform, Crailsheim carried Prince Luitpold's letter to the king, informing him of the Bavarian government's decision. But Crailsheim never had a chance to deliver the letter. As soon as the commission members alighted from their carriages, they were surrounded by a brigade of soldiers who had taken up defensive positions on the king's orders. Crailsheim began to explain that Prince Luitpold had ordered the king taken into custody, but the commander, Sergeant Heinz, refused to listen. The sentries guarding the gatehouse tried to push the commission members back to their carriages, causing one of the orderlies to drop a bottle of chloroform he had been hiding in his jacket. In the midst of this conflict, an elderly woman hurled herself at the group of commissioners, parasol in hand, in an attempt to drive them back to their carriages. This was Baroness Spera von Truchess, a prominent member of Munich society who had actually been certified insane by Gudden himself. A great admirer of the king, the baroness frequently followed him as he moved from residence to residence, hoping to catch a glimpse of him. She let forth a torrent of verbal abuse on the commission members: "Count Toerring, your children will be ashamed of you!" and "Are you not ashamed of betraying your King? A glorious legacy you will leave your children!"[6] Then, after berating the commission members, the baroness did what the commission members had failed to do: She forced herself past the soldiers blocking the gatehouse and succeeded in gaining admission to the castle, saying, "I shall not leave my King to these traitors!"[7]

Ludwig had just dressed after a short nap when a servant knocked on the door and presented the baroness. She begged him to leave the castle at once for Munich and there to appeal to his people for support. Ludwig still refused to believe that a plot existed, and it took several hours for the king to convince her that he was in no danger. Eventually, the baroness was escorted from his presence. At first, Ludwig found the incident amusing. But from the windows of his new castle, he could look down on the commission members at the gatehouse and at the angry crowd of local peasants who, hearing tales of the goings-on, had come to Neuschwanstein to defend their king.

The crowd which gathered at Neuschwanstein's gatehouse had come with axes, rifles, knives, and swords. Their presence so unnerved the commission members that they finally gave up hope and, led by Gudden, climbed into their carriages and returned to Hohenschwangau. But soon after their arrival there, a group of local police stormed the castle and, on the king's orders, arrested them. The only member not caught was Rumpler, who somehow managed to escape to Munich, where he sounded the alarm to Lutz. The others were not so fortunate; surrounded by guards, the commission members were forced to walk up the mountain roadway to Neuschwanstein. Lining the road, groups of angry peasants jeered the commission members as they passed. One lady was heard to say to her children, "Take a good look at them, and when you grow up you'll be able to say you've seen some genuine traitors."[8]

At Neuschwanstein, the prisoners were locked in a few sparsely furnished rooms in the gatehouse. Ludwig had ordered them put in chains, but Sergeant Heinz could not locate any. Instead, they were divested of their uniforms and placed under constant observation. As the day wore on, Ludwig worked himself into such a rage that he issued another series of bizarre orders—the commission members were to be flogged; each one was to lose an eye, they were to be skinned alive, starved to death, left to "decay in their own filth."[9] Under normal circumstances, such peculiar orders would have simply been ignored by the king's household; now, however, his wishes were taken as further evidence of his insanity. There was never any question of the orders being carried out, and the king obviously knew this, for by noon, he had ordered the commission members set free. Frightened, the men fled back to the relative safety of Hohenschwangau.

The regency had been declared that morning in Munich. When Ludwig learned of this, he finally became worried and gave the order that horses were to be harnessed and a carriage prepared so that he might return at once to Munich. But Count Dürckheim, his aide-de-camp, who had just arrived at Neuschwanstein from the capital, advised against such action; he feared that Ludwig would be arrested in the streets if he tried to make his way to the Residenz. Both Dürckheim and Sergeant Boppeler suggested that the king should escape across the border into Austria and seek the protection of Emperor Franz Josef. But Ludwig refused, saying that he was too tired and that he could not imagine what he would do in Austria. He had no desire to flee, and his honor would not permit him to be driven from his own country, only to beg for protection from his crowned cousin. "We are not living in an age of Might before Right," the king said calmly. "I shall make use of my rights and shall not leave. My subjects shall judge whether I am crazy or not."[10] He did consent to sending several telegrams to those who might help him. The telegrams intended for the emperors of Germany and Austria were intercepted by authorities at the Department of Posts and Communications in Munich, where they were thrown into a wastebasket.[11] But Dürckheim wisely dispatched several cables from Reutte across the Austrian border and thus avoided interception by the Bavarian authorities. One cable went to Bismarck, who replied that the king should immediately go to Munich and appear before his subjects. Another was sent to Baron von Franckenstein, whom the king asked to form a new government to replace the existing Lutz regime.

Dürckheim also urged the king to draft an appeal to his subjects, in which he argued his case with great persuasion. It read:

> I, Ludwig II, King of Bavaria, am under the necessity of addressing this appeal to my Faithful and beloved people, as well as to the whole German Nation. My Uncle, Prince Luitpold, designs, without My Consent, to have himself proclaimed as Regent of My Kingdom, and My former Ministry has, by means of false reports about the state of My Health, deceived My Beloved People and thus rendered itself guilty of High Treason. I enjoy perfect health, and My Mind is as sound as that of any other Monarch, but the contemplated High Treason is so sudden and astounding that I have not had time to take the necessary measures to meet it, or to frustrate the criminal designs of My former Ministers.
>
> Should this conspiracy against My Person succeed and Prince Luitpold assume, against My Will, the Government of this Country, I beseech My Faithful Friends and Subjects to try to uphold My Rights by all means in their power. I adjure all state officials, and especially all honourable Bavarian Soldiers, to remember the oath they have taken to Me and to remain faithful to it in this painful hour, when I have to contend with an unscrupulous usurper.
>
> I enjoin every Bavarian Citizen, true to his King, to fight against Prince Luitpold and the Ministry until now in power, as against dangerous traitors. I have confidence in My People and feel sure they will not desert Me in the Hour of My Need.

I address Myself to the whole German Nation and to the allied German Princes to support Me. As far as was in My Power I have worked for the good of the German Empire and I expect that it will not suffer a German Prince to become the victim of High Treason.

Should I not be allowed an opportunity of appealing directly to His Majesty the German Emperor, then I commit the justice of My Cause to public opinion. My Brave and True Bavarians will surely not foresake Me, and in case I am prevented by violence from upholding My Rights, then let this appeal be a reason to My People to help Me defeat the plans of the traitors in arms against Me.[12]

This was a convincing appeal, perfectly sane and well reasoned. If nothing else, it clearly demonstrated that the king, when he chose to apply himself, remained intelligent, thoughtful, and clear-sighted. With this declaration, the king had crossed a dangerous line; if the Bavarian government had expected him to go quietly, they were now in for a fight. Ludwig II had called for open rebellion against the sitting prime minister; this determination to hold on to his throne was to prove fatal to the king.

Count Dürckheim took the king's declaration and had ten thousand copies printed; only a few, however, made it into the hands of the public. The Bavarian government soon learned of its existence and managed to confiscate nearly all of the known copies, but the letter was published in full in a Bamberg newspaper. Neither Lutz nor Luitpold could risk the possibility of a popular uprising in favor of the king. Ludwig's declaration amounted to a call for civil war if he should be forcibly removed; now, the very survival of the Lutz regime was threatened.

Ludwig remained confused by the rapidly unfolding events. Sitting in his green study at Neuschwanstein, Ludwig also wrote a letter to his cousin Prince Ludwig Ferdinand. He related that amazing things were taking place. The king told of Osterholzer's confrontation with Holnstein and the attempts apparently being made by the government to depose him on the grounds that he was no longer capable of ruling. "I cannot think who is behind it," the king wrote. "Someone must be. Can you discover? For some time I have known that people have been paid for going about saying that I am ill and unfit to rule. Such infamy."[13] By the time the letter reached its destination, however, the King had already been toppled from power.

Ludwig's delay in leaving Neuschwanstein proved fatal. That afternoon, a heavily armed detachment arrived from Munich and sealed off all entrances to the castle. The king was now trapped. "Here

I am—a prisoner, without committing any crime!" he said to Boppeler. "What have I done to my subjects to be forsaken like this? Wretched King that I am, have I no friends to help me?" Naively, he continued to believe that the situation would resolve itself in his favor; he was too tired, too despondent to fight against the forces moving against him. Fearful that his personal property might somehow fall into the hands of his enemies and be used against him, Ludwig spent the afternoon sorting through his papers; Dürckheim burned letters from several of the king's favorites, hoping to maintain the secrecy of their relationships.[14]

On Thursday, 10 June, Count Dürckheim received an order from the ministry of war demanding that he report at once to Munich. Uncertain of what position to take, the aide-de-camp turned to the king, and Ludwig asked him to remain at Neuschwanstein. The count wired this information back to the capital but soon received a cable in the name of Prince Luitpold, threatening prosecution with high treason unless the soldier returned to Munich at once. "You know how much I'd like to keep you with me," Ludwig said to Dürckheim. "Why don't you wire my uncle and ask him if he wouldn't leave you here?"[15] This admission from the king of his uncle's supremacy was the first clear indication that Ludwig realized the hopelessness of his situation. Dürckheim did as the king had requested, but soon enough the answer came: "Count Dürckheim must obey the orders of the War Office."[16] The aide-de-camp later wrote:

> I had to inform the King of the contents of the telegram and his appeal to me not to abandon him was heart-rending. But finally he said, "I realize that you must go back, or your career and your future will be ruined." Then he asked me to obtain poison for him, and the more I refused the more he implored me. How could I get poison, I asked—even supposing that I was willing to agree to doing anything so criminal? The King replied: "From the nearest chemist; you can get poison from anywhere. I cannot continue to live."[17]

Dürckheim left Neuschwanstein that same day. On his arrival in Munich, the aide-de-camp was placed under arrest at the railway station. Fortunately for the count, no charge was made, and he subsequently went on to become a general in the Bavarian army.

Ludwig had only a few servants left with him at Neuschwanstein. Most of the retainers had left the castle, abandoning the king; their loyalty had simply evaporated with the turn of events. There was no one to whom Ludwig could turn for advice. He had no will left to fight against the government; at one time, he had envisioned himself in the role of his illustrious and heroic ancestors such Charlemagne and Ludwig the Bavarian, controlling the destiny of his country through sheer might. Now, however, he had lost faith in even this remote fantasy. He felt himself surrounded by traitors and cowards. It had been some time since Ludwig had slept; now he wandered through his castle, drinking heavily as the evening wore on. He lingered in the still unfinished throne room, its marble dais empty. The castle was completely isolated from the rest of the world; the Bavarian government had cut the telephone lines and the power supply from the turbine generators.

Earlier that day, Ludwig had summoned the district medical officer, Dr. B. Popf. When the doctor arrived, he greeted him coolly, asking, according to Boppeler, "whether he thought him crazy, as others seemed to." Popf seemed at a loss for words, then declared, "In that case we are all crazy. I have been in practice for many years and have rarely come across anyone completely normal." This seemed to satisfy him. "It seems that I am no crazier than other people," he said in a low voice before dismissing the doctor.[18] Trapped in his castle, awaiting the inevitable end, Ludwig's thoughts turned to suicide. To Welcker, he declared, "Tell Hoppe when he comes tomorrow to fix my hair, he will find my head in the Pollat Gorge. I hope that God will forgive me for this step."[19]

That evening, Ludwig had a long conversation with Mayr. He asked if he believed in the immortality of the soul, and the valet answered that he did. Ludwig agreed, saying:

> I believe in the immortality of the soul, and in the justice of God. I have read much about materialism and its doctrines and they have not satisfied me. It puts men on the level of beasts and this is not consistent with human dignity. . . . I am going to be precipitated from the highest position a man can occupy in the world to the lowest depths. I shall not bear it; life would be worthless afterwards. . . . I could endure their taking my crown away but I could never survive being declared insane. I did not suffer to be reduced to the condition of my brother Otto, whom any keeper can order about and threaten with his fists when he does not choose to listen.[20]

As night fell, the king ordered the entire castle illuminated. He continuously asked Mayr for the key to the main tower, but the valet, fearing that the king intended to jump from the balcony and commit suicide, pretended that it had been lost. Whatever his intentions, the king certainly expressed himself in suicidal terms. "Half-past twelve I was born and half-past twelve I shall die," he declared.[21] Later: "No blood shall be shed for my sake. I shall settle my account with Heaven."[22] And, finally: "I hope God will forgive me this step."[23]

Shortly before midnight, the king called Welcker to his Study, where he gave the valet 1,200 marks. "Here's my last, you deserve it, you've been the most loyal one," the king declared. "You just take it, I shall need no more money."[24] Overwhelmed, Welcker burst into tears, and the king, deeply moved, gave him one of the diamond agrafes which he customarily wore on his hats. He also wrote out a note saying that Welcker, if forced to return the clasp, should be compensated by the royal treasury for the sum of 25,000 marks—"surely evidence that his mind was not wholly unhinged," writes Wilfrid Blunt.[25]

At midnight, the commission members, again led by Dr. Gudden, arrived for a second time at Neuschwanstein. This time, however, there was no resistance. With Gudden leading Dr. F. Müller, Dr. Grashey, and a group of asylum orderlies, they made their way through the gatehouse and up into the palace block. There they were met by a frantic Mayr, who anxiously told the doctors of the king's suicidal tendencies and his repeated demands for the key to the main tower. A plan to apprehend him was quickly worked out: Mayr would tell the king that the key to the tower had been found. Orderlies would be stationed halfway up the staircase of the main tower, while Gudden and the rest of the doctors were to hide in a corridor through which he would pass on his way to the tower. Thus, Ludwig would be surrounded. Some of the orderlies were armed with strait-jackets. Mayr disappeared and the men hid themselves. Müller recalled:

> Suddenly we heard a firm tread, and a man of imposing height stood at the entrance of the corridor and conversed in short, decisive sentences with a servant, who exhibited an almost slavish deference. The Keepers came from their places above and below. At the same moment we went towards the room the King had left and cut off his return. With great promptitude two of the keepers had seized the King by his arms. Dr. Gudden came forward and said: "Majesty, this is the saddest task that has ever fallen to my lot; Your Majesty's case has been studied by four specialists on madness, and from the report made by them Your Majesty's uncle, Prince Luitpold, has been entrusted with the Regency. I shall have the honour of conducting Your Majesty to the Castle of Berg. We shall start this very night.[26]

Ludwig said nothing. He looked from one man to the next in stunned silence. Then he let out a long and pathetic "Ahh!" followed quietly by "Yes, what is it that you want? Yes, what does it all mean?"[27] The group of doctors and orderlies escorted him back to his bedroom, where Gudden ghoulishly introduced the members of the commission and reminded the king that he himself had been in charge of Prince Otto some years before and had been received in an audience. Ludwig remembered the occasion. He sat in silence for a moment. Then, he asked Gudden the most obvious and sensible question: "How can you certify me insane without seeing me and examining me beforehand?"

Gudden replied by stating that there was "overwhelming" documentary evidence of the king's mental illness and that this had provided sufficient means to undertake a judgment.

Ludwig paced back and forth, clearly agitated. He was calm but angry. Finally, he stopped and stared at Gudden for a long time without comment. Then, he asked: "Listen, as an experienced neurologist, how can you be so devoid of scruple as to make out a certificate that is decisive for a human life? You have not seen me for the last twelve years!"

"I took this step," Gudden answered, "on the strength of the servants' evidence."

"Ah!" Ludwig cried. "On the strength of the evidence of these paid lackeys that I have raised from nothing and they betray me in return! And how long, assuming that I am really sick, do you think my cure will take?"

"That will depend upon Your Majesty," the doctor replied. "It will be necessary for Your Majesty to submit to my instructions."

"No Wittelsbach—let me tell you once and for all—need never submit to anything!" Ludwig bellowed. He continued to walk up and down the room, occasionally muttering to himself or cursing the doctors and their orderlies who stood by and watched him in silence as they awaited their departure.[28]

There was no more conversation. The doctors let Ludwig gather a few things together, which Mayr packed. The uncomfortable silence was broken by the sound of three carriages which arrived in the castle courtyard. With members of the commission walking before and after him to prevent any attempt at escape, Ludwig descended the grand staircase. As he left his private apartments, he turned to Niggl, one of the castle staff, and whispered, "Preserve these rooms as a sacred precinct, and let no curious eyes profane them!" When Mayr helped him with his greatcoat, he asked in a whisper for poison, but the valet could do nothing. He walked down the courtyard steps, turning to gaze back upon his fairytale castle, and saying in a voice scarcely above a whisper, "Farewell Schwanstein, child of my sorrows!" As Ludwig prepared to climb into the carriage indicated by Gudden, a sentry reached out to guide him in, only to be met with an icy glare and an angry "Don't put your hands on me! I can go alone!"[29]

A large crowd of peasants and local villagers had gathered before the castle gatehouse and lined the roadway to Hohenschwangau. Just after four in the morning, the gates swung open and Ludwig II left Neuschwanstein for the last time. The crowd tossed flowers as his carriage passed, and the king, deeply moved, bowed in silence. Standing in the courtyard, Sergeant Boppeler watched as the equipage disappeared into the rain and fog. "I shall never forget," he later sadly recalled, "this funeral procession for a living ruler."[30]

37

Götterdämmerung

The journey from Neuschwanstein to Castle Berg took eight hours. Ludwig traveled alone in the second of three carriages; the door handles had been removed from the interior so that he could not attempt an escape. When the carriages came to a halt at Weilheim so that the commission members might refresh themselves, he was not allowed out of his vehicle for fear that he would flee. At Seeshaupt, the procession stopped to change horses at the Gasthof zur Post, and Ludwig asked for a glass of water. The wife of the postmaster, Frau Anna Vogl, brought it to the carriage, and he took it from her hand, whispering, "Thank you, thank you, thank you."[1] As soon as the carriages had left, Frau Vogl sent a messenger to Possenhofen, where Ludwig's cousin Empress Elizabeth was visiting.[2] This curious, sad procession finally arrived at Lake Starnberg at noon on Saturday, 12 June and proceeded swiftly round the perimeter of the shore to the confines of the royal estate.

Originally the king was to have been confined at Linderhof. It was secluded, easy to guard, and the only one of the king's estates which was completed. Preparations had been made to this end; then, at a meeting of the commission members soon after Ludwig issued his counter-proclamation, Count Holnstein suddenly objected to Linderhof. According to the count, the loyalty and devotion of the local populace for the king made it unsuitable as a place of secure confinement. Several options were discussed, including Castle Furstenried, where Prince Otto was confined, and the former lodge at Berchtesgarten. In the end, however, Holnstein prevailed and arranged for Castle Berg as the king's new prison. He argued that Berg, because of its proximity to the capital, would allow the commission members and doctors to come and go as they wished. The numerous dangers of keeping the deposed king so close to his capital seemed not to have been discussed at all. With Ludwig's call for armed resistance against the prime minister and the new prince regent, the possibility of his rescue and restoration at the hands of loyalists was very real; imprisoning him so close to Munich exposed the king not only to the increased chance of a rescue but also to any potential assassination attempt. Nevertheless, Count Holnstein had his way, and Berg was duly prepared to receive its new prisoner.

By the time he arrived at Berg, the king had not been to bed for more than a day; nevertheless, when his carriage came to a halt, he seemed remarkably calm. He spotted the guard on duty, Sergeant S. Sauer, and greeted him with a friendly, "Ah, Sauer, it's nice to see that you are in service here again."[3]

Workmen had been busy at Berg since the previous afternoon, transforming the castle into a prison. It had been decided that the king was to be allowed free use of his former study and bedroom on the first floor; the anteroom to these apartments, however, had its door fixed so that the handle could be opened only from the outside with a key. Small holes had been cut into the panels and into walls so that the king could be kept under observation. The threat of constant surveillance deeply offended the misanthropic king. As Ludwig arrived, he also noticed that the window frames were being drilled with holes for iron bars. His only comment was, "Everything is in fine shape."[4]

Berg was filled with unfamiliar faces, and the king was immediately suspicious, fearing an assassination attempt. He was particularly distrustful of both Prussians and Catholics, believing that one or the other—or even a coalition of both—had been responsible for his deposition. After meeting Bruno Mauder, the chief orderly appointed to look after him, the king was introduced to his three assistants, Braun, Schneller, and Hack. He appeared to trust Mauder but remained uncertain where the other men were concerned. When Mauder was alone with him, the king asked in a whisper, "Where do they come from? Are they Prussians?"

"No, Your Majesty, they are Bavarians," Mauder replied.

"And what is their religion?"

"Why, they are both Catholic, Your Majesty."[5]

At three in the afternoon, the king finally lay down for a rest. He had not slept for nearly two days, and the fatigue had finally caught up with him. He left orders with Mauder that he should be woken at midnight. But Dr. Müller, hearing this, forbade it, wishing to regulate the king's daily schedule. At first, the king slept soundly; then, as the night wore on, he began to toss in his bed and mumble in his sleep. He finally awoke at two in the morning. Looking at his watch, he immediately called for a servant. Two warders were on night duty at Berg that evening, Braun and Schneller. Ludwig demanded to know why his orders had not been carried out, and they informed him that the doctors wished him to sleep through the night. Ludwig asked that his clothes be brought to him, but this was refused. He rose, pacing up and down the length of the room in his nightshirt. He asked for an orange and for some bread, and these items were duly brought to his room, where the king slowly ate them. Finally, however, the chill forced him to return to his bed.

The following day, 13 June 1886, was to be the last of Ludwig's life. He awoke at six that morning, called for Gudden, and asked for permission to attend mass at Aufkirchen. But the doctor refused to allow him this, and Ludwig took this denial in silence. He then asked for his favorite valet, Mayr, and his barber, Hoppe, but he was informed that they were no longer in his personal service. With resignation, Ludwig allowed Mauder to shave and dress him, then sat down to breakfast. When he had finished, he handed his pocket watch to Mauder and asked him to wind it, but Schneller, also on duty, was immediately suspicious and seized the watch from Mauder's hands, insisting that he perform the duty instead.

Both Gudden and Grashey had several conversations with the king that morning. Ludwig was calm, though he repeatedly asked about the nature of his proposed cure. Grashey informed him that he must begin to live his life with moderation; he was to keep to a regular schedule, drink moderately, occupy himself, and cooperate fully with the wishes of the doctors assigned to his case. Ludwig seemed to accept most of this advice and even asked that his personal library be transported from Neuschwanstein to Berg, but he voiced his displeasure that Count Holnstein had been appointed as one of his guardians. It was obvious that the king not only disliked his former Oberstallmeister but distrusted him as well. He also made repeated inquiries about the nationality and loyalties of the warders and orderlies the government had installed at Berg.

Gudden had suggested that the king take a walk in the gardens, and Ludwig, eager to escape the confines of his new prison, agreed.[6] At half past eleven, the two men began their stroll, returning at a quarter past twelve. They were followed by orderlies at a discreet distance. The presence of the guards excited Ludwig, who inquired of Gudden if there was any danger. The doctor reassured him that there was not and, to appease the king, waved the orderlies away several times. Once back at Berg, Gudden gave the other doctors a favorable report, saying that all had gone well with the walk and that the king had impressed him with his calm behavior. Another walk was planned for the evening. The other commission members found this incredible. They believed the king to be a dangerous, unpredictable lunatic, and Gudden's unquestioning trust seemed irresponsible. That afternoon, Gudden cabled to Lutz: "So far, everything here has gone marvelously."[7]

That afternoon, Ludwig had a long talk with Friedrich Zanders, the head of the royal household at Berg. Gudden had stipulated that Zanders must promise not to discuss any rescue plans with the king, and he agreed. Ludwig greeted Zanders, who had been in his personal service for fifteen years, warmly; as soon as they were left alone, he pointed out the holes in the doorways and the bolts which had been placed on the windows of his rooms. According to Zanders, his "eyes blazed with energy and life as in his best days and very different from forty-eight hours before." Ludwig began the conversation by asking Zanders, "Do you think that they will keep me locked up for over a year just as I am today?" Zanders replied that, although he was not a doctor, he was certain that a cure could be effected in less than a year and that, in any case, it was highly unlikely that the king would remain incarcerated for more than a year.

"Do you actually think that is so?" Ludwig asked. "*L'appetit vient en mangeant.* My uncle Luitpold will get accustomed to ruling and come to enjoy the power so much that he will never let me out again." The conversation ended with an inquiry from the king as to how many guards there were on duty on the castle grounds and if they were armed. Zanders informed him that there were between six and eight policemen but that they were not armed. This news seemed to relieve Ludwig greatly. Before Zanders left, Ludwig motioned him into the corner of the room where they were out of sight of the holes drilled into the doors. Zanders later testified that he thought the king was about to confide something important and, remembering his pledge to Dr. Gudden, asked that Ludwig dismiss him. "That dark expression suddenly clouded the King's face, the expression he always had when his mistrust was aroused. He said nothing more and signalled me to leave."[8] Before he left, however, Zanders handed the king a number of papers, including the menus and the orders of the day. Ludwig took these, glanced through them, and then handed Zanders a sealed envelope, which he said was a letter for his cousin Empress Elizabeth. He asked that his servant take the letter to Possenhofen, and Zanders agreed. Surprisingly, no one from the government commission questioned Zanders about this conversation or even knew of the secret letter to the empress.

Ludwig had one last recorded conversation that day, this time with Dr. Müller. The doctor later recalled: "The King was standing when I entered; he examined me from head to foot, but he could not bear to look at me, nor I at him. During our conversation he grew more and more restless, and walked about in a nervous manner. The conversation itself was nothing but a game of hide-and-seek between a patient and his doctor."

"For the last year you have been my brother's medical attendant," Ludwig declared. "How is he?"

"During the last year there has been no particular change in his condition."

"Isn't it the case that you have orders to send the same report about me as you used to send to me about the Prince."

"I have received no such order," Müller replied.

"You will write sometimes that I am very bad—very bad indeed, and everyone will be delighted to hear that I am so bad."

"I am convinced, Your Majesty," Müller answered, "that every one will rejoice when they hear that Your Majesty is better."

"Yes, yes," Ludwig agreed. "But isn't it very easy to give a man something in his soup—something that will prevent his ever waking?"

Müller did not reply to this question, and Ludwig sensed his unease.

"What is a good sleeping draught?" he asked.

"There are several—opium, morphia, chloral, baths, washing, gymnastics, exercises."

"Will you remain here always?" Ludwig inquired.

"I will change places every month with a colleague."

"Who is he?"

"He is not yet appointed."

"Ah," Ludwig nodded, "he will know some means by which I can be put out of the way."

"Your Majesty," Müller said, "I can answer for my colleagues as well as for myself: the duty of a doctor is to cure, not to kill." There was some further, inconsequential conversation between the two men, but Ludwig's attention seemed directed to Lake Starnberg, where he watched as a small boat continually rowed back and forth along the shoreline. Finally, he nodded to Müller and dismissed him. According to the doctor, "I was with the King for about three-quarters of an hour and during that time I had more questions put to me than in the State Examinations. If I had not already been informed of the patient's bearing by Dr. Gudden and convinced of his illness during our first and second visits to Neuschwanstein, then I would never have had occasion to make my diagnosis."[9]

When Mauder entered his rooms that afternoon to inquire about Ludwig's dinner wishes, he found the king standing at the window, staring out at the lake. The orderly sensed that he was anxious about the continued rain, fearing that it might postpone or even cancel his planned evening walk with Dr. Gudden. He asked Mauder to fetch his opera glasses from a nearby bureau, and Ludwig used them to scan the surface of the lake. Finally, he turned from the window and asked the orderly if the sentries on duty in the castle park had been given any fresh instructions, again inquiring if they were armed.

The afternoon at Berg was calm, with commission members discreetly discussing the situation. There was some talk that further precautions were needed to guard the king, and Holnstein suggested that the shoreline of the lake might somehow be enclosed. But no more was said, and Holnstein left, declaring that he was returning to Munich for the evening. At four-thirty, Ludwig consumed an enormous meal. As if to bolster his courage, he drank a large amount of alcohol: a glass of beer, two glasses of spiced wine, three glasses of regular Rhine wine, and two glasses of arrack.[10] When he had finished, he sent for Dr. Gudden, asking that they take their evening walk as planned. It was raining heavily, but the weather seemed not to deter the king. Gudden agreed, and Ludwig changed his clothing.

Although he had consented to the planned walk, Gudden was less than enthusiastic about the prospect. He complained to several of the commission members not only of the inclement weather but also of the king's incessant questioning on their earlier walk. Nevertheless, Gudden felt honor-bound to abide by his earlier promise. The doctor told his colleagues that he and the king would return to Berg by eight o'clock.

The sky over Lake Starnberg was thick with gray clouds as the two men prepared to leave for their walk, but the rain had temporarily stopped. Ludwig had dressed in a thick black double-breasted overcoat with a velvet collar, and a bowler hat. As he stood on the steps of the castle, he carefully undid the buttons on his suit jacket and left the buttons of his greatcoat open as well. Gudden wore a gray wool overcoat and black silk top hat. Both the king and Gudden carried umbrellas. Ludwig handed his umbrella to Mauder and asked that he roll it up. Mauder did as Ludwig had asked, and handed the rolled umbrella back to the king, who descended the steps and began to walk down the garden path. Gudden was still buttoning his overcoat as the king took to the path, and hurriedly rushed to join him. As the pair departed, the two orderlies began to follow, but Gudden quickly turned round and whispered, *"Es darf kein Pfleger mitgehen"*—"The nurses must not go with the King."[11] Ludwig had selected the lower garden path, which skirted the shoreline of the lake, and Gudden followed without hesitation. Lauterbach, one of the policemen on sentry duty at the castle, watched as Ludwig and Gudden walked toward the shoreline of the lake, finally disappearing into the mist and fog. They were never seen alive again.

38

The Mystery of Lake Starnberg

$\mathbf{B}$y eight o'clock that Sunday evening, Ludwig and Gudden had not yet returned to Castle Berg, and a growing apprehension quickly spread among the staff there that something had gone wrong. Three guards had been on their regular patrols around the castle park, but each reported that he had seen or heard nothing unusual. Lauterbach, the chief of police assigned to Berg, ordered a quick search of the gardens surrounding the castle. There was no sign of either the king or Gudden, though one of the guards did report that he had seen fresh carriage tracks just beyond the main gates, on the road which led back to Munich.

Nearly an hour passed before Dr. Müller ordered a general search of the entire estate. The sky had darkened considerably, and the now incessant rain and wind made the task even more difficult. Police, orderlies, servants, and doctors all joined in the search for the missing men. Along the shoreline, a group of men began a slow hunt among the reeds, their flaming torches and lanterns flickering in the dim twilight.

A little over a half mile from the castle, along the path which skirted the shore of Lake Starnberg, one of the guards spotted the king's rolled umbrella, laid across a park bench. On further examination, he also discovered the king's overcoat and suit jacket. These garments must have been removed rather quickly, for they were turned inside out, with the arms of the suit jacket still inside those of the overcoat. Both coats were drenched. The view from the path to the lake was partially hidden by a number of bushes and small trees. Several of the branches here were broken, as though someone had fallen or been pushed into the foliage. Farther down the path, the hedges parted, allowing access to the shoreline. The guard stepped to the water; there, floating among the reeds, were two hats, the king's bowler and Dr. Gudden's silk top hat.

These ominous discoveries seemed to indicate the worst to Müller, who raced to a nearby fisherman's hut, woke the occupant, Jacob Lidl, and ordered him to row up and down the shoreline in search of the missing men. Müller and Leonhard Huber, the assistant castle steward, joined Lidl in his boat, followed by Jakob Wimmer, the chief castle steward, two servants called Schuster and Liebmann, and the kitchen assistant, Gumbiller. Just down the lake from the spot where the two hats had been found, Huber spotted a dark object floating among the reeds, some ten feet from the shore. Lidl rowed close enough for Huber to see that it was a body, floating facedown, arms outstretched toward the shore. Lidl anchored the boat with his oars, and Huber and Gumbiller jumped into the lake to turn the body over: It was Ludwig. His eyes were open, staring vacantly, and he was cold to the touch. The lake was only four feet deep here, and the king's feet had caught in the loose pebbles of the bottom, anchoring his lower body while the current had carried his upper body toward the shoreline. Müller and Liebmann helped pull him into Lidl's boat, Huber having ordered Wimmer and Schuster back to the castle to bring a stretcher.

Lidl turned his boat and in the darkness almost immediately collided with a second corpse floating face down in the lake. Müller and Huber reached out and turned over Dr. Gudden. They had found him in a curious half-kneeling, half-sitting position, his feet, like those of the king, embedded in the stones on the lake bed. Müller and Huber pulled the second body into Lidl's boat and ordered him to row to shore. Although it was apparent that both men had been dead for some time—rigor mortis had begun to set in—a frantic effort was made to revive them. Müller worked on the king, giving him mouth-to-mouth resuscitation; he also removed the king's shoes and socks and made cuts along the soles of his feet to check his responses. Two policemen attended to Dr. Gudden. When Baron Washington came upon this scene, he apparently assumed that there was still hope and quickly cabled the prime minister: "The King and Gudden both alive. Müller carrying out artificial respiration."[1]

At midnight, after nearly an hour, Müller finally gave up and pronounced the king dead. The two corpses were wrapped in blankets brought from the castle, placed in Lidl's boat, and conveyed back along the shoreline to the castle dock. They were laid out in two different rooms, carefully covered with sheets. Local officials were summoned and a quick examination conducted. Gudden had fought hard for his life. His face showed a number of scratches on the nose and forehead. There was a large bruise over his right eye and, just above it, a deep cut in his forehead. His right cheek also had a gash. The nail of the middle finger on his right hand had been torn off. There were no reported injuries to the king; according to Müller, his face bore "a dark, domineering, almost tyrannical expression."[2]

✳　✳　✳

No part of Ludwig's life is as clouded in legend as his death. Almost as soon as it was announced in Munich, rumors spread that he had strangled Dr. Gudden and then committed suicide, that he had been the victim of an assassination plot, or that he had drowned while trying to escape. The Bavarian government eventually announced that the king had most likely killed Dr. Gudden and then himself, but the space describing cause of death was left blank on Ludwig's autopsy protocol. The intervening years, along with the destruction of many relevant documents, have effectively cloaked the king's death in mystery, a mystery which remains to this day.

The Prussian envoy to Bavaria, Count Philipp zu Eulenburg, happened to be at Lake Starnberg on 13 June 1886. He visited the castle soon after learning of the tragedy and later made several questionable statements which have now passed into the canonical body of literature surrounding the king's death. Eulenburg wrote to his friend Fritz von Farenheid-Beynuhnen:

> I have well endured the great excitement that has attended the royal drama. It was of remarkable interest to personally witness this most unbelievable of recent catastrophes. Privy to the plans of the State to depose the unfortunate King, I was also involved in the events at Hohenschwangau where the King, in his madness, condemned to death the commission which had come to announce his deposition. I was also woken in that night at Starnberg when the King and Dr. Gudden were found in the water near Berg. I will never forget that impression as I rowed across the lonely lake with the fisherman Jakob Ernst in the early morning mist. The silence of death shrouded Schloss Berg; pale and numb stood the servants in the courtyard and in the corridors as I hurried, with a beating heart, to the room where the legendary King had just been laid to rest, an insane smile on his ashen lips, his black curls defiant upon his white forehead. My dismayed questions remained unanswered. I had to piece together for myself what had transpired. In the next room lay Dr. von Gudden, dead, a sombre look upon his face. I saw the scar upon his forehead, the frightful marks of strangulation on his thick neck. He had been strangled by the King when attempting to prevent his suicide. I was the first to examine the scene of the struggle by daylight. I saw the King's footprints deep below the surface. They could not have been made by someone attempting to flee towards the center of the lake. The King, who was a strong swimmer, could have escaped to the left or right of the shore and left no marks on the lake bed. He

had purposefully driven himself to his own death. From the point where the unmistakable signs of the struggle with Dr. Gudden could be seen, the steps of the King traced a line away from the shore towards his death.[3]

There are several problems with Eulenburg's statement. First, he firmly declared that he had seen clear marks of strangulation around Gudden's throat, suggesting that the doctor had been murdered by the king. But neither Müller, who discovered and then examined the bodies, nor the officials who conducted the autopsy, observed any such marks. Eulenburg is the only person who claimed to have seen such marks. Therefore, his testimony must be viewed with suspicion.

Even more unreliable are Eulenburg's assertions regarding the actual scene of the tragedy. He later wrote that he had examined the area on the shore where the park sloped down to the lake, and seen sets of footprints which he identified as those of the king and of Dr. Gudden leading into the water. Eulenburg further claimed that he observed footprints on the muddy lake bed, indicating a terrific struggle between the king and Gudden before Ludwig had managed to drown himself. But Eulenburg's assertions are without truth. He declared that he had visited the lakeshore at four in the morning and observed the footprints leading from the garden path to the water; yet, by this time, it had been raining incessantly for at least eight hours, and the rain and wind had turned the slope into a morass. It is absurd to think that two sets of footprints, hastily made by two men presumably running toward the shore, would remain to be seen in the soft mud after an eight-hour storm. Nor is Eulenburg's testimony concerning the footprints in the lake bed any more trustworthy. Contrary to the count's declaration, the bottom of the lake where the king died was covered not with mud but with loose stones and pebbles. No impression of footprints would thus have remained, only unsettled stones. Even being generous to Eulenburg, one might ask how he managed to see footprints four feet below the surface on the bottom of the lake bed during a storm. Tales of footprints along the shore and on the lake bed itself are inaccurate, a conclusion also reached by the Starnberg Examining Commission, which reported that "the wind, rain and strong waves made conditions such that no footprints could possibly have remained undisturbed."[4]

Nor is the information concerning the time of the king's death any more conclusive. Ludwig and the doctor left Berg for their walk at a quarter to seven that evening, taking the lakeside path, and were expected to return by eight. Both men carried pocket watches. When their bodies were found, it was said that the king's watch had stopped at 6:54 P.M., while Gudden's watch showed 8:00 P.M. If Ludwig's watch is assumed to have stopped when it first came into contact with the water, this suggests that Gudden outlived the king by an hour. The principal problem with this evidence is that there is no independent confirmation to support the time shown on the king's watch: It was viewed very quickly and disappeared later that night, apparently into the pocket of Baron Washington, and was never seen again. Although many writers have offered speculation to account for the difference, this timing problem has remained a mystery.

It has been suggested that Gudden simply forgot to wind his watch and that it had stopped prior to his death. This is ludicrous. Gudden was a man of exacting habits, who made much of his intention to keep the king to a regular schedule. With consultations, telegrams to the government, reports and meetings with fellow commission members, and scheduled meals, it is absurd to think that Gudden would simply have forgotten to tend to his pocket watch. Assuming that his watch stopped for this reason, as several authors have argued, it would mean that from 8:00 A.M. that morning until the time of his death nearly twelve hours later, the doctor never once looked at his watch and noticed that it had stopped. It could not have stopped at eight o'clock at any other time that day had he neglected to wind it. Overwhelmingly, the evidence mitigates against such a conclusion.

It is entirely possible that the king's watch was hastily misread in the confusion following his discovery; it is equally likely that the king's watch stopped of its own accord before it came into contact with the water. Earlier that morning, Ludwig had handed his pocket watch to Mauder and asked him to wind it; the nurse Schneller, who was present, had immediately snatched the item from Mauder's hands and insisted on doing this task himself. The possibility that Schneller suspected some form of secret communication and wished to examine the watch himself is therefore high; he might very well have fumbled with it, turning it over in his hands without bothering to wind it before handing it back to the waiting king. If Schneller neglected to fully wind the watch, then it could very well have stopped at some point during the evening walk. If this is the case, then the time shown on Gudden's watch would most probably be the actual time of death.

It has been suggested that Dr. Gudden carried a bottle of chloroform with him during the evening walk and that this was responsible for the king's death. When Ludwig tried to escape, so this theory runs, the doctor used the chloroform on the king, accidentally killing him. Gudden is then supposed to have suffered a heart attack from the shock and died from accidental drowning. It is known that Gudden did indeed boast that he always had the ability to overpower the much stronger king, and there is a comment from the Reverend Martin Beck from nearby Aufkirchen, who viewed the bodies, that Ludwig's features were not those of a drowned man.[5] While this theory sounds attractive, it also stretches probability to its limits. The sheer coincidence of Gudden suffering a heart attack at just that moment mitigates against acceptance of this scenario. In addition, there surely would have been some evidence that chloroform had been used—a bottle or a handkerchief soaked with the substance; no such evidence was ever found at Lake Starnberg.

From the testimony of Dürckheim, Welcker, Mayr, and others who were with the king during the last week of his life, it is known that Ludwig had often expressed thoughts of suicide. He asked both Dürckheim and Mayr for poison at Neuschwanstein; according to Mayr, he also asked for the key to the main tower there, presumably so that he could jump from its balcony. At Berg, the king made no mention of himself ending his life, though Dr. Müller later declared that he believed Ludwig wished to obtain poison.

The suicide theory has always been popular. Ernest Newman declared, "To us, today, the murder and suicide explanation seems the correct one, but it surely proves not the King's madness but his complete sanity. He knew that, for him, life was over."[6] On the surface, at least, the available evidence seems to support this conclusion. And yet the suicide theory rests almost entirely on the presumption that Ludwig would have acted on his threats. Throughout the king's life, there are repeated examples of both threats and statements made by him which he never had any intention of carrying out. For example, he often declared his intention of abdicating the throne but never followed through with his threat. Nor was he any more attentive to the various orders he gave that his servants be punished, that loans be raised, or, later, that the commission members sent to arrest him be flogged or skinned alive.

Had Ludwig really wished to end his life, he had ample opportunity to do so while still at Neuschwanstein. Although he demanded the key to the main tower presumably so that he could then jump to his death, there was nothing to prevent him, had he so wished, from leaping out a window. Likewise, a plunge from the balcony outside his bedroom would have ended in his death on the rocks of Pollat Gorge below.

Rumors that Ludwig had been murdered began to circulate within hours of his death. The mysterious circumstances of his end, together with a near silence on the subject from both the Bavarian government and the Wittelsbach family, led many to believe the worst. The surreptitious manner in which the government conspired to remove the king raised suspicions; it did not require much imagination to assume that his death might have resulted from a similiar plot. No one in Catholic Bavaria wanted to believe that their anointed sovereign had perished by his own hand. Ludwig's most vehement supporters saw the government's declaration of his suicide as the final injustice inflicted on their beloved monarch. The king's deposition had turned him into a hero; his suspected murder created a martyr.

If there is little evidence to support the suicide and accidental drowning theories, there is even less reliable information to bolster the increasingly popular idea that Ludwig may have been murdered. The fisherman Jacob Lidl left an ambiguous deathbed statement hinting that something mysterious had happened that night; only later did his surviving friends proclaim that he had seen the king shot by an assassin while trying to escape. Although stories that Ludwig was shot circulated among certain elements of the Munich court, all seem to have been second- or thirdhand at best; no one at the scene when the bodies were discovered, nor any of the numerous officials who examined the bodies, reliably reported any evidence of violence. Allegations of widespread conspiracy, involving Lutz, Bismarck, and the royal family themselves, only began to surface much later, when sons and daughters, friends and acquaintances made tearful confessions claiming that Ludwig had been murdered.

The Bavarian government certainly found itself in a perilous situation immediately after the king's deposition; Ludwig's open call for armed resistance against Lutz and his uncle Luitpold amounted to a declaration of civil war. Under such circumstances, it is not difficult to think that the Lutz ministry might possibly have moved to eliminate the popular figure of Ludwig II. But any government plot would almost certainly have involved figures capable of eliminating such inconvenient witnesses as simple fishermen and untrustworthy orderlies. Despite the extravagant claims made over the years, there is no direct evidence that Ludwig may have been assassinated.

Overwhelmingly, the evidence suggests that plans for a rescue of the king existed. Empress Elizabeth spent the afternoon of 13 June 1886 wandering along the shoreline of Starnberg at Possenhofen, across the lake from Berg. She insisted on remaining outside into the evening, even though the impending storm had broken, staring across the lake at the distant castle.[7] It was widely believed that she had arranged for her cousin to be rescued, and she is said to have had a carriage waiting for him just down the lake, ready to spirit him to Munich or across the border into Austria.[8]

It is possible that this was the mysterious carriage said to have belonged to a certain Baron M. Beck. Beck reportedly sent to Munich for a team of his fastest horses and kept them harnessed to a carriage all afternoon and evening. Inside, the carriage was filled with hundreds of handbills, copies of the king's proclamation of the week before, calling for his restoration and armed resistance to both Lutz and Prince Luitpold.[9] Several men were supposed to have been hidden in the park at Berg that evening to direct the king to this carriage; this would also explain the fresh carriage tracks discovered outside the gates later that evening.[10]

According to several sources, the carriage is also tied to the boats observed by both the king and the commission members that evening sailing up and down Lake Starnberg. One or two of these boats was said to have contained up to twenty armed men from neighboring Leoni, Ammerland, and Seeshaupt, there to assist the king in his escape and to defend him from the sentries on duty at Berg.[11] One of the boats also apparently contained Richard Hornig's brother and a relative, Count A. Rambaldi. Hornig, who lived down the shoreline at Seeleiten, later maintained that Ludwig had been trying to reach his house when he died. These men reportedly spent the afternoon and evening of the thirteenth sailing before the park at Berg, waiting to rescue the king. That night, Count Rambaldi returned to his wife, soaked to the skin, and exclaimed, "We found a hat! It's all over!"[12]

What happened that dark, rainy Sunday evening at Lake Starnberg? That afternoon, Ludwig passed a letter for his cousin Elizabeth to Friedrich Zanders, and it is likely that he informed the empress of the planned second walk that evening. After Zanders left, Ludwig seemed preoccupied; he sat by the window of his room, scanning the surface of the lake with a pair of opera glasses, searching for something. Later that afternoon, his attention was rewarded when he spotted several small boats, sailing purposefully back and forth before the castle. He called for Mauder and asked if the guards on duty had been given any new instructions. At half past four, he consumed a large meal, washed down with a considerable amount of alcohol; as the hour of his proposed second walk with Gudden approached, Ludwig appeared extremely anxious, fearful that the excursion would be canceled due to the increasingly inclement weather.

Ludwig and Gudden left Berg at 6:45 P.M. As he stood on the castle steps in the pouring rain, Ludwig carefully undid the buttons on his overcoat and suit jacket. The only logical conclusion is that he was preparing himself for a moment when he could quickly strip off the cumbersome clothes to ease his swim to safety. The king himself elected to follow the lakeside path through the garden which skirted the shoreline. He had already walked several hundred yards by the time Gudden managed to catch up. A quarter mile from the castle, hidden by a bend in the shore and dense foliage, the lakeside path divided: To the right, the walk continued to skirt the reed-choked shoreline, while the path to the left climbed the hillside and wound through a grove of trees. The two paths merged again just under a half mile from the castle garden.

One of the sentries on duty at Berg that evening, Lauterbach, later reported that he had patrolled along the upper path and had seen nothing unusual; the king and Dr. Gudden, therefore, must have remained on the lower path, the one closest to the lakeshore. This choice would also place Ludwig in proximity to the shoreline, important if he expected to be rescued by boat.

It was growing dark when Ludwig and Gudden reached the end of the lakeside path. Here, the trees parted, opening to Lake Starnberg; as Ludwig walked, the beckoning waters spread before him, their rain-dappled surface reflecting the distant shoreline and the vague outline of Possenhofen. He had been betrayed, declared mad, imprisoned like his brother, Otto. At Neuschwanstein he had not the strength to fight; now, staring out across the lake, he made his decision. He turned to Dr. Gudden, struggling to keep up with the king's rapid pace; his servants, his prime minister, and his uncle had deceived and humiliated him, but the elderly man at his side had proclaimed him incurably insane. With his rolled umbrella, Ludwig swung at the doctor, hitting Gudden in the forehead before throwing it upon a nearby bench. Startled, Gudden reached out to the king, grabbing his overcoat and jacket in an effort to halt his flight. Free of his heavy outer garments, Ludwig ran toward the shoreline, with Gudden stumbling behind; the doctor grabbed him again at the edge of the path, sending both men tumbling into a clump of bushes, but the king, taller and more powerful than his keeper, pushed him away and plunged into the lake. Gudden somehow managed to reach him again, but Ludwig would not be stopped. He struck the doctor in the face, bruising his right eye and scratching him in an effort to break free. Gudden fought back, tearing the nail from his right middle finger, before he finally succumbed. He may have lost consciousness from the blows to his head during the struggle and thus drowned, or suffered a heart attack or stroke. His grip on Ludwig eased, and the king pushed him aside into the water.

In his youth, Ludwig had been an excellent swimmer. But his struggle with Gudden had left him exhausted. Overweight, plunged into a cold lake, possibly still drunk and with a full stomach, Ludwig was suddenly overwhelmed. Whether it was a heart attack or fatigue, he could continue no longer. Drenched by the incessant rain, he slowly slipped beneath the cool waters of Lake Starnberg, the distant lights of Possenhofen growing dim, sinking further and further until the blackness closed over him.

Epilogue

News of King Ludwig II's death, coming so soon after his forced deposition and declaration of madness, plunged Bavaria into profound shock and mourning. Word of the tragedy at Lake Starnberg spread quickly. Queen Marie was staying at Elbigenalp at the time of her son's arrest and incarceration at Berg. The staff and suite were notified early Monday morning, but no one could summon the courage to inform the queen that Ludwig was dead. Her personal confessor found Marie sitting with a few of her ladies-in-waiting and asked if he might read to her a particular Bible passage. As he read, the queen noticed the strained faces of her suite and suddenly asked if something had happened to her son Ludwig. One of her ladies-in-waiting answered that he was seriously ill. But their tear-stained faces gave the terrible secret away. "Is King Ludwig dead?" his mother asked in a whisper. No one was able to speak; finally, Princess Thérèse nodded yes, and the queen burst into tears.[1]

A provisional report had already been commissioned by the Lutz government to confirm Prince Otto's insanity. Although he technically became king on the moment of his brother's death, Otto remained locked away at Castle Furstenreid, unaware of the drama being played out at Lake Starnberg. A delegation sent by the Wittelsbach family visited him and sadly informed the prince of Ludwig's death. But Otto, according to the report, seemed completely unaware of this grave news and quickly changed the subject.[2]

Empress Elizabeth of Austria was visiting her family at Possenhofen when she learned of the king's death. On hearing the news, the empress cried out to her mother, "The King was no madman, only an eccentric living in a world of dreams! They might have treated him more gently and spared him such a terrible end."[3] Prince Luitpold, the new prince regent and the man who, along with Prime Minister Lutz, had brought down his nephew and thus precipitated the tragedy, burst into tears on learning of Ludwig's death.[4]

Early that Monday morning, Ludwig's body was washed and laid out in his bedroom at Berg. Wilhelm von Rumann and Max Gube created a death mask, sculpted his hands, and cut a lock from the side of his carefully arranged hair.[5] Since midnight the previous evening, groups of local residents had been gathering at the castle gates, waiting to pay their respects to their much loved king. They were finally admitted to Berg at three Monday afternoon. Ludwig lay in his bed, beneath a canopy of his favorite blue brocade; his body was completely surrounded by bunches of roses and potted palms, and by fragrant votive candles. On his breast lay a simple bouquet of jasmine, picked by his cousin Empress Elizabeth herself and sent from Possenhofen early that afternoon. The peasants who filed past his body repeatedly crossed themselves, dropped to their knees in prayer, and tore at the sheets which covered him, hoping to carry away a last precious souvenir of their sovereign.[6]

At eight that evening, court ecclesiastics finally arrived at Castle Berg to bless Ludwig's body. Four grooms placed him in a casket and carried it out of the castle to a waiting hearse. The hearse itself was almost entirely covered with flowers, many of which had been brought by residents of the neighboring villages on Lake Starnberg. Against the scarlet-and-gold backdrop of the setting sun and the light of the flaming torches, Ludwig left Berg for the last time as the procession slowly made its way out of the castle gates and along the road toward Munich.

Midway through the journey, the cortege passed by the dark windows of Castle Furstenreid, where the new king, Otto, remained confined, oblivious to the sad scene below. By one o'clock, the procession had reached the outskirts of the capital. Hundreds of people had simply joined the entourage along the way, walking silently behind the hearse with its wreath-covered casket. At the city limits, a cavalry squadron of Chevaux Legers met the cortege and formed an honor guard, riding before the seemingly endless string of mourners and officials as it made its way through the twisting streets to the Residenz.

On the following day, a group of royal physicians conducted the king's autopsy, and in an effort to support their findings of insanity, the Bavarian government took the unprecedented step of releasing the findings to the national press. According to the report, several interesting discoveries were made as to the state of Ludwig's brain. There was evidence of repeated attacks of inflammation of the skull cavity and the skin surrounding it. The skin covering the skull was found to be extremely thin, while the skull cavity itself was quite small. A small growth near the frontal bone appeared at times to have cut off some of the flow of blood through the main artery. A number of smaller deformations in the brain itself tend to confirm the conclusion that the king was suffering from some degenerative brain disease. This, in turn, supports Biermann's theory that Ludwig may have had syphilis.[7]

Ludwig's enormous popularity soon became apparent. Buildings in the capital were draped in black crepe, flags were lowered to half-mast, and church bells tolled mournfully, summoning his former subjects to pray for his soul. Shops quickly sold out of commemorative busts of the king, along with special postcards, photographs, and cheaply printed pamphlets hinting at Ludwig's possible murder. Coverage of his death saturated the newspapers, and special editions—sometimes as many as four a day—were printed to satisfy the heavy public demand.[8] Thousands of Bavarians from all across the kingdom came to Munich to pay their last respects. One newspaper reported on 17 June: "The crush of mourning folk to the Old Chapel in the Residenz was without end. A lady who had fainted was almost trampled to death. Yesterday a total of twenty people fainted and a mountain of lost tresses, bustles, and broken umbrellas bore testimony to the rigours to which people subjected themselves."[9]

From Wednesday, 16 June through his funeral on Saturday, Ludwig's body lay in state in the Hofkapelle of the Munich Residenz. The walls of the chapel were draped in black; from the center of the ceiling, a canopy of black silk fell away in folds to the four corners of the room, and above the high altar hung a large white cross and the Wittelsbach coat of arms. Banks of flowers, laurel and cypress trees, and garlands of Malmaison roses decorated the church, overwhelming the room with their exotic scents, while flickering shadows from the hundreds of tall votive candles played upon the black-draped walls. General-adjutants of the king's suite, along with Knights of the Order of St. George, formed the honor guard, heads bowed in silence. Ludwig's coffin rested on an inclined bier, covered with a black velvet pall and his ermine robe of state. He was dressed in the robes of the grand master of the Order of St. Hubertus: black silk knee breeches, black velvet cloak, and a white silk shirt with heavy ruffles at the collar and cuffs. Around his neck were the collar and chain of the order. His left hand lay at his side, embracing the jeweled hilt of a sword. Clutched between the stiff fingers of his right hand was Empress Elizabeth's bouquet of jasmine. Ludwig's face had a strange, almost waxen look, and his hair had been carefully swept up at the sides to conceal the autopsy scars. In death, he seemed to have regained his famous youthful beauty. Crown Prince Friedrich Wilhelm of Prussia wrote to Queen Marie: "Today I saw the face of your dear son for the last time, fifteen years having elapsed since I had seen him previously. Peace and tranquility rested upon his features, the beauty of which death could not take from him."[10]

The king's state funeral took place on Saturday, 19 June, a brilliant, cloudless summer day. Thousands of people lined the procession route from the Residenz to St. Michael's Church, where Ludwig was to be interred, standing solemnly between the lines of soldiers guarding the route. Places at windows overlooking the route commanded rental fees of as much as 100 marks.[11]

A thunderous last salute announced that the funeral procession had at last departed the Wittelsbach palace for the king's final place of rest. The muffled drumbeats of the royal musicians joined the tolling of the church bells and the booming of the distant guns to create a cacaphony, shattering the somber stillness of the late Saturday morning. Ludwig's funeral was the largest state occasion ever held in the Bavarian capital. The procession was headed by the servants of the Bavarian nobility, bearing flaming torches. They were followed by representatives of the city's religious orders; the schools; officials of the court staff in full dress uniforms; the secular and regular clergy; the court clergy; the chapter; and the bishops of Bavaria. A delegation of black-cowled figures known as Gugelmänner came next, each holding crossed tapers and carrying the royal coat of arms.[12]

Eight white horses draped in black palls and equipped with black liveries drew the king's hearse through the streets of Munich, preceded by officials in gold braid carrying the sword of state and swords of office. The hearse itself was a large vehicle, draped in black, with wreaths of garlanded flowers hung at each of the four peaked corners. At the center, above the bier, rose a gilded base on which stood a replica of the Wittelsbach state crown. On either side of the hearse walked the king's adjutants, the court chamberlains in their gold-braided costumes, and the Knights of the Order of St. George.[13] Ludwig's coffin was covered with the royal standard; the state crown, and the scepter, along with the king's orders and awards, lay atop the coffin. Ludwig's favorite horse, saddle empty and draped in black, followed. A cross bearer and two pages carrying lighted tapers followed the hearse, with a squadron of soldiers behind them. The royal mourners who walked in the procession included Prince Luitpold, the new prince regent; the crown prince of Prussia in the uniform of a German field marshal; and the crown prince of Austria. The princes of the royal house came next, followed by Bavarian noblemen, the foreign ambassadors, high officials of the crown, the ministry, and deputations from various Bavarian towns and associations. Detachments of cavalry and infantry closed the procession, their regimental bands playing the funeral marches of Frédéric François Chopin and Beethoven.[14] It took two and a half hours for the procession to reach St. Michael's Church.

Huge mourning banners draped the entrance to the church. The archbishop, assisted by members of the clergy, blessed the coffin, while mourners sank upon their knees, and the people looking on from the sidewalks sobbed openly. Members of the Gugelmänner carried the coffin inside to the high altar as the choir chanted a psalm. A large black tapestry hung behind the altar, decorated with a large white cross inscribed in Latin: "*Ludovicus II Rex Bavariae nat. 25.8.1845, denat. 13.6.1886.*" Above the altar hung a baldachin surmounted by a gilded crown; from its rim, black crepe was hung in swags to the four corners of the church, forming a canopy. The king's coffin rested on an inclined bier before the altar, surrounded by tall white candles and banks of flowers. The Bavarian state crown and all of Ludwig's orders and insignia lay on top of the coffin. After a short service, Capuchin monks carried Ludwig's coffin through the nave and down a flight of stone steps into the crypt below. As they did so, the blue sky above suddenly clouded over and, without warning, a bolt of lightning split the sky, nearly striking the church. "The Heavens shed a tear," one of Munich's newspapers declared sadly.[15]

In October of 1886, Ludwig II was finally interred in his finished tomb, a magnificent neoclassical green marble sarcophagus resting on four heavily carved lion's paws. At each of the four corners, raised finials were topped with gilded representations of the Wittelsbach lion. The center of the sarcophagus was raised to form a platform on which rested a gilded replica of the Bavarian state crown; at the front was a carved relief of the royal coat of arms. Following Wittelsbach tradition, Ludwig's heart, which had been removed at the time of autopsy, was taken to the Votive Chapel at Altotting to join the hearts of other Bavarian kings, including his father, Maximilian II, and his grandfather Ludwig I. His heart was placed in a tall silver urn of classical design, decorated in gilt with Ludwig's intertwined initials and carved wreaths of edelweiss and Alpine roses.[16]

The day after Ludwig's death, a pole was anchored in the bottom of Lake Starnberg at the spot where his body had been discovered. Just up the hillside, Queen Marie had a small, temporary chapel erected in memory of her son, and Prince Regent Luitpold built a twisted Gothic column containing a watch light near the shoreline. On the tenth anniversary of the king's death, Luitpold presided over the laying of a foundation stone for a permanent votive chapel to Ludwig's memory. His former court architect Julius Hofmann designed the Romanesque structure, with its steeply pitched roof and high dome decorated with frescoes. Every year, on the anniversary of his death, the king's admirers gather at the shoreline of the lake before the cross. They bring wreaths, Bavarian flags, and Wittelsbach standards to cast on the water where Ludwig died.

The king's mother survived him by only three years, dying at Hohenschwangau on 17 May 1889 at the age of sixty-four. Following Ludwig's death, she withdrew completely from public life, finding comfort only in her conversion to Catholicism. Although Otto had always been her favorite son, the queen could not bear to visit him at Castle Furstenried. She died alone, surrounded only by the members of her small court.

Otto ruled Bavaria as king only in name; his condition did not allow any meaningful conversation, and no one ever knew if he understood his position.

Otto died on 11 October 1916 of a stomach hemorrhage at the age of sixty-eight. His impotent reign had lasted thirty years—ironically, the longest of all the Wittelsbach kings. Despite World War I, Otto was given a full state funeral befitting his position. Members of Europe's royal families came to pay their respects, and the Wittelsbach court went into mourning for three months. Otto was interred in the crypt of St. Michael's Church, in a large sarcophagus next to that of his brother Ludwig.

Prince Luitpold, the prince regent who actually ruled Bavaria during the reign of his nephew Otto, died in 1912 at the age of ninety-two. His son acceded to the Bavarian throne as Ludwig III, thus providing the unusual circumstance of two reigning kings in the same country. In 1918, when Kaiser Wilhelm II abdicated the German throne, the Wittelsbachs' thousand-year rule in Bavaria also came to an end. A republic was declared, and the royal family quietly accepted their loss of royal status. There was, however, no revolution: Members of the royal family remained welcome Bavarians, though they lost most of their regal trappings, including the Residenz and Nymphenburg, to a nationalization scheme. Today, they remain respected and loved within the country, strong symbols of a proud heritage and tradition which many Bavarians openly wish to restore.

Ludwig's former fiancée, Princess Sophie in Bavaria, never quite recovered from the scandalous gossip which circulated about her at the time the king broke off the engagement. Her marriage to the Duc d'Alençon appears to have been a happy one, and their daughter, Princess Louise d'Orléans, married Prince Alfonso of Bavaria in 1891. In May of 1897, Sophie was supervising a charity bazaar in Paris when a fire erupted among the stalls. Rather than flee, Sophie helped some of the young girls to escape, returning again and again into the increasing inferno. Finally, however, she failed to return. When her body was discovered, it was so badly burned that she could be identified only by her teeth.[17]

"I feel so foresaken and lonely on this earth, like a left-over from better times, blown into the present which I hate, and where I shall always feel a stranger," Ludwig once wrote.[18] It was a sentiment which aptly described the king's life, and one with which his cousin Empress Elizabeth could easily identify. She, more than anyone else—more than the queen, Wagner, Taxis, or Hornig—understood the king's strange nature, his romantic ideals, and the forsaking of the realities of the nineteenth century for a world of dreams where there were no unfriendly voices. She alone would have understood the famous words of her cousin, which serve as his epitaph to history: "It is surely understandable that I am sometimes attacked by an absolute fever of anger and hatred, and that I turn away in disgust from the world around me which has so little to offer me. Perhaps one day I shall be at peace with this earth, when all the ideals whose sacred flames I cherish are destroyed. But do not ever wish this! I wish to remain an eternal enigma, to myself and to others."[19]

Source Notes

In the source notes, the following abbreviations have been used: BWL: Richard Wagner, *Briefwechsel zwischen Wagner und Liszt;* C-H: Desmond Chapman-Huston, *Bavarian Fantasy: The Story of Ludwig II;* CW: Cosima Wagner, *Die Tagebucher;* FKLB: Eugen Frantz, editor, *König Ludwig II von Bayern, das königliche Kabinett, das Ministerium und das Bayerische Volk, 1864–1866* ; KLRWB: Otto Strobel, editor, *König Ludwig II und Richard Wagner, Briefwechsel;* and Letters: Stewart Spencer and Barry Millington, editors, *Selected Letters of Richard Wagner.*

Chapter One

1. This description of the Residenz is drawn from Herbert Brunner, *Residenz Guide* and *Altes Residenztheatre Guide* and from personal visits.
2. Gerard, xxxi.
3. Ibid, xxxvi.

Chapter Two

1. Steinberger, 14.
2. C-H, 5.
3. Steinberger, 25.
4. C-H, 14.
5. Ibid, 298–99.
6. Steinberger, 21.
7. C-H, 14.
8. Richter, 7.
9. Gerard, 14.
10. Hacker, 25–6.

11. Ibid, 26.
12. Richter, 11.
13. Channon, 69.
14. C-H, 15.
15. This description of Hohenschwangau draws on information from *Guide Book, Neuschwanstein and Hohenschwangau*, Kreisel, *Schloss Hohenschwangau*, Des Cars, Mennett, Nohbauer, and personal visits.
16. Gerard, xlvii.
17. Richter, 5.
18. C-H, 26.
19. Richter, 6.

Chapter Three

1. C-H, 15.
2. Ibid, 17.
3. McIntosh, 19–20.
4. Richter, 4.
5. C-H, 16.
6. Ibid, 23.
7. Ibid, 23.
8. Richter, 7.
9. C-H, 21.
10. Ibid, 19.
11. Gerard, 17.
12. McIntosh, 22.
13. C-H, 18.
14. Hacker, 26.

Chapter Four

1. Zareck, 27.
2. Newman, 3:231–2.
3. Ibid, 3:206.
4. Zareck, 27.
5. Ibid, 29.
6. Ibid.
7. C-H, 30.
8. Newman, 3:265.
9. KLRWB, 3:6.
10. C-H, 30.
11. Newman, 3:214.

Chapter Five

1. Blunt, 20.
2. C-H, 58.
3. Ibid, 59.
4. Ibid, 38–9.
5. Bohm, 1:19.
6. Newman, 1:243.
7. Ibid, 3:384–5.
8. C-H, 38.
9. Ibid, 36.
10. Ibid, 45.
11. Ibid, 49–50.
12. Ibid, 48.

Chapter Six

1. C-H, 33.
2. Bismarck, 388–9.
3. C-H, 55.
4. Ibid, 52.
5. Ibid, 52.
6. Ibid, 52.
7. Ibid, 52.
8. Zareck, 39.
9. Steinberger, 17.
10. Ibid, 34.
11. Hacker, 43.
12. Bohm, 1:16.

Chapter Seven

1. C-H, 60.
2. Ibid, 58–9.
3. Zareck, 45.
4. Bismarck, 389.
5. Bohm, 1:15.
6. Ibid, 1:18–9.
7. Steinberger, 36.
8. Richter, 20.
9. C-H, 75.

10. Zareck, 42.
11. Ibid, 43.
12. Bismarck, 1:165.
13. Kissinger, 129.
14. Palmer, 131.
15. C-H, 53.

Chapter Eight

1. Haslip, 11.
2. Hamann, 9; 21.
3. Cited, Hamann, 267.
4. Hacker, 133.
5. Haslip, 176–77.
6. Ibid, 245.
7. Ibid, 216.
8. Cited, Hamann, 267.
9. C-H, 72.
10. Richter, 21.

Chapter Nine

1. Bohm, 1:43.
2. Zareck, 57.
3. Ibid, 57.
4. Newman, 3:218.
5. KLRWB, 1:xxxv.
6. KLRWB, 1:xxxv.
7. Ibid, 186.
8. Newman, 3:222.
9. Zareck, 58.
10. KLRWB, 1:xxxv.
11. Hacker, 65.
12. Wagner, 197.
13. Newman, 3:217.
14. KLRWB, 1:12.

Chapter Ten

1. C-H, 134.
2. CW, 1:74.
3. Cited, Letters, 587.
4. Letters, 587.
5. KLRWB, 1:21.

6. Ibid, 1:36.
7. Gerard, 66.
8. Ibid, 2:223.
9. BWL, 2:4.
10. Newman, 3:467-68.
11. Cited, Newman, 3:468.
12. Letters, 591.
13. Newman, 3:228.

Chapter Eleven

1. Newman, 3:229–30.
2. Ibid, 3:308.
3. Ibid, 3:309–10.
4. Ibid, 3:388.
5. Richter, 63–4.
6. Ibid, 61.
7. Ibid, 53.
8. Newman, 3:340.
9. Ibid, 3:335.
10. KLRWB, 4:48–51.
11. Newman, 3:336.
12. KLRWB, 4:43.
13. Newman, 3:337.
14. KLRWB, 4:45.
15. Newman, 3:339.
16. KLRWB, 4:47–51.
17. Ibid, 1:60–1.
18. Ibid, 1:68–9.
19. Ibid, 1:71–2.
20. Newman, 3:364.

Chapter Twelve

1. Ibid, 3:369.
2. Ibid, 3:353.
3. Ibid, 3:370.
4. KLRWB, 1:03.
5. Ibid, 1:95.
6. Quoted, Sabor, 351.
7. KLRWB, 1:105.
8. Newman, 3:406.

Chapter Thirteen

1. Ibid, 3:390.
2. Ibid, 94–5.
3. C-H, 85.
4. Ibid, 84.
5. Richter, 62.

Chapter Fourteen

1. KLRWB, 1:143.
2. Newman, 3:456.
3. KLRWB, 1:144–8.
4. Newman, 3:461.
5. Ibid, 3:488.
6. Ibid, 3:488.
7. Ibid, 3:487.
8. KLRWB, 4:107–9.
9. Newman, 3:495.
10. Ibid, 1:231–2.
11. Newman, 3:494.
12. Ebenthal, 74-5.

Chapter Fifteen

1. Newman, 3:497.
2. Ibid, 3:497–8.
3. Zareck, 116.
4. Richter, 72.
5. Newman, 3:499.
6. Ibid, 3:499.
7. Ibid, 3:499.
8. KLRWB, 4:124.
9. Newman, 3:514–5.

Chapter Sixteen

1. Crankshaw, 192.
2. Cited, Palmer, 133.
3. Richter, 78.
4. Ibid, 78.
5. Gerard, 93.
6. Richter, 47.
7. Ibid, German edition, 310.

8. Hohenlohe, 1:145.
9. Richter, 77.
10. FKLB, 97–8.
11. KLRWB, 2:xiv.
12. Ibid, 2:34.
13. Ibid, 2:37–8.
14. Corti, Elizabeth, 147.
15. Newman, 3:542.
16. Hohenlohe, 1:147.

Chapter Seventeen

1. Richter, 64.
2. Ibid, 93.
3. Corti, 147.
4. KLRWB, 2:63.
5. Richter, 92.
6. Hohenlohe, 1:149–51.
7. KLRWB, 2:65.
8. Hacker, 121.
9. Richter, 94.
10. Gerard, 92.
11. Ibid, 93-4.
12. KLRWB, 2:73.

Chapter Eighteen

1. Ibid, 3:545.
2. KLRWB, 2:53–5.
3. Ibid, 3:549.
4. Ibid, 3:548.
5. Ibid, 3:456.
6. Newman, 4:85–6.
7. KLRWB, 2:177.
8. Ibid, 4:196.
9. Newman, 4:103.
10. KLRWB, 2:120.
11. Newman, 4:44.
12. KLRWB, 2:212–5.
13. Ibid, 2:213–5.
14. Ibid, 2:216.

Chapter Nineteen

1. KLRWB, 2:232.
2. KLRWB, 2:255.
3. Newman, 4:222.
4. KLRWB, 5:102.
5. Ibid, 5:102–3.
6. Ibid, 4:210–2.
7. Richter, 145.
8. Newman, 4:224.
9. KLRWB, 2:290.
10. Ibid, 2:305.
11. Ibid, 2:296.
12. KLRWB, 2:311.

Chapter Twenty

1. Gerard, 158.
2. Haslip, 176.
3. Ibid, 94–5.
4. Ibid, 96.
5. Ibid, 112.
6. Zareck, 163.
7. Bohm, 1:353.
8. Hacker, 138.
9. Steinberger, 58.

Chapter Twenty-one

1. Hacker, 140.
2. C-H, 117.
3. Ibid, 117.
4. Zareck, 165.
5. Haslip, 208.
6. KLRWB, 2:155–6.
7. C-H, 124–5.
8. Haslip, 216.
9. Schmid, 33–4.
10. Richter, 127.
11. Hacker, 141.

12. C-H, 125.
13. Bohm, 2:369.
14. Gerard, 102.
15. Richter, German edition, 172.
16. C-H, 134–5.
17. Ibid, 135.
18. Ibid, 135-7.
19. Bohm, 2:402.
20. Sailer, 49.
21. Hacker, 139–40.
22. C-H, 137.
23. Bertram, 47.
24. Corti, *Downfall*, 196.
25. Corti, Elizabeth, 174–5.

Chapter Twenty-two

1. Corti, Elizabeth, 179.
2. Ibid, 152–3.
3. Blunt, 93.
4. Bohm, 1:385.
5. Ibid, 1:385.
6. Ibid, 1:385–8.
7. Zareck, 240.
8. Richter, 129.
9. Zareck, 240.
10. Ibid, 154.

Chapter Twenty-three

1. Hohenlohe, 1:136.
2. Bohm, 2:176.
3. Hohenlohe, 1:130.
4. Ibid, 1:353.
5. Ibid, 1:201.
6. Ibid, 1:224–5.
7. Hohenlohe, 1:244.
8. Ibid, 1:244–5.
9. Ibid, 1:248–9.
10. Ibid, 1:278.

Chapter Twenty-four

1. Bohm, 2:224.
2. Richter, German edition, 216.
3. Gerard, 115.
4. Hohenlohe, 2:15.
5. Friedrich Wilhelm, 12.
6. Ibid, 17.
7. Richter, 168.
8. Ibid, 163–4.
9. Zareck, 203.
10. Hohenlohe, 2:27.

Chapter Twenty-five

1. Richter, 171.
2. Ibid, 171.
3. Crankshaw, 291.
4. Richter, German edition, 248.
5. C-H, 164.
6. Ibid, 164.
7. Richter, 23.
8. Bohm, 1:139.
9. Sailer, 75, reproduces Ludwig's original draft.
10. Bismarck, 1:391.
11. Richter, 183.
12. Bismarck, 1:392.
13. Friedrich Wilhelm, 210.
14. C-H, 165.
15. Richter, German edition, 258–9.
16. C-H, 167.
17. Ibid, 170–1.
18. C-H, 169.
19. Sailer, 81.

Chapter Twenty-six

1. Hohenlohe, 1:327.

Chapter Twenty-seven

1. Hacker, 264.
2. Gerard, 136.

3. Ibid, 240.
4. Richter, 228.
5. Hamann, 269.
6. Hacker, 261–2.
7. Nohbauer, 141.
8. Zareck, 243.
9. Richter, 148.

Chapter Twenty-eight

1. Quoted, Blunt, 166–7.
2. Bohm, 2:103.
3. Zareck, 228.
4. Hacker, 289.
5. Ibid, 292.
6. C-H, 200.
7. Ibid, 204.
8. Hacker, 279–80.
9. See McIntosh, Chapter 13, for further information.

Chapter Twenty-nine

1. Newman, 4:284.
2. Gerard, 140.
3. Ibid, 3:83.
4. Newman, 4:468.
5. C-H, 247.
6. Richter, 240.
7. Newman, 3:240.

Chapter Thirty

1. C-H, 254.
2. Ibid, 168–9.
3. Ibid, 174.
4. Ibid, 174–5.
5. Ibid, 208.
6. Richter, 252.
7. C-H, 183.
8. Ibid, 189.

9. Ibid, 186.
10. Ibid, 188.
11. Ibid, 217.
12. Ibid, 220.
13. Ibid, 220.
14. Blunt, 192.
15. C-H, 221.
16. Blunt, 197.
17. Zareck, 255.
18. Zareck, 257.
19. Blunt, 201.
20. Newman, 3:344.
21. C-H, 227.

Chapter Thirty-one

1. Kreisel, 11.
2. Hojer, *König Ludwig II.-Museum Herrenchiemsee, Katalog*, 154–86.
3. Ibid, 62–94.
4. Paz, 117–22.
5. Haslip, 229.
6. *Guide Book, Neuschwanstein and Hohenschwangau*, 10.
7. KLRWB, 2:224–5.
8. Ebenthal, 213.
9. Petzet, *The Castle of Neuschwanstein*, 34.
10. Ibid, 21.
11. Nohbauer, 145.
12. Desing, *Royal Castle, Neuschwanstein*, 8.
13. Petzet, *Neuschwanstein*, 23.

Chapter Thirty-two

1. C-H, 147.
2. Kreisel, 25.
3. Petzet, *Linderhof Castle*, 36.
4. Kreisel, *The Castles of Ludwig II of Bavaria*, 39.
5. Gerard, 202.
6. Kreisel, *The Castle of Ludwig II of Bavaria*, 50.
7. Nicolson, 316; Petzet, *The Royal Palace of Herrenchiemsee*, 16.
8. Zareck, 220.
9. Hojer, *König Ludwig II.-Museum*, 401.

10. Petzet, *Die Welt des Bayerischen*, 90.
11. *Designs for the Dream King*, 15.

Chapter Thirty-three

1. C-H, 245.
2. Hacker, 319.
3. C-H, 263.
4. Hacker, 322–3.
5. C-H, 266.
6. Quoted, McIntosh, 182.

Chapter Thirty-four

1. Hamann, 270.
2. Zareck, 263.
3. Richter, 12.
4. C-H, 166–7.
5. Ibid, 168.
6. Ibid, 168.
7. Ibid, 171.
8. Ibid, 172.
9. Ibid, 176–7.
10. Rall and Petzet, *King Ludwig II*, 47–8.
11. C-H, 178.
12. Ibid, 201.
13. Channon, 111.
14. Blunt, 174.
15. Hacker, 340.
16. Richter, 212.
17. Channon, 96.
18. Hacker, 302.
19. Blunt, 211.
20. Ibid, 208.
21. Hacker, 305.
22. Ibid, 305.
23. Richter, 253.
24. Blunt, 207.
25. Quoted, Desing, 35–6.
26. Ibid, 38–40.
27. C-H, 244.

28. See Von Burg, *Ludwig II of Bavaria* for further speculation on Ludwig's drug use.
29. Biermann.
30. Ibid.
31. Quoted, Desing, 21–2.

Chapter Thirty-five

1. Rall and Petzet, *King Ludwig II*, 30.
2. Hacker, 339–40.
3. Richter, 256.
4. Rall and Petzet, 33–4.
5. C-H, 275–6.
6. Hacker, 343.
7. Ibid, 343–4.

Chapter Thirty-six

1. Rall and Petzet, *King Ludwig II*, 33–4.
2. Ibid, 35.
3. Ebenthal, 284.
4. C-H, 279.
5. Richter, 264.
6. Ebenthal, 287.
7. Richter, 265.
8. Ibid, 266.
9. Ibid, 266.
10. Rall and Petzet, 37.
11. Ibid, 38.
12. Ebenthal, 291–2.
13. C-H, 281.
14. Rall and Petzet, 39.
15. Richter, 272.
16. Ebenthal, 293.
17. Hacker, 360.
18. Rall and Petzet, *King Ludwig II*, 40.
19. Hacker, 362.
20. Ebenthal, 298.
21. Richter, 273.
22. Hacker, 361.
23. Richter, 273.
24. Ibid, 273.
25. Blunt, 223.

26. Gerard, 272–73.
27. Ibid, 274.
28. Rall and Petzet, *King Ludwig II. Wirklichkeit und Rätsel*, 93–4.
29. Ibid, 44.
30. Ibid, 44.

Chapter Thirty-seven

1. Nohbauer, 192–93.
2. Sailer, 139.
3. Richter, German edition, 386.
4. Richter, 275.
5. Hacker, 388.
6. C-H, 288.
7. Richter, 277.
8. Hacker, 383–5.
9. Gerard, 278–80.
10. Blunt, 226.
11. C-H, 289.

Chapter Thirty-eight

1. Von Burg, *Ludwig II of Bavaria*, 311.
2. Hacker, 400.
3. Sailer, 146.
4. Quoted, Von Burg, 322–3.
5. Sailer, 167.
6. Hacker, 421–2.
7. Haslip, 353.
8. Hamann, 272.
9. Sailer, 158.
10. Von Burg, 314.
11. Hacker, 421–2.
12. Von Burg, *Ludwig II of Bavaria*, 313–4.

Epilogue

1. Steinberger, 131–32.
2. Ibid, 132.
3. Corti, 347.
4. C-H, 290.
5. Hojer, *Konig Ludwig II.-Museum*, 150–2.
6. Sailer, 145.

7. Gerard, 291–2.
8. Sailer, 146.
9. Ibid, 152.
10. Ibid, 151.
11. Ibid, 155.
12. Ibid, 152.
13. Steinberger, 138.
14. Ibid, 138–9.
15. Sailer, 155.
16. Nohbauer, 30.
17. C-H, 303.
18. Ibid, 163.
19. Zareck, 242.

Bibliography

Arthaud, Claude. *Enchanted Visions: Fantastic Houses and Their Treasures.* New York: G. P. Putnam's Sons, 1972.

Bainville, Jacques. *Louis II de Bavière.* Paris: Perrin, 1900.

Bertram, Werner. *Der einsame König.* Munich: Herpich, 1936.

Biermann, Cristoph. "Leiden eines Königs," *Deutsches Arzteblatt,* 45 (8 November 1973): pp. 36–52.

Bismarck, Prince Otto von. *Memoirs.* Two vols. London: Harper & Brothers, 1940.

Blunt, Wilfrid. *The Dream King.* London: Hamish Hamilton, 1970.

Bohm, Gottfried von. *Ludwig II. König von Bayern.* Two vols. Berlin: Engelmann, 1921–24.

Brunner, Herbert. *Altes Residenztheater in Munich.* Munich: Bayerische Verwaltung der Staatlichen Schlösser, Garten und Seen, 1987.

_____. *Residenz, Munich.* Munich: Bayerische Verwaltung der Staatlichen Schlösser, Garten und Seen, 1991.

Channon, Henry. *The Ludwigs of Bavaria.* London: Methuen, 1933.

Chapman-Huston, Desmond. *Bavarian Fantasy: The Story of Ludwig II.* London: John Murray, 1955.

Corti, Count Egon. *Elizabeth, Empress of Austria.* New Haven: Yale University Press, 1936.

_____. *Downfall of Three Dynasties.* Freeport, N.Y.: Books for Libraries Press, 1970.

Crankshaw, Edward. *Bismarck.* New York: Viking, 1981.

Darmstaedter, F. *Bismarck and the Creation of the Second Reich.* London: Methuen, 1948.

Des Cars, Jean. *Les Chateaux fous de Louis II de Bavière.* Paris: Perrin, 1986.

Designs for the Dream King: The Castles and Palaces of Ludwig II of Bavaria. London: Debrett's Peerage, 1978.

Desing, Julius. *King Ludwig II, His Life, His End.* Lechbruck: Verlag Kienberger, 1976.

_____. *Royal Castle, Neuschwanstein.*

Ebenthal, Hildegarde [Princess Catherine Radziwill]. *The Tragedy of a Throne.* London: Cassell, 1917.

Ellis, Ashton, ed. *Wagner Letters to Wesendonck.* London: Grant Richards, 1899.

Fischer-Dieskau, Dietrich. *Wagner and Nietzsche.* Translated by Joachim Neugroschell. New York: Seabury Press, 1976.

Frantz, Eugen, ed. "König Ludwig II. von Bayern, das königliche Kabinett, das Ministerium und das Bayerische Volk, 1864–1866." In *Staat und Volkstum.* Munich: 1933.

Friedrich Wilhelm III. *War Diary, 1870–1871.* London: Stanley Paul, 1927.

Gerard, Francis. *The Romance of Ludwig II of Bavaria.* London: Jarrold, 1899.

Grein, Edir, ed. *Tagebuch-Aufzeichnungen von Ludwig II. König von Bayern.* Liechtenstein: Schaan, 1925.

Guide Book, Neuschwanstein and Hohenschwangau. Lechbruck: Verlag Kienberger, 1978.

Hacker, Rupert. *Ludwig II. von Bayern in Augenzeugenberichten.* Düsseldorf: Rauch Verlag, 1966.

Hamann, Brigitte. *The Reluctant Empress: A Biography of Empress Elizabeth of Austria.* New York: Knopf, 1986.

Haslip, Joan. *The Lonely Empress: A Biography of Elizabeth of Austria.* New York: World Publishing Co., 1965.

Heigel, Karl von. *König Ludwig II. von Bayern. Ein Beitrag zu seiner Lebensgeschichte.* Stuttgart: Bonz, 1893.

Heindl, Hannes. *Marie, Königin von Bayern.* Munich: Herpich Verlag, 1989.

Hibbert, Christopher. *Versailles.* New York: Newsweek Books, 1972.

Hierneis, Theodor. *The Monarch Dines.* London: Werner Laurie, 1972.

Hohenlohe, Prince Chlodwig von. *Memoirs.* Two vols. London: Heinemann, 1907.

Hojer, Gerhard. *Nymphenburg: Palace, Park and Pavilions.* Munich: Bayerische Verwaltung der Staatlichen Schlösser, Garten und Seen, 1991.

_____. *Treasury in the Munich Residenz.* Munich: Bayerische Verwaltung der Staatlichen Schlösser, Garten und Seen, 1988.

_____. *Schloss Linderhof.* Munich: Bayerische Verwaltung der Staatlichen Schlösser, Garten und Seen, 1994.

_____, ed. *König Ludwig II.-Museum Herrenchiemsee, Katalog.* Munich: Hirmer Verlag, 1986.

Hollweck, Ludwig. *Er war ein König.* Munich: Hugendubel, 1979.

Hommel, Kurt. *Die Separatvorstellungen vor König Ludwig II. von Bayern.* Munich: Laokoon Verlag, 1963.

Kissinger, Henry. *Diplomacy*. New York: Simon & Schuster, 1994.

Kobell, Luise von. *Unter den vier ersten Königen Bayerns. Nach Briefen und eigenen Erinnerungen*. Munich: C. H. Beck, 1894.

Kreisel, Heinrich. *The Castles of Ludwig II of Bavaria*. Darmstadt: Schneekluth, 1955.

_____. *Schloss Hohenschwangau*. Munich: Hirmer Verlag, 1992.

Listowel, Judith. *A Habsburg Tragedy: Crown Prince Rudolf*. New York: Dorset Press, 1978.

McIntosh, Christopher. *The Swan King: Ludwig II of Bavaria*. London: Allan Lane, 1982.

Mennett, Arthur. *Die Königsphantasien: Eine Wanderung zu den Schlössern König Ludwigs II. von Bayern*. Leipzig: Verlag der Literarischen Gesellchaft, 1892.

Mignot, Claude. *Architecture of the Nineteenth Century*. Cologne: Evergreen, 1994.

Newman, Ernest. *The Life of Richard Wagner*. Four vols. London: Cassell, 1933–47.

Nicolson, Nigel. *Great Houses of the Western World*. New York: G. P. Putnam's Sons, 1968.

Nohbauer, Hans F. *König Ludwigs II. Ein Führer zu Schlössern und Museen Lebens-und Erinnerungsstätten des Märchenkönigs*. Munich: Prestel, 1986.

Palmer, Alan. *The Chancellories of Europe*. London: George Allen & Unwin, 1983.

Paz, Infanta of Spain [HRH Princess Ludwig Ferdinand]. *Through Four Revolutions*. London: John Murray, 1933.

Perouse de Montclos, Jean-Marie. *Versailles*. New York: Abbeville Press, 1991.

Petzet, Detta. *Linderhof Castle*. Munich: Herpich & Sohn, 1990.

_____. *The Royal Palace of Herrenchiemsee*. Munich: Herpich & Sohn, 1990.

Petzet, Michael. *The Castle of Neuschwanstein*. Munich: Bayerische Verwaltung der Staatlichen Schlösser, Garten und Seen, 1977.

_____, and Werner Neumeister. *Die Welt des Bayerischen Märchenkönigs*. Munich: Prestel, 1980.

Possart, Ernst von. *Die Separatvorstellungen für König Ludwig II*. Munich: C. H. Beck, 1901.

Rall, Hans, and Michael Petzet. *King Ludwig II*. Munich: Verlag Schnell & Steiner, 1980.

_____. *König Ludwig II. Wirklichkeit und Rätsel*. Munich: Schnell & Steiner, 1986.

Richter, Werner. *Ludwig II., König von Bayern*. Leipzig: Rentsch, 1939.

_____. *The Mad Monarch*. Chicago: Regnery, 1954.

Ridley, Jasper. *Napoleon III and Eugenie*. London: Constable, 1979.

Rockel, Sebastian. *Ludwig II. und Richard Wagner*. Munich: 1913, 1920.

Russ, Sigrid. *Die Schlössern König Ludwigs II*. Munich: Süddeutscher Verlag, 1990.

Sabor, Rudolph. *The Real Wagner*. London: Cardinal, 1987.

Sailer, Anton. *Castles, Mystery and Music: The Legend of Ludwig II*. Munich: Bruckmann, 1992.

Schad, Martha. *Bayerns Königshaus*. Munich: Verlag Friedrich Pustet, 1994.

Schmid, Elmar D., and Luisa Hager. *Marstallmuseum, Schloss Nymphenburg in Munich*. Munich: Bayerische Verwaltung der Staatlichen Schlösser, Garten und Seen, 1992.

Sitwell, Sacheverell. *Great Palaces of Europe*. London: Spring Books, 1969.

Skelton, Geoffrey. *Richard and Cosima Wagner: Biography of a Marriage*. Boston: Houghton Mifflin, 1982.

Spencer, Stewart, and Barry Millington, ed. *Selected Letters of Richard Wagner*. New York: Norton, 1988.

Steinberger, Hans. *The Life of Ludwig II of Bavaria*. Munich: United Arts Establishment, 1930.

Strobel, Otto, ed. *König Ludwig II. und Richard Wagner, Briefweschsel*. Five vol. Karlsruhe: Braun, 1936–39.

Taylor, Ronald. *Richard Wagner: His Life, Art and Thought*. New York: Taplinger, 1979.

Van der Kemp, Gerald. *Versailles*. New York: Park Lane, 1981.

Von Burg, Katerina. *Ludwig II of Bavaria, The Man and the Mystery*. London: Windsor Publications, 1989.

_____. *Elizabeth of Austria: A Life Misunderstood*. London: Windsor Publications, 1995.

Wagner, Cosima. *Die Tagebücher*. Edited by M. Gregor-Dellin and D. Mack. Two vols. Munich: 1976–77.

Wagner, Richard. *The Letters of Richard Wagner*. Edited by Wilhelm Altmann. London: J. M. Dent & Sons, 1927.

_____. *Briefwechsel zwischen Wagner und Liszt*. Two vols. Leipzig: Stein und Mark, 1900.

_____. *Brown Book*. Edited by J. Bergfeld. Zurich: Schweigler, 1975.

Walton, Guy. *Louis XIV's Versailles*. Chicago: University of Chicago Press, 1986.

Wille, E. *Briefe von Richard Wagner*. Berlin: Tieziplinger, 1894.

Zareck, Otto. *The Tragic Idealist: Ludwig II of Bavaria*. New York: Harper, 1939.

Acknowledgments

A great number of people have helped to make this book possible, and each deserves my utmost thanks and admiration.

First, I must once again acknowledge the support and assistance of my parents, Roger and Helena King; without their continued indulgence, my pursuit of writing would be far more of a burden. Their valuable sympathy for my somewhat peculiar choice of a career enables me to pursue my research in ways too numerable to list.

Many other people have assisted me through their friendship and encouragement: Sharlene Aadland, Kathryn Glennie, Dan Kaufman, Angela Manning, Cecelia Manning, Cynthia Melin, Denis Meslans, Linda Tillmann, and Edd Vick have provided me with the support necessary for the completion of this book. Laura Enstone helped to ensure my research in Germany, at the cost of her own personal inclinations and desires. And Russell Minugh has proved especially understanding, remaining at my side through what I can only describe as a trying year, and his friendship continues to amaze me.

I have been able to call on the wisdom and advice of several friends throughout the writing of this book: Princess Pamela Cantacuzène, Edward Dorian, Marlene Eilers, Bill Melin, and Susanne Meslans gave freely of their time during the various stages of development. Their translations, suggestions, and corrections have helped transform the story in large and small ways, but the responsibility for any mistakes which may remain is solely mine. And Allan J. Wilson, my editor at Carol Publishing Group, has been a constant source of encouragement through his unfailing support for my projects.

Last, I again have the privilege of thanking Gabriel Glennie. His work as my research assistant helped uncover new areas to explore and new directions to examine, and inspired me to look beyond the obvious. He sacrificed his own valuable time to read and reread the manuscript, and together we spent many long nights sitting before a computer, tearing apart pages and composing paragraphs and chapters. Every sentence and page reflects his skill and encouragement, and it would be impossible for me to exaggerate his contribution.

Index